A remarkable analysis of data collection – "not neutral and inert but powerful and potentially dangerous" – combined with a profound quest to fight the discrimination against refugees with disabilities, ultimately providing an innovative conceptual framework in international law, based on the relationship between visibility, control and power.

François Crépeau, *Full Professor, Faculty of Law, McGill University*

This book brilliantly propounds an alternative reading of Article 31 *CRPD*, with a focus on refugee context. It is a timely and thought-provoking contribution, which calls for a more intersectional approach to data collection and suggests a greater focus on attitudinal and environmental barriers.

Delia Ferri, *Professor of Law at the School of Law and Criminology and Co-director of the Assisting Living and Learning (ALL) Institute, Maynooth University*

I0888255

Refugee Displacement, Disability and Human Rights

This book presents a timely and innovative exploration of one of the first human rights articles about data production and processing: the Convention on the Rights of Persons with Disabilities article 31, 'Statistics and data collection'.

The study provides detailed explorations of the legal and practical demands of article 31, how these have been interpreted and the practice of human rights research with marginalised communities. It describes the history of the article's drafting in detail, uncovering the tensions at its heart today. This analysis provides the foundations for an alternative doctrinal reading of the obligations in article 31 and an exploration of a potential group right. The book's detailed analysis is assisted by a new conceptual framework that illustrates the relationship between visibility and power. The work demonstrates that data is not inert but powerful and may be used in ways that are helpful and harmful to rights holders. Through closely examining disability human rights data practices in refugee contexts, it concludes that human rights protections are being ignored in the urgency to create more data to identify and address inequality. The author identifies immediate actions that may be taken to remediate current practices.

The book will be an invaluable resource for academics, researchers and policy-makers working in disability studies, human rights law, refugee and migration studies, technology and society.

Philippa Duell-Piening is a socio-legal researcher specialising in the human rights of people who are refugees with disability.

Routledge Research in Human Rights Law

The European Convention on Human Rights and the COVID-19 Pandemic
Ronagh J.A. McQuigg

International Human Rights and Local Courts
Human Rights Interpretation in Indonesia
Edited by Aksel Tømte and Eko Riyadi

Defamation and the Right to Freedom of Speech
The UK in Comparative Perspective
Mariette Jones

Bulk Surveillance, Democracy and Human Rights Law in Europe
A Comparative Perspective
Marcin Rojszczak

Surveillance Law, Data Retention and Human Rights
A Risk to Democracy
Matthew White

Domestic Abuse and the European Court of Human Rights
Ronagh J.A. McQuigg

Human Rights Law and Corporate Regulation
A Neo-Concession Approach
Jonathan Barrett

Refugee Displacement, Disability and Human Rights
The Production, Processing and Power of Data
Philippa Duell-Piening

For more information about this series, please visit: www.routledge.com/Routledge-Research-in-Human-Rights-Law/book-series/HUMRIGHTSLAW

Refugee Displacement, Disability and Human Rights

The Production, Processing and Power of Data

Philippa Duell-Piening

Routledge
Taylor & Francis Group
LONDON AND NEW YORK

First published 2025
by Routledge
4 Park Square, Milton Park, Abingdon, Oxon OX14 4RN

and by Routledge
605 Third Avenue, New York, NY 10158

Routledge is an imprint of the Taylor & Francis Group, an informa business

British Library Cataloguing-in-Publication Data
A catalogue record for this book is available from the British Library

ISBN: 978-1-032-82771-1 (hbk)
ISBN: 978-1-032-82773-5 (pbk)
ISBN: 978-1-003-50614-0 (ebk)

DOI: 10.4324/9781003506140

Typeset in ITC Galliard Pro
by Apex CoVantage, LLC

For Mum, Dave and Matt, who sensitise me to injustice, inspire me to learn and provide me the space to toil, thank you.

Contents

Figures

Tables

Acknowledgements

This monograph was mostly written on the unceded lands of the Wurundjeri people of the Kulin Nation, where I have lived, worked and studied most of my life. I also had the privilege of tutoring alongside an Indigenous cultural mentor, Nicole, in the first year of my research. During this formative part of my research, we spoke about Indigenous identity and the importance of the right not to identify.

Over the four-year journey, thousands of conversations with hundreds of people have shaped this research. These conversations have sparked ideas, provided space to talk things through and helped me make connections that would have otherwise gone unnoticed. My research did not and could not have occurred in a vacuum. I know because I spent months in lockdown during the COVID-19 pandemic, where seemingly little work progressed. I now take this opportunity to acknowledge some of these people.

My PhD research, which forms the basis of this monograph, was supported by the Melbourne Social Equity Institute with an Australian Government Research Training Program Scholarship. I was privileged to be supervised by Professor Michelle Foster and Associate Professor Anna Arstein-Kerslake, whom I thank for their mentorship. Thank you also to Professor Christiaan van Veen for allowing me to audit the Human Rights and the Digital State class. Thank you to my examiners, Professor Francois Crépeau and Professor Delia Ferri, whose feedback progressed the intellectual rigour of the research and who kindly provided endorsements for this monograph.

Thank you to my research advisory group, Amir, Grace, Elizabeth and Jubran. Your generous contributions and participation in our meetings were pivotal to my research. Thank you to Donna Chesters for mentoring me in community advisory group facilitation and grounding my work.

I have been the beneficiary of the generosity of practitioners and scholars around the world. In 2019, I was fortunate enough to intern for Rosemary Kayess, the chair of the Committee on the Rights of Persons with Disabilities. I met with scholars working on the Washington Group Questions on Disability and with Humanity and Inclusion in Germany, who are working with people fleeing Syria. I hope these conversations and relationships have not prevented me from honestly reporting what I saw emerging from my research but, instead, to say it with respect and nuance.

Thank you to my Zoom Shut Up & Write! buddies – Toerien, Azadah, Ash, Tess and Jo – for your daily companionship as I toiled at this writing. Thank you to André and Karin for your thoughtful comments on my workshop papers. Thank you to Rasika for the helpful advice you provided from your experience of publishing your research.

Thank you to my family and friends for your care and for reminding me of life outside my research. You will forgive me for not naming you all. You know you are important to me.

Lastly, and most importantly, thank you to my favourite COVID-19 lockdown buddy and co-author of my life for the past 28 years, my husband, Matt.

Language and Formatting Note

I acknowledge people identify in various ways and have preferred language to communicate their identity. This monograph follows People with Disability Australia's advice in describing disability.[1] In doing so, it mainly uses a person-first approach, that is, people with disability. In some cases, communities prefer identity-first language. When I was aware of this, I followed this convention, for example, autistic people.

Similarly, it is important to recognise that people seeking protection are people, not a status. To that end, I have also used person-first language to describe people who are refugees. Further, as a person's gender is not always known, I have generally used gender-inclusive pronouns throughout this monograph, they/them/their.

I have used first-person pronouns to refer to myself throughout the monograph. This approach acknowledges my role in shaping the research and is consistent with my critique of knowledge construction throughout the monograph. I have made choices throughout this research about what I believe is important and what is not, 'making known one reality among many possibilities'.[2]

1 People with Disability Australia, *What Do I Say? A Guide to Language About Disability* (Guidelines, 2019) <https://pwd.org.au/resources/disability-info/language-guide/>.

2 Sally Engle Merry, *The Seductions of Quantification: Measuring Human Rights, Gender Violence, and Sex Trafficking* (University of Chicago Press, 2016) 5.

Abbreviations and Short Titles

ABS	Australian Bureau of Statistics
CRPD	*Convention on the Rights of Persons with Disabilities*
CRPD Committee	Committee on the Rights of Persons with Disabilities
DPO	disabled persons organisation
ExCom	Executive Committee of the High Commissioner (for Refugees)'s Programme
IASC	Inter-Agency Standing Committee
ICF	International Classification of Functioning, Disability and Health
ICIDH	International Classification of Impairments, Disabilities and Handicaps
NGO	non-government organisation
OHCHR	Office of the High Commissioner for Human Rights
Refugee Convention	*Convention Relating to the Status of Refugees* (as amended by the 1967 Protocol)
UNHCR	Office of the United Nations High Commissioner for Refugees
UNHCR Statute	*Statute of the Office of the United Nations High Commissioner for Refugees*
Vienna Convention	*Vienna Convention on the Law of Treaties*
WHO	World Health Organization

Convention on the Rights of Persons With Disabilities Article 31
Statistics and Data Collection

1. States Parties undertake to collect appropriate information, including statistical and research data, to enable them to formulate and implement policies to give effect to the present Convention. The process of collecting and maintaining this information shall:

   (a) Comply with legally established safeguards, including legislation on data protection, to ensure confidentiality and respect for the privacy of persons with disabilities;
   (b) Comply with internationally accepted norms to protect human rights and fundamental freedoms and ethical principles in the collection and use of statistics.

2. The information collected in accordance with this article shall be disaggregated, as appropriate, and used to help assess the implementation of States Parties' obligations under the present Convention and to identify and address the barriers faced by persons with disabilities in exercising their rights.
3. States Parties shall assume responsibility for the dissemination of these statistics and ensure their accessibility to persons with disabilities and others.

Preface

Four encounters significantly informed my research proposal. These encounters took place at my work, through my study and in conversations with friends and colleagues. I have described them here to explain why this research about the *Convention on the Rights of Persons with Disabilities* ('*CRPD*') article 31 explores the intersectionality of refugee experiences and disability rather than other intersectionalities, which may be equally important in deepening our understanding of article 31.

Before commencing this research, I worked at a non-government organisation ('NGO') that provides services to people who are survivors of torture and trauma from refugee backgrounds in Victoria, Australia. As a policy advisor at this organisation, I noted the importance of data for communicating clients' situations with governments to advocate for appropriate services. I also noted the care taken to transmit the smallest amount of identifiable information necessary to the government because of the potential for information to impact individuals adversely. Negotiating this balance often involved thoughtful contractual arrangements with the Australian government which funded services. Great care was also taken with the security and confidentiality of the database held by the NGO, as there was recognition that the information in the database, if obtained by persecuting states, could harm clients of the services.

When more people with disability began arriving through the Australian Refugee and Humanitarian Program post-2012,[3] naturally, as a policy advisor, I sought information about this population to understand their needs and advocate for accessible services. While doing this work, I undertook graduate studies in international law in which I wrote a research paper about the influence of the *CRPD* on the Australian Refugee and Humanitarian Program.[4] During this research, I was excited to find *CRPD* article 31 contained state obligations to produce and process information, seemingly, about people with

3 See generally Philippa Duell-Piening, 'Refugee Resettlement and the Convention on the Rights of Persons with Disabilities' (2018) 33(5) *Disability & Society* 661.

4 This was during a refugee law subject taught by Professor Michelle Foster. A rewritten version of that research paper was published in *Disability and Society*. IBid. 661.

disability. On the face of it, I felt that article 31 supported my work in refugee health policy by obligating governments and their funded services to routinely collect and disaggregate data by variables such as migration status.

Nonetheless, I felt an internal tension grow, as I was increasingly unable to reconcile the care taken with clients' data by the organisation I worked for and my work advocating that governments and funded services routinely collect more information about people with disability from refugee backgrounds. I also appreciated that the risk posed by information production and processing was not experienced equally. People with various disability and migration statuses experience risks from state information production and processing differently. A person seeking asylum who is not yet recognised as a refugee and who has a mental illness may face more significant risks in sharing their information than a person with a permanent protection visa with a physical disability. These nuances were challenging to communicate in our advocacy.

Around this time, I received an evening phone call from a friend who was distressed that their family had been selected by the Australian Bureau of Statistics ('ABS') to undertake the National Health Survey. The ABS had informed them that their family's participation was compulsory.[5] Their family were required by law to participate in a survey that asked them to disclose their health information. My friend's early life experience of fleeing a government that persecuted and imprisoned their family undoubtedly made them aware of the dangers of disclosing information. When I rang the ABS with a general enquiry about my friend's situation, the representative provided me with specific information about my friend. I can only imagine that, in doing so, they hoped to co-opt me into viewing my friend's concerns as irrational and unwarranted.

This disclosure and the institutional culture of an unwavering adherence to and belief in data's value over individual autonomy to choose whether to disclose personal information led me to question my faith in the ABS, an institution Australians revere as impartial and working in our best interest. These drastic powers to demand information about the private lives of people within their jurisdiction comes with significant responsibility that can easily be forgotten when dangers are not imminent. Nonetheless, the information collected today has implications for the future when we may have a populist government that vilifies certain groups for their own political gain or are in times where emergency powers allow the bypass of protections. The health information of my friend's children was collected and will be stored by the ABS for the rest of their lives, we hope with scrupulous protections. Nevertheless, this was not

5 'Is the survey compulsory? Ultimately, yes. The questions included in this survey are being asked under the authority of the Census and Statistics Act 1905, which has provisions to make surveys compulsory. Under the Act, you are obliged to provide the information being requested, unless otherwise specified by your interviewer'. 'National Health Survey', *Australian Bureau of Statistics* (Online Survey) <https://www.abs.gov.au/participate-survey/household-survey/national-health-survey>.

a minor intrusion into the private lives of their family and yielded no direct benefit to them. This event took place in a politically stable liberal democracy where we can have some confidence about the separation of powers and subsequent protections. However, my friend's previous experiences sensitised them to how quickly things may change.

During this period, I worked with a colleague with a disability who held a temporary protection visa. We were working together to document the gaps in service provision for people with disability on temporary visas. We have now worked together for some years, but I remember being struck in our first meeting when they said (and I paraphrase due to the passage of time): 'Ask me anything. As a refugee, there is no privacy'. This comment reflected, I assume, the countless times they had to share their story with others and the fact that they no longer felt in control of their own information. It struck me that, after people have reached safety from persecution, we perpetuate actions that are invasive and remind them of their uncertain and precarious situation (even if this is no longer the case). In my work, some people fervently rejected the title 'refugee' post-resettlement. It perhaps was a constant reminder that their safety resulted from 'burden sharing' or charity rather than their humanness and the inalienable rights attached. Further, others argued that classification as a 'refugee' does not recognise their valuable contribution to the community.

These encounters fuelled my growing unease about the data evangelism I was undertaking as a policy advisor. I could no longer ignore the niggling tension every time I advised governments that they needed to collect more information about people with disability from refugee backgrounds. This unease informed my decision in 2019 to leave my job and spend four years researching the implications of *CRPD* article 31 for people with disability who are refugees or from refugee backgrounds.

1 Introduction

Enthusiasm for data to measure disparity in human rights attainment is unprecedented.[1] Data hold the potential to measure inequalities, inform the targeting of special measures and assess states' compliance with obligations. Omission from datasets is characterised as having no identity;[2] to count, you must be counted. Many human characteristics, experiences and 'statuses' are being counted in the name of human rights implementation: immigration status, health conditions, education, livelihoods and experiences of violence, to name a few.[3] Further, the data production and processing landscape has changed tremendously over the last decades, so much so that one scholar characterised it as giving rise to the 'fourth industrial revolution'.[4]

Increasingly, scholars are writing about the potential harms that may result from this new data landscape, such as harms resulting from data linking,[5] algorithmic bias,[6] data asymmetries[7] and governments' lack of motivation and

1 As will be demonstrated throughout this monograph, particularly in Section 3.3.1 and Chapter 7. Nonetheless, by way of introductory example, see generally 'Disability Data', *CBM* (Web Page) <https://www.cbm.org.au/stories/disability-data>. See also 'Data2X: Partnering for Better Gender Data', *Data2X* (Web Page) <https://data2x.org/>.

2 Carmen Barroso and Katell Le Goulven, 'A Rights-Based Data Revolution?', *UN Data Revolution* (online, 14 October 2014) <https://www.undatarevolution.org/2014/10/14/rights-based-revolution/>.

3 See, eg, the Committee on the Rights of Persons with Disabilities' Concluding Observations to Hungary: 'Collect data on persons with disabilities, disaggregated by age, sex, health status, race, ethnicity, income, migration and/or asylum-seeking or refugee status, level of education, employment situation, place of residence and services received, as well as on the barriers that persons with disabilities face in society, including data related to deinstitutionalization, legal capacity status and victims of violence, abuse and ill-treatment'. This formulation is very similar to other recent Concluding Observations issued by the committee. Committee on the Rights of Persons with Disabilities, *Concluding Observations on the Combined Second and Third Periodic Reports of Hungary*, UN Doc CRPD/C/HUN/CO/2-3 (20 May 2022) [61(a)].

4 Klaus Schwab, *The Fourth Industrial Revolution* (World Economic Forum, 2016).

5 Mason Marks, *Algorithmic Disability Discrimination* (SSRN Scholarly Paper No ID 3338209, Social Science Research Network, 19 February 2019).

6 AI Now, *Algorithmic Accountability Policy Tool Kit* (Report, October 2018).

7 Shoshana Zuboff, *The Age of Surveillance Capitalism: The Fight for a Human Future at the New Frontier of Power* (Profile Books, 2019).

DOI: 10.4324/9781003506140-1

ability to protect the rights of data subjects.[8] Despite this activity, scarce scholarly work exists about the addition to the human rights framework, in 2006, of an article dedicated to data and statistics, article 31 of the *Convention on the Rights of Persons with Disabilities* ('*CRPD*').[9] Scholarly work related to this article generally focuses on operationalising data production and processing about the bodies and lives of people with disability.[10]

As described in the Prologue, this research project emerged from tensions I observed in my study, work and relationships. In increasingly digitised states where data knowledge is paramount, there is widespread advocacy for representative data to inform data-driven policy to address discrimination and marginalisation.[11] However, this movement for representative data has not adequately engaged with the impacts of data production and processing on data subjects and the broader community. This research sought to explore these tensions and to understand why a human rights treaty included an article that seemingly promotes the surveillance of rights-holders.[12]

This chapter introduces the research project in four sections. Section 1.1 introduces the *CRPD*. It describes the model of disability adopted by the convention and some of the treaty's innovations, including the codification of multiple discrimination and an article about the production and processing of data, article 31. Section 1.2 defines refugee contexts and explains why these are important and productive sites for exploring disability rights. Section 1.3 contextualises the research project, outlines the research questions and summarises the project's four substantial and original contributions to human rights scholarship and practice. Section 1.4 provides an overview of this monograph and summarises the chapters.

8 Virginia Eubanks, *Automating Inequality: How High-Tech Tools Profile, Police, and Punish the Poor* (St Martin's Press, 2018); Philip Alston, *Report of the Special Rapporteur on Extreme Poverty and Human Rights*, UN Doc A/74/48037 (11 October 2019).

9 The treaty text was adopted in 2006 by the United Nations General Assembly. *Convention on the Rights of Persons with Disabilities*, opened for signature 24 January 2007, 2515 UNTS 3 (entered into force 3 May 2008) ('*CRPD*').

10 Mads Pedersen and Federico Ferretti, 'Article 31: Statistics and Data Collection' in Ilias Bantekas, Michael Ashley Stein and Dimitris Anastasiou (eds), *The UN Convention on the Rights of Persons with Disabilities: A Commentary* (Oxford University Press, 2018) 924. See also Mads Pedersen, 'Article 31: Statistics and Data Collection' in Valentina Della Fina, Rachele Cera and Giuseppe Palmisano (eds), *The United Nations Convention on the Rights of Persons with Disabilities: A Commentary* (Springer International Publishing, 2017) 557.

11 See earlier n 1.

12 While surveillance is often associated with totalitarian regimes who seek to control the population through knowledge of their activities, surveillance is also used in public health to understand the activities of a population to formulate interventions to improve health outcomes. Surveillance is also entering development and human rights methodologies as well, though it is often not termed surveillance due to the political connotations. The role of data in population control is explored further in Chapter 3.

1.1 The *Convention on the Rights of Persons With Disabilities*

Following World War II, there was great resolve to ensure that the atrocities the world witnessed were never repeated. The non-binding 1948 *Universal Declaration of Human Rights* was adopted within this context.[13] Over time, these rights were translated into two binding treaties the *International Covenant on Civil and Political Rights* and the *International Covenant on Economic, Social and Cultural Rights.*[14] These treaties, together with the *Universal Declaration of Human Rights*, are sometimes called the International Bill of Human Rights or 'bill of rights'.

The subsequent rise of the civil rights movement and feminism problematised the drafting of these documents by white adult males without disability.[15] Disability studies and human rights law scholars Rosemary Kayess and Philip French explained the impact of the drafters' homogeneity:

> the traditional human rights paradigm is based on an 'able-bodied' norm. In most cases it is not self-evident how traditional human rights are to be interpreted and applied in a manner that will penetrate to the specific human rights violations to which persons with disability are subject.[16]

In response to the new consciousness that some people experience specific human rights violations, treaties that focused on ameliorating the unique harms experienced by sections of the community were negotiated. These treaties included the *International Convention on the Elimination of All Forms of Racial Discrimination*,[17] the *Convention on the Elimination of All Forms of Discrimination against Women*,[18] the *Convention on the Rights of the Child*[19] and most recently, the *CRPD*.[20]

13 *Universal Declaration of Human Rights*, GA Res 217A (III), UN GAOR, UN Doc A/810 (10 December 1948).

14 *International Covenant on Civil and Political Rights*, opened for signature 16 December 1966, 999 UNTS 171 (entered into force 23 March 1976). *International Covenant on Economic, Social and Cultural Rights*, opened for signature 16 December 1966, 993 UNTS 3 (entered into force 3 January 1976).

15 See, eg, Philip Alston and Ryan Goodman, *International Human Rights* (Oxford University Press, 2013) 166–220, 531–681; Dianne Otto, 'Women's Rights' in Daniel Moeckli, Sangeeta Shah and Sandesh Sivakumaran (eds), *International Human Rights Law* (Oxford University Press, 2nd ed, 2014) 345.

16 Rosemary Kayess and Phillip French, 'Out of Darkness into Light – Introducing the Convention on the Rights of Persons with Disabilities' (2008) 8 *Human Rights Law Review* 1, 14.

17 *International Convention on the Elimination of All Forms of Racial Discrimination*, opened for signature 21 December 1965, 660 UNTS 195 (entered into force 4 January 1969).

18 *Convention on the Elimination of All Forms of Discrimination against Women*, opened for signature 18 December 1979, 1249 UNTS 13 (entered into force 3 September 1981).

19 *Convention on the Rights of the Child*, opened for signature 20 November 1989, 1577 UNTS 3 (entered into force 2 September 1990).

20 *CRPD* (n 9).

The *CRPD* was not intended to create new rights but to ensure that people with disability are able to realise their existing human rights.[21] All rights have foundations in the bill of rights. Nonetheless, in codifying state obligations to ensure rights realisation for people with disability, mounting evidence demonstrates that the *CRPD* has contributed innovations to the human rights framework. Some of these innovations are only beginning to be understood. This section describes three of the *CRPD*'s innovations: a new model of disability in international law, greater recognition of multiple and aggravated discrimination and the inclusion of a procedural article entitled 'Statistics and data collection'.

1.1.1 *The Evolution of the Conceptualisation of Disability*

Many scholars have written detailed accounts of the changing models of disability, what informed those changes and their impact.[22] It cannot be overemphasised how important the progression in the model of disability has been to disability rights. This conceptual change is fundamental to understanding the *CRPD*, and it is necessary to reiterate it briefly here. This subsection will briefly describe the charity, medical, social and human rights models of disability and demonstrate how this evolution is reflected in international law.

The *charity model of disability* characterises people with disability as passive objects of kind acts. People with disability are characterised as suffering and needing charity.[23] Disability is seen as an individual problem. People with disability are viewed as a burden on their families and the community. In some cultures, people with disability are taken away from their families and put in institutions. People with disability under this model have no control over their life, and others make decisions on their behalf. The charity model is still prominent in telethons and organisations using photographs of people with disability in difficult and undignified situations to illicit financial donations. Charity model organisations are invested in providing care rather than promoting the autonomy of people with disability.

The *medical model of disability* equates disability with a person's impairment, individualising the experience of disability. People with disability are

21 Theresia Degener, 'Disability in a Human Rights Context' (2016) 5(3) *Laws* 35, 1–24, 4.

22 See especially Jane Campbell and Michael Oliver, *Disability Politics: Understanding Our Past, Changing Our Future* (Routledge, 1996); Michael Oliver, *Understanding Disability: From Theory to Practice* (Macmillan, 1996); James I Charlton, *Nothing About Us Without Us: Disability Oppression and Empowerment* (University of California Press, 1998); Tom Shakespeare, 'The Social Model of Disability' in Lennard J Davis (ed), *The Disability Studies Reader* (Routledge, 5th ed, 2017) 195; Degener (n 21); Gerard Quinn and Theresia Degener (eds), *Human Rights and Disability: The Current Use and Future Potential of United Nations Human Rights Instruments in the Context of Disability* (Report, United Nations, 2002); Office of the High Commissioner for Human Rights (OHCHR), *The Convention on the Rights of Persons with Disabilities: Training Guide* (2014).

23 OHCHR (n 22) 8–9.

defined by the medical treatment 'provided (or imposed) on them'.[24] The medical model aims to 'fix' people with disability through medical intervention and rehabilitation in order for them to participate in society.[25] Because disability is characterised as a medical problem, medical professionals are provided significant power over people with disability to assess their needs, goals and progress. They are often gatekeepers to entry and exit from institutions. Under this model, people with disability have limited or no power over their lives. This model is often mixed with the charity model, as charities often raise funds and run rehabilitation programs.[26]

According to the *social model*, disability is a consequence of an interaction between an individual and an environment that does not accommodate individual differences. Disability, according to the social model, is the experience of exclusion that is socially constructed and, therefore, socially remediated.[27] The social model emerged from the early disability rights movement (in the 1970s), which defined the problems that people with disability experience in terms of 'social oppression, cultural discourse and environmental barriers'.[28] Disability was no longer conceptualised as a defect within a person but as an issue caused by environments that do not accommodate human diversity. Environments were conceptualised as physical and social, which may include attitudinal barriers exacerbating disability. The inequality experienced by people with disability was due to the 'inability of society to eliminate barriers' obstructing people with disability.[29] This model was instrumental in framing disability as oppression and making a case for a human rights treaty to address disparities experienced by people with disability.

As a result of the *CRPD*, the *human rights model of disability* emerged. This model acknowledges people with disability as rights-holders with inherent dignity.[30] Like the social model, the location of 'the main "problem" [is] outside the person and in society'.[31] A person with disability has control over decisions about their life, barriers within society are discriminatory, and states are responsible for removing these barriers.

In a 2016 paper, the former chair of the Committee on the Rights of Persons with Disabilities ('CRPD Committee'), Theresia Degener, explained

24 OHCHR (n 22) 9.
25 OHCHR (n 22) 9.
26 OHCHR (n 22) 9. See later Section 5.1.1 for more on the *CRPD*'s break from the medical model.
27 For more about the social model of disability, see, eg, Shakespeare (n 22).
28 Shakespeare explained that '[t]he social model emerged from the intellectual and political arguments of the Union of Physically Impaired Against Segregation (UPIAS) . . . the aim of UPIAS was to replace segregated facilities with opportunities for people with impairments to participate fully in society, to live independently, to undertake productive work, and to have full control over their own lives'. Shakespeare (n 22) 195–196.
29 OHCHR (n 22) 9.
30 Quinn and Degener (n 22) 14.
31 Quinn and Degener (n 22) 14.

that the human rights model does not 'abandon the social model of disability, but . . . develop[s] it further'.[32] Jenny Morris highlighted the social model 'insist[s] that our physical differences and restrictions are *entirely* socially created'.[33] Degener suggests that the human rights model addresses this somewhat, 'valu[ing] impairment as part of human diversity and human dignity'.[34] Further, Degener argues that the human rights model of disability created space to acknowledge intersectional identities and the experience of multiple and aggravated discrimination (explored later in the next subsection).

The conceptual evolution of the model of disability is apparent in international law when comparing two instruments drafted 30 years apart. Firstly, the 1975 *Declaration on the Rights of Disabled Persons* states that people with disability are 'unable to ensure by himself or herself . . . the necessities of a normal individual and/or social life, as a result of deficiency . . . in his or her physical or mental capabilities'.[35] In contrast, the *CRPD* text adopted in 2006 describes people with disability as 'those who have . . . impairments which in interaction with various barriers may hinder their full and effective participation in society'.[36] The *CRPD* was the culmination of work that framed people with disability no longer as defective humans who are objects of charity but as full humans who are legitimately part of human diversity and rights-holders.[37]

1.1.2 Multiple and Aggravated Forms of Discrimination

The drafters of the *CRPD* were concerned about equality and non-discrimination for people with disability 'on all grounds'.[38] It is the first human rights treaty to include 'multiple discrimination' in the treaty text: 'States Parties recognize that women and girls with disabilities are subject to multiple discrimination'.[39] The Preamble of the *CRPD* also enumerates a larger number of grounds on which people may experience multiple discrimination: 'race, colour, sex, language, religion, political or other opinion, national, ethnic, indigenous or social origin, property, birth, age or other status'.[40]

32 Degener (n 21) 14.
33 Jenny Morris, *Pride Against Prejudice: Transforming Attitudes to Disability* (New Society, 1991) 10 (emphasis in original).
34 Degener (n 21) 8.
35 *Declaration on the Rights of Disabled Persons*, GA Res 3447(XXX), UN GAOR Supp (No 34) at 88, 30th sess, 2433rd plen mtg, UN Doc A/RES/3447(XXX) (adopted 9 December 1975) para 1.
36 *CRPD* (n 9) art 1.
37 Degener (n 21).
38 *CRPD* (n 9) art 5.
39 *CRPD* (n 9) art 6.
40 *CRPD* (n 9) art 6 Preamble para p.

Drawing on the work of the Committee on the Elimination of Discrimination against Women,[41] the CRPD Committee defined multiple discrimination in *General Comment No 3 (2016) on Women and Girls with Disabilities* ('*General Comment 3*'):

> 'Multiple discrimination' refers to a situation in which a person can experience discrimination on two or more grounds, leading to discrimination that is compound or aggravated. 'Intersectional discrimination' refers to a situation where several grounds interact with each other at the same time in such a way that they are inseparable. Grounds for discrimination include age, disability, ethnic, indigenous, national or social origin, gender identity, political or other opinion, race, refugee, migrant or asylum status, religion, sex, or sexual orientation.[42]

This General Comment introduced further grounds on which people may experience multiple discrimination, including refugee or asylum seeker status, and introduced the term 'intersectional discrimination' to the committee's work. While multiple discrimination is described as the additive effect of two or more discriminatory grounds, intersectional discrimination occurs when it is impossible to isolate one discriminatory ground's impact from another.[43]

Recognising and wanting to address multiple and aggravated forms of discrimination can be directly linked to the drive to produce and process more data about people and their lives. According to early intersectional methodology scholars, data are integral to 'describ[ing] women's realities more accurately and to determin[ing] what factors contribute to women's discrimination'.[44] The inference is that the more data available, the more accurately problems may be understood

41 Committee on the Elimination of Discrimination against Women, *General Recommendation No 25 (2004) on Temporary Special Measures*, UN Doc HRI/GEN/1/Rev.7 at 282 (2004) [12]; Committee on the Elimination of Discrimination Against Women, *General Recommendation No 28 (2010) on the Core Obligations of States Parties Under Article 2 of the Convention on the Elimination of All Forms of Discrimination Against Women*, UN Doc CEDAW/C/GC/28 (16 December 2010) [18].

42 Committee on the Rights of Persons with Disabilities, *General Comment No 3 (2016) on Women and Girls with Disabilities*, UN Doc CRPD/C/GC/3 (25 November 2016) [11] (citations omitted).

43 A growing body of scholarly work explores disability's intersection with other identities and life experiences. See, eg, Chris Bell, 'Is Disability Studies Actually White Disability Studies?' in Lennard J Davis (ed), *The Disability Studies Reader* (Routledge, 5th ed, 2017) 406; Nirmala Erevelles and Andrea Minear, 'Unspeakable Offenses: Untangling Race and Disability in Discourses of Intersectionality' in Lennard J Davis (ed), *The Disability Studies Reader* (Routledge, 5th ed, 2017) 381; Liat Ben-Moshe and Sandy Magaña, 'An Introduction to Race, Gender, and Disability: Intersectionality, Disability Studies, and Families of Color' (2014) 2(2) *Women, Gender, and Families of Color* 105.

44 Center for Women's Global Leadership, *A Women's Human Rights Approach to the World Conference Against Racism* (2001).

and effectively addressed. *General Comment 3* also linked data production and disaggregation to addressing multiple and intersectional discrimination:

> The concept of intersectional discrimination . . . acknowledges the lived realities and experiences of heightened disadvantage of individuals caused by multiple and intersecting forms of discrimination, which requires targeted measures to be taken with respect to disaggregated data collection.[45]

General Comment 3 proposes that data disaggregation is intrinsically linked to monitoring multiple and intersectional discrimination. Therefore, it is unsurprising that the first human rights treaty to contain multiple discrimination in the text is the first treaty to have an entire article dedicated to statistics and data collection, *CRPD* article 31.

1.1.3 Article 31 Statistics and Data Collection

The main focus of this monograph is *CRPD* article 31, entitled 'Statistics and data collection'.[46] Article 31 is the first article in a United Nations human rights treaty entirely dedicated to the production and processing of data.[47] Also of interest to this monograph is that it contains several underexamined tensions that were apparent at the research's outset.[48] These tensions, including data's concurrently beneficial and harmful effects and the transfer of power to the data controller, are elaborated throughout the monograph.

1.2 Refugee Contexts

This monograph situates the exploration of *CRPD* article 31 in refugee contexts. The following briefly defines refugee contexts and explains why refugee contexts are important and productive sites for considering disability rights.

1.2.1 What Are Refugee Contexts?

Refugee contexts, to various extents, are regulated by the *Convention Relating to the Status of Refugees ('Refugee Convention')* and associated

45 CRPD Committee, *General Comment No 3* (n 42) [16].

46 The full text may be found in the front pages of this monograph.

47 However, it is not completely novel, as the 1951 *Convention Relating to the Status of Refugees* ('*Refugee Convention*') article 35 references statistics in paragraph 2. *Convention Relating to the Status of Refugees*, opened for signature 28 July 1951, 189 UNTS 150 (entered into force 22 April 1954) art 35(2) ('*Refugee Convention*'). See later Section 6.3.1 for a comparison between *CRPD* art 31 and the *Refugee Convention* art 35(2). See also the International *Convention for Protection of All Persons From Enforced Disappearance*, opened for signature 6 February 2007, 2716 UNTS 3 (entered into force 23 December 2010) art 19. This article has a focus on individual data protection.

48 See earlier Prologue.

protocol,[49] which contain a definition of refugee and provide rights and protections.[50] Refugee contexts are not restricted to states that are parties to the *Refugee Convention*, as states not party to the convention have customary international law *non-refoulement* obligations.[51] While the convention and customary international law obligations are directed to states, certain actors have responsibilities in refugee contexts, such as the Office of the High Commissioner for Refugees ('UNHCR').[52] Other actors have established expertise in these contexts, for example, civil society organisations. Several non-binding instruments, such as the *Global Compact on Refugees*,[53] serve as guidelines or policies for working in these contexts.

Refugee contexts exist in nearly all jurisdictions, as the UNHCR Global Trends reports show.[54] Nevertheless, the low- and middle-income countries host more people living in these contexts.[55] More people in refugee contexts live in urban settings,[56] and most live in protracted situations that last five or more years.[57]

49 The 1951 *Refugee Convention* and it's 1967 protocol are interrelated treaties, as the intent of the latter was to increase the temporal and geographical reach of the earlier instrument. The latter instrument includes all the rights from the earlier, so it is a standalone instrument. Both will be referred to as the *Refugee Convention*, unless there is a reason to differentiate them. *Refugee Convention* (n 47); *Protocol Relating to the Status of Refugees*, opened for signature 31 January 1967, 606 UNTS 267 (entered into force 4 October 1967).

50 A refugee is defined as a person who, 'owing to well-founded fear of being persecuted for reasons of race, religion, nationality, membership of a particular social group or political opinion, is outside the country of his nationality and is unable or, owing to such fear, is unwilling to avail himself of the protection of that country; or who, not having a nationality and being outside the country of his former habitual residence, is unable or, owing to such fear, is unwilling to return to it'. *Refugee Convention* (n 47) art 1(A)(2), as modified by *Protocol Relating to the Status of Refugees* (n 49) art 1(2).

51 *Non-refoulement*, while not explicitly stated in the *Refugee Convention*, is viewed as a core principle of the convention and 'embedded in customary international law'. Ministerial Meeting of State Parties, *Declaration of States Parties to the 1951 Convention and/or Its 1967 Protocol Relating to the Status of Refugees* (12 December 2001) Preamble para 4. See also Cathryn Costello and Michelle Foster, 'Non-Refoulement as Custom and Jus Cogens? Putting the Prohibition to the Test' in Maarten den Heijer and Harmen van der Wilt (eds), *Netherlands Yearbook of International Law 2015: Jus Cogens: Quo Vadis?* (TMC Asser Press, 2016) 273, 282–306. For the UNHCR's guidance on the matter, see United Nations High Commissioner for Refugees, *The Principle of Non-Refoulement as a Norm of Customary International Law. Response to the Questions Posed to UNHCR by the Federal Constitutional Court of the Federal Republic of Germany in Cases 2 BvR 1938/93, 2 BvR 1953/93, 2 BvR 1954/93* (31 January 1994) <https://www.refworld.org/docid/437b6db64.html>.

52 *Statute of the Office of the United Nations High Commissioner for Refugees*, UNGA Res 428(V), UN Doc A/RES/428(V) (adopted 14 December 1950).

53 *Report of the United Nations High Commissioner for Refugees: Part II Global Compact on Refugees*, UN Doc A/73/12 (Part II) (13 September 2018, adopted 2 August 2018).

54 UNHCR, *Global Trends: Forced Displacement in 2023* (Report, 2024).

55 IBid., 21.

56 'Refugee Camps Explained', *USA for UNHCR* (Web Page, 6 April 2021) <https://www.unrefugees.org/news/refugee-camps-explained/>.

57 Protracted situations are defined by UNHCR as 'where more than 25,000 refugees from the same country of origin have been in exile in a given low- or middle-income host country for at least five consecutive years' UNHCR (n 54) 21. See later Section 6.1 for a discussion about the experiences of people with disability in refugee contexts.

1.2.2 Refugee Contexts as Sites to Explore Disability Human Rights

There are several reasons why refugee contexts are important and productive sites for exploring disability human rights. As described earlier, the *CRPD* is more explicit about multiple and aggravated forms of discrimination than earlier human rights instruments. People who are refugees with disability experience multiple and aggravated discrimination that can manifest in many ways, for instance, in greater barriers to accessing refugee *or* disability support services.

Human rights are not premised on citizenship rights. Nonetheless, many states provide disability services exclusively to citizens and certain permanent residents.[58] This service access criterion has a cascading effect on the ability of people who are refugees with disability to access their rights. Those who can access services must often contend with material, language and cultural barriers to accessing their rights.[59] Despite people who are refugees with disability experiencing specific barriers to accessing their rights, there are few or no disabled persons organisations ('DPOs') speaking on behalf of this group.

Further, while we often view refugee contexts as emergencies, as discussed earlier, many people have lived in these settings for over five years. This prolonged period requires consideration of when emergency settings, such as those that allow for derogation or suspension of human rights, cease and people's rights may be restored. Emergency response power dynamics resemble the medical model with a tension between paternalism and self-determination. Given the history of the disability rights movement and the evolution of the model of disability, disability studies and disability human rights scholars may make interesting contributions to practice and theory in prolonged emergency contexts. Contributions may also stem from scholarship around *CRPD*

58 See, eg, Soldatic et al who discuss the complexity of different service entitlements according to visa migration category. Karen Soldatic et al, 'Disability and Migration in Urban Australia: The Case of Liverpool' (2020) 55(4) *Australian Journal of Social Issues* 456. In an earlier piece, Soldatic uses doctrine and theory to argue that 'While the CRPD was made at the international level, the claiming of disability justice and the realization of disability rights firmly depends on one being a citizen of a nation state and making claims for justice upon that state'. Karen Soldatic, 'The Transnational Sphere of Justice: Disability Praxis and the Politics of Impairment' (2013) 28(6) *Disability & Society* 744, 746. In a submission, I described the gap in services for people with disability who are temporary protection visa holders. Philippa Duell-Piening, *Response to a Discussion Paper of the Victorian State Disability Plan 2017–2020* (Victorian Refugee Health Network, July 2016). For a description of service access for people with disability who are refugees or seeking asylum in the UK, see Jennifer Harris and Keri Roberts, '"Not Our Problem": The Provision of Services to Disabled Refugees and Asylum-Seekers' in Debra Hayes and Beth Humphries (eds), *Social Work, Immigration and Asylum: Debates, Dilemmas and Ethical Issues for Social Work and Social Care Practice* (Jessica Kingsley, 2004) 151.

59 See, eg, Samantha Furneaux and Dina Korkees, *'We Need to Raise Our Voices': Advice From People of Refugee Backgrounds Living with Disabilities and Their Carers* (Report, Victorian Foundation for Survivors of Torture, 2019).

article 11, 'Situations of Risk and Humanitarian Emergencies',[60] despite article 11 not referencing refugee contexts or the *Refugee Convention*.[61]

Another reason research on disability rights in refugee contexts is important is that there has been greater attention to this space since the adoption of the *CRPD*. While the 1951 *Refugee Convention* does not mention people with disability,[62] the 2018 *Global Compact on Refugees* contains 20 references to disability across many areas.[63] Further, shortly after the *CRPD* entered into force, the UNHCR released a practice guide, *Working with Persons with Disabilities in Forced Displacement: Need to Know Guidance*, in 2011, with an update in 2019.[64]

Several other instruments have been drafted demonstrating the commitment of a broad range of actors to working more inclusively with people with disability in refugee contexts. These instruments include the 2016 *Charter on Inclusion of Persons with Disabilities in Humanitarian Action*,[65] the 2018 *Humanitarian Inclusion Standards for Older People and People with Disabilities*[66] and the 2019 *Inclusion of Persons with Disabilities in Humanitarian Action*.[67] Of import to this monograph, these instruments and resources all refer to producing and processing data about the bodies and lives of people with disability in refugee contexts.[68]

Often, these instruments use *CRPD* article 31 as the legal basis to produce and process data about people with disability in refugee contexts:

> In recent years, there have been considerable efforts to collect, analyse and use data on persons with disabilities catalysed by data collection requirements called for in Article 31 of the UN Convention on the Rights of Persons with Disabilities (CRPD) . . . Consequently, disaggregation of data by disability is now a core principle included in many global frameworks.[69]

60 *CRPD* (n 9) art 11.

61 See later Section 6.2.2 for a discussion about the missed opportunity to include a reference to the *Refugee Convention* or the situations of people who are refugees in the *CRPD* during the drafting.

62 *Refugee Convention* (n 47).

63 *Report of the United Nations High Commissioner for Refugees: Part II Global Compact on Refugees* (n 53).

64 Office of the United Nations High Commissioner for Refugees (UNHCR), *Working with Persons with Disabilities in Forced Displacement: Need to Know Guidance* (2011); Office of the United Nations High Commissioner for Refugees (UNHCR), *Working with Persons with Disabilities in Forced Displacement: Need to Know Guidance* (2019).

65 *Charter on Inclusion of Persons with Disabilities in Humanitarian Action* (2016) <http://humanitariandisabilitycharter.org/>.

66 CBM International, HelpAge International and Handicap International, *Humanitarian Inclusion Standards for Older People and People with Disabilities* (Report, 2018).

67 Inter-Agency Standing Committee (IASC), *Guidelines on Inclusion of Persons with Disabilities in Humanitarian Action* (2019).

68 See later Section 6.3 for an examination of the provisions in these instruments for data production and processing.

69 Handicap International, *Data on Persons with Disabilities in Humanitarian Action: Collecting Quantitative Data with the Washington Group Questions* (May 2019) 2.

Further, the CRPD Committee has used article 31's authority to recommend disaggregating data by refugee status in Concluding Observations to 15 states.[70] In addition to the guidance provided under the heading of article 31 in the Concluding Observations, the committee have also recommended data production and processing about people who are refugees with disability to support the realisation of substantive rights,[71] including article 6, 'Women with Disabilities',[72] article 7, 'Children with Disabilities',[73] article 11, 'Situations of Risk and Humanitarian Emergencies',[74] article 16,

70 Committee on the Rights of Persons with Disabilities, *Concluding Observations on the Combined Second and Third Periodic Reports of Azerbaijan*, UN Doc CRPD/C/AZE/CO/2-3 (22 March 2024) [66]; Committee on the Rights of Persons with Disabilities, *Concluding Observations on the Initial Report of Kazakhstan*, UN Doc CRPD/C/KAZ/CO/1 (22 March 2024) [65]–[66]; Committee on the Rights of Persons with Disabilities, *Concluding Observations on the Combined Second and Third Periodic Reports of Sweden*, UN Doc CRPD/C/SWE/CO/2-3 (22 March 2024) [67]–[68]; Committee on the Rights of Persons with Disabilities, *Concluding Observations on the Combined Second and Third Periodic Reports of Austria*, UN Doc CRPD/C/AUT/CO/2-3 (8 September 2023) [69]–[70]; Committee on the Rights of Persons with Disabilities, *Concluding Observations on the Combined Second and Third Periodic Reports of Germany*, UN Doc CRPD/C/DEU/CO/2-3 (8 September 2023) [69]–[70]; Committee on the Rights of Persons with Disabilities, *Concluding Observations on the Initial Report of Israel*, UN Doc CRPD/C/ISR/CO/1 (8 September 2023) [65]–[66]; Committee on the Rights of Persons with Disabilities, *Concluding Observations on the Initial Report of Bangladesh*, UN Doc CRPD/C/BGD/CO/1 (9 September 2022) [59]; Committee on the Rights of Persons with Disabilities, *Concluding Observations on the Combined Second and Third Periodic Reports of Hungary* (n 3) [61(a)]; Committee on the Rights of Persons with Disabilities, *Concluding Observations on the Initial Report of Iraq*, UN Doc CRPD/C/IRQ/CO/1 (19 September 2019) [59]–[60]; Committee on the Rights of Persons with Disabilities, *Concluding Observations on the Initial Report of the Former Yugoslav Republic of Macedonia*, UN Doc CRPD/C/MKD/CO/1 (29 October 2018) [54]; Committee on the Rights of Persons with Disabilities, *Concluding Observations on the Initial Report of the United Kingdom of Great Britain and Northern Ireland*, UN Doc CRPD/C/GBR/CO/1 (3 October 2017) [65]; Committee on the Rights of Persons with Disabilities, *Concluding Observations on the Initial Report of the Islamic Republic of Iran*, UN Doc CRPD/C/IRN/CO/1 (10 May 2017) [58]–[59]; Committee on the Rights of Persons with Disabilities, *Concluding Observations on the Initial Report of Morocco*, UN Doc CRPD/C/MAR/CO/1 (25 September 2017) [59]; Committee on the Rights of Persons with Disabilities, *Concluding Observations on the Initial Report of Uganda*, UN Doc CRPD/C/UGA/CO/1 (12 May 2016) [60]; Committee on the Rights of Persons with Disabilities, *Concluding Observations on the Initial Report of Kenya*, UN Doc CRPD/C/KEN/CO/1 (30 September 2015) [56].

71 This makes sense as art 31's purpose is to enable the implementation of the *CRPD*. Therefore, it is necessary to make clear what data would be useful in implementing the substantive rights in the treaty.

72 Committee on the Rights of Persons with Disabilities, *Concluding Observations on the Initial Report of Bangladesh* (n 70) [14(a)]; Committee on the Rights of Persons with Disabilities, *Concluding Observations on the Initial Report of Germany*, UN Doc CRPD/C/DEU/CO/1 (13 May 2015) [16(b)].

73 Committee on the Rights of Persons with Disabilities, *Concluding Observations on the Combined Second and Third Periodic Reports of Germany* (n 70) [15]–[16].

74 Committee on the Rights of Persons with Disabilities, *Concluding Observations on the Initial Report of Canada*, UN Doc CRPD/C/CAN/CO/1 (8 May 2017) [25]–[26].

'Freedom from Exploitation, Violence and Abuse',[75] article 17, 'Protecting the Integrity of the Person',[76] article 18, 'Liberty of Movement',[77] article 24, 'Education',[78] and article 28, 'Adequate Standard of Living and Social Protection'.[79] Extraterritorial data production and processing in refugee contexts has also been recommended by the committee: 'Collect disaggregated data on disability in all humanitarian and development programmes'.[80] Nonetheless, there is growing evidence data production and processing may harm individuals and groups.[81] Urgent attention and discussion about data's beneficial and harmful effects and how to mediate this tension are required. The following outlines how this research engages with this tension.

1.3 About This Research Project

This section contextualises this monograph within a field of scholarly work and describes the gap into which this project intervenes. It then outlines the project's research questions. This section concludes with a summary of the monograph's main contributions.

1.3.1 Contextualising This Project Within a Field of Scholarly Work

Refugee law scholar Mary Crock and colleagues have undertaken the most comprehensive study of disability rights in refugee contexts. Their research involved fieldwork across six jurisdictions documenting the implications of the

75 Committee on the Rights of Persons with Disabilities, *Concluding Observations on the Combined Second and Third Periodic Reports of Azerbaijan* (n 70) [38(c)], Committee on the Rights of Persons with Disabilities, *Concluding Observations on the Initial Report of Switzerland*, UN Doc CRPD/C/CHE/CO/1 (13 April 2022) [33]–[34].

76 Committee on the Rights of Persons with Disabilities, *Concluding Observations on the Initial Report of France*, UN Doc CRPD/C/FRA/CO/1 (4 October 2021) [39].

77 Committee on the Rights of Persons with Disabilities, *Concluding Observations on the Combined Second and Third Periodic Reports of Hungary* (n 3) [37(e)], [38(e)]; Committee on the Rights of Persons with Disabilities, *Concluding Observations on the Combined Second and Third Periodic Reports of Mexico*, UN Doc CRPD/C/MEX/CO/2-3 (20 April 2022) [48]–[49]; Committee on the Rights of Persons with Disabilities, *Concluding Observations on the Initial Report of Turkey*, UN Doc CRPD/C/TUR/CO/1 (9 April 2019) [38]–[39].

78 Committee on the Rights of Persons with Disabilities, *Concluding Observations on the Combined Second and Third Periodic Reports of Germany* (n 70) [55]–[56]; Committee on the Rights of Persons with Disabilities, *Concluding Observations on the Initial Report of the Islamic Republic of Iran* (n 70) [47(b)].

79 Committee on the Rights of Persons with Disabilities, *Concluding Observations on the Combined Second and Third Periodic Reports of Azerbaijan* (n 70) [62(a)].

80 Committee on the Rights of Persons with Disabilities, *Concluding Observations on the Initial Report of Switzerland* (n 85) [60(c)].

81 See later Chapter 3 for a discussion of data and power as well as Part 3 for an exploration of some of the particular harms that people who are refugees with disability may encounter through visibility in datasets.

CRPD for people who are refugees.[82] Many of Crock's publications have been co-authored with the former chair of the CRPD Committee, Ron McCallum. While Crock, McCallum and colleagues demonstrated significant interest in identifying people with disability in refugee contexts using article 31 as the legal basis,[83] their legal analysis of *CRPD* article 31 is not apparent in their published work.

Crock, McCallum and colleagues described the data systems used by the UNHCR in each jurisdiction they studied without critique.[84] They did not identify the possible harms and measures in place to protect data subjects. The breadth of Crock, McCallum and colleagues' work is impressive, and their scholarly contribution about the rights of people who are refugees with disability is important. Nonetheless, gaps in scholarship remain, particularly concerning the nature of the state obligations in *CRPD* article 31, how refugee contexts may impact these and an exploration of the potential harms caused by data production and processing.

Article 31 is often cited as a legal basis for surveilling people with disability.[85] Yet the legal obligations in article 31 are underexamined. The CRPD Committee's authoritative advice and the two scholarly commentaries on article 31 read like technical manuals for producing and processing data about the bodies and lives of people with disability rather than doctrinal interpretations of the article's obligations.[86] While no General Comment exists on article 31, the primary advice from the committee on the article may be found in Concluding Observations to states. This advice often contains indicators by which states should consider disaggregating data. For example, the committee recommended to China:

> The Committee recalls the Washington Group short set of questions on disability and recommends that the State party develop data collection systems on the situation of persons with disabilities with the data

82 Mary Crock et al, *The Legal Protection of Refugees with Disabilities: Forgotten and Invisible?* (Edward Elgar Publishing, 2017); Mary Crock and Laura Smith-Khan, 'Swift and Systematic? Identifying and Recording Disability in Forced Migration' in Barbara M Altman (ed), *International Measurement of Disability: Purpose, Method and Application* (Springer, 2016) 305; Mary Crock, Christine Ernst and Ron McCallum, 'Where Disability and Displacement Intersect: Asylum Seekers and Refugees with Disabilities' (2012) 24(4) *International Journal of Refugee Law* 735; Mary Crock et al, *Syrian Refugees with Disabilities in Jordan and Turkey* (University of Sydney, 2015).

83 See especially Crock and Smith-Khan (n 82) 305; Crock et al, *The Legal Protection of Refugees with Disabilities: Forgotten and Invisible?* (n 82) 62–88.

84 Crock et al, *The Legal Protection of Refugees with Disabilities: Forgotten and Invisible?* (n 82).

85 For an explanation of the use of the word surveillance in this monograph, see earlier n 12.

86 Pedersen (n 10); Pedersen and Ferretti (n 10). The CRPD Committee has not issued a general comment on art 31; however, every Concluding Observation to states about their performance implementing the *CRPD* recommends further disaggregation of data and some include instruments that may be used.

> disaggregated by a range of factors, such as age, sex, sexual orientation and gender identity, place of residence, socioeconomic status and ethnicity. These systems should cover all areas of life and should include information on violence against persons with disabilities.[87]

As illustrated earlier, the CRPD Committee's advice may include tools states should use for disaggregation. Since 2017, the *Washington Group Short Set of Questions on Disability* has featured in 65 of 82 of the committee's Concluding Observations to states.[88]

The article 31 commentaries justify the legal basis for data production about the bodies and lives of people with disability by citing a guideline developed by the Office of the High Commissioner for Human Rights ('OHCHR') regarding human rights indicators: 'In the [OHCHR's] human rights-based approach to data the purpose of disaggregation is to reveal underlying discrimination recognized in international human rights law, such as sex, age, ethnicity, and more'.[89] Likely, the lack of attention to the legal interpretation of article 31 is because the article is seen as a procedural article that works to aid the implementation of the substantive rights within the convention. Further, being a novel article, the commentaries and the CRPD Committee have scarce jurisprudence to draw upon.

There is considerable need and urgency for a debate about the article 31 obligations and how these are being operationalised. As described in the Prologue, clear tensions exist within article 31 that need more investigation. These tensions include the beneficial and harmful effects of data, the impost on the privacy of data subjects and the accumulation of power by the data controller. This article, with procedural obligations, must not be viewed as giving a broad mandate to data technocrats without examination of the legal basis and the nature of the obligations for data production and processing.

This monograph seeks to contribute to the disability human rights scholarship regarding *CRPD* article 31. Furthermore, its examination of disability data practices in refugee contexts seeks to contribute to refugee law scholarship and practice. Lastly, this research may also contribute to scholarship on the social impact of data production and processing. The following outlines the research questions formulated to respond to the gap in scholarship described in this section.

87 Committee on the Rights of Persons with Disabilities, *Concluding Observations on the Combined Second and Third Periodic Reports of China*, UN Doc CRPD/C/CHN/CO/2-3 (10 October 2022) [59].

88 These numbers are from the time of writing August 2024. See the CRPD Committee website for access to all their Concluding Observations: 'Committee on the Rights of Persons with Disabilities', *Office of the High Commissioner for Human Rights* (Web Page) <https://www.ohchr.org/en/treaty-bodies/crpd>. See later Sections 7.2.2 and 7.3.1 for a critique of the human rights compliance of the *Washington Group Short Set of Questions on Disability*.

89 Pedersen and Ferretti (n 10) 945.

1.3.2 *Research Hypothesis and Questions*

CRPD article 31 – an under-explored and innovative human rights provision entitled 'Statistics and data collection' – may be beneficial to people with disability who are refugees because it renders individuals and their rights more visible. However, information production and processing may also be harmful. Drawing on these hypotheses, this research asks the following:

A. How should *CRPD* article 31 be interpreted?
B. How do refugee contextual considerations inform the interpretation of the state obligations and (potential) group right in *CRPD* article 31?
C. Does the international human rights framework adequately balance the potential benefits of information production and processing with the potential harms?

1.3.3 *Main Contributions*

This monograph makes at least four contributions to legal scholarship. These interventions are (1) a doctrinal argument and demonstration of participatory treaty interpretation, (2) a *Vienna Convention on the Law of Treaties* ('*Vienna Convention*') adherent interpretation of article 31 that emphasises data production and processing of state actions in contrast to the more accepted interpretation that focuses on data production and processing about the bodies and lives of people with disability,[90] (3) a doctrinal argument for a group right to be counted (or not) and (4) a conceptual framework that describes the relationship between visibility and power. Each intervention is described here.

a) Participatory Treaty Interpretation

In Chapter 2, this monograph presents doctrinal reasoning behind a state obligation to include rights-holders in interpreting the *CRPD*. In addition, it describes a participatory approach to treaty interpretation that was designed and trialled during this research. The participatory approach drawing on Freire's work on dialogue is depicted in Figure 2.3.[91] Four advocates with disability who had lived in refugee contexts met with me eight times over two years to engage in dialogue about article 31 and other questions that emerged from the research. I kept minutes of the meetings, which acted as an archive for the research. I also kept a research diary that demonstrated

90 For the general rule of interpretation see *Vienna Convention on the Law of Treaties*, opened for signature 23 May 1969, 1155 UNTS 331 (entered into force 27 January 1980) arts 31–3 ('*Vienna Convention*'). For a description of the prevailing understanding of the *CRPD* art 31 obligations, see Pedersen and Ferretti (n 10); Pedersen (n 10).
91 Paulo Freire, *Pedagogy of the Oppressed*, tr Myra Bergman Ramos (Penguin Classics, 1970).

the group had an indirect influence in shaping the research in addition to the direct contribution made through the advisory group meeting minutes cited in this monograph.

b) An Alternative Interpretation of CRPD *Article 31*

In Chapter 5, using the general rules of interpretation from the *Vienna Convention*,[92] this monograph interprets the state obligations in *CRPD* article 31. Information produced and processed under the authority of *CRPD* article 31 is to be used to assess how states should implement their obligations to identify and address barriers to people with disability realising their rights.[93] One reading of this article may lead to extensive surveillance of people with disability to ensure they have not encountered barriers to realising their rights.

This monograph proposes an alternative reading of *CRPD* article 31, interpreted in context and consistent with the treaty's object and purpose. It argues that article 31 emphasises information production and processing about *state actions* and *barriers* to rights attainment, not about the bodies and lives of people with disability. Barriers may be identified through close consultation and active involvement of people with disability through their representative organisations and disability human rights research methods.[94]

c) A Group (Human) Right to Be Counted

Information's power comes through aggregation, the grouping of data. Therefore, it is possible that rights, harms and protections associated with data must be conceptualised at a group rather than individual level. Group rights, which individuals cannot realise apart from a group,[95] are controversial and under-theorised in human rights law. Nevertheless, it has been argued that one of the *CRPD*'s contributions to the human rights framework is the progression of group rights.[96]

This monograph presents doctrinal reasoning for a group (human) right to be counted (or not). The group (human) right to be counted (or not) is a subsidiary right to *CRPD* article 4(3), which requires people with disability through their representative organisations to be actively involved and closely

92 *Vienna Convention* (n 90) arts 31–33.

93 *CRPD* (n 9) art 31(1), (2).

94 *CRPD* (n 9) art 4(1)(f), (g), 4(3). See also Anna Arstein-Kerslake et al, 'Introducing a Human Rights-Based Disability Research Methodology' (2020) 20(3) *Human Rights Law Review* 412.

95 Peter Jones, 'Human Rights, Group Rights, and Peoples' Rights' (1999) 21(1) *Human Rights Quarterly* 80.

96 Kayess and French (n 16) 32.

consulted in the implementation of the *CRPD*.[97] The group (human) right allows a pre-existing group to control their visibility within datasets produced and processed for *CRPD* article 31.

To further understand the nature of this right, I applied it to refugee contexts where it has been identified that even aggregated data may be sensitive and used to target groups at risk of persecution.[98] The monograph concluded that, for people who are refugees with disability to exercise this group right, they need to be included in existing DPOs or self-organise DPOs. Nonetheless, they face many barriers to doing so.

d) Visibility and Locus of Power Conceptual Framework

People who are refugees with disability have been legally and programmatically invisible.[99] Visibility is often seen as an antidote or at least a step along the path to remedy marginalisation. Nonetheless, visibility alone cannot achieve human rights. In some instances, visibility may be counter-productive to human rights attainment.

This monograph argues that the locus of power over an individual must be considered to understand whether visibility may benefit or harm the rights-holders. Visibility combined with state power over an individual may lead to subjugation, for example, Kimlik (Temporary Protection Identification) being used by Turkish police to identify and detain people who are refugees from Syria.[100] This monograph argues that greater visibility with greater individual autonomy creates human rights–promoting conditions. Conversely, greater visibility with greater state control creates conditions that lead to the subjugation of people with disability. The locus of power is influenced by laws, citizenship and other mechanisms of control.

Figure 1.1, developed during this research, depicts a conceptual framework that illustrates the interaction between visibility and locus of power. The conceptual framework differentiates the conditions created by changes in the locus of power and visibility. This conceptual framework enabled the identification of conditions that should be promoted to ensure human rights–consistent data production and processing.

The contributions outlined earlier are made through six substantive chapters. The following summarises the chapters' content.

97 *CRPD* (n 9) art 4(3).

98 Christopher Kuner and Massimo Marelli (eds), *Handbook on Data Protection in Humanitarian Action* (International Committee of the Red Cross, 2nd ed, 2020) 24.

99 Women's Refugee Commission, *Disabilities Among Refugees and Conflict-Affected Populations* (Report, June 2008).

100 Human Rights Watch, 'Syrian Refugees in Turkey Fear Turkish Police' (YouTube, 25 October 2022) <https://www.youtube.com/watch?v=4_HoMO0PMz4&t=16s>.

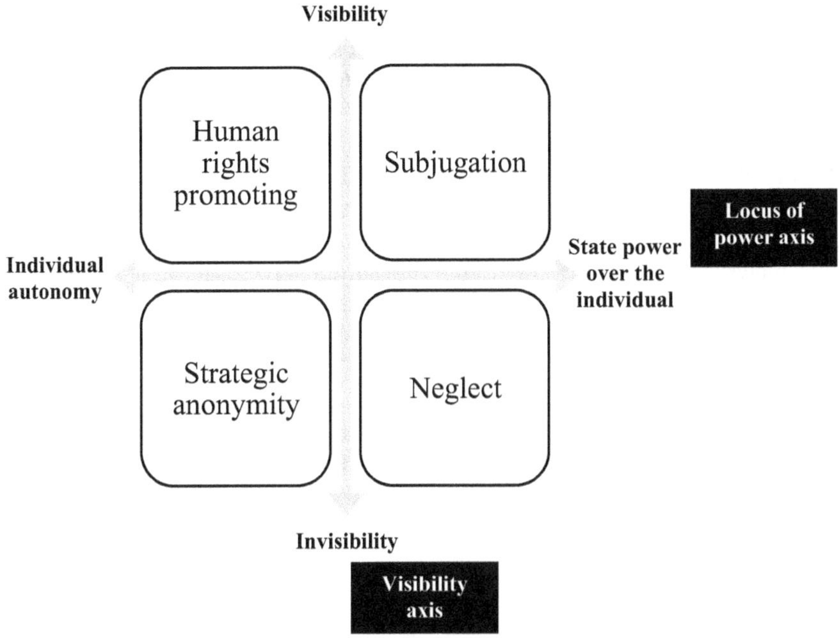

Figure 1.1 Conceptual framework depicting the intersecting axes of locus of power and visibility

1.4 Chapter Summaries

This monograph is divided into three parts. *Part I* is broadly about knowledge production and control. It outlines the research methodology and contains a theoretical chapter that problematises data production and processing. *Part II* focuses on *CRPD* article 31 by reviewing the drafting debates and undertaking a doctrinal interpretation to determine the rights and obligations in the article. *Part III* then considers the implications of *CRPD* article 31 in refugee contexts and explores methods to prevent and mitigate harm from data. The substantive chapters that make up these sections are described here.

Chapter 2, Participatory Treaty Interpretation, deconstructs knowledge production and demonstrates the critical role of rights-holders in implementing the *CRPD*. It does so by describing the legal research methods used in the project in detail. This description of methods includes a doctrinal argument for rights-holders to be involved in interpreting the *CRPD*. This chapter then describes the participatory approach to treaty interpretation adopted in this research.

Chapter 3, Data and Power, explains data and statistics' role in justifying eugenics, forced sterilisation and murder of many people with disability. It then draws on the work of philosophers, sociologists and disability studies scholars to argue that data are not neutral and inert but powerful and potentially dangerous.[101] Chapter 3 concludes by engaging with the work of theorists and human rights scholars who critique the rising digitisation of the state and its implications.

Chapter 4, Drafting CRPD Article 31, identifies the core tensions evident during the drafting of *CRPD* article 31. These tensions include data production and processing's unresolved role in society, its concurrently harmful and useful effects and its function of amassing power to the data controller. The analysis demonstrates the drafters' willingness to settle on language with considerable scope for various interpretations. The chapter argues that it is problematic that these tensions have not been adequately engaged with since the treaty came into force.

Chapter 5, Interpreting CRPD Article 31, proposes an alternative legal interpretation of article 31 from the dominant one held by disability human rights scholars and supported by the CRPD Committee. The dominant view is that article 31 obligates states to produce and process data about the bodies and lives of people with disability. Chapter 5, adhering to the *Vienna Convention* interpretive rules, argues that the *CRPD* article 31 obligations emphasise information production and processing about *state actions* and *barriers to rights attainment*, not the bodies and lives of people with disability. This chapter also introduces the possibility of article 31 containing a group (human) right to control the visibility of identity in datasets, a group right to be counted or not.

Chapter 6, People With Disability in Refugee Contexts as Rights-Holders and Data Subjects, describes the multiple and aggravated forms of discrimination experienced by people who are refugees with disability. It then outlines the development of international human rights and refugee law and policy that seeks to remedy the discrimination experienced by this population. This chapter explains that making this population and their rights more visible was one of the strategies employed to advance the rights of people who are refugees with disability. Nonetheless, the chapter describes how the operationalisation of article 31 obligations has omitted an important safeguard that requires data only to be produced and processed if 'appropriate'.[102] The chapter introduces a framework that considers the relationship between power and visibility. The framework is useful for analysing the implications of *CRPD* article 31 in refugee contexts and identifying interventions to restore autonomy to people with disability.

Chapter 7, A Balancing Act: Mitigating the Harms of Human Rights Data Production and Processing, takes a slightly different position from earlier

101 See, eg, Sally Engle Merry, *The Seductions of Quantification: Measuring Human Rights, Gender Violence, and Sex Trafficking* (University of Chicago Press, 2016); Shelley Tremain, 'Foucault, Governmentality, and Critical Disability Theory: An Introduction' in Shelley Tremain (ed), *Foucault and the Government of Disability* (University of Michigan Press, 2005) 1; Shakespeare (n 22).

102 Art 31 requires that data are disaggregated 'as appropriate'. *CRPD* (n 9) art 31(2).

chapters in accepting the premise that data production and processing about the bodies and lives of people with disability may improve human rights attainment. Nonetheless, the chapter argues that data production and processing often omit critical human rights protections because they are incompatible with comprehensive, harmonious and interoperable data. In making this argument, the chapter observes that the *CRPD* has contributed to the normative understanding of these protections. The protections the chapter explores include a *CRPD* test for 'appropriate' data production and the human rights principles of self-defining and self-identifying. This chapter also highlights that the *CRPD* has underutilised tools that work alongside data production and processing to facilitate the convention's implementation, such as awareness raising, participation, disability human rights research and universal design.[103]

1.5 Conclusion

This monograph is a timely exploration of *CRPD* article 31, 'Statistics and data collection'. The article is being used as an authority to justify the production and processing of data about the bodies and lives of people with disability, including in refugee contexts. As explained in this chapter, this research sought to explore the legal basis for these claims and understand their implications in refugee and broader human rights contexts. In doing so, it has made at least four contributions to legal scholarship. These interventions include a doctrinal argument and demonstration of participatory treaty interpretation, an alternative legal interpretation of article 31 that emphasises data production and processing of state actions, a doctrinal argument for a group right to be counted or not and a conceptual framework that describes the relationship between visibility and power. The next chapter outlines the research's methodology adopted to interrogate article 31's tensions.

103 *CRPD* (n 9) arts 4, 8.

Part I

Knowledge Production and Control

> Data is used to target us. [It] makes us feel unsafe.
>
> Stakeholder Advisory Group meeting minutes, 16 July 2021

DOI: 10.4324/9781003506140-2

2 Participatory Treaty Interpretation

Research questions and methods are not generated in a vacuum. They are shaped by a range of assumptions that are not always explicit. Research outcomes are often described as common sense,[1] reflections of the true order of nature[2] and scientific without attention to the assumptions that shaped that knowledge.[3] In their work to bring greater attention to the construction of knowledge about disability, disability studies scholar Lennard Davis explained that 'the "problem" is not the person with disabilities; the problem is the way that normalcy is constructed to create the "problem" of the disabled person'.[4] Lack of attention to how knowledge is constructed has maintained the marginalisation of people with disability for centuries.[5] Research findings have been used to justify segregation, eugenics and 'the systematic denial of human rights'.[6]

The drafters of the *Convention on the Rights of Persons with Disabilities* ('*CRPD*') were acutely aware of the implications of the power to shape knowledge.[7] The import of knowledge construction is explicit in how the *CRPD* frames disability,[8] and the role of rights-holders in knowledge

1 See, eg, Paul Chynoweth, 'Legal Research' in Andrew Knight and Leslie Ruddock (eds), *Advanced Research Methods in the Built Environment* (Wiley-Blackwell, 2008) 28, 32.
2 See, eg, the primate case study in Donna Jeanne Haraway, *Primate Visions: Gender, Race, and Nature in the World of Modern Science* (Routledge, 1989) 9–13.
3 Sheila Jasanoff has written extensively about how knowledge is constructed. See, eg, Sheila Jasanoff, *States of Knowledge: The Co-Production of Science and the Social Order* (Taylor & Francis Group, 2004); Sheila S Jasanoff, 'Contested Boundaries in Policy-Relevant Science' (1987) 17(2) *Social Studies of Science* 195.
4 Lennard J Davis, *Enforcing Normalcy: Disability, Deafness, and the Body* (Verso, 1995) 24.
5 For an example of how the statistics movement in the mid-19th century led to the eugenics movement, remnants of which still exist in law and policy around the world, see Davis (n 4).
6 Emma Stone and Mark Priestley, 'Parasites, Pawns and Partners: Disability Research and the Role of Non-Disabled Researchers' (1996) 47(4) *British Journal of Sociology* 699, 701, citing Marcia Rioux and Michael Bach (eds), *Disability is Not Measles: New Research Paradigms in Disability* (L'Institut Roeher, 1994).
7 *Convention on the Rights of Persons with Disabilities*, opened for signature 24 January 2007, 2515 UNTS 3 (entered into force 3 May 2008) ('*CRPD*').
8 IBid., ('*CRPD*'). Preamble para e, art 1. See earlier Section 1.1.1.

DOI: 10.4324/9781003506140-3

production to implement and monitor the treaty.[9] Disability human rights scholars know that the *CRPD*'s approach to knowledge has implications for how they work.[10]

During this research, I developed a participatory methodology to include and respect the knowledge of rights-holders. I convened a Stakeholder Advisory Group ('advisory group') of people with disability from refugee backgrounds living in Australia.[11] The group assisted with interpreting the rights and obligations in article 31 and explored the implications of data production and processing for people with disability who are refugees or from refugee backgrounds.

This chapter explains that the *CRPD* places new demands on international law methods.[12] These demands include greater participation of people with disability at all stages and levels of research 'relating to persons with disabilities'.[13] Legal research methods must also evolve to accommodate these new demands. Given that this research seeks to understand how *CRPD* article 31 should be interpreted, the chapter demonstrates that doctrinal research methods can and should be participatory. Moreover, it makes the doctrinal argument that people with disability have a role in interpreting *CRPD* rights and obligations more broadly. While it is widely understood that participatory research is complex due to people's diverse lives and experiences, this chapter illustrates that doctrinal research can accommodate multiple perspectives. Nonetheless, marginalised communities' access to forums where people may engage in doctrinal debates is challenging. This chapter engages with these challenges and presents a methodology to overcome some of these barriers.

These arguments are progressed by first examining the doctrinal contribution the *CRPD* has made to treaty interpretation practices in Section 2.1. Section 2.2 introduces a legal research methodology and the theoretical frames employed in this research: ***data and power*** and ***disability human rights research***. Section 2.3 locates the participatory methodology in a field of legal research, followed by engaging with the practicalities of representation and sites for discussions about 'what is the law'. Section 2.4 describes the theoretical basis for the advisory group facilitation method and then describes the advisory

9 *Convention on the Rights of Persons with Disabilities*, opened for signature 24 January 2007, 2515 UNTS 3 (entered into force 3 May 2008) ('*CRPD*'). Preamble para e, arts 4(3), 33(3).

10 See, eg, Anna Arstein-Kerslake et al, 'Introducing a Human Rights-Based Disability Research Methodology' (2020) 20(3) *Human Rights Law Review* 412.

11 The term 'people from refugee backgrounds' is a broad term that encompasses people who have had refugee experiences or refugee-like experiences. It also acknowledges that some people continue to identify as 'refugees' after they have resettled while others do not. 'Backgrounds' plural is used to denote multiple refugee experiences. See generally Department of Health, *The Victorian Refugee and Asylum Seeker Health Action Plan 2014–2018* (Action Plan, 2014) 5.

12 Arstein-Kerslake et al (n 10).

13 *CRPD* (n 7) art 4(3).

group process in detail. The chapter concludes by drawing together how the doctrine and theory in the proceeding sections are reflected in the research methodology.

2.1 Human Rights Treaty Interpretation: The Doctrinal Case for a Participatory Method

The *Vienna Convention on the Law of Treaties* ('*Vienna Convention*') embodies the rules that govern treaty interpretation.[14] Human rights treaties are agreements between states that bestow rights on humans, who are not parties to the conventions. While the extent of the specialist nature of human rights law and the need for specialised interpretive methods is not settled,[15] it appears widely accepted that the *Vienna Convention* provides a 'flexible enough' framework for interpreting human rights treaties.[16] Accepting that these rules apply to international human rights treaties does not deliver a definitive approach to their interpretation. It is widely accepted that the *Vienna Convention* allows significant latitude for various interpretations to be produced from the same text.[17]

Since states are the primary subjects of international law, and the decentralised system is based on state consent, treaty interpretation is generally the domain of states and courts to which states have granted jurisdiction (eg, the International Court of Justice).[18] Nonetheless, with human rights law, state primacy in treaty interpretation is somewhat counterintuitive, as states are accountable for their actions or inactions towards individual humans. Therefore, human rights committees, civil society organisations and legal scholars often make reasoned arguments about rights and obligations within human rights treaties.[19] These bodies and individuals have varying success in gaining

14 *Vienna Convention on the Law of Treaties*, opened for signature 23 May 1969, 1155 UNTS 331 (entered into force 27 January 1980).

15 See generally James Crawford and Amelia Keene, 'Interpretation of the Human Rights Treaties by the International Court of Justice' (2020) 24(7) *International Journal of Human Rights* 935, 938–940.

16 Çalı Başak, 'Specialized Rules of Treaty Interpretation: Human Rights' in Duncan B Hollis (ed), *The Oxford Guide to Treaties* (Oxford University Press, 2nd ed, 2020) 504.

17 Gardiner describes the *Vienna Convention* rules as 'a quite loose structure for developing interpretations, rather than a straightjacket or formulaic set of requirements'. Richard Gardiner, 'The Vienna Convention Rules on Treaty Interpretation' in Duncan B Hollis (ed), *The Oxford Guide to Treaties* (Oxford University Press, 2nd ed, 2020) 459, 476. Tobin argued that the *Vienna Convention* provides a 'frame' for the interpretive process, 'but it is ultimately unable to choose a meaning for the text of a treaty from among the inevitable range of potential meanings'. John Tobin, 'Seeking to Persuade: A Constructive Approach to Human Rights Treaty Interpretation' (2010) 23(1) *Harvard Human Rights Journal* 1, 3.

18 *Statute of the International Court of Justice* art 36.

19 Note the Court statute makes provision for subsidiary means of interpretation through 'the teaching of the most highly qualified publicists'. *Statute of the International Court of Justice* art 38(1)(d).

traction for their interpretation and ultimately require state or court agreement with the interpretation to have wide-ranging authority.

As discussed in Chapter 1, the *CRPD* has brought several innovations to the human rights framework, one of which may bring greater legitimacy to diverse voices in treaty interpretation. The *CRPD* requires states to 'closely consult with and actively involve' people with disability '[i]n the development and implementation of legislation and policies to implement' the *CRPD*,[20] as well as requiring that states ensure that people with disability 'participate fully in the monitoring process'.[21] Implicit in implementing and monitoring the treaty is the need to interpret 'What is the law?' Therefore, it could reasonably be read that people with disability should be closely consulted and actively involved in interpreting the *CRPD*'s rights and obligations.

This reading is consistent with the *CRPD*'s drafting process, in which people with disability were actively involved in the writing of the treaty.[22] The inclusion of people with disability in the drafting process was essential to understanding the way that people with disability experience human rights violations.[23] The same rationale exists in interpreting the rights and obligations of the treaty. To ensure that provisions are understood correctly, people with disability need to be actively involved in interpreting the *CRPD*.

2.2 Legal Research Methodology

The *CRPD* makes demands on legal research to change. In order to change, legal scholars need to be conscious of their practice and the embedded assumptions that shape the outcomes of their research. This part of the

20 *CRPD* (n 7) art 4(3). While the *CRPD* formulation is new, the *Convention on the Rights of the Child* includes a right to participation in art 12: 'the right to express those views freely in all matters affecting the child, the views of the child being given due weight in accordance with the age and maturity of the child'. *Convention on the Rights of the Child*, opened for signature 20 November 1989, 1577 UNTS 3 (entered into force 2 September 1990) art 12(1). The Committee on the Rights of the Child clarified in its *General Comment 5* that 'This principle, which highlights the role of the child as an active participant in the promotion, protection and monitoring of his or her rights, applies equally to all measures adopted by States to implement the Convention'. Committee on the Rights of the Child, *General Comment 5: General Measures of Implementation of the Convention on the Rights of the Child*, UN Doc CRC/GC/2003/5 (27 November 2003) [12].

21 *CRPD* (n 7) art 33(3).

22 'Juan Manuel Gómez Robledo, Mexico's Under-Secretary for Multilateral Affairs and Human Rights, said . . . the negotiating process had been unprecedented in the history of the United Nations because disability-rights activists and representatives of non-governmental organizations had participated in the talks on a nearly similar footing as Member States'. United Nations, 'Press Conference by High Commissioner for Human Rights on Signing of Convention' (Media Release, 30 March 2007) <https://www.un.org/press/en/2007/070330_Disabilities.doc.htm>.

23 The *CRPD* is a translational tool that ensures existing human rights 'based on "able-bodied" norm[s]' may be realised by people with disability. Rosemary Kayess and Phillip French, 'Out of Darkness into Light – Introducing the Convention on the Rights of Persons with Disabilities' (2008) 8 *Human Rights Law Review* 1, 14.

chapter introduces an approach to legal scholarship that promotes cognisance of research practice. It then describes the two lenses employed throughout this research, also known as epistemologies.

2.2.1 The Object of Enquiry and the Archive

International law scholar Sundhya Pahuja undertook to describe the process of legal research.[24] Part of this process was naming and differentiating different elements of the research process. Pahuja described the primary 'thing' being investigated by the research questions as the 'object of the enquiry'.[25] This research's object of enquiry was article 31 of the *CRPD*. Further, this research was interested in how refugee contexts may impact the interpretation and application of article 31.

The object of the enquiry is constructed through what Pahuja termed an 'archive'.[26] This project's archive consisted of the *CRPD* and its drafting history, human rights committees' documents, scholarly works, NGO reports, the *Convention Relating to the Status of Refugees* (as amended by the 1967 Protocol) ('*Refugee Convention*')[27] and United Nations documents. In addition, meeting documents from the advisory group (described later in this chapter) provided a unique 'lived experience' expertise in the archive. The archive's content and the materials' hierarchy were determined by the *Vienna Convention* rules of interpretation,[28] the advisory group's input and the theoretical lenses described in the next section.

2.2.2 Research Lenses

Pahuja described the theoretical approaches that inform the analysis of the archive as lenses.[29] In other fields of research, these lenses are referred to as epistemologies. Pahuja explains the lens may be described as: 'what literatures will I draw on to help both to study and to describe my object?'[30] The lenses adopted in this research included the following: data and power and disability human rights research. Both of these lenses are introduced here, with the next chapter elaborating on the data and power lens in detail.

24 Sundhya Pahuja, 'Methodology: Writing About How We Do Research' in Rossana Deplano and Nicholas Tsagourias (eds), *Research Methods in International Law: A Handbook* (Elgar, 2021) 60.

25 Ibid., 71.

26 Ibid., 71.

27 *Convention Relating to the Status of Refugees*, opened for signature 28 July 1951, 189 UNTS 150 (entered into force 22 April 1954); *Protocol Relating to the Status of Refugees*, opened for Signature 31 January 1967, 606 UNTS 267 (entered into force 4 October 1967). See earlier Chapter 1 n 49 for more on the relationship between these treaties.

28 *Vienna Convention* (n 14).

29 Pahuja (n 24) 74.

30 Pahuja (n 24) 73–74.

a) Data and Power

This monograph takes the view that data are not inert or neutral. In Chapter 3, this lens is elaborated and framed through the work of several theorists, including disability studies scholar Lennard Davis, philosopher Michel Foucault and anthropologist Sally Engle Merry. Chapter 3 examines several examples to demonstrate how power is deployed through the production and processing of data. One such example is how statistics legitimised the eugenics movement that stripped people with disability of their humanity, autonomy and lives.[31] More contemporary examples of powers operation through data are also explored in considering the creation of human rights indicators and the emergence of the digital state. The data and power lens enabled this research to problematise data production and processing and consider how *CRPD* article 31 may be helpful and harmful. It provided a foundation for exploring data's power and how various actors may harness it.

b) Disability Human Rights Research

For decades, disability advocates have exposed the significant role that research has played in the marginalisation of people with disability.[32] Advocates have confronted powerful research institutions by reframing their practices using the social model of disability lens.[33] They argued that these institutions were often informed by epistemologies that objectified, excluded and harmed people with disability, such as medical, positivist and neoliberal approaches to research.[34] Since the *CRPD* has come into force, work has been undertaken in the research community to establish practices that are congruent with disability human rights.

The second lens I adopted for this project's methodology is the disability human rights research lens as described by the Disability Human Rights Research Network. The Network, a group of academics that sought to 'end marginalisation through research, and to ensure that research is playing an emancipatory role',[35] developed and published a protocol highlighting how research enhances or undermines human rights.[36] The *Protocol for Rights-Based Disability Research in All Fields* ('*Rights-Based Disability Research Protocol*') employs the human rights model of disability theoretical

31 For a discussion about the impact of eugenics on people with disability, see Davis (n 4); Michael Robertson, Astrid Ley and Edwina Light, *The First into the Dark* (University of Technology Sydney ePress, 2019).

32 Mike Oliver, 'Changing the Social Relations of Research Production?' (1992) 7(2) *Disability, Handicap & Society* 101; Stone and Priestley (n 6) 3.

33 See earlier Section 1.1.1 for an overview of the models of disability.

34 Stone and Priestley (n 6).

35 Arstein-Kerslake et al (n 10) 425.

36 Disability Human Rights Research Network, *Protocol for Rights-Based Disability Research in All Fields* (February 2018).

frame and draws on emancipatory, participatory and inclusive research theory and methods.[37] The *Rights-Based Disability Research Protocol* outlines *CRPD*-consistent research methods 'to guide both research design and objectives',[38] transforming people with disability from being the 'objects of research' into rights-holders.[39] It positions people with disability as leaders in the research process, whereby they take on the role of co-researcher, set research agendas and are universally accepted as having the legal capacity to participate in research.[40]

The *Rights-Based Disability Research Protocol* significantly shaped this project's methodology by limiting the scope and demanding attention to previously neglected areas. By adopting this lens, I did not seek to question the legitimacy of human rights. Nonetheless, I did not shy away from critiquing the practices of states, human rights bodies, disabled persons organisations ('DPOs') and others charged with implementing and monitoring human rights treaties.[41] This lens also demanded that I venture into spaces previously uncharted by legal research and make genuine efforts to design a research methodology in which people with disability were involved 'in all stages' of the research process.[42]

Inclusive, participatory research processes require significant attention to methodological design. This research engaged with additional complexity, as it was interested in the impact of *CRPD* article 31 on people with disability who experience multiple and aggravated forms of discrimination: people with disability in refugee contexts. Attention was paid to accessibility, reciprocity and remuneration to address some of the barriers faced by this community.[43]

Despite considerable effort, this research necessarily fell short of some of the principles of the *Rights-Based Disability Research Protocol*. While this research project was 'consistent with the *CRPD*' and did not 'conflict with, undermine or contradict the *CRPD*',[44] elements could not be reconciled with the protocol. For example, this research was not 'initiated and led by voices from the disability community'.[45]

37 Arstein-Kerslake et al (n 10) 422.
38 Arstein-Kerslake et al (n 10) 413.
39 Arstein-Kerslake et al (n 10) 413.
40 *CRPD* (n 7) art 12.
41 For a discussion on the importance of challenging conventional thinking about human rights even when it is uncomfortable, see Fons Coomans, Fred Grünfeld and Menno T Kamminga, 'Methods of Human Rights Research: A Primer' (2010) 32(1) *Human Rights Quarterly* 179, 183.
42 Arstein-Kerslake et al (n 10) 423.
43 See later Section 2.4.2.
44 Arstein-Kerslake et al (n 10) 426.
45 Arstein-Kerslake et al (n 10) 426.

The lack of disability community leadership was partly due to the structure of PhD programs, which require ethics approval ahead of engaging with communities and, further, the need for the candidate to demonstrate their unique contribution to scholarship. The research questions emerged from my work with people with disability from refugee backgrounds in Australia;[46] for a description of this, see the Prologue. People with disability from refugee backgrounds are under-represented in mechanisms for consultation and advocacy.[47] This under-representation raises the issue of how these communities may be actively involved in leading a disability human rights research agenda.[48]

The traditions of legal scholarship were another barrier to the research being 'initiated and led by voices from the disability community'.[49] Legal methods 'read' perspectives into the law but do not traditionally include participatory methods unless they are socio-legal research methods to review the law's impact.[50] While the *Rights-Based Disability Research Protocol* has been developed for an interdisciplinary audience, consideration must be given to how the protocol, and the *CRPD*, impact research methods in international law beyond socio-legal methods.

The role and responsibilities of international law scholars extend beyond interpreting the *CRPD* for others; scholars must also examine their methods and practice. The knowledge acquired through the 'lived experience' of people with disability is recognised in the *CRPD* as vital for the implementation of the convention.[51] Therefore, this research engaged with how to include people

46 Victorian Refugee Health Network, *Service Responses for People with Disabilities From Refugee Backgrounds in Northern Melbourne* (Victorian Foundation for Survivors of Torture, 2018); Samantha Furneaux and Dina Korkees, *'We Need to Raise Our Voices': Advice From People of Refugee Backgrounds Living with Disabilities and Their Carers* (Report, Victorian Foundation for Survivors of Torture, 2019); Philippa Duell-Piening, *Response to a Discussion Paper of the Victorian State Disability Plan 2017–2020* (Victorian Refugee Health Network, July 2016). And other advocacy work that is not in the public domain.

47 This was most recently demonstrated in the number of submissions made to the Disability Royal Commission, only 8% coming from culturally and linguistically diverse communities. Royal Commission into Violence, Abuse, Neglect and Exploitation of People with Disabilities, *Connect* (Newsletter, 14 July 2020) <https://comms.external.royalcommission.gov.au/em/message/email/view.php?id=1559316&a=89073&k=gVRNtlWjstBVnI2h_teU0on0vniz1dMUvjjyNBNjaEk>; Nas Campanella, 'Disability Royal Commission Data Shows Indigenous and Culturally Diverse Groups Under-Represented in Submissions', *ABC News* (online, 23 July 2020) <https://www.abc.net.au/news/2020-07-23/disability-royal-commission-indigenous-cald-submissions-lacking/12476358>.

48 Recognising this, I invested time and resources in building the disability rights advocacy skills of the advisory group participants. Representation is discussed throughout this monograph, see especially Section 7.4.

49 Disability Human Rights Research Network (n 36).

50 This is discussed further in Section 2.3.1.

51 *CRPD* (n 7) art 4(3).

with disability in interpreting the rights and obligations in *CRPD* article 31 as explained in the following sections.

2.3 Legal Research Methods and Participation

Though not always explicit, law, like other disciplines, has research methods that govern 'how to find relevant information, how to organize it, and how to interpret the results'.[52] As discussed in the previous section, the *CRPD* requires that we examine these practices. This section first argues that doctrinal methods can be participatory. The remainder of this section examines how to develop practices to 'closely consult and actively involve' people with disability in interpreting the *CRPD* by attending to representation, processes for accommodating diverse views and the sites of participation in treaty interpretation.

2.3.1 Locating This Project in a 'Field' of Legal Research

This research project used a mixture of doctrinal and interdisciplinary methods.[53] Interdisciplinary methodologies, 'research about the law' and doctrinal methodologies, 'research in the law', are often seen as polar opposites on a spectrum of legal research methods.[54]

Doctrinal research is not about presenting a definitive truth. At the heart of doctrinal research is the 'development of legal argument[s]',[55] which are often subsequently critiqued and reworked by other scholars. There are rules, conventions and discourses that shape the reasoning of these arguments, the rigour of which are appraised by peers. Those qualified to articulate a view, critique and respond are schooled in the necessary traditions, accept certain tenets about the world and speak in a language developed for the purpose. They form the legal scholar discipline.

While disciplines have many strengths, public policy scholar David Adams cautioned that they are in danger of becoming hermetic knowledge systems, not knowing 'what knowledge looks like because . . . [it has] become self-referential – that is, the way we work and the tools we use largely define what is good and proper'.[56] Recently, popular culture has labelled this

52 Coomans, Grünfeld and Kamminga (n 41) 183–184.

53 HW Arthurs, *Law and Learning: Report to the Social Sciences and Humanities Research Council of Canada by the Consultative Group on Research and Education in Law* (Social Sciences and Humanities Research Council of Canada, 1983) 67.

54 Chynoweth's 2008 adaptation of Arthurs' 1983 framework depicts legal research as four quadrants created by two intersecting axes. Chynoweth (n 1) 29.

55 Chynoweth (n 1) 35.

56 David Adams, 'Usable Knowledge in Public Policy' (2004) 63(1) *Australian Journal of Public Administration* 29.

phenomenon an echo chamber.[57] Anything that is outside or that challenges established knowledge is dismissed as an anomaly. Participatory methods, such as the one adopted in this research, provide pathways for new perspectives and knowledge.

The advisory group of people with disability from refugee backgrounds convened for this research was engaged in doctrinal and interdisciplinary research.[58] They contributed to discussions about 'What is the law?' and 'What is the impact of the law?' or 'the law in context'. It is usual practice in legal scholarship to assume that, when an ethics application is made and a research project involves talking to people who are not legal scholars, the research must be socio-legal or research about the law.

As discussed in Section 2.1, the *CRPD* provides for rights-holders to have a role in interpreting the treaty to determine 'What is the law?' The next step for legal scholars is to determine how this is done by carefully developing and critiquing methods. While some may argue that participatory methods are not legal methods, it is notable that they were not accepted methods in education or medicine until they were pioneered, studied and refined in those fields. Further, since involving people with disability in *CRPD* interpretation is an act of treaty implementation,[59] people with disability should be involved in co-designing these participatory methods. Some guidance about representation and sites for participation already exist, as covered next.

2.3.2 Representation and Accommodating Diverse Views

Questions that often follow discussions about participation include: Who represents people with disability? Furthermore, how do we ensure that they represent the views of all people with disability? The following explains that guidance exists about steps to closely consult and actively involve people with disability. This guidance outlines that it is imperative to consider diverse opinions, including those from people who are refugees with disability. Consideration must be given to the barriers that people who are refugees with disability experience to participating in representative organisations and, therefore, *CRPD* implementation. Once people have access to these forums, this subsection concludes that legal scholarship can accommodate diverse perspectives and that consensus is not a prerequisite to engaging in doctrinal discussions.

57 The *Macquarie Dictionary* defines an echo chamber as 'a figurative chamber created in social media where like-minded people reinforce each other's views and opinions'. *Macquarie Dictionary: Australia's National Dictionary Online* (Electronic Resource, Macquarie Library, 2003) <www.macquariedictionary.com.au>. Oxford Advanced Learner's Dictionary defines an echo chamber as 'an environment in which somebody encounters only opinions and beliefs similar to their own, and does not have to consider alternatives'. 'Oxford Advanced Learner's Dictionary', *Oxford University Press* (online, 2023) <https://www.oxfordlearnersdictionaries.com/>.

58 See later Section 2.4.2 for more on the advisory group.

59 *CRPD* (n 7) art 4(3).

The Committee on the Rights of Persons with Disabilities ('CRPD Committee'), which monitors the implementation of the *CRPD*, has provided guidance in its *General Comment No 7* about governance and processes to enable the participation of people with disability in matters affecting them.[60] The *CRPD* identifies DPOs, for the most part,[61] as the vehicle for participation. DPOs are organisations that are led by and have a majority membership of people with disability.[62] The committee importantly distinguishes those who provide opinions on disability issues (like service providers and carers) from the advice of people with disability.

The *CRPD* highlights that people with disability and the situations in which they live are heterogeneous.[63] States must engage diverse participants in the implementation and monitoring of the treaty. The intersectional experiences of many people with disability in realising their rights are acknowledged in *General Comment 7*, which describes state obligations to

> 'ensure the close consultation and active involvement of organizations of persons with disabilities, which represent *all* persons with disabilities, including but not limited to . . . *refugees, asylum seekers*, internally displaced persons, undocumented and stateless persons'.[64]

The committee also highlighted that participation is possible, even vital, in situations of risk and humanitarian emergencies, during which 'State parties should promote the establishment of organizations of internally displaced persons or refugees with disabilities that are enabled to promote their rights in any situation of risk, including during armed conflict'.[65]

Nonetheless, this project discovered that DPOs representing people in refugee contexts are scarce.[66] This scarcity of DPOs representing people in refugee contexts may be because systemic advocacy is a low priority for people with disability seeking protection. Priorities for these communities commonly include housing, medication, education, livelihood activities and other things necessary to survive and thrive. In 2019, when I met with representatives of Humanity and Inclusion in Germany, they described their efforts to establish self-advocacy groups with people with disability who had recently

60 Committee on the Rights of Persons with Disabilities, *General Comment No 7 (2018) on the Participation of Persons with Disabilities, Including Children with Disabilities, through Their Representative Organizations, in the Implementation and Monitoring of the Convention*, UN Doc CRPD/C/GC/7 (9 November 2018) ('*General Comment 7 Participation*').

61 The provisions in art 33(3) are for 'persons with disabilities and their representative organizations', in contrast to art 4(3), which states 'persons with disabilities . . . through their representative organizations'. *CRPD* (n 7).

62 CRPD Committee, *General Comment 7 Participation* (n 60) [11].

63 *CRPD* (n 7) Preamble para p, arts 6, 7. See earlier Section 1.1.2.

64 CRPD Committee, *General Comment 7 Participation* (n 60) [50] (emphasis added).

65 CRPD Committee, *General Comment 7 Participation* (n 60) [78].

66 See later Section 7.4.1.

sought protection in Germany. They noted that people had other priorities early in their settlement, such as connecting with services.[67] Further, when self-advocacy groups were established, there was greater interest in mutual support than systemic and political advocacy. The mutual support aspect of self-advocacy groups was also a key finding of Furneaux and Korkees' work.[68]

As a result of the under-representation of people from refugee backgrounds in Australian DPOs,[69] I decided to establish an advisory group of people with disability from refugee backgrounds for this research project. Interestingly, when discussing barriers to participating in representative organisations with the advisory group, they echoed the learnings from the project described earlier: 'Food, work, and school are priorities. As well as saving money to send back home'.[70] Moreover, 'People who have been here longer can engage in self-advocacy groups because they are more financially stable'.[71]

The research advisory group did not, and could not, represent all the views of people with disability from refugee backgrounds. As feminist legal scholar Hilary Charlesworth noted on representation, 'I clearly cannot speak for all women participants in and observers of the international legal system'.[72] The expectation is that other views may be added over time to build a fuller picture of women's experiences, in Charlesworth's case, or people with disability from refugee backgrounds in the case of this project.

A consequence of wide-ranging life experiences is the difficulty in finding common ground. Troublingly, emphasising the requirement for consensus among groups is sometimes a way to invalidate the reasonable conclusion that there are multiple lived experiences and views and to support the claim that participatory processes are too hard. Eva Lövbrand and colleagues, who research knowledge politics of the environment, identified the double standard in requiring consensus amongst citizens about environmental issues when scientists provide varying perspectives and dissenting views.[73] Consensus is not demanded of legal scholars either. Legal scholar Jan Smits highlighted:

> in finding what normatively belongs, there is not one objective truth . . . Law is about conflicting normative positions: if law is regulating

67 Author's meeting notes, meeting with Dr Susanne Schwalgin and Wolfram Buttschardt, *Humanity and Inclusion Germany* (Formerly Handicap International Germany, Berlin, 3 September 2019).

68 Furneaux and Korkees (n 46).

69 A peak body, National Ethnic Disability Alliance, does exist in the Australian capital; however, it represents the diverse interests of all migrants and established ethic communities. See also later Section 7.4.1.

70 Stakeholder Advisory Group meeting minutes, 30 September 2022.

71 Stakeholder Advisory Group meeting minutes, 30 September 2022.

72 Hilary Charlesworth, 'Feminist Methods in International Law' (1999) 93(2) *American Journal of International Law* 379.

73 'Many scholars of science and technology . . . tend to emphasize the virtue of disagreement and dissensus'. Eva Lövbrand, Roger Pielke and Silke Beck, 'A Democracy Paradox in Studies of Science and Technology' (2011) 36(4) *Science, Technology, & Human Values* 474, 479.

> society and opinions on how to do this differ – which is necessarily the case – there also has to be differing opinions about what the law should say. The academic-legal method must reflect this important characteristic of law.[74]

Thus, a consensus is unnecessary among those participating in treaty interpretation, including rights-holders contributing to the process.[75] Disagreements within the interpretive community are inevitable with such diverse interests. International human rights scholar Tobin argued that engagement with diverse views strengthens reasoning and analysis:

> This does not mean that these views must always be accommodated or reconciled before offering an interpretation. However, a careful consideration of such views, to the extent that they can be identified, contributes to a deeper and more rigorous analysis, thus strengthening the coherence in the reasoning used to support an interpretive exercise.[76]

As discussed in the next subsection, people with disability, through DPOs, already engage with and challenge states', scholars' and other civil society organisations' interpretation of the *CRPD*.

2.3.3 Sites for Participatory Human Rights Law Interpretation

Perhaps the best normative example of how states and people with disability engage in treaty interpretation is during the periodic reviews of states undertaken by the CRPD Committee. During this process, national DPOs submit shadow reports and attend closed hearings where participants actively interpret the *CRPD* by detailing concerns about human rights violations.[77] Furthermore, the committee charged with monitoring the implementation of the *CRPD* must include 'representation of experts with disabilities'.[78] Most of the experts on the committee have disability and routinely question states about their performance in implementing the *CRPD*, again presenting a powerful example of rights-holders engaging in treaty interpretation.

In 2019, I attended the 22nd session of the CRPD Committee and witnessed how the committee worked firsthand. Among many experiences,

74 Jan M Smits, 'Redefining Normative Legal Science: Towards an Argumentative Discipline' in Fons Coomans, Fred Grünfeld and Menno T Kamminga (eds), *Methods of Human Rights Research* (Intersentia, 2009) 45, 50.

75 Lövbrand, Pielke and Beck (n 73) 479.

76 Tobin (n 17) 11.

77 Committee on the Rights of Persons with Disabilities, 'Annex II: Guidelines on the Participation of Disabled Persons' Organizations and Civil Society Organizations in the Work of the Committee' in *Report of the Committee on the Rights of Persons with Disabilities on Its Eleventh Session* (31 March–11 April 2014) 9.

78 *CRPD* (n 7) art 34(4).

witnessing committee member Sir Robert Martin, the first man with an intellectual disability to be elected to a United Nations human rights committee, question Australia on its performance in implementing the *CRPD* was profound. Sir Martin asked questions about implementing article 12 about legal capacity, article 17 about the forced sterilisation of people with disability and article 19 about living independently and being included in the community. Regarding article 19, Sir Martin stated:

> can you tell us why there are young people living in aged care facilities and what is your plan to end this practice? . . . what have you in place to prevent new institutions being created, and how are you making article 19 real for persons with disabilities, including persons with intellectual disabilities, so that all persons can live in the community and choose where, how and with whom they live?[79]

Sir Martin's unique insight from living in institutions has informed how he interprets the *CRPD*'s rights and obligations and what questions he poses about the realisation of rights.[80] Furthermore, the CRPD Committee demonstrates that people with disability can interpret the *CRPD*. Therefore, it is difficult for states to deny that it is possible to include people with disability in interpreting the *CRPD* during implementation and monitoring.[81] While the CRPD Committee represents various lived experiences and knowledge that informs their work,[82] no CRPD Committee members are refugees. Given that the process for electing CRPD Committee members is through the Conference of the States Parties,[83] it is unlikely that a person with lived experience of multiple discrimination of disability in a refugee context would ever be a committee member.

Another forum where human rights treaties are interpreted is academia.[84] Due to the historical (and continued) marginalisation of people with disability and the significant barriers that exist, people with disability are under-represented in academia. This research methodology aimed to address

79 *Consideration of Australia – 499th Meeting 22nd Session Committee on Rights of Persons with Disabilities* (Video, Directed by UN Web TV, 12 September 2019) 2:34:00–2:35:00 <https://media.un.org/en/asset/k1i/k1i5jtj8yk>.

80 For an account of Sir Robert Martin's life, see John McRae, *Becoming a Person: The Biography of Robert Martin* (Craig Potton Publishing, 2014).

81 *CRPD* (n 7) arts 4(3), 33(3).

82 Committee members have a lived experience of a diversity of disability, gender and world region.

83 See, eg, 'Thirteenth Conference of States Parties and 2020 Elections', *Office of the High Commissioner for Human Rights* (Web Page) <https://www.ohchr.org/en/events/events/2020/thirteenth-conference-states-parties-and-2020-elections>.

84 The International Court of Justice's statute provides for the 'teachings of the most highly qualified publicists' to be 'subsidiary means for the determination of rules of law'. *Statute of the International Court of Justice* art 38(1)(d).

this gap by including rights-holders in interpreting *CRPD* article 31 to contribute to the scholarly community's interpretive debate. The next section describes the methods used to engage with people with disability from refugee backgrounds and facilitate dialogue.

2.4 A Participatory Treaty Interpretation Method

People with disability should be partners in research rather than the objects of research, as highlighted by the *Rights-Based Disability Research Protocol*. Careful attention was paid to engaging advisory group participants in this research. Considering the advisory group's focus on rights, the under-representation of people from refugee backgrounds in DPOs, and acknowledging the multiple and aggravated forms of discrimination that this community experiences, the approach to participation was modelled on Brazilian educational theorist and philosopher Paulo Freire's method of dialogue.[85] This section first introduces Freire's work, followed by a detailed description of the advisory group's methodology and a reflection on the impact of the group on the research project. The final subsection draws links between the methodology, theory and doctrine discussed throughout this chapter.

2.4.1 Freire's Approach to Dialogue

Freire developed a cooperative teacher – student education model that used the method of dialogue. Freire's account of this work was published in *Pedagogy of the Oppressed* and has been highly influential in many fields.[86] Freire's dialogue with people who were poor, illiterate and working class paid careful attention to the impact of a person's context on their ability to engage in dialogue.[87] When working with marginalised communities, such as people with disability from refugee backgrounds, this attention to contextual considerations is very important – bearing in mind that disability varies according to the social and physical environment.

Freire's passion for accessible and engaged dialogue was such that they likened the denial of forums to express oneself as 'dehumanizing aggression'.[88] The converse of this must also be true: participation in dialogue, as conceived by Freire, is a humanising process. Freire strongly advocated for all people's

85 See specifically, Paulo Freire, *Pedagogy of the Oppressed*, tr Myra Bergman Ramos (Penguin Classics, 1970).

86 Ibid.

87 Freire, holding a keen sense of the material reality of poverty and illiteracy, noted that we need to be mindful of people's context, the reality of their lives: 'a naively conceived humanism often overlooks the concrete, existential, present situation of real people'. Ibid., 66.

88 Ibid., 61.

right to participate in dialogue,[89] and they also viewed participation in dialogue as a method of awakening people to their rights:

> Dialogue . . . requires an intense faith in humankind, faith in their power to make and remake, to create and re-create, faith in their vocation to be more fully human (which is not the privilege of an elite, but the birthright of all).[90]

In this research, Freire's intense faith in people's ability to engage in dialogue stood in contrast to international law's intimidating and impenetrable discourse.

Freire argued that those who have the power to describe, define and interpret transform the world: 'If it is in [expressing oneself] . . . that people, by [describing] . . . the world, transform it, dialogue imposes itself as the way by which they achieve significance as human beings'.[91] A person gains significance by participating in dialogue, describing, defining and interpreting the world. The humanising impact of dialogue is important for people with disability who have been marginalised and dehumanised in many forums.

Understanding Freire's approach to dialogue involves being clear about their views on what dialogue is not. Dialogue for Freire was not 'a crafty instrument for the domination of one person over another' nor was it ' "depositing" ideas in another', 'a simple exchange of ideas to be "consumed" by the discussant', 'a hostile, polemical argument between those who are committed neither to [describing] . . . the world, nor searching for truth, but rather the imposition of their own truth' or 'a situation where some name on behalf of others'.[92]

Freire's approach to dialogue positioned the facilitator and participants as co-learners and co-teachers and created critical spaces for discussion.[93] According to Freire, establishing trust between the participants through a horizontal relationship is fundamental to dialogue.[94] Trust is gained when dialoguers are transparent about and act according to their intentions.[95] Dialogue also requires hope. Freire stated: 'if the dialoguers expect nothing to come of their efforts, their encounter will be empty and sterile, bureaucratic and tedious'.[96] Critical thinking is the last element necessary for dialogue: 'thinking that

89 See Ibid., particularly ch 3.

90 Ibid., 63.

91 Ibid., 61. The original quotation contained ableist language, and these words have been substituted with those with a similar meaning. People express themselves and communicate in a range of ways, including by speaking, signing and utilising assistive technologies.

92 Ibid., 62.

93 Margaret Ledwith, 'Emancipatory Action Research as a Critical Living Praxis: From Dominant Narratives to Counternarratives' in Lonnie L Rowell et al (eds), *The Palgrave International Handbook of Action Research* (Palgrave Macmillan, 2017) 56.

94 Freire (n 85) 64.

95 Freire (n 85) 64.

96 Freire (n 85) 65.

perceives reality as process, as transformation, rather than a static entity – thinking that does not separate itself from action, but constantly immerses itself in temporality without fear of the risks involved'.[97]

The previous section argued that doctrinal research is a practice of dialogue between scholars. Freire's approach to dialogue challenges some of the tenets and practices of international law, which are hierarchical, often opaque, bureaucratic and aim to maintain stability. Nonetheless, to create spaces and overcome barriers to participation in discussions about 'What is the law?' a new approach is necessary. The following describes how dialogue was undertaken in this legal research project.

2.4.2 Stakeholder Advisory Group

The advisory group that informed this research met eight times via video conference from January 2021 to October 2022. As outlined in this section, I paid careful attention to the engagement process to enhance participation. Before recruiting group members, I gained research ethics approval from the University of Melbourne Humanities, Law and Social Science Human Ethics Sub-Committee.[98] The meetings ranged from one to two hours, and I provided secretariat support. The group's small size, the length of time over which the meetings took place and the safe (online) social space of the meetings supported the development of the trusting relationships required for dialogue.[99] This subsection provides a detailed description of the advisory group's methodology and some critique of the methods used. This subsection is divided into three sub-subsections that describe the participants, meetings and data collection and analysis processes.

a) Participants

The advisory group had four members, which was adequate to meet the group's purpose – providing the perspectives of a range of rights-holders. The participants were recruited based on the following inclusion criterion: they were adults with disability, from refugee backgrounds,[100] living in Australia and interested in disability human rights advocacy. I recruited the members of the advisory group using purposive sampling through my existing networks.[101] A Plain Language Statement about the research and a Script for Verbal Consent

97 Freire (n 85) 65.

98 Ethics ID: 2056906.1.

99 Freire (n 85).

100 They included people who had arrived in Australia with humanitarian visas and those who had arrived in Australia and then sought humanitarian protection.

101 'Purposive sampling (also known as judgment, selective or subjective sampling) is a sampling technique in which researcher relies on his or her own judgment when choosing members of population to participate in the study'. John Dudovskiy, 'Purposive Sampling', *Business Research Methodology* (Web Page) <https://research-methodology.net/sampling-in-primary-data-collection/purposive-sampling/>. My networks included DPOs and refugee organisations.

were provided directly to the potential participants via mail or email, and I followed up with a phone call to confirm the documents had been received and offered the opportunity for the documents to be reviewed with a confidential telephone interpreter funded by the project. Informed consent was gained verbally from all participants.

Two males, one female and one gender non-binary person were recruited to the advisory group. The group members ranged in age from 20 to 59. Some had sought protection from countries in the Middle East and North Africa region and others from the broader African continent. They ranged in the length of time since they arrived in Australia[102] and in their Australian citizenship and visa status. All participants spoke English, identified as having disability, were experienced advocates and had refugee backgrounds.

In line with the *Rights-Based Disability Research Protocol*,[103] all advisory group members who participated outside their regular work duties were remunerated for their time. The Melbourne Social Equity Institute's *Guidelines for Equitable and Fair Remuneration for Community Research Participants* guided the amount of remuneration,[104] which was AUD62.67 for a 90-minute meeting.[105] This amount accounted for preparation and prereading time for the meetings. Due to university accounting practices and audit requirements, paying group members was administratively burdensome to participants. Therefore, the remuneration was provided via a retail voucher of a group member's choosing. I was concerned about this remuneration method, as it is often used in welfare programs to control how people spend their money.[106] For this reason, I tried to provide maximum flexibility to participants.[107]

102 The participants had arrived in the past 20 years. Initially, the inclusion criterion was 10 years, but this was expanded due to the difficulties in recruiting participants.

103 Arstein-Kerslake et al (n 10) 427.

104 The rate of remuneration was indexed according to inflation over the years. I opted to pay the higher rate for the entire project. Melbourne Social Equity Institute, *Guidelines for Equitable and Fair Remuneration for Community Research Participants* (Guidelines, 2019).

105 This amount was adjusted for shorter or longer meetings. It also should be noted that my scholarship included funding for research expenses such as remuneration for participation and other accessibility requirements.

106 A quotation from a recent newspaper article said: 'I hate the card, it's demeaning, it's racist, it's dehumanising, and it gives you no independence to make your own decisions'. Hannah Barry, Isabel Moussalli and Evelyn Leckie, 'A Trial of the Controversial Cashless Welfare Card Will Run for Two More Years. Here's What People Think', *ABC News* (online, 10 December 2020) <https://www.abc.net.au/news/2020-12-10mixed-response-to-cashless-debit-card-extension/12971626>. An entry from my journal on 17 September 2020 stated: 'I feel that the gift card re-imbursement is somewhat condescending in this study and had argued for a cash remuneration – but the university did not allow this'.

107 Examples of strategies used to provide flexibility included allowing participants to choose which voucher they wanted after each meeting, holding the fund for some participants to enable to them to save for a large voucher that they wanted to use at a store of their choice to purchase a specific item (eg, an electric shaver) and sending an e-voucher or cards in the mail.

b) Meetings

Due to public health measures responding to the COVID-19 pandemic, meetings were facilitated over the video conference platform Zoom. The meetings were held at a time that enabled the participation of most group members. An agenda was circulated before the meeting so group members could prepare for the meetings. A discussion was promoted on each agenda item through various facilitation strategies (see later). I took minutes and circulated them following the meeting. Group discussions were also recorded on an online whiteboard and added to each meeting with differently coloured notes. This process provided the sense that the group's knowledge was growing, and new ideas could be linked with previous meetings. The following describes the strategies used to improve group accessibility and promote dialogue and summarises the meetings.

ACCESSIBILITY

As observed earlier in this chapter, people from refugee backgrounds face a range of barriers to participating in DPOs, including language, cultural differences in understanding disability and, at a practical level, eligibility for funding to pay for measures needed to access meetings.[108] Measures were taken to ensure that the research advisory group meetings were accessible to people with disability from refugee backgrounds. The online meetings likely assisted with accessibility, as all participants used video conferencing for other activities. Video meetings enabled participants located in three different states of Australia to participate in the advisory group.

It should be noted that interpreter funding was available for this project, and two potential participants with low English proficiency showed some interest in the project. Nonetheless, following the ethics process, they opted to withdraw from the project. It is difficult to pinpoint the exact reason for withdrawal, but it illustrates some of the complexities of gaining trust and informed consent in video interpreter-mediated sessions.

FACILITATION

I brought substantial relevant experience to this project, including group facilitation skills, trauma-informed approaches and working cross-culturally. I am trained as an occupational therapist, have a Master of Community and International Development and have worked with people from refugee backgrounds for over a decade. I had to be mindful of the group's purpose and my role in facilitating the meetings. As is common in clinical practice, I obtained advisory group mentoring from a senior social worker with extensive experience

108 These measures vary depending on the disability a person experiences. For detailed discussions on barriers to participation for people with disability from refugee backgrounds, see Furneaux and Korkees (n 46); Victorian Refugee Health Network (n 46).

facilitating community advisory groups. This mentoring provided a space to debrief about the group dynamics and to discuss facilitation strategies to promote dialogue during the meetings while keeping all participants safe.

The meeting facilitation approach drew upon Freirean dialogical principles and the democratic processes of DPOs.[109] Aside from meeting several times to develop rapport, strategies adopted to build trust and transfer power from myself to the meeting participants included enabling participants to frame some of the aims of the meetings, identify useful outcomes, structure the discussions, ask for more information and build on ideas and discussions across meetings.[110] The most common approach to generating dialogue in the advisory group meetings was posing curious questions and confirming that the right question was asked. The group also reviewed and critiqued current practices and tools and compared them to the obligations in *CRPD* article 31. Similarly, scenario-based discussions took the abstract concept of data production and processing and applied it to real-world scenarios, such as COVID-19 contact tracing and the Australian census.

CAPACITY BUILDING (MEETINGS 1–3 [3 MEETINGS])

Time was allocated in advisory group meetings for capacity building, focusing on building the skills and knowledge of group members. Capacity building is in line with recommendations from the CRPD Committee, which stated in its *General Comment 7*:

> States parties should also support persons with disabilities and their representative organizations in the development of the competencies, knowledge and skills required to independently advocate for their full and effective participation in society, and in developing stronger democratic governance principles, such as respect for human rights, the rule of law, transparency, accountability, pluralism and participation.[111]

The capacity-building process responds to barriers faced by people with disability in accessing education and the unemployment and underemployment of many people with disability.[112] Given the multiple discrimination experienced by people with disability from refugee backgrounds, this experience is likely compounded.[113] These meetings utilised the Office of the High Commissioner for Human Rights training package about the *CRPD*.[114] I presented the

109 See earlier Section 2.4.1; CRPD Committee, *General Comment 7 Participation* (n 60).
110 Ledwith (n 93) 56.
111 CRPD Committee, *General Comment 7 Participation* (n 62) [60].
112 CRPD Committee, *General Comment 7 Participation* (n 62) [59].
113 Harley and Hobbs argue that 'leadership training and other capacity-building activities' are crucial to improving refugee participation in decision-making. Tristan Harley and Harry Hobbs, 'The Meaningful Participation of Refugees in Decision-Making Processes: Questions of Law and Policy' (2020) 32(2) *International Journal of Refugee Law* 200, 213.
114 United Nations Office of the High Commissioner for Human Rights (OHCHR), *The Convention on the Rights of Persons with Disabilities: Training Guide* (2014).

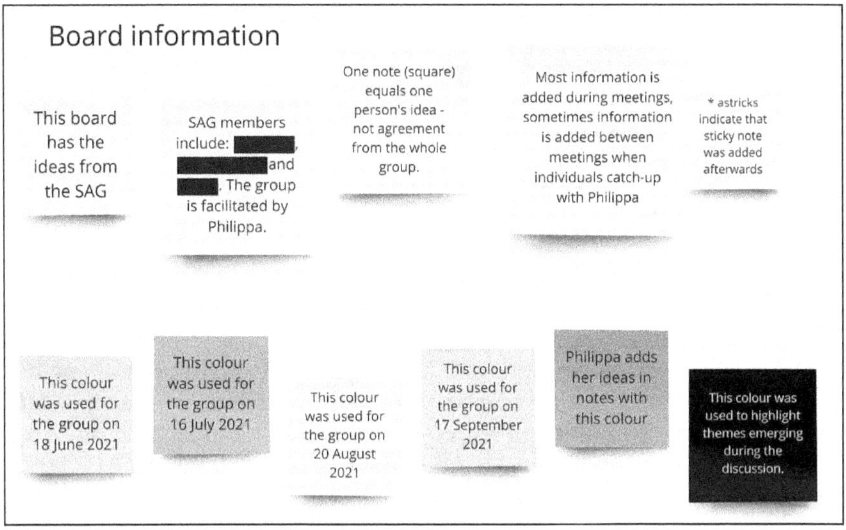

Figure 2.1 A canvas from the Stakeholder Advisory Group's ('SAG') Miro board that describes how the tool will be used and group processes

introductory module and then the group chose from various topics, including national implementation. In my journal, I noted surprise about the lack of knowledge about the *CRPD* amongst the advisory group, as all members were very experienced advocates.[115]

DIALOGUE (MEETINGS 4–8 [5 MEETINGS])

As the meetings were online, I introduced an online whiteboard tool called Miro to support the dialogue and demonstrate that all group member's ideas were recorded.[116] The Miro board was viewed as a method to build continuity between meetings and to enable people who could not attend to add their ideas afterwards. Figure 2.1 is an image of a section of the Miro board, a canvas with information about the board.

This project had to be concluded within a time frame. Progress of the group dialogue was promoted through transparency. Transparency was achieved partly by including a canvas showing the group process stage (see Figure 2.2).

Aside from these Miro canvases, which provided structure and signposting, additional canvases were added to capture the ideas raised by group members at

115 'Reading Shakespeare's book (2014), it is clear the disconnect between disability activists and the broader community re: models of disability, disability identity. This prompted me to think of the advisory group who are all experienced activist and their lack of knowledge of disability models and the *CRPD*'. Extract from the researcher's journal, 23 February 2021.

116 Please note one group member required audio description of the notes, which was accommodated in the group process.

Figure 2.2 Image from the advisory group's Miro board with the meeting numbers and process

each meeting. The dialogue explored various substantive themes using the facilitation techniques described earlier. These themes included: how data are helpful and harmful, whether there is a difference in disclosing disability status compared with other personal information, such as gender, the Australian census and how data about disability status are collected, group interests as opposed to individual interests and the functioning of representative organisations, among other topics. The group also spent time dissecting the text of *CRPD* article 31 – raising questions and providing examples of best practice from their experience.

DISSEMINATION OF GROUP KNOWLEDGE (MEETINGS 9–10 [2 MEETINGS])

These meetings were scheduled to develop resources to communicate the findings of the group meetings and build group members' profiles as content area experts. These meetings and the products developed were not part of the research process; rather, they formed the 'reciprocity' acts of the research. I set aside time and resources for these meetings. However, advisory group members had competing priorities for their advocacy time. On reflection, the acts of reciprocity that responded to the group member's interests and contributed to their projects were more well-received. Supporting group members' other advocacy projects, I delivered training to a youth advocacy network about the *CRPD* and co-authored a submission to the CRPD Committee on the right to work. When I planned these meetings at the start of the project, I assumed that group members would want to share their knowledge and be known as experts in the research area. Instead, it proved that group members had their own projects for which they preferred to have input and support.

c) Data Collection and Analysis

Data collected throughout this research included demographic and logistics information in a 'commencement survey', advisory group minutes and a researcher's journal. The researcher's journal was a tool through which I reflected on, synthesised and analysed the information from the advisory group meetings and began to draw links with my research.[117] The journal also enabled greater continuity between meetings, reflections on facilitation

117 Based on Graham Gibbs, *Learning by Doing: A Guide to Teaching and Learning Methods* (Oxford Centre for Staff and Learning Development, Oxford Brookes University, 1988).

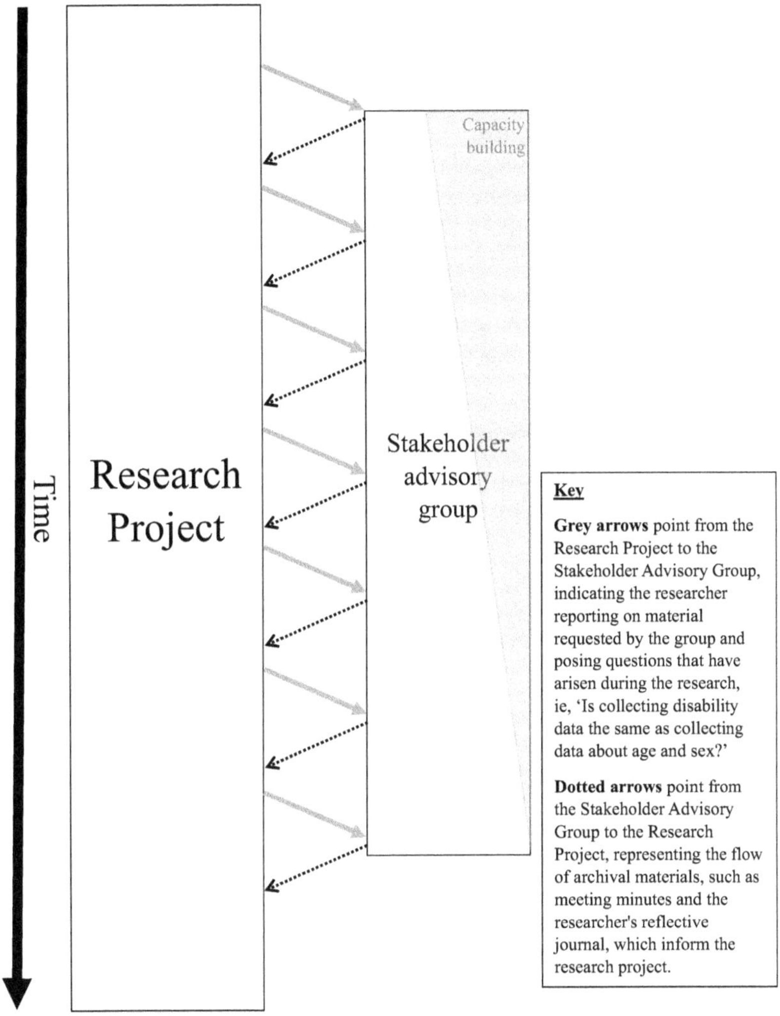

Figure 2.3 Depiction of the relationship and information flow between the advisory group and the research project

techniques and problem-solving, for example, of issues related to group attendance.[118]

Data were analysed through iterative cycles between the research and the advisory group (see Figure 2.3, which illustrates the information flow). The

118 'It is important to maintain the relationships for the long term. This is why I do not put too much pressure on people who say they are unavailable for meetings due to other commitment. Nonetheless, this does impact group members who are regular and good attenders'. Reflection from the researcher's journal, 3 August 2021.

advisory group engaged with questions and materials emerging from my research. Advisory group meeting documents were analysed in the research, alongside materials in the research archive from other sources, such as the United Nations, states parties to the *CRPD* and civil society organisations (including DPOs). The advisory group meeting minutes are cited in the monograph alongside other research archive documents.

The advisory group and the research were parallel processes that informed each other's work. Maintaining the advisory group knowledge as distinct and separate from the rest of the research enabled the contribution of the advisory group to be appropriately acknowledged and not subsumed by the research project. The meeting documents reflected the group's collective knowledge and contribution to exploring *CRPD* article 31.

2.4.3 The Impact of the Stakeholder Advisory Group on the Research

The advisory group shaped this research directly and indirectly. The direct contributions are noted in the meeting minutes and subsequently cited throughout the chapters in this monograph. The indirect contributions are recorded, to a degree, in my journal. The group also created a form of indirect accountability through my regular reporting at group meetings. These regular conversations kept me in touch with the experiences of people with disability from refugee backgrounds and shaped my world view – much as Freire anticipated that dialogue changes how the dialoguers view the world.[119]

The advisory group meeting minutes demonstrate that the group had essential expertise necessary for interpreting *CRPD* article 31. The group members understood the tensions within article 31 well. They argued that disaggregated data was necessary for advocacy.[120] They described the cost, risk and degradation experienced by people with disability who are asked to disclose personal data across various contexts.[121] Group members differentiated

119 Freire (n 85) 63.

120 The group identified that disaggregated data are necessary to justify funding and to understand how COVID-19 is impacting people with disability. Stakeholder Advisory Group meeting minutes, 18 June 2021. The group identified that disaggregated data are necessary to assist with understanding community need. Stakeholder Advisory Group meeting minutes, 16 July 2021. The group felt that data reflecting people with disability's strengths, demographics and needs are necessary. Stakeholder Advisory Group meeting minutes, 8 July 2022.

121 For example, the group expressed concern about where data are being stored and who has access to it and that when the government has access to information about individuals it may use this information to discriminate against them. The group expressed concern that data protection might extend to some communities but not the whole community and that data may be misused. Stakeholder Advisory Group meeting minutes, 18 June 2021. The group expressed concern that people with disability are more exposed and less supported to protect themselves against data abuse. The group discussed the additional barriers of non-citizens having disability: 'Disability is a barrier for many visas'. Stakeholder Advisory Group meeting

the capacity and trustworthiness of different jurisdictions.[122] They identified the flexibility in the article 31 text 'as appropriate' and asked, 'How and who decides what is appropriate?'[123] The group provided examples of categorisation leading to exclusion.[124] These and other contributions recorded in the meeting minutes respond to both legal research questions 'What is the law?' and 'What is the impact of the law?' The advisory group meeting minutes are cited in the footnotes throughout the monograph.

a) Limitations of the Advisory Group Method to Participatory Treaty Interpretation

There were, of course, limitations to the advisory group approach. Data and the harms associated with data are somewhat abstract concepts. Overall, the advisory group members were less enthusiastic about discussing data than I was. Group members were more animated in discussions about their direct experiences of data, such as privacy imposts, or its use in advocacy. However, abstract discussions about the harms of data were more difficult. Nevertheless, observing this mismatched enthusiasm to talk about data enabled me to gain insight into the abstract nature of this topic and that it was unlikely to be a pressing issue in people's daily life unless there were significant and imminent harms, such as a data breach.

Perhaps participatory treaty interpretation may be more engaging for rights-holders when exploring more tangible rights, such as access to education, the right to work, right to accessible health care and so on. Furthermore, if research is led by people with disability, as stipulated by the *Rights-Based Disability Research Protocol*, one imagines that their interest and motivation for the topic will be greater.

2.4.4 Linking the Methodology to the Theory and Doctrine

Participatory doctrinal methods do not require abandoning principled approaches to treaty interpretation. Rather, participatory approaches demand greater attention to how knowledge is produced and interrogating the

---

minutes, 16 July 2021. One group member was a victim of the Australian Immigration Department data breach and stated: 'No one told us what data was taken'. Stakeholder Advisory Group meeting minutes, 8 July 2022.

122 For example, group members expressed a belief that Australia has strong protection for consumers. Stakeholder Advisory Group meeting minutes, 16 July 2021. However, they did not trust other state officials. Stakeholder Advisory Group meeting minutes, 20 August 2021.

123 Stakeholder Advisory Group meeting minutes, 18 June 2021.

124 For example, one group member referenced that the Australian Government policy to prioritise Christian Syrian refugees was a reason not to disclose religion and be 'categorised' as such. See Anna Henderson and Chris Uhlmann, 'Syrian Migrant Crisis: Christians to Get Priority as Abbott Faces Pressure to Take in More Refugees', *ABC News* (online, 8 September 2015) <https://www.abc.net.au/news/2015-09-08/christians-to-get-priority-in-syrian-refugee-intake/6757110>. Stakeholder Advisory Group meeting minutes, 8 July 2022.

assumptions used to generate that knowledge. As feminist and Global South legal scholars have effectively demonstrated, people's life experiences affect their perception of the world.[125] In this project, attention was paid to creating spaces for diverse opinions and lived experience knowledge to be valued alongside other forms of knowledge.

The disability human rights research lens, informed by the *Rights-Based Disability Research Protocol*, centred the *CRPD* in this research's methodology. The *CRPD* requires that people with disability are actively involved in all matters affecting them.[126] The CRPD Committee's *General Comment 7* explains that diverse representation is necessary to meet this obligation. Nonetheless, some people with disability who experience multiple and aggravated forms of discrimination due to their intersecting identities or life experiences face greater barriers to participating in DPOs. This project was concerned with the rights and obligations in *CRPD* article 31 and the implications for people who are refugees. Therefore, due to the under-representation of people from refugee backgrounds in Australian DPOs, I convened an advisory group of people with this intersecting identity.

This project's adoption of an advisory group strategically addressed the power dynamic between myself and the group members. The advisory group provided a more horizontal structure than that obtained between researchers and focus group subjects. Discussions were recorded as meeting minutes rather than transcripts. In the meeting minutes, the group's knowledge was recorded. This knowledge may be added to, amended, engaged with and critiqued by the group. In contrast, transcripts of focus groups are static after they are captured and thematically analysed by researchers. Research participants' power in focus groups is primarily in withdrawing their unprocessed data. The dynamic exchange in the advisory group approach is congruent with the *Rights-Based Disability Research Protocol*, positioning group members as rights-holders and not 'objects of research'.[127]

This research also invested significant time in building trust and the capacity of the group to have conversations about the law. Trust and a 'horizontal relationship' were also key to Freire's method of dialogue.[128] The content of the dialogue was a significant barrier to establishing a horizontal relationship. Inviting advisory group members to discuss 'What is the law?' was overwhelming; it took time for them to be confident and feel that their knowledge was valid. Many people with disability and from refugee backgrounds are conditioned to 'having the law done to them' rather than shaping 'What is the law?' Therefore, capacity building was an important part of the process, as was grounding the abstract discussion in real-world examples.

125 'Feminist methods seek to expose and question the limited bases of international law's claim to objectivity and impartiality and insist on the importance of gender relations as a category of analysis'. Charlesworth (n 72) 379.

126 *CRPD* (n 7) art 4(3).

127 Arstein-Kerslake et al (n 10) 413.

128 Freire (n 85) 64.

Freire said that in dialogue, 'we must pose this existential, concrete, present situation to the people as a problem which challenges them and requires a response – not just at the intellectual level, but at the level of action'.[129] In this research, data collection around COVID-19 and the national census were two 'existential, concrete and present situation[s]' that enabled dialogue with the group that could be used to open discussion about some of the more abstract ideas in article 31.

Keeping the group engaged over the 24 months was difficult at times. Sometimes my interests and the group members' interests did not align. A group member consoled me about the difficulty in maintaining attendance at the group by offering 'the community English classes emptied after people seeking asylum were granted work rights'. This brief story highlights that aligning interests is necessary for groups to come together. The research project adopted several strategies to keep group members engaged – foremost, valuing group members' time and acknowledging the multiple demands placed on them. Valuing group members' time was achieved by providing flexibility, reciprocity[130] and remuneration. The ongoing engagement was also achieved by being transparent about the group's purpose; all participants knew the group was for a research project. Concurrently, I promoted a sense of hope by demonstrating that the group's knowledge was useful. The relevance of the group knowledge was highlighted by linking it to the treaty text, the object of enquiry for this investigation.

2.5 Conclusion

The *CRPD* introduced new requirements around knowledge production. It requires international law scholarship to interrogate legal research methods to include avenues for people with disability to participate in research concerning their lives. This chapter presented doctrinal reasoning, theory and methods to contribute to developing participatory approaches in doctrinal and socio-legal research.

Doctrinal research methods have a tradition of dialogue between scholars where consensus is unnecessary, and critique is encouraged. Therefore, it is possible to add human rights-holders' perspectives; indeed, it is already the case in human rights practice through shadow reporting to committees. Nonetheless, academia is somewhat impenetrable to those not schooled in the necessary traditions. This project provided a pathway for people under-represented in other forums to interpret *CRPD* article 31 and discuss the impacts of data production and processing via an advisory group.

The next chapter draws on scholarship about data, knowledge construction, disability and power to deconstruct how power operates through data. This critique about data and power serves as the second lens this research utilises to explore *CRPD* article 31 in refugee contexts.

129 Freire (n 85) 68–69 (citations omitted).

130 An example of reciprocity I engaged in was taking time to present about *CRPD* rights at one of the advisory group members' advocacy network meetings.

3 Data and Power

Content note: this chapter discusses the eugenics movement, forced sterilisation and the Nazi regime's murder of people with disability.

Data create knowledge that is used to legitimise and deploy power. As sociologist Michel Foucault and his followers observed, '[b]ecause government refers to strategic, regulated and rationalized modes of power that have to be legitimized through forms of knowledge, the idea of critique as a form of resistance now becomes crucial'.[1] Disability studies scholars of last century knew that critique of knowledge and its construction is necessary to hold power to account.[2] The drafters of the *Convention on the Rights of Persons with Disabilities* ('*CRPD*') demonstrated considerable insight into the role of knowledge in legitimising power over people with disability.[3] This awareness of the power of knowledge construction was demonstrated in the drafters' reframing disability in international law and ensuring rights-holders' participation in matters affecting them.[4] *CRPD* article 31, entitled 'Statistics and data collection', seemingly contradicts the drafters' intent to regain control over how knowledge is constructed, as it is often interpreted as obligating, and in turn providing power to, states to categorise and count the bodies and lives of people with disability.[5]

1 Gary Gutting and Johanna Oksala, 'Michel Foucault' in Edward N Zalta (ed), *The Stanford Encyclopedia of Philosophy* (Metaphysics Research Lab, Stanford University, Spring 2019) <https://plato.stanford.edu/archives/spr2019/entries/foucault/>.

2 See earlier Sections 1.1.1 and 2.2.2(b) for a description of the work of disability scholars and advocates that challenges the dominant 'knowledge' about disability.

3 *Convention on the Rights of Persons with Disabilities*, opened for signature 24 January 2007, 2515 UNTS 3 (entered into force 3 May 2008) ('*CRPD*').

4 Ibid., art 4(3). See later Section 5.1.1 for a discussion about how the *CRPD* breaks from the medical model.

5 See, eg, leading civil society organisations that observed that, 'in recent years, there have been considerable efforts to collect and analyse data on persons with disabilities. . . . This has been catalysed by data collection requirements called for in the UN Convention on the Rights of Persons with Disabilities. . . . Consequently, disaggregation of data by disability is now a core

DOI: 10.4324/9781003506140-4

Article 31 has been used to justify considerable data production and processing about the bodies and lives of people with disability, including in refugee contexts.[6] This increased activity is supported by the Committee on the Rights of Persons with Disabilities, which monitors the *CRPD*'s implementation. It has recommended increased data production and processing about the bodies and lives of people with disability in all its Concluding Observations to states parties.[7] Data production and processing, including disability categorisation, has also been a significant project of the United Nations to facilitate the realisation of the Sustainable Development Goals, which pledge to 'leave no one behind'.[8] Nonetheless, while these bodies seek to harness the power of data for good, there are reasons to proceed with caution.

The function of this chapter is to develop the research lens about data and power.[9] In doing so, it seeks to disrupt the narrative about data being scientific and objective, arguing that data are not neutral and inert but powerful and potentially dangerous. The lens will be used to critique the object of this enquiry, *CRPD* article 31, and scholarly work and practices that draw on its authority.[10]

---

principle'. Leonard Cheshire and Humanity & Inclusion, *Disability Data Collection: A Summary Review of the Use of the Washington Group Questions by Development and Humanitarian Actors* (Report, 2018) 4.

6 See later Part 3 of this monograph for more about disability data production in refugee contexts.

7 The International Disability Alliance (IDA) compilations of the CRPD Committee's Concluding Observations are useful for reviewing all the committee's recommendations by article. The IDA compilation on art 31 identifies that the CRPD Committee has recommended in all but one Concluding Observation that states should increase data production and processing under art 31's authority. The exception is the CRPD Committee's Concluding Observations to the Czech Republic, where the committee recommends increased data collection under art 6 'Women with Disabilities'. 'IDA's Compilations of CRPD Committee's Concluding Observations', *International Disability Alliance* (Web Page) <https://www.internationaldisabilityalliance.org/content/ida%E2%80%99s-compilations-crpd-committee%E2%80%99s-concluding-observations>; Committee on the Rights of Persons with Disabilities, *Concluding Observations on the Initial Report of Czech Republic*, UN Doc CRPD/C/CZE/CO/1 (15 May 2015) [13]–[14]. All the CRPD Committee's Concluding Observations are available on the CRPD Committee's website: 'Committee on the Rights of Persons with Disabilities', *Office of the High Commissioner for Human Rights* (Web Page) <https://www.ohchr.org/en/treaty-bodies/crpd>.

8 United Nations Economic Commission for Europe, 'UNECE Launches Knowledge Hub on Statistics for SDGs to Support Evidence-Driven Policies' (Press Release, 2 December 2019) <https://www.unece.org/info/media/presscurrent-press-h/statistics/2019/unece-launches-knowledge-hub-on-statistics-for-sdgs-to-support-evidence-driven-policies/doc.html>.

9 See earlier Section 2.2.

10 In line with Pahuja's approach to legal research (detailed in Section 2.2), this theory chapter serves as a lens to see the archival material presented in subsequent chapters from new perspectives. Sundhya Pahuja, 'Methodology: Writing About How We Do Research' in Rossana Deplano and Nicholas Tsagourias (eds), *Research Methods in International Law: A Handbook* (Elgar, 2021) 60, 74.

This chapter constructs this lens through three distinct sections. Section 3.1 explores the relationship between disability and statistics in the 19th and early 20th centuries. It explains how statistics were used to categorise and marginalise people with disability with horrific outcomes, including forced sterilisation and state-directed murder. This section draws on the work of disability studies scholar Lennard Davis to describe the mechanism of power deployed through statistics that resulted in these dire outcomes. Section 3.2 examines philosopher Michel Foucault's observations about how power operates over and through humans. Section 3.3 explores the politics of quantification. It first turns to anthropologist Sally Engle Merry's work deconstructing human rights indicators. It then engages in the emerging literature on the digital state, including a report on the digital welfare state by Special Rapporteur on Extreme Poverty and Human Rights Philip Alston.[11] Key threads from each substantive section of the chapter inform a succinct explanation of the data and power research lens in the chapter's conclusion.

3.1 Data and Disability in the 19th and Early 20th Centuries

Governments have long produced and processed data on people within their jurisdictions,[12] but the last two decades have seen significant changes in the scale and the stakeholders involved. The technology used for data production and processing has enabled enormous growth in the amount of data produced and processed through increasingly affordable digital storage capacity, processing power and the proliferation of sensors. One commentator reported in 2018 that '[o]ver the last two years alone 90 per cent of the data in the world was generated'.[13]

In a time of rapid development in the production and processing of data, reflection on some of the harmful impacts on people with disability is important. This section revisits the history of human categorisation to challenge notions that data are neutral, scientific and factual. It will use this history to highlight assumptions that shape data production and processing and describe

11 Philip Alston, *Report of the Special Rapporteur on Extreme Poverty and Human Rights*, UN Doc A/74/48037 (11 October 2019).

12 Political arithmetic emerged in the 1660s to promote 'sound, well-informed state policy'. Theodore M Porter, *The Rise of Statistical Thinking, 1820–1900* (Princeton University Press, 1986) 18. 'The term "political arithmetic" . . . was coined by Sir William Petty, a founder member of the Royal Society [United Kingdom], who – being a scientist by education and a government economic adviser by career choice – deliberately set out to apply the new scientific methodology of the 17th century to the practical economic problems of the modern nation state'. Phyllis Deane, 'Political Arithmetic' in Matias Vernengo, Esteban Perez Caldentey and Barkley J Rosser Jr (eds), *The New Palgrave Dictionary of Economics* (Palgrave Macmillan UK, 2017) 1 <https://doi.org/10.1057/978-1-349-95121-5_1313-2>.

13 Bernard Marr, 'How Much Data Do We Create Every Day? The Mind-Blowing Stats Everyone Should Read', *Forbes* (online, 21 May 2018) <https://www.forbes.com/sites/bernardmarr/2018/05/21/how-much-data-do-we-create-every-day-the-mind-blowing-stats-everyone-should-read/>.

their impact. These arguments will be progressed by first describing how data production and processing were used to categorise people with disability as abnormal. The second subsection will describe how this scientific reasoning was used by the totalitarian Nazi regime and liberal democracies to implement eugenics laws and policies.

3.1.1 Creating '(Ab)Normal'

In 1838, the council of the Statistical Society of London viewed its new endeavour, statistics, as 'pure facts' and held that 'opinion was to be excluded from this science'.[14] According to the society, measuring phenomena enabled factual categorisation and ranking. This world view does not account for the reality that units of measurement and categorisation are socially constructed frameworks from which people derive meaning.[15] Anthropologist Sally Engle Merry argued that '[r]ather than revealing the truth, indicators create it . . . making known one reality among many possibilities'.[16] Merry observed that '[i]t is important to see *who* is creating the indicators'[17] to understand the assumptions, motivations and limitations that informed their construction.

One of the pioneers of statistics was Adolphe Quetelet (1796–1847), a French-Belgian astronomer whose interest turned to social physics. Quetelet applied a statistical approach used by astronomers to human characteristics to make sense of human diversity.[18] In response to the French government publishing crime statistics, Quetelet expressed their surprise at the 'frightening regularity with which the same crimes are reproduced'.[19] This statistical regularity awakened Quetelet's curiosity about what other social phenomena may conform to statistical patterns. Through collecting physical measurements of height, weight and limbs, Quetelet demonstrated that some human population characteristics adhere to the same statistical bell curve ('bell curve') used in astronomy. Those who fell under the mean, or centre of the bell curve, Quetelet termed the 'average man', *l'homme moyen*.

Quetelet concluded that the 'average man' was the ideal, and those that deviated constituted 'ugliness in body as well as vice in morals and a state of sickness with regard to the constitution'.[20] Though data were scarcer, Quetelet proposed that the same bell curve applied to moral traits such as courage,

14 Porter (n 12) 40.

15 See, eg, the primate case study in Donna Jeanne Haraway, *Primate Visions: Gender, Race, and Nature in the World of Modern Science* (Routledge, 1989) 9–13.

16 Sally Engle Merry, *The Seductions of Quantification: Measuring Human Rights, Gender Violence, and Sex Trafficking* (University of Chicago Press, 2016) 5.

17 Ibid., 5 (emphasis added).

18 Porter (n 12) 42.

19 Quetelet, 1829, cited in Porter (n 12) 49.

20 Porter (n 12) 103.

criminality and affection.[21] This so-called discovery, categorising and ranking human diversity, had significant implications that will be explored further in the next section, but it is important to pause and understand what shaped these ideas. Science historian Theodore Porter observed that Quetelet's interpretation of the data was shaped by a world view that venerated moderation[22] and regarded any deviation from the mean 'as flawed'.[23]

Quetelet's categorisation of human traits created those who were average or normal and those who were deviants or abnormal. Disability studies scholar Lennard Davis critiqued this proclaimed scientific advancement: 'When we think of bodies, in a society where the concept of the norm is operative, then people with disabilities will be thought of as deviants'.[24] The terms *norm* and *average* entered European languages in the 19th century through the rise of statistics.[25] At this time, human bodies, intellect and behaviour began to be categorised as normal or abnormal.

3.1.2 *The Role of Data and Statistics in the Pursuit of a Superior Race: Eugenics*

Frances Galton (1822–1911), the author of the book that first used the word *eugenics*,[26] was Charles Darwin's cousin. Galton wrote to Darwin of their 'awakening' when reading *On the Origin of Species*: 'your book drove away the constraint of my old superstition as if it had been a nightmare and was the first to give me Freedom of thought'.[27] Like Quetelet before them, Galton became an evangelist for a society ordered by science, even calling for 'the establishment of a sort of scientific priesthood . . . whose duties would have reference to the health and well-being of the nation in its broadest sense'.[28]

Porter noted that Galton's 'tendency to approach problems statistically seemed to be so thoroughly ingrained in his character that he attributed it to genetic inheritance'.[29] Porter instead attributed Galton's fervour for numbers to their studies in meteorological and geographical statistics, the unprecedented activity of the European statistical movement at the time and their father's habits that they ingrained in their child as a successful businessperson and banker.[30] With this statistical propensity, Galton looked to contribute to the theory of evolution by natural selection, and eugenics was born.[31]

21 Porter (n 12) 53.
22 Porter notes that Quetelet 'was enthralled by Cousin's ideal of moderation and compromise'. Porter (n 12) 102.
23 Porter (n 12) 104.
24 Lennard J Davis, *Enforcing Normalcy: Disability, Deafness, and the Body* (Verso, 1995) 29.
25 Ibid., 25–26.
26 Francis Galton, *Inquiries into Human Faculty and Its Development* (Macmillan, 1883).
27 Galton, letter to Darwin, cited in Porter (n 12) 133.
28 Galton, *English Men of Science: Their Nature and Nurture* (1874), cited in Porter (n 12) 133.
29 Porter (n 12) 135.
30 Porter (n 12) 135.
31 Porter (n 12) 134.

Galton, like Quetelet, believed the bell curve was applicable to all human characteristics.[32] Nonetheless, Galton needed data to test their theory. They gathered anthropometric data from 9,000 subjects, parents and their grown children, to test their theories of heredity.[33] Measurements of 'talent' were harder to come by in the mid-19th century.[34]

No doubt, Galton's values and other contextual considerations influenced their work. Kevles noted: 'Hardly a liberal, he [Galton] did not believe in natural equality; he held that people deserved equal protection but not equal political rights'.[35] Galton did not idealise the 'average man' like Quetelet. Galton instead believed in a hierarchy of 'man'. This belief translated into Galton's work, where they assumed the small area to the right end of the bell curve represented '250 of every million men [who] are properly eminent'.[36] The result was a theory that proposed the right end of the bell curve reflected the 'desirably' exceptional, and the left end reflected the 'undesirably' exceptional.

Substituting a median average in place of the mean at the centre of the bell curve,[37] Galton divided the curve into 14 intervals that ranked 'the grades of intelligence or statesmanship, as defined by mathematics'.[38] With this, the 'desirable' were identified, and a selective breeding program could be implemented to improve the human race. Galton described the rationale behind eugenics: 'What Nature does blindly, slowly and ruthlessly, man may do providently, quickly and kindly'.[39] Galton proselytised marriages between genetically preferred people and the collection of information about family heredity to improve matches to breed more genetically preferable future generations.[40]

Following Galton's death, the Great Depression (1929–1939) led to poor people being problematised and blamed for their poverty.[41] Further, nations wanted to rebuild with what was viewed as *genetically preferred stock* following the Great War (1914–1918).[42] Within this context, eugenics had a renewed audience.

32 Porter (n 12) 141.

33 Anthropometric data included height, weight, arm span and breathing power, amongst others. See Daniel J Kevles, *In the Name of Eugenics: Genetics and the Uses of Human Heredity* (Harvard University Press, 1995) 14.

34 Ibid., 14.

35 Ibid., 9.

36 Porter (n 12) 142.

37 Davis (n 24) 38.

38 Porter (n 12) 142.

39 Francis Galton, *Essays in Eugenics* (Eugenics Education Society, 1909) 42

40 Ibid.

41 For a discussion about the problematisation of the poor throughout modern history, including during the Great Depression, see Virginia Eubanks, *Automating Inequality: How High-Tech Tools Profile, Police, and Punish the Poor* (St Martin's Press, 2018).

42 Kevles (n 33) 57–69.

This era saw the rise of advocates promoting forced sterilisation of people who were perceived as holding back the advancement of society.[43] Forced sterilisation of people who lived in institutions and those receiving state welfare payments gained wide support.[44] A book review in *Nature* in 1930 noted that 20 states in the United States of America allowed 'legal sterilisation of sexual perverts, and imbecile and insane patients in public institutions . . . to aid Nature in eliminating the unfit'.[45] In addition to the United States of America,[46] the practice was carried out in countries such as Sweden, Denmark, Finland and Switzerland[47] and infamously under the National Socialist German Workers' Party, *Nationalsozialistische Deutsche Arbeiterpartei* ('Nazi regime'), through their 1933 *Gesetz zur Verhütung erbkranken Nachwuchses* (Law for the Prevention of Genetically Diseased Offspring).[48]

The Nazi regime, which held power in Germany from 1933 to 1945, ordered the forced sterilisation of the following:

> all people, institutionalized or not, who suffered from allegedly hereditary disabilities, including feeblemindedness, schizophrenia, epilepsy, blindness, severe drug or alcohol addiction, and physical deformities that seriously interfered with locomotion or were grossly offensive.[49]

The Nazi regime forcibly sterilised 250,000 people in the first three years of this law.[50] It also implemented its eugenics program by controlling marriage, promoting marriages between preferred 'stock' and making other marriages unlawful. The Nazi regime's eugenics program culminated in the state-directed murder of people identified as belonging to 'certain classes of the mentally diseased or disabled in German asylums'.[51] Over 600,000 people living in institutions because of illness, disability or poverty were murdered by medical professionals working for the Nazi regime under a 'medical euthanasia' program.[52]

Disability studies scholar Lennard Davis observed that Darwin's theory of evolution by natural selection 'serve[d] to place disabled people along the

43 Kevles (n 33) 114.
44 See Kevles (n 33) 115–116.
45 EW Macbride, 'Sterilisation for Human Betterment: A Summary of Results of 6000 Operations in California, 1909–1929' (1930) 125(3141) *Nature* 40, 41.
46 Eubanks reported that eugenics resulted in more than 60,000 people being forcibly sterilised in the United States of America. Eubanks (n 41) 24.
47 Kevles (n 33) 115.
48 See Michael Robertson, Astrid Ley and Edwina Light, *The First into the Dark* (University of Technology Sydney ePress, 2019) 31; Kevles (n 33) 115.
49 Kevles (n 33) 116.
50 Kevles (n 33) 117.
51 Kevles (n 33) 118.
52 See Robertson, Ley and Light (n 48) 23 who account for approximately 660,000 people who were killed in the Nazi party's 'medical euthanasia' program. This is in addition to those murdered because they were Jewish who may have also had a disability.

wayside as evolutionary defectives to be surpassed by natural selection'.[53] Davis explained that the number of statisticians that were eugenicists was striking, almost all of them. However, Davis was not surprised by this, stating that 'we must remember that there is a real connection between figuring the statistical measure of humans and then hoping to improve humans so that deviations from the norm diminish'.[54] It is important to note that eugenics was not a fringe movement but enjoyed support from many powerful people.[55] Davis gravely concluded: 'We have largely forgotten that what Hitler did in developing a hideous policy of eugenics was just to implement the theories of the British and American eugenicists'.[56]

As we see the rapid expansion of data production and processing in society, it is important to turn to history to understand some of the potential harms of data. Historically, statistics and human categorisation have created difference and division and ranked human characteristics. While human categorisation may be seen as a way of identifying people who need targeted measures, motivations can rapidly change in times of austerity and fear for human security. During these times, difference is problematised, those receiving targeted or special measures may be viewed as a burden on the state, and this group may be forced to comply with certain measures. This history of human categorisation informs this monograph's data and power research lens.

The next section examines philosopher Michel Foucault's (1926–1984) observations on power. Foucault also used history as a device to understand power. Nonetheless, Foucault's work focused on the seemingly subtle uses of power to control populations in liberal democracies. Foucault illustrated how knowledge production and documentation are methods of exerting power. This work is useful for examining how data production and processing about humans can act to marginalise and control them.

3.2 Power According to Michel Foucault

The purpose of describing power is to make visible something that is pervasive across every life domain yet rarely apparent. This section explores Foucault's philosophical concepts of power to provide an analytical lens to uncover how data are used as an instrument of power and how power shapes data. Foucault reflected that 'the role of philosophy is . . . to keep watch over the excessive powers of political rationality'.[57] Extending this same critique to scientific

53 Davis (n 24) 31.

54 Davis (n 24) 30.

55 Davis identified Alexander Graham Bell, citing a 'eugenics speech' that Bell delivered called 'Memoir upon the Formation of a Deaf Variety of the Human Race'. Other prominent supporters of eugenics he identified were John D Rockefeller, Prime Minister AJ Balfour, Neville Chamberlain, Winston Churchill, President Theodore Roosevelt, HG Wells, John Maynard Keynes and HJ Laski. Davis (n 24) 32, 37.

56 Davis (n 24) 38.

57 Michel Foucault, 'The Subject and Power' (1982) 8(4) *Critical Inquiry* 777, 779.

reasoning, Foucault employed history to question the sciences' 'naturalistic explanatory framework'.[58]

According to Foucault, power became more dispersed at the start of the 17th century, as sovereigns ceded some of their power over people's lives.[59] At the same time, humankind gained more control over famine and wars, allowing them more time to focus on living rather than dying.[60] Foucault observed that different and more diffuse power systems soon subjugated these newly free individuals.

Foucault's body of work, largely presented as a lecture series in French, introduced several, at times overlapping and incomplete, accounts of power that do not form one single coherent framework. Nonetheless, each theory provides insights into how power operates. This section does not contain a full description of Foucault's work, as much has been written elsewhere.[61] Rather, it summarises aspects of Foucault's critiques to contribute to the monograph's data and power research lens.[62]

3.2.1 Biopolitics, Biopower and Subjectivity

One system of power Foucault identified, biopower, emerged in the second half of the 18th century. Biopower's primary focus is power over life.[63] Biopower is particularly concerned with conditions that enable reproduction and longevity.[64] It may be exercised at a macro level, that is, through government

58 Gutting and Oksala (n 1). Foucault argued: 'We have to know the historical conditions which motivate our conceptualization. We need a historical awareness of our present circumstances'. Foucault, 'The Subject and Power' (n 57) 778.

59 Foucault qualified that they were critiquing 'some western countries', rather than regimes worldwide.

60 '[D]eath was ceasing to torment life so directly. But at the same time, the development of the different fields of knowledge concerned with life in general, the improvement of agricultural techniques, and the observations and measures relative to man's life and survival contributed to this relaxation: a relative control over life averted some of the imminent risks of death. In the space for movement thus conquered, and broadening and organizing that space, methods of power and knowledge assumed responsibility for the life processes and undertook to control and modify them'. Michel Foucault, 'Chapter 1 (Reproduction) Right of Death and Power over Life' in Timothy Campbell and Adam Sitze (eds), *Biopolitics: A Reader* (Duke University Press, 2013) 41, 46.

61 See, eg, Mitchell Dean, *Governmentality: Power and Rule in Modern Society* (Sage, 2nd ed, 2010).

62 See Section 2.2 for a description of the research methodology and the role of research lenses.

63 'Now it is over life, throughout its unfolding, that power establishes its dominion', Foucault, 'Chapter 1 (Reproduction) Right of Death and Power Over Life' (n 60) 43.

64 Foucault said that biopolitic/biopower involved 'a set of processes such as the ratio of births to deaths, the rate of reproduction, the fertility of a population, and so on. It is these processes – the birth rate, the mortality rate, longevity, and so on – together with a whole series of related economic and political problems . . . which, in the second half of the eighteenth century, become biopolitics' first objects of knowledge and the targets it seeks to control'. Foucault, 'Chapter 1 (Reproduction) Right of Death and Power Over Life' (n 60) 64.

regulation to ensure clean water, or at a micro level, that is, by individuals controlling their bodies through exercise and dieting.[65] This endeavour for human improvement also carries with it significant elements of control.

Biopower is 'a power that exerts a positive influence on life, that endeavours to administer, optimize, and multiply it, subjecting it to precise controls and comprehensive regulations'.[66] According to Foucault, these precise controls and comprehensive regulations are biopolitics of the population.[67] Biopolitics emerged with the work of the first demographers, who began to measure the ratio of births to deaths, the rate of reproduction and the population's fertility in statistical terms.[68] Shelley Tremain, disability studies and Foucauldian scholar, described these regulatory controls: 'bio-politics involves the introduction of mechanisms whose functions include forecasts, statistical estimates, and overall measures, and whose purpose is to intervene at the level of generality'.[69] Biopolitics is a political rationality that regulates life.[70]

Foucault observed that the beginning of the era of biopower was marked by 'an explosion of numerous and diverse techniques of achieving the subjugation of bodies and the control of populations'.[71] Foucault identified three mechanisms of subjectivity: objectification by science, 'dividing practices' where the 'subject is either divided inside himself or divided from others' and the process of turning oneself into a subject.[72] Objectification and classification by scientists, Tremain argued, has subjugated people with disability for the past two centuries:

> during the past two centuries, in particular, a vast apparatus, erected to secure the well-being of the general population, has caused the contemporary disabled subject to emerge into discourse and social existence. Among the items that have comprised this expansive apparatus are asylum, income support programs, quality of life assessments . . . These (and a host of other) practices, procedures, and policies have created, classified, codified, managed, and controlled social anomalies through which some people have been divided from others and *objectivized* as

65 Foucault, 'Chapter 1 (Reproduction) Right of Death and Power Over Life' (n 60) 44–47.

66 Foucault, 'Chapter 1 (Reproduction) Right of Death and Power Over Life' (n 60) 42.

67 Foucault, 'Chapter 1 (Reproduction) Right of Death and Power Over Life' (n 60) 44.

68 Shelley Tremain, 'Foucault, Governmentality, and Critical Disability Theory: An Introduction' in Shelley Tremain (ed), *Foucault and the Government of Disability* (University of Michigan Press, 2005) 1, 4.

69 Ibid., 5.

70 For more about biopolitics and biopower, see Rachel Adams, 'Michel Foucault: Biopolitics and Biopower', *Critical Legal Thinking* (online, 10 May 2017) <http://criticallegalthinking.com/2017/05/10/michel-foucault-biopolitics-biopower/>.

71 Foucault, 'Chapter 1 (Reproduction) Right of Death and Power Over Life' (n 60) 44–45.

72 Foucault, 'The Subject and Power' (n 57) 777–778.

> (for instance) physically impaired, insane, handicapped, mentally ill, retarded, and deaf.[73]

Much like Davis' argument describing how categorisation enabled the eugenics movement,[74] Tremain utilised Foucault's critique to explain that categorisation created the disabled subject. Tremain further argues that creating this category of people becomes self-serving for the institutions created to administer and 'care' for people with disability.[75]

Disability studies scholar Tom Shakespeare observed that medicine intrinsically 'seek[s] to count the numbers of people with impairments, or . . . reduce the complex problems of disabled people to issues of medical prevention, cure, or rehabilitation'.[76] Disability prevention, cure and rehabilitation are all preoccupied with longevity and biological peak performance. Biopower was deployed in the framing of disability for many years under the medical model of disability, where medical professionals held significant power over the lives of people with disability.[77]

Foucault's descriptions of biopower, biopolitics and subjectivity are pertinent to this monograph's data and power research lens as they highlight that data about individuals' bodies and lives are collected to exert control. Control is deployed through political rationality informed by averages and norms to ensure the 'greater good of humanity'. Nonetheless, not all individuals benefit from biopolitics or biopower's goal of longevity and biological optimisation. Foucault's description of subjectivity suggests that the control mechanisms reduce individuals' humanity through objectification. People are corralled, and their autonomy is reduced.

3.2.2 *Mechanisms of Power and Knowledge*

Biopower is exercised through mechanisms of power and knowledge that are the domain of scientists and administrators. These mechanisms of power and knowledge assume 'responsibility for the life process in order to optimize, control, and modify it. The exercise of power over living beings no longer carries the threat of death, but instead takes charge of their lives'.[78] Foucault identified many problematic aspects of science and those that had the power to define the truth and exercise power over others, for example, doctors examining patients and teachers setting exams for students.

73 Tremain (n 68) 5–6 (emphasis in original).
74 See earlier Section 3.1.
75 Tremain argued that 'the category of impairment emerged and, in many respects, persists in order to legitimise the governmental practices that generated it in the first place'. Tremain (n 68) 11.
76 Tom Shakespeare, 'The Social Model of Disability' in Lennard J Davis (ed), *The Disability Studies Reader* (Routledge, 5th ed, 2017) 195, 197.
77 See earlier Section 1.1 for more on the medical model of disability.
78 Gutting and Oksala (n 1).

To illustrate the mechanisms of power and knowledge, Foucault used the example of a patient examination. Foucault described the expert gaze as combining hierarchical observations and 'normalising judgements . . . the deployment of force and the establishment of truth'.[79] The medical professional can define 'the truth about those who undergo the examination' and direct a course of treatment 'controlling their behaviour'.[80] Gutting and Oksala suggested that, for Foucault, 'the goals of power and the goals of knowledge cannot be separated: in knowing we control and in controlling we know'.[81] Foucault problematised medicine's notions of knowledge, competence and quantification, observing that this was often accompanied by 'secrecy, deformation, and mystifying representations imposed on people'.[82]

Foucault's reflections on power and knowledge are supported by the success of the methods that progressed the disability rights movement. As discussed earlier in Section 1.1, which explored models of disability, the disability rights movement resisted the power of experts to define the 'truth' about their lives to regain the power to define their circumstances through the social model of disability. Foucault explained that power is diffuse and dynamic, moving between actors, and 'is exercised and exists only in action'.[83] *CRPD* article 4(3) obligates states to ensure people with disability are actively involved in matters affecting them. This obligation transfers power from the state to disabled persons organisations to enable people with disability to regain some power to define knowledge and truth about their lives.

The power of knowledge creation and the actors who have access to this power are important elements of this monograph's data and power research lens. The *CRPD*'s drafters recognised the power of defining truth and knowledge and provided mechanisms to ensure that people with disability gained some of that power. Assessing who holds the power of knowledge and 'truth' creation throughout data production and processing is vital in understanding how power is exerted.

3.2.3 Disciplinary Power and Documentation

Foucault observed that, at the beginning of the 19th century, biopower came together with disciplinary power. Foucault explained that disciplinary power is concerned with 'what people have not done', including 'a person's failure to reach a required standard . . . the primary function of modern disciplinary

79 Michel Foucault, *Discipline and Punish: The Birth of the Prison*, tr Alan Sheridan (Vintage Books, a Division of Penguin Random House, 2nd ed, 1995) 184.

80 Gutting and Oksala (n 1).

81 Gutting and Oksala (n 1).

82 Foucault clarified: 'There is nothing "scientistic" in this (that is, a dogmatic belief in the value of scientific knowledge), but neither is it a skeptical or relativistic refusal of all verified truth'. Foucault, 'The Subject and Power' (n 57) 781.

83 Tremain (n 68) 4 (emphasis omitted).

systems [is] to correct deviant behaviour'.[84] The main goal of discipline is not revenge, like in previous centuries, but reform: discipline through imposing precise and detailed norms ('normalization').[85]

Deviant behaviour is monitored and addressed in part through metrics and documentation. Gutting and Oksala explained:

> The examination also situates individuals in a 'field of documentation'. The results of exams are recorded in documents that provide detailed information about the individuals examined and allow power systems to control them (e.g., absentee records for schools, patients' charts in hospitals). On the basis of these records, those in control can formulate categories, averages, and norms that are in turn a basis for knowledge. The examination turns the individual into a 'case' – in both senses of the term: a scientific example and an *object of care.* Caring is always also an opportunity for control.[86]

Monitoring creates records and documentation that enable the creation of knowledge in the form of categories and averages used to mould people's behaviour. This reasoning is strikingly similar to the origins of the eugenics movement, described earlier,[87] in that it seeks to reform those seen to deviate from the norm. This process of examination, documentation and knowledge creation diminishes a person's autonomy and translates them into an object of care.

Foucault's conceptualisation of disciplinary power and its subtle moulding of behaviour is a powerful description that resembles the experiences of people with disability. People with disability commonly undergo examinations in which professionals assess and document findings that position people with disability as objects of care. Foucault's apt description of the power dynamics in these contexts results from studying the workings of institutions and how power operates within them.[88] Foucault's observations are relevant to this monograph's data and power research lens, particularly considering the role of documentation, information and data in disciplinary power and control.

3.2.4 *Governmentality*

Power exists within a broader framework that Foucault called governmentality. Governmentality refers to government rationality.[89] Governmentality does

84 Gutting and Oksala (n 1).

85 'This idea of normalization is pervasive in our society: e.g., national standards for educational programs, for medical practice, for industrial processes and products'. Gutting and Oksala (n 1).

86 Gutting and Oksala (n 1) (emphasis added).

87 See earlier Section 3.1.

88 Institutions such as prisons, hospitals, schools and 'asylums'. See, eg, Foucault, *Discipline and Punish: The Birth of the Prison* (n 79).

89 'A rationality of government, as Foucault explained it, is a system of thinking about the practice of government that has the capacity to rationalize some form of that activity to those who

not, exclusively or even primarily, operate at the level of the state. Foucault argued that governments within liberal democracies aim 'to maximize [their] effect and diminish [their] political and economic cost'.[90]

Maximising effect at minimal political and economic cost is achieved through systems of control that go well beyond government and include 'the governing of a wide array of objects and persons such as entire populations at the most abstract level and one's own desire and thoughts at a more micro level'.[91] As Campbell and Sitze summarised, Foucault proposed:

> the 'rights of man' could not materialize in the absence of very specific administrative apparatuses – apparatuses whose structures needed to be just as variable and expansive as the life they proposed to govern was unpredictable and unbounded. The result was that human life entered into law at the very moment that biopower 'grasped' life as a series of indefinite, enigmatic processes, and handed life over to apparatuses of governmentality whose operation then quickly began to exceed law from within.[92]

The idea of governmentality ***exceeding the law from within*** mirrors anthropologist Sally Engle Merry's appraisal that human rights indicators operate as soft law transferring 'responsibility from judicial and political decision makers to the experts in quantification who develop and implement measurement systems'.[93]

The idea that the state can exercise maximum impact through seemingly innocuous administrative apparatuses is another area of Foucault's work that is highly relevant to this monograph's data and power research lens. Further, it brings to light more of those who influence these dispersed power systems. From Foucault and Merry's account, power is held by bureaucrats and technocrats.

3.2.5 *Pastoral Power*

Foucault argued that remote sovereign power was replaced by an intimate pastoral power enacted through the 'development of knowledge of man' at the population and individual level.[94] This required 'globalising and quantitative' and 'analytical' means and methods.[95] According to Foucault, the state administered an individualising and totalising form of power concurrently.[96] Foucault

---

practice it and to those upon whom it is practiced, where this capacity entails to render thinkable and to render applicable or acceptable'. Tremain (n 68) 11.

90 Tremain (n 68) 12.

91 'Power/Knowledge: Michel Foucault', *Social Theory Re-Wired* (Web Page, 2016) <http://routledgesoc.com/category/profile-tags/powerknowledge>.

92 Timothy Campbell and Adam Sitze, 'Introduction: Biopolitics an Encounter' in Timothy Campbell and Adam Sitze (eds), *Biopolitics: A Reader* (Duke University Press, 2013) 1, 23.

93 Merry (n 16) 12. See later Section 3.3.1 for more on Merry's work on indicators.

94 Foucault, 'The Subject and Power' (n 57) 784.

95 Foucault, 'The Subject and Power' (n 57) 784.

96 Foucault, 'The Subject and Power' (n 57) 782.

likened this to the power exercised by the Christian church from the pulpit and in the confessional.[97] Gutting and Oksala observed that pastoral power 'relies on individualizing knowledge about a person's life. The modern state required the development of power technologies oriented towards individuals in an attempt to govern their conduct in a continuous and permanent way'.[98]

Data technologies are growing in their capacity to individualise knowledge about a person's life. The push for granular, detailed data is currently supported by private, public and civil society organisations with diverse motivations. In describing Foucault's work, Tremain characterised the power of the modern state as an 'ever-expanding and increasingly totalizing web of social control . . . inextricably intertwined with, and dependent upon, its capacity to generate an increasing specification of individuality'.[99] This characterisation of power and control informs this monograph's data and power research lens in considering the ubiquity of the data produced and processed about intimate aspects of people with disability's bodies and lives. Power is enacted through detailed knowledge of people.

Foucault's critiques of power and the mechanisms through which it is deployed are important in the development of the data and power lens for this research monograph, particularly when read alongside the accounts from people with disability who have had to fight for control over their bodies and lives throughout modern history. People with disability routinely experience state control over their lives. The totalising yet subtle mechanisms of power through administrative interactions, 'expert' assessments and documentation are important in exploring *CRPD* article 31, 'Statistics and data collection'.

Power was about control for Foucault. Foucault's work sometimes speaks to the consequences of power but often only highlights its potential – the potential to be used for helpful or harmful ends. Power is dangerous; therefore, those in positions of power must first recognise their power and proceed with caution. This is perhaps one of the most important messages of this research lens: proceed with caution.

3.3 The Politics of Quantification

Politics is closely related to power. Politics recognises that actors and institutions have different interests and will act accordingly to secure those interests. This chapter has explained that quantification is about translating a complex world into binary – the categorisation of phenomena. Politics shapes the choices about what data are produced and processed and what data are not.

This section has two distinct subsections that reveal aspects of the politics of quantification. The first describes anthropologist Sally Engle Merry's work on human rights indicators. The second examines some of the literature about

97 Foucault, 'The Subject and Power' (n 57) 783.
98 Gutting and Oksala (n 1).
99 Tremain (n 68) 6.

the digital or dataist state and examines the report from Special Rapporteur on Extreme Poverty and Human Rights Philip Alston on the digital welfare state. Both subsections serve to develop this monograph's data and power research lens and further the argument that data are not neutral and inert.

3.3.1 Human Rights Indicators, According to Sally Engle Merry

Like Foucault, anthropologist Sally Engle Merry's work on human rights indicators focused on knowledge construction and those with the power to create knowledge. Merry explained: 'The technical is always political because there is always interpretation and judgment in systems of classifications, in the choice of things to measure'.[100] Merry argued that '[a]ll indicators are framed by implicit theories about what is important to count and what is not, as well how social change happens'.[101]

During Merry's six years of research into international human rights indicator development in gendered violence and human trafficking, Merry demonstrated that indicators, rather than objective measures of phenomena, 'reflect the social and cultural worlds of the actors and organizations that create them'.[102] Similarly, Veronika Flegar, a socio-legal and policy researcher, found the following in reviewing the Office of the United Nations High Commissioner for Refugees' (UNHCR) framing of people with disability during the World Refugee Year (1960) and International Year of Disabled People (1981):

> UNHCR's engagement with disabled refugees during the two UN observances is characterized by the economic rationale of self-sufficiency and the humanitarian rationale of vulnerability – depending on what was perceived as the bestselling frame in light of the political climate at the time. Both cases therefore highlight the political nature of classifications and frames for the international protection of disabled refugees.[103]

Information and data reflect the world view of those constructing them as well as their desired outcomes.

Merry illustrated the different motivations that various actors have in producing and processing data, summarising that '[a]dvocates use indicators to make problems visible, social science scholars to produce scientific knowledge,

100 Merry (n 16) 21. Earlier Merry explained: 'By "political," I do not mean the kinds of pressures political leaders exert on official statistical bureaus to produce data they wish. My analysis of the politics of indicator production refers to the way in which indicators are subtly and even unconsciously shaped by the assumptions, motivations, and concerns of those who carry them out': at 20.

101 Merry (n 16) 16.

102 Merry (n 16) 4–5.

103 Veronika Flegar, 'UNHCR's Shifting Frames in the Social Construction of Disabled Refugees: Two Case Studies on the Organization's Work During the World Refugee Year (1959–1960) and the International Year of Disabled Persons (1981)' (2019) 1(2) *Diplomatica* 157.

and businesses and government to monitor and control behaviour'.[104] Often, there are multiple motivations for producing and processing the same data, either from a range of actors involved or as actors change over time. Data produced by international organisations or states for one purpose may be used for different purposes later. This data reuse may be justified and widely supported in a climate of austerity and heightened national security.[105]

Those measured are often not involved in developing the categories for measurement. Merry noted that local knowledge is often not valued in the development of global indicators explaining that 'it is important to track what forms of expertise are involved in creating an indicator'.[106] Further, global indicators assume that human identity and characteristics are universal. The notion of universal characteristics was contested by Nira Yuval-Davis, an intersectionality scholar, who cautioned that 'each social division has a different ontological basis, which is irreducible to other social divisions', highlighting the complexity of the human experience.[107]

Even when categories are well defined, Merry found that what was being measured was not always clear. Data often contain gaps and proxies that are not always apparent in the final neat quantification. There may be many compromises and vagaries, often not visible in final outputs, such as proxies taken from other national datasets, ambiguous categories, assumptions made to repair errors in counting or missing data and a lack of commensurability.[108]

Merry attributed the lack of communication about the nuances and shortfalls of quantitative data to crowded information spaces where decision-makers are rapidly trying to build an understanding of complex social issues. Merry summarised: 'the simplest and most coherent [indicators] often prevail'.[109] Recognising the limitations of indicators, Merry did not advocate discarding indicators but rather better literacy of quantitative measures and caution in interpreting them: 'By recognising the politics of producing quantitative data,

104 Merry (n 16) 13.

105 For a case study on UNHCR data being used by the United States of America government to identify terrorists, see Katja Lindskov Jacobsen, *The Politics of Humanitarian Technology: Good Intentions, Unintended Consequences and Insecurity* (Routledge, 2015). Eubanks describes how welfare data that showed where cash was withdrawn was used by a candidate for governor to suggest that welfare recipients were using their money to buy alcohol and cigarettes and to gamble. Eubanks (n 41) 7. Aratani reported that 'information from the 1940 [US] Census was secretly used in one of the worst violations of constitutional rights in U.S. history: the internment of Japanese Americans during World War II'. Lori Aratani, 'Secret Use of Census Info Helped Send Japanese Americans to Internment Camps in WWII', *Washington Post* (online, 7 April 2018) <https://www.washingtonpost.com/news/retropolis/wp/2018/04/03/secret-use-of-census-info-helped-send-japanese-americans-to-internment-camps-in-wwii/>.

106 Merry (n 16) 7.

107 Nira Yuval-Davis, 'Intersectionality and Feminist Politics' (2006) 13(3) *European Journal of Women's Studies* 193, 195.

108 Merry (n 16) 19–20.

109 Merry (n 16) 20.

it is possible to see how particular choices about how to categorize and count shape the knowledge that is produced as well as what is missed, ignored, and not counted'.[110]

Merry's work contributes to this monograph's data and power research lens in three significant ways. Firstly, Merry highlights the influence of data creators' social and political context on data variables.[111] Secondly, Merry problematises universal indicators by questioning whether data variables can be truly universal.[112] On this point, Merry's investigation of regional differences and conclusion about the importance of data subjects' involvement in defining the data categories are particularly useful to this research. Lastly, Merry's work contributes to the data and power research lens by underscoring the limitations of quantitative data and emphasising that caution should be exercised when using data to inform policy decisions.

3.3.2 *The Digital State*

The digital state differs from previous iterations of the state in that it has a greater reliance on technology and a belief in technology's supremacy in solving social problems.[113] The digital state reduces society and people's individual lives to data variables. The locus of control for the digital state is concentrated with a few powerful technology companies that created the tools that enable the digital state.[114] States and these technology companies avoid accountability by hiding behind commercial arrangements.[115] Commentators have observed that, ultimately, digital conversion serves those in power and not individual rights-holders.[116] This subsection explores the literature on the digital state that problematises data-driven policy and reviews a United Nations Special Rapporteur's report that explains the implications of the digital welfare state for people who experience extreme poverty.[117] The analysis contributes further to the data and power research lens.

110 Merry (n 16) 20.
111 Merry (n 16) 4–5.
112 Merry (n 16) 21.
113 For more about the digital state, see Marion Fourcade and Jeffrey Gordon, 'Learning Like a State: Statecraft in the Digital Age' (2020) 1(1) *Journal of Law and Political Economy* 78.
114 See, eg, Oscar Williams, 'How Palantir is Quietly Extending Its Reach Through the British State', *New Statesman* (online, 5 January 2021) <https://www.newstatesman.com/science-tech/2021/01/how-palantir-quietly-extending-its-reach-through-british-state>.
115 See, eg, Fourcade and Gordon (n 113) 93.
116 See, eg, Yuval Noah Harari, 'Why Technology Favors Tyranny' *The Atlantic* (online, October 2018) <https://www.theatlantic.com/magazine/archive/2018/10/yuval-noah-harari-technology-tyranny/568330/>; Robert Booth, 'Benefits System Automation Could Plunge Claimants Deeper into Poverty', *The Guardian* (online, 14 October 2019) <https://www.theguardian.com/technology/2019/oct/14/fears-rise-in-benefits-system-automation-could-plunge-claimants-deeper-into-poverty>. '[C]itizens become ever more visible to their governments, but not the other way around': Alston (n 11) [3] (citations omitted).
117 Alston (n 11).

a) Data-Driven Policy

Sociologists Fourcade and Gordon argue that the digital or, as they termed it, the ***dataist state*** 'declares that a society consists of data flows, and the state's responsibility is to collect and process that data'.[118] Fourcade and Gordon explained that this new order leads to a 'transportation of political rationality, in which data affordances increasingly drive policy strategy'.[119] They observed:

> what can be measured is not necessarily what really matters. The institutional relevance of measures is often defined by affordability, ease of collection, or political preference rather than by real-world pertinence . . . more often than not, useable measures propose an inaccurate representation of the underlying policy goal.[120]

Data affordance's critical role in policy development in the digital state has an immediately apparent implication: you and your needs must be counted for the state to respond. If this cannot be done, then some proxy or approximate measure must be determined. Things that cannot be measured or counted are valued less and neglected. This rationale no doubt informs a common advocacy slogan: 'to count, you must be counted'.[121] Further, this approach to policy proposes that ineffective policy responses are fixed with more data, legitimising greater surveillance of people within a state's jurisdiction.

Another characteristic of the dataist state observed by Fourcade and Gordon is that it is responsive rather than proactive. Drawing on Evgeny Morozov's work, they illustrate how reductive this approach to policy-making is by using the example of the intelligence services approach to terrorism, relying on surveillance of threats to the exclusion of contextual information, such as history and foreign policy.[122] Responsive policy development increases the drive for rapid production and processing of data. Furthermore, it undervalues other sources of knowledge in the development of policy.

These two observations from Fourcade and Gordon illustrate the enormous value the digital state places on data for policy development. These observations are important contributions to this monograph's data and power research lens used to critique *CRPD* article 31, which is about producing and processing appropriate information to 'formulate and implement ***policies*** to give effect' to the *CRPD*.[123] Rather than data being one source of information

118 Fourcade and Gordon (n 113) 81.

119 Fourcade and Gordon (n 113) 78.

120 Fourcade and Gordon (n 113) 88.

121 A variation of this slogan exists on the Disability Data Advocacy Working Group webpage: 'if persons with disabilities are not counted, then they don't count'. 'Disability Data Advocacy Working Group', ***International Disability Alliance*** (Web Page) <https://www.internationaldisabilityalliance.org/content/disability-data-advocacy-working-group>.

122 Fourcade and Gordon (n 113).

123 *CRPD* (n 3) art 31(1) (emphasis added).

to inform policy development, the digital state gives it primacy as the only source or at least the most important source of information despite the quality of data available on some social issues. This critique provides insight into why advocates call for greater data production in their work to influence policy and is also important context in considering how states devalue people's lived experience knowledge.

b) *The Digital Welfare State*

Philip Alston, Special Rapporteur on Extreme Poverty and Human Rights, in a 2019 report identified a lack of attention to the human rights implications of the digital welfare state.[124] The digital welfare state is the administrative element of the welfare state, which uses technology to verify the identity of individuals, assess their eligibility for social security entitlements, calculate the entitlements, detect and prevent fraud and 'facilitate' communication between the individual and the state.[125] Alston assessed that, in the transition to the digital welfare state, '[v]alues such as dignity, choice, self-respect, autonomy, self-determination, privacy, and a range of other factors are all traded off without being factored into the overall equation'.[126] The report concluded that there are significant gaps in research, discourse and advocacy related to the human rights of those impacted by the emerging digital welfare state.

Alston debunked the notion that digitisation is 'an essentially benign initiative'.[127] They observed that, while technology is 'presented as being "scientific" and neutral', it is imbued with 'values and assumptions that are far removed from, and may be antithetical to, the principles of human rights'.[128] Further, technology and digitisation are often presented as the 'inevitable result of "scientific" progress' without acknowledging the political choices that have been made.[129]

The digital welfare state is less transparent and accountable. While claims are made that digital welfare tools are 'putting more power in the hands of citizens and being more responsive to their needs',[130] the digital welfare state is opaque and elusive. Alston argued that 'citizens become ever more visible to their governments, but not the other way around'.[131] The digital welfare state places the burden of accountability on the 'applicant': 'Rather than the ideal of the State being accountable to the citizen to ensure . . . an adequate standard of living, the burden of accountability has in many ways been reversed'.[132]

124 Alston (n 11).
125 Alston (n 11) [10]–[31].
126 Alston (n 11) [63].
127 Alston (n 11) [4].
128 Alston (n 11) [6].
129 Alston (n 11) [74].
130 Alston (n 11) [4] (citations omitted).
131 Alston (n 11) [3].
132 Alston (n 11) [50].

People who receive government services have little bargaining power and recourse to hold the digital welfare state accountable.[133]

The opaqueness of the digital welfare state is partly due to a change in the actors that hold power in welfare administration and provision. Alston's report described the new actors as 'a handful of powerful executives replacing governments and legislators'.[134] These new actors lack democratic accountability and participation in mechanisms to enforce human rights norms. Alston argued that many industry codes of ethics contain references to human rights, but 'the substance of human rights law is invariably lacking'.[135]

Those designing the digital welfare systems are far removed from the lived experience of those engaged with the systems, 'often ill-equipped to anticipate the sort of problems that are likely to arise'.[136] Alston recommended that, 'in order to reduce the harm caused by incorrect assumptions and mistaken design choices, digital welfare systems should be co-designed by their intended users and evaluated in a participatory manner'.[137] Co-design is consistent with the *CRPD*'s participatory obligations.[138]

The increasing asymmetry in power between the state and the welfare recipient was a major theme of Alston's report. Alston conceded: 'That the poor suffer from more intense levels of scrutiny, monitoring, surveillance, is hardly an original observation'.[139] Nonetheless, the Special Rapporteur highlighted the coercive and exploitative nature of the relationship between the welfare recipient and the state: 'there is a real risk that beneficiaries are effectively forced to give up their right to privacy and data protection to receive their right to social security as well as other social rights'.[140] Alston bleakly forecasts:

> as humankind moves, perhaps inexorably, towards the digital welfare future it needs to alter course significantly and rapidly to avoid stumbling zombie-like into a digital welfare dystopia. Such a future would be one in which: unrestricted data matching is used to expose and punish

133 An example of the power differentials between individuals and the digital welfare state is seen in the Robodebt Scheme, where individuals had illegal and erroneous debt notices served by the state with few or no avenues for review. The consequence of a class action lawsuit was the restitution of $1.8 billion dollars. The stress caused by this illegal debt collection system was much greater. 'At least seven families believe the suicide of people they loved was partly or directly linked to the program. Thousands were thrust further into penury, prevented from leaving violent living situations or so mentally traumatised that their disadvantage was all but guaranteed'. Rick Morton, 'The Transmission of Shame: What the Robodebt Royal Commission Tells Us About Who Knew What and Why It Matters', *The Monthly* (December 2022–January 2023) 42.
134 Alston (n 11) [36].
135 Alston (n 11) [40].
136 Alston (n 11) [48].
137 Alston (n 11) [49].
138 *CRPD* (n 3) art 4(3).
139 Alston (n 11) [57].
140 Alston (n 11) [59] (citations omitted).

> the slightest irregularities in the record of welfare beneficiaries (while assiduously avoiding such measures in relation to the well-off); evermore refined surveillance options enable around the clock monitoring of beneficiaries; conditions are imposed on recipients that undermine individual autonomy and choice in relation to sexual and reproductive choices, and in relation to food, alcohol and drugs and much else; and highly punitive sanctions are able to be imposed on those who step out of line.[141]

This critique of the digital welfare state is important to this monograph's data and power research lens because people with disability rely on the state for reasonable accommodations to realise their rights. In accessing services necessary to fulfil their human rights, people with disability are often characterised not as rights-holders but as welfare recipients or service recipients. Therefore, people with disability are more likely to be engaged with the (digital) welfare state than those without disability.

Alston's critique, echoing the theorists earlier in this chapter, challenges the notion that data and technology are neutral, raises concerns about the lack of state transparency and accountability, highlights the new actors in this space pursuing their interests (technology companies) and vividly explains the growing asymmetry between the rights-holder and the state. A point of difference from the earlier theorists is Alston's international human rights law frame, which demonstrates the digital welfare state's departure from human rights norms. This analysis is useful for this monograph in considering points of intervention.

3.4 Conclusion

Data are dangerous. Foucault explains:

> [m]y point is not that everything is bad, but that everything is dangerous, which is not exactly the same as bad . . . I think that the ethico-political choice we have to make every day is to determine which is the main danger.[142]

Data must be treated with caution. As this chapter has highlighted, historically, statistics and human categorisation have created difference and division and ranked human characteristics with disastrous outcomes. While human categorisation may be seen as a way of identifying people who need targeted measures, history demonstrates that motivations can rapidly change in times of austerity and fear for human security. During these times, difference is problematised. Those receiving targeted or special measures may be viewed as a burden on the state, and this group may be punished.

141 Alston (n 11) [72].

142 Foucault, 'On the Genealogy of Ethics: An Overview of Work in Progress', cited in Tremain (n 68).

Foucault's observations of power systems are important, as people with disability routinely experience state control over their lives. The totalising yet subtle mechanisms of power through administrative interactions, 'expert' assessments and documentation are used to subjugate people with disability. Assessing who holds the power to create knowledge and 'truth' is vital in understanding how power is exerted. Documentation, information and data are used to define truth and exert control. Foucault's work sometimes speaks to the consequences of power but often only highlights its potential – the potential to be used for helpful or harmful ends. Considering that what may be helpful to one person may be harmful to another, those outcomes are rarely universal.

Data creation is political. Merry underscores the significance of understanding the data creators' social and political context, questions whether data variables can be truly universal and recommends that data subjects be involved in defining the data categories. Merry warns of the limitations of quantitative data and cautions against its uncritical use to inform policy decisions. Data-driven policy is being developed based on what data are available rather than other methods of identifying pressing social issues. In this context, it is understandable that advocates call for greater data production. Nonetheless, as Alston argues, this should be done assiduously because the digital welfare state is becoming less compliant with human rights norms.

This monograph's data and power research lens draws on the work of the earlier theorists and recognises that data and statistics have historically been used to create divisions and differences and to rank people. Administrative processes and expert assessments that categorise people lead to hierarchies and value judgments. Data, information and documentation are used to exert power over individuals and groups. Critique is important to uncover how knowledge is produced and keep power in check. Institutions and individuals, including myself, must recognise their power and proceed cautiously.

The next part of the monograph focuses on *CRPD* article 31. Employing this research lens on data and power, along with the disability human rights research lens,[143] Chapter 4 analyses the tensions that emerged from the drafting debates that remain in the article. This then informs Chapter 5's interpretation of article 31, which proposes an alternative reading to the dominant one used to justify the production and processing of data about the bodies and lives of people with disability.

143 See earlier sub-subsection 2.2.2(b).

Part II

CRPD Article 31

The group highlighted the word 'appropriate' in the text of [CRPD Article 31] paragraph 1 and wrote the note: 'appropriate' – this is vague, defined by who?

Stakeholder Advisory Group meeting minutes, 18 June 2021

DOI: 10.4324/9781003506140-5

4 Drafting *CRPD* Article 31

The *Convention on the Rights of Persons with Disabilities* ('*CRPD*') is the first United Nations-facilitated human rights treaty to have an entire article dedicated to 'Statistics and data collection'.[1] Despite broad consensus amongst the *CRPD* drafters about the need for data, the exact nature of these obligations was the subject of significant debate. Drafters grappled with data production and processing's unresolved role in society and human rights law, its concurrently harmful and useful effects and its function of amassing power to the data controller. The negotiators endeavoured to harness the great potential of data production and processing to realise the human rights of people with disability without causing harm.

According to the *Vienna Convention on the Law of Treaties*, reference to the drafting history is a supplementary means of interpretation.[2] At this point of the monograph, reviewing the drafting history, or *travaux preparatoires*, is not intended as a means to interpret the article. Rather, the review is to provide context about the inclusion of a novel human rights obligation regarding data production and processing. By exploring the origins of *CRPD* article 31, 'Statistics and data collection', this chapter also builds on the monograph's introduction and Part I examination of the critical role of knowledge production in asserting and maintaining power over others.

An inductive approach was employed to review the *CRPD*'s *travaux preparatoires* to identify the themes that emerged during the article 31

1 *Convention on the Rights of Persons with Disabilities*, opened for signature 24 January 2007, 2515 UNTS 3 (entered into force 3 May 2008) ('*CRPD*'). However, it is not completely novel as the 1951 *Convention Relating to the Status of Refugees* ('*Refugee Convention*') article 35 references statistics in paragraph 2. *Convention Relating to the Status of Refugees*, opened for signature 28 July 1951, 189 UNTS 150 (entered into force 22 April 1954) art 35(2) ('*Refugee Convention*'). See later Section 6.2.1 for a comparison between *CRPD* art 31 and the *Refugee Convention* art 35(2). See also the International *Convention for Protection of All Persons from Enforced Disappearance*, opened for signature 6 February 2007, 2716 UNTS 3 (entered into force 23 December 2010) art 19. This article has a focus on individual data protection.

2 *Vienna Convention on the Law of Treaties*, opened for signature 23 May 1969, 1155 UNTS 331 (entered into force 27 January 1980) art 32.

DOI: 10.4324/9781003506140-6

negotiations.[3] Unsurprisingly, the major themes reflect the text of article 31 and its core tensions. This chapter presents these findings in four sections. Section 4.1 describes the drafting process, the *CRPD* negotiations' participants and the *travaux preparatoires* archive. The following three sections present a thematic analysis of the negotiations. Section 4.2 describes the difficulty in drafting the obligations due to a lack of clarity or agreement about data's evolving role in society and human rights law. Section 4.3 illustrates useful and harmful elements of data production and processing by focusing on the debates about defining disability and the disaggregation of data. Finally, Section 4.4 examines how the drafters tried to diffuse and regulate the power amassed by the data controller: states.

4.1 The Drafting of the *CRPD*

The Ad Hoc Committee on a Comprehensive and Integral International Convention on the Protection and Promotion of the Rights and Dignity of Persons with Disabilities ('Ad Hoc Committee') met from 2002 to 2006 over eight sessions to negotiate the text of the *CRPD*.[4] As shown in Table 4.1,

Table 4.1 Timeline of *CRPD* drafting negotiations

Date	*Drafting activity*
2001 December	UNGA Resolution A/RES/56/168 establishes the Ad Hoc Committee
2002 August	1st session of the Ad Hoc Committee
2003 June	2nd session of the Ad Hoc Committee
2004 January	Drafting Working Group
2004 May/June	3rd session of the Ad Hoc Committee
2004 August/September	4th session of the Ad Hoc Committee
2005 January/February	5th session of the Ad Hoc Committee
2005 August	6th session of the Ad Hoc Committee
2006 January	7th session of the Ad Hoc Committee
2006 May/August	8th session of the Ad Hoc Committee commences and is adjourned
2006 September/November	Technical review of the draft treaty text
2006 December	Resumed 8th session of the Ad Hoc Committee
2006 December	UNGA Resolution A/RES/61/106 adoption of the text for the *Convention on the Rights of Persons with Disabilities*

3 'Inductive analysis is a process of coding the data without trying to fit it into a preexisting coding frame or the researcher's analytic preconceptions'. Lorelli S Nowell et al, 'Thematic Analysis: Striving to Meet the Trustworthiness Criteria' (2017) 16(1) *International Journal of Qualitative Methods* 1, 8.

4 Established by *Comprehensive and Integral International Convention to Promote and Protect the Rights and Dignity of Persons with Disabilities*, GA Res 56/168, UN Doc A/RES/56/168 (26 February 2002, adopted 19 December 2001).

the Drafting Working Group met between the second and third sessions to develop text to progress the negotiations. Significant attempts were made to include people with disability and organisations that represented and worked with people with disability in the negotiation process. The unprecedented numbers of opening signatories and swift ratification implied a broad acceptance of the text that the Ad Hoc Committee negotiated. This section briefly looks at who participated in the negotiations, the quality of the negotiations' archives and factors that may have influenced the negotiations' speed.

4.1.1 Participants in the Treaty Negotiations

The Ad Hoc Committee's participants were United Nations member states, observers of the United Nations and a larger group of stakeholders 'with an interest in the matter'.[5] Civil society participation was encouraged, and they were active in the negotiations. Civil society organisations could attend meetings, make statements, receive written documents and make written submissions.[6] The success of this initiative was reflected in the number of accredited organisations growing over consecutive sessions.[7]

Measures were taken to facilitate access to the Ad Hoc Committee meetings, indicating a genuine and assertive attempt to engage a broad range of stakeholders in drafting the treaty.[8] The Ad Hoc Committee repeatedly extended invitations to relevant stakeholders to participate in future meetings, including 'regional commissions, United Nations bodies and mechanisms, experts, national human rights institutions and national disability institutions'.[9]

5 *Comprehensive and Integral International Convention to Promote and Protect the Rights and Dignity of Persons with Disabilities*, GA Res 56/168, UN Doc A/RES/56/168 (26 February 2002, adopted 19 December 2001) [3].

6 Ad Hoc Committee, *Report of the Ad Hoc Committee on a Comprehensive and Integral International Convention on Protection and Promotion of the Rights and Dignity of Persons with Disabilities*, UN Doc A/57/357 (27 August 2002) [10(a)] ('*Report of the Ad Hoc Committee's First Session*').

7 Eg, 22 additional non-government organisations were accredited to the Ad Hoc Committee in just the 7th session. Ad Hoc Committee, *Report of the Ad Hoc Committee on a Comprehensive and Integral International Convention on the Protection and Promotion of the Rights and Dignity of Persons with Disabilities on Its Seventh Session*, UN Doc A/AC.265/2006/2 (13 February 2006) annex 1.

8 Human Rights Commission, *Human Rights of Persons with Disabilities*, CHR Res 2002/61, UN Doc E/CN.4/2002/61 (adopted 25 April 2002) 15. This was followed by a General Assembly resolution about the accreditation and participation of non-government organisations in the Ad Hoc Committee providing high-level details about how non-government organisations could apply for accreditation. *Accreditation and Participation of Non-Governmental Organizations in the Ad Hoc Committee on a Comprehensive and Integral International Convention on Protection and Promotion of the Rights and Dignity of Persons with Disabilities*, UNGA Res 56/510, UN Doc A/RES/56/510 (26 July 2002, adopted 23 July 2002).

9 Ad Hoc Committee, *Report of the Ad Hoc Committee's First Session* (n 6) [11]; Ad Hoc Committee, *Ad Hoc Committee on a Comprehensive and Integral International Convention on Protection and Promotion of the Rights and Dignity of Persons with Disabilities*, UN Doc A/58/118 & Corr.1 (3 July 2003) [15] ('*Report of the Ad Hoc Committee's Second Session*').

Special measures were also put in place to fund the participation of civil society organisations and experts from 'developing countries, in particular from the least developed countries'.[10] Committee documents were also to be 'published to the fullest extent possible in formats accessible to persons with disabilities'.[11]

Civil society organisations' advocacy during the negotiations was informed by their membership, work and history. There are diverse views amongst disabled persons organisations ('DPOs'). Further, not all civil society organisations participating in the negotiations were DPOs.[12] Some organisations 'worked with' people with disability and, therefore, spoke from their perspective of providing services or 'care'. Understanding the membership, work and history of the delegations to the *CRPD* negotiations is further complicated because some were coalitions created for the negotiations.[13] Discerning who was represented in the negotiations is challenging when reviewing the negotiations' archive.

4.1.2 Record of the CRPD *Treaty Negotiations*

The official records (those with UN document numbers) of the *CRPD* negotiations are brief and include, among others, high-level reports (some with appendices with draft text), documents submitted by states and other delegations with draft text and expert reports.[14] Alongside these official records, the United Nations Enable website has transcripts of most of the plenary negotiation sessions, labelled 'Daily summary of discussions' ('daily summaries').[15] These do not comprise the 'official record' of the negotiations. While this archive provides invaluable insights into the negotiations, its limitation must be acknowledged.

10 Ad Hoc Committee, *Report of the Ad Hoc Committee's Second Session* (n 9) [15(3)].

11 Ad Hoc Committee, *Report of the Ad Hoc Committee's Second Session* (n 9) [15(5)].

12 DPOs are organisations that are led by and have a majority membership of people with disability. Committee on the Rights of Persons with Disabilities, *General Comment No 7 (2018) on the Participation of Persons with Disabilities, Including Children with Disabilities, Through Their Representative Organizations, in the Implementation and Monitoring of the Convention*, UN Doc CRPD/C/GC/7 (9 November 2018) ('*General Comment 7 Participation*') [11].

13 Maria Veronica Reina explained that the International Disability Caucus (IDC) 'was composed of more than 70 world-wide, regional and national Disabled People's Organizations (and allied NGOs) who had decided to work together and coordinate their efforts. The IDC included all the different disability groups and had organizations from all regions of the world'. Maria Veronica Reina, 'How the International Disability Caucus Worked During Negotiations for a UN Human Rights Convention on Disability', *Global Action on Aging* (Web Page, 6 February 2008) <http://globalag.igc.org/agingwatch/events/CSD/2008/maria.htm>.

14 See, eg, draft text in Working Group to the Ad Hoc Committee, *Report of the Working Group to the Ad Hoc Committee*, UN Doc A/AC.265/2004/WG.1 (27 January 2004).

15 For all of the formal and informal Ad Hoc Committee documents, see 'Ad Hoc Committee on a Comprehensive and Integral International Convention on the Protection and Promotion of the Rights and Dignity of Persons with Disabilities', *United Nations Department of Economic and Social Affairs* (Web Page) <https://www.un.org/development/desa/disabilities/resources/ad-hoc-committee-on-a-comprehensive-and-integral-international-convention-on-the-protection-and-promotion-of-the-rights-and-dignity-of-persons-with-disabilities.html>.

Civil society organisations transcribed the negotiations from audio recordings of the session. Session 8 transcripts do not exist,[16] and many side conversations and breakout sessions are not documented. The transcripts are also incomplete and sometimes summarised rather than documenting verbatim what was said by delegates. The daily summaries were posted on the committee's website, suggesting their purpose was to support continuity between the meetings. Therefore, the rigour applied in producing these records was less than the official ones. Nonetheless, the daily summaries are the richest source of information about the treaty negotiations and are the primary materials that inform this chapter.

4.1.3 Rapid Negotiations and Wide Adoption

A significant amount of the negotiations and drafting of the *CRPD* was led by New Zealand Ambassador Don MacKay as Coordinator and then Chair.[17] Ambassador MacKay's influence through facilitating the discussions and guiding the drafting cannot be underestimated. The Ad Hoc Committee daily summaries indicate that, as the sessions progressed, Ambassador MacKay facilitated the discussions with urgency to avoid losing institutional knowledge and draining the organisations' resources.[18] There was no significant pushback to the negotiations' speed and wide adoption of the treaty subsequently; therefore, it does not appear that this speed was reckless. The decades of international discussions about the rights of people with disability and skilled negotiators likely contributed to this success.[19]

At the resumed 8th session of the Ad Hoc Committee,[20] the committee 'decided to recommend to the General Assembly for adoption a draft resolution

16 If we take the view that the transcripts were to support continuity in conversations and debates between meetings, transcripts of the 8th session may not exist because a ninth session was unlikely.

17 Ambassador MacKay also reformulated the draft text between the 6th and 7th session. Don MacKay, *Letter Dated 7 October 2005 From the Chairman to All Members of the Committee*, UN Doc A/AC.265/2006/1 (14 October 2005).

18 Rehabilitation International, 'Daily Summary of Discussion at the Sixth Session 1 August 2005', *UN Convention on the Human Rights of People with Disabilities Ad Hoc Committee – Daily Summaries* (United Nations Enable, 1 August 2005) <https://www.un.org/esa/socdev/enable/rights/ahc6sum1Aug.htm>.

19 Eg, during the 4th session, the Coordinator raised concerns during negotiations on draft article 6 (data and statistics) about the speed of the negotiations and how long it would take to negotiate a treaty at this rate: 'The Coordinator therefore recommended to delegations who still wished to raise issues, both in this and forthcoming AHC sessions, that if their proposals were not garnering support, or raising opposition, they should be prepared to seriously reconsider their positions and yield on their text, unless these issues were of fundamental importance to them'. Disabled Peoples' International, Handicap International and International Service for Human Rights, 'Daily Summary of Discussion at the Fourth Session 02 September 2004', *UN Convention on the Human Rights of People with Disabilities Ad Hoc Committee – Daily Summary* (United Nations Enable, 2 September 2004) <https://www.un.org/esa/socdev/enable/rights/ahc4sum02sep.htm>.

20 See Table 4.1 for the timeline of the *CRPD* drafting negotiations.

entitled "Convention on the Rights of Persons with Disabilities", containing the draft Convention and draft Optional Protocol'.[21] On 13 December 2006, the United Nations General Assembly adopted the *CRPD* and the Optional Protocol by consensus.[22] The *CRPD* came into force on 3 May 2008 after the 20th ratification or accession.[23]

People with disability now had an instrument that more clearly articulated how they experienced human rights abuses that 'afforded freedom, but also the means to take advantage of it'.[24] The means to promote, protect and ensure rights for people with disability were included in the *CRPD* in the form of newly expressed state obligations. Among these obligations were requirements for data production and processing to give effect to the convention.[25] The following sections will focus on the drafting debates that led to the creation of article 31, 'Statistics and data collection'.

4.2 Data's Unresolved Role in Society and Human Rights Law: Negotiating an Article About Statistics and Data Collection

Leading up to and during the *CRPD*'s drafting negotiations, the nature of data production and processing was evolving due to technological advancements, expanding its possible uses in society. In 2002, the Organisation for Economic Co-operation and Development reported, '[i]nformation and communications technologies (ICTs) are increasingly ubiquitous and firms, industries and countries are reaping greater benefits from their ongoing investments in ICTs and the more widespread use of the Internet'.[26] As society was embracing a connected and technologically enhanced future, there was growing interest in data's role in human rights law.[27]

21 Ad Hoc Committee, *Final Report of the Ad Hoc Committee on a Comprehensive and Integral International Convention on the Protection and Promotion of the Rights and Dignity of Persons with Disabilities*, UN Doc A/61/611 (6 December 2006) [7].

22 *CRPD* (n 1).

23 *CRPD* (n 1) art 45(1); 'Entry into Force', *United Nations Enable* <https://www.un.org/development/desa/disabilities/convention-on-the-rights-of-persons-with-disabilities/entry-into-force.html>.

24 Gerard Quinn and Theresia Degener (eds), *Human Rights and Disability: The Current Use and Future Potential of United Nations Human Rights Instruments in the Context of Disability* (Report, United Nations, 2002) 4.

25 *CRPD* (n 1) art 31.

26 Organisation for Economic Co-Operation and Development (OECD), *OECD Information Technology Outlook* (2002) 3.

27 See especially the Committee on the Rights of the Child's *General Comment 5*, which states: 'Collection of sufficient and reliable data on children, disaggregated to enable identification of discrimination and/or disparities in the realization of rights, is an essential part of implementation'. Note this general comment was released during the *CRPD* negotiations. Committee on the Rights of the Child, *General Comment 5: General Measures of Implementation of the Convention on the Rights of the Child*, UN Doc CRC/GC/2003/5 (27 November 2003) [48]. Earlier advice about data and human rights fulfilment was provided in the Committee

Despite data production and processing's growing utility, its potential function and purpose in society were not fully conceived. Much like the ancient fable about the people in a dark room describing the same elephant they are touching at different locations,[28] consensus about data's role (purpose and function) in 'giv[ing] effect to the . . . Convention' was hindered by the divergent experience of data production and processing amongst delegations.[29] This section considers the tensions around defining data's role in society and how it should be regulated in human rights law. These tensions will be explored by examining the advocacy for a standalone article on 'Statistics and data collection', the negotiations about the form of data/information to be collected and the dissent about the classification of people.

4.2.1 A Standalone Article About 'Statistics and Data Collection'

Early submissions to the Ad Hoc Committee included proposed texts containing state duties to collect data.[30] The most comprehensive of these submissions

---

on the Elimination of Discrimination Against Women's *General Recommendation 9*, which states 'that statistical information is absolutely necessary in order to understand the real situation of women'. Committee on the Elimination of Discrimination Against Women, *General Recommendation No 9: Statistical Data Concerning the Situation of Women*, 148th, 149th and 150th Comm, 8th sess, UN Doc A/44/38 V (13 February 1990, adopted 1989); and the Committee on the Elimination of Racial Discrimination's *General Recommendation 24*, which states: 'Some States parties fail to collect data on the ethnic or national origin of their citizens or of other persons living on their territory, but decide at their own discretion which groups constitute ethnic groups or indigenous peoples that are to be recognized and treated as such'. Committee on the Elimination of Racial Discrimination, *General Recommendation XXIV Concerning Article 1 of the Convention*, 55th sess, 1371st mtg, UN A/54/18 annex V (adopted 27 August 1999).

28 'Some Hindoos were exhibiting an elephant in a dark room, and many people collected to see it. But as the place was too dark to permit them to see the elephant, they all felt it with their hands, to gain an idea of what it was like. One felt its trunk, and declared that the beast resembled a water-pipe; another felt its ear, and said it must be a large fan; another its leg, and thought it must be a pillar; another felt its back, and declared the beast must be like a great throne. According to the part which each felt, he gave a different description of the animal'. Rumi, 'The Elephant in a Dark Room', *Myth-Folklore* (Web Page, 9 October 2004) <http://www.mythfolklore.net/3043mythfolklore/reading/rumi/pages/01.htm>.

29 *CRPD* (n 1) art 31.

30 A working paper by Mexico suggested that to monitor the rights of people with disability states parties should submit 'an annual report . . . [with] data' to a committee of experts. *Comprehensive and Integral International Convention to Promote and Protect the Rights and Dignity of Persons with Disabilities: Working Paper by Mexico*, UN Doc A/AC.265/WP.1 (2002) art 20(g). China proposed: 'States Parties shall take necessary administrative measures to promote overall improvement of status of persons with disabilities and to realize all rights of persons with disabilities, in particular: . . . 3. To collect disability-related information through national census and other means, and to develop specific statistic data-collection mechanism related to persons with disabilities'. *Convention on the Rights of Persons with Disabilities: A Proposed Draft Text by China: For the Working Group of the Ad Hoc Committee on a Comprehensive and Integral International Convention on Protection and Promotion of the Rights and Dignity of Persons with Disabilities* (January 2004) art 13 <https://www.un.org/esa/socdev/

included an entire article on the 'Collection of data and statistics' with five paragraphs providing guidance on 'harmonising national classification systems', frequency of data collection, disaggregation of data, consultation and participation of people with disability, storage and processing of data, accessibility of data, data privacy and research activities.[31] Delegations at the Drafting Working Group progressed the advocacy for the inclusion of duties about data production and processing,[32] but there were also dissenting voices. Amongst the dissenting, the Swedish delegation questioned the support for including state obligations related to data production and processing.[33] This intervention perhaps had an effect contrary to their intention, consolidating the Coordinator's view that '[i]t seems that balance of debate has shifted somewhat to favor its inclusion'.[34] The following briefly describes the negotiations for a standalone article about 'Statistics and Data Collection'.

Delegations to the negotiations generally agreed that data production and processing were not individual rights and, hence, initially raised these

---

enable/rights/wgcontrib-china.htm>. The International Labour Organization submission stated under a heading 'Provision concerning the right to decent work' that: 'The role of the ILO in the field of vocational rehabilitation and employment of persons with disabilities to be promoted, particularly with regard to: . . . the improvement of reliable and valid statistical and other information'. International Labour Organization, *ILO Submission to Working Group Set Up by the United Nations Ad Hoc Committee to Consider Proposals for a Comprehensive and Integral International Convention on Protection and Promotion of the Rights and Dignity of Persons with Disabilities* (January 2004) <https://www.un.org/esa/socdev/enable/rights/wgcontrib-ilo.htm>.

31 Regional Workshop towards a Comprehensive and Integral International Convention on Protection and Promotion of the Rights and Dignity of Persons with Disabilities, 14–17 October 2003, Bangkok, Thailand, *Bangkok Draft: Proposed Elements of a Comprehensive and Integral International Convention to Promote and Protect the Rights of Persons with Disabilities* (2003) <https://www.un.org/esa/socdev/enable/rights/bangkokdraft.htm>.

32 The delegation from India stated: 'Without the data, it is impossible to provide the necessary services, programs and support to PWD [people with disability]'. The delegation from Morocco said: 'In order for governments to address the needs of PWD [people with disability] and allocate adequate resources, they need data and statistics'. The delegation from the Asia Pacific Disability Forum said: 'With the competing demands for resources in all countries, this kind of information becomes a valuable tool for PWD to advocate for proper resource allocation to disability issues and for the development of national policies that address their concerns'. Landmine Survivors Network, 'Daily Summary Related to Draft Article 6 Statistics and Data Collection (14–15 January 2004)', *UN Convention on the Human Rights of People with Disabilities Ad Hoc Committee – Daily Summaries* (United Nations Enable, 15 January 2004) <https://www.un.org/esa/socdev/enable/rights/wgsuma6.htm> ('Drafting Working Group Daily Summaries 14–15 January 2004'). Morocco proposed that 'a databank would give states a picture on the needs of PWD'. Landmine Survivors Network, 'UN Convention on the Rights of People with Disabilities: Working Group Daily Summary', *Disability Information Resources* (Web Page, 7 January 2004) <https://www.dinf.ne.jp/doc/english/rights/040107.html> ('Drafting Working Group Daily Summary 7 January 2004').

33 Landmine Survivors Network, 'Drafting Working Group Daily Summaries 14–15 January 2004' (n 32).

34 Landmine Survivors Network, 'Drafting Working Group Daily Summaries 14–15 January 2004' (n 32).

provisions in discussions about the draft general obligations article.[35] The Coordinator, identifying the divergent views of delegations about the inclusion of provisions for data production and processing,[36] stated that 'a provision for data collection could be included if appropriate language could be developed'.[37] The Colombian delegation undertook this task and convened an informal group to develop draft text.[38] They returned to the plenary with draft text, including several footnotes that detailed the delegations' varying perspectives. Draft article 6, 'Statistics and data collection',[39] was created to progress the negotiations and avoid this detailed text overloading the draft general obligations article.[40]

Historically, human rights law has used data production and processing for monitoring the realisation and violations of rights.[41] Therefore, to some, it was unexpected that significant time was taken debating the purpose of the 'Statistics and data collection' obligations during the *CRPD* negotiations. During the 3rd and 4th sessions of the Ad Hoc Committee, there was considerable discussion about whether draft article 6, 'Statistics and data collection', should be merged with draft article 25, 'Monitoring'. The European Union, a powerful voting bloc,[42] strongly advocated for statistics and data collection to be part of draft article 25.[43] Nonetheless, the daily summaries reported that 'The

35 These submissions were generally in discussions about the placement of the article within the convention. Eg, in the 3rd session of the Ad Hoc Committee, the delegation from PWD Australia/NACLC/Australian Federation of Disability Organizations argued that 'statistics and data collection are not human rights; they are operational and should therefore appear at the end of the Convention'. Landmine Survivors Network, 'Daily Summary of Discussion at the Third Session 25 May 2004', *UN Convention on the Human Rights of People with Disabilities Ad Hoc Committee – Daily Summaries* (United Nations Enable, 25 May 2004) <https://www.un.org/esa/socdev/enable/rights/ahc3sum25may.htm> ('Ad Hoc Committee Daily Summary 25 May 2004'). For a discussion on a possible group right in art 31, see later Section 5.3.

36 'The Coordinator noted that the issue of statistics has already been raised, some delegations were opposed to its inclusion, for reasons of infringement on the privacy of PWD [people with disability], but this broader issue would be revisited'. Landmine Survivors Network, 'Drafting Working Group Daily Summary 7 Jan 2004' (n 32).

37 Coordinator of the Drafting Working Group. Landmine Survivors Network, 'Drafting Working Group Daily Summary 7 Jan 2004' (n 32).

38 Landmine Survivors Network, 'Drafting Working Group Daily Summaries 14–15 Jan 2004' (n 32).

39 Working Group to the Ad Hoc Committee (n 14) annex 1 art 6, n 23.

40 By the delegation from Ireland. See Landmine Survivors Network, 'Drafting Working Group Daily Summary 7 Jan 2004' (n 32).

41 Committee on the Elimination of Discrimination Against Women (n 27); Committee on the Rights of the Child (n 27) [48]; Committee on the Elimination of Racial Discrimination (n 27).

42 See generally Gráinne de Búrca, 'The EU in the Negotiation of the UN Disability Convention' (2010) 35(2) *European Law Review* 2010.

43 During the discussions about draft article 25, 'Monitoring', the Netherlands representing the European Union said that 'the EU proposed replacing the contents of Article 6 (Data and Statistics) and inserting it into Article 25 (Monitoring)'. Disabled Peoples' International,

vast majority of States supported retaining this [draft article 6] as a separate Article'.[44] Over time, the European Union changed its position to supporting 'a short and concise separate article provided it is moved near the article on monitoring (Article 25)'.[45] Many delegations supported this compromise.[46] After the Ad Hoc Committee's 6th session, the article on 'Statistics and data collection' moved to article 31,[47] immediately before 'International cooperation' (article 32) and 'Monitoring' (article 33), but it remained an independent article.

As this is the first human rights treaty article of its kind, the implications of a standalone article about statistics and data collection are not fully understood. Further, it is unclear how changing the article's position in the treaty affects how it is interpreted. Nevertheless, retaining the independence of the article means that it can work horizontally within the treaty more effectively, like *CRPD* article 4, 'General obligations'. If the statistics and data collection obligations were subsumed into the 'Monitoring' article, they would be subservient to that article's purpose. Instead, article 31 has its own purpose: states are 'to collect appropriate information . . . to formulate and implement policies to give effect to the . . . Convention'.[48]

Delegations that argued for a standalone article on statistics and data collection appeared to accept the utility of these obligations for monitoring; however, they viewed the obligations as having a broader application.[49] The

Handicap International and International Service for Human Rights, 'Daily Summary of Discussion at the Fourth Session 23 August 2004', *UN Convention on the Human Rights of People with Disabilities Ad Hoc Committee – Daily Summary* (United Nations Enable, 23 August 2004) <https://www.un.org/esa/socdev/enable/rights/ahc4sum23aug.htm> ('Ad Hoc Committee Daily Summary 23 August 2004').

44 Disabled Peoples' International, Handicap International and International Service for Human Rights, 'Daily Summary of Discussion at the Fourth Session 25 August 2004', *UN Convention on the Human Rights of People with Disabilities Ad Hoc Committee – Daily Summary* (United Nations Enable, 25 August 2004) <https://www.un.org/esa/socdev/enable/rights/ahc4sum25aug.htm> ('Ad Hoc Committee Daily Summary 25 August 2004').

45 Ibid., ('Ad Hoc Committee Daily Summary 25 August 2004').

46 Delegations that voiced support for the European Union proposal included New Zealand, Eritrea, Canada, Serbia Montenegro, Republic of Korea, Thailand, Costa Rica, Lebanon and the International Disability Caucus. Ibid., ('Ad Hoc Committee Daily Summary 25 August 2004').

47 MacKay (n 17) annex II.

48 *CRPD* (n 1) art 31(1). See later Chapter 5 for an examination of art 31's purpose.

49 The Guatemalan delegation 'asserted the usefulness of this Article both for monitoring purposes as well as for providing data for the design of policies and programs', and the delegation from the Philippines 'supported a stand-alone article given the crucial role of statistics in giving effect to the convention'. Disabled Peoples' International, Handicap International and International Service for Human Rights, 'Ad Hoc Committee Daily Summary 25 August 2004' (n 44). The Coordinator summarised the discussions from the 4th session, stating: 'Many delegations supported moving the article to Article 25 on monitoring, but others expressed opposition on the grounds that the data should be used for more than just monitoring'. Disabled Peoples' International, Handicap International and International Service for Human Rights, 'Daily Summary of Discussion at the Fourth Session

sentiment behind the support for keeping a standalone article was captured in this statement by the delegation from Jordan: 'this Article would serve all other articles'.[50] Merging the articles was viewed as having the potential to 'weaken' the data production and processing obligations.[51] Nonetheless, delegations that viewed the purpose of statistics and data collection as broader than monitoring did not clearly describe the broader application. These negotiations were a microcosm of contemporaneous societal discussions about data production and processing's role in society.[52] The drafters and global commentators had a sense of data's omnipresence and the promise of what data could deliver to society, yet this could not be fully defined or articulated.[53]

4.2.2 Form of Information or Data

The unsettled role of data in society and human rights law was also evident in the negotiations about how to describe the form of data to be produced and processed by states. The *CRPD* drafters were not data experts, and part of the difficulty of reaching a consensus in these negotiations was a lack of shared terminology. Beyond common language, the sometimes detailed proposals about data forms reflected delegations' different data experiences. The drafters were divided about how detailed the article should be and what it should prescribe.[54] Delegations called for the collection of quantitative data and the production of statistics, qualitative data, universal indicators and, simply, information. Some delegations believed that the draft article's text was weighted towards quantitative data, proposing: 'The chapeau should reflect the fact that it is equally important to collect qualitative data, on behaviors, attitudes, beliefs and experiences'.[55] Several delegations raised concerns that

---

31 August 2004', *UN Convention on the Human Rights of People with Disabilities Ad Hoc Committee – Daily Summary* (United Nations Enable, 31 August 2004) <https://www.un.org/esa/socdev/enable/rights/ahc4sum31aug.htm> ('Ad Hoc Committee Daily Summary 31 August 2004').

50 Landmine Survivors Network, 'Ad Hoc Committee Daily Summary 25 May 2004' (n 35).

51 Delegation from Uganda. Disabled Peoples' International, Handicap International and International Service for Human Rights, 'Ad Hoc Committee Daily Summary 25 August 2004' (n 44).

52 See, eg, Zuboff's description of the 'Aware Home' project. Shoshana Zuboff, *The Age of Surveillance Capitalism: The Fight for a Human Future at the New Frontier of Power* (Profile Books, 2019) 5.

53 See earlier Section 3.3.2 for a critique of the digital state.

54 See later, especially Section 4.3.3.

55 Delegation from Eritrea. Disabled Peoples' International, Handicap International and International Service for Human Rights, 'Daily Summary of Discussion at the Fourth Session 01 September 2004', *UN Convention on the Human Rights of People with Disabilities Ad Hoc Committee – Daily Summary* (United Nations Enable, 1 September 2004) <https://www.un.org/esa/socdev/enable/rights/ahc4sum01sep.htm> ('Ad Hoc Committee Daily Summary 1 September 2004').

'statistics' and 'data', as named in the draft article's title and text,[56] were too limiting and suggested broader terms such as 'information'.[57]

The Chair favoured the term information in the updated draft between the 6th and 7th sessions of the Ad Hoc Committee. The Chair's proposed brief two-paragraph article had many similarities to the final text and was broadly formulated to balance the importance of competing forms of information. Nonetheless, the changes made following this draft steered the obligations towards the requirement to produce and process quantitative data. For instance, the second paragraph of the Chair's draft article had the following formulation:

> 2. The information collected in accordance with this article shall be used to help assess the implementation of States Parties obligations under the present Convention, and shall also be used to identify and address the barriers faced by persons with disabilities in exercising their rights.[58]

Although the Chair's draft attempted to broadly formulate the obligations and not prescribe the form of data to be collected, the article's final text has four additional words inserted between 'shall be' and 'used'. These additional words are: 'disaggregated, as appropriate, and'. In addition, the final text has a third paragraph about 'dissemination of these statistics'. Both of these additions describe quantitative processes.[59]

56 The article title 'Statistics and Data Collection' remained unchanged from the Drafting Working Group's text, despite the article number changing. Interestingly, fn 23 of the Working Group's draft text states: 'Other delegations suggested that the draft article should be re-titled. One suggestion was "Collection and protection of statistics and data"'. Working Group to the Ad Hoc Committee (n 14) 12 n 23.

57 A European Union proposal removed all references to 'statistics' and 'data' from the chapeau, replacing it with the word 'information'. The only reference to data was within the provision on safeguards which specified that states should 'comply with legally established safeguards . . . including legislation on data protection'. 'Contributions Submitted by Governments in Electronic Format at the Fourth Session: Proposed Modifications to Draft Article 6', *United Nations Enable* (Web Page, 2004) <https://www.un.org/esa/socdev/enable/rights/ahc4da6.htm>. During the 4th session, the delegation from the European Union argued that the focus 'on statistical data is too limiting . . . Likewise, referring only to safeguards for statistics . . . would not do justice to the intention of the Article'. Likewise, the delegation from Israel argued that 'the chapeau was . . . of concern because it implies a focus on statistics, when in fact the focus should be to collect reliable information, which better serves the purpose of this Article'. Disabled Peoples' International, Handicap International and International Service for Human Rights, 'Ad Hoc Committee Daily Summary 1 September 2004' (n 55).

58 MacKay (n 17) 32.

59 See later Section 4.3 for a discussion about the drafting of the second paragraph about disaggregation, and Section 4.4.3 for a discussion about the drafting of the paragraph on dissemination.

Article 31's final formulation reflects the compromises made during the negotiations about the form of data to be produced and processed. A product of these compromises is the conceptual discontinuity about the form of information or data that states must collect, complicating the interpretation of article 31. Despite the form of data being broadly formulated in the chapeau to the first paragraph, the subsequent text steers the obligations towards producing and processing quantitative data and statistics.[60] Perhaps this distinction is less important 20 years after these negotiations in light of evolving technology, where the traditional distinction between quantitative and qualitative data is becoming blurred.[61]

4.2.3 *Counting People or Rights Violations?*

In collecting data 'to formulate and implement policies to give effect to the' *CRPD*,[62] states are giving effect to human rights. Motivated by the desire to fulfil this duty, the inclination of state actors may be to increase surveillance and systematically produce data about everyone's situation to ensure they have benefited from their rights. In turn, where states are not motivated to do so independently, non-state actors may call upon states to collect such data.[63] The World Network of Users and Survivors of Psychiatry anticipated and cautioned against this practice at the Drafting Working Group, stating: 'There is a difference between collecting information on disabilities and on collecting information on the enjoyment of human rights by PWD [people with disability]. The former is of concern for inclusion in a human rights treaty'.[64] The network stated that, for data production and processing duties to gain its support, 'the focus of the data collected should be on access and rights, rather than disability per se'.[65]

Collecting data about the realisation of the rights of people with disability without identifying people with disability is much more straightforward within a program that only caters to people with disability. For instance, during the 6th session of the Ad Hoc Committee, Mental Disability Rights International, in its description of monitoring deinstitutionalisation, cited the European monitoring guidelines that require the conditions of people still in institutions to be closely

60 See later Chapter 5 which interprets the text of art 31.

61 Consider that at least 95% of big data is unstructured data. Unstructured data is difficult-to-categorise data, such as the content of videos, photos, audio recordings, emails and web pages. AC Beduschi, 'The Big Data of International Migration: Opportunities and Challenges for States Under International Human Rights Law' (2018) 49 *Georgetown International Law Journal* 981, n 7; Steven Finlay, *Predictive Analytics, Data Mining and Big Data: Myths, Misconceptions and Methods* (Palgrave Macmillan, 2014) 13.

62 *CRPD* (n 1) art 31(1).

63 See later. This is explored further in Sections 5.2.6 and 7.4.3.

64 Landmine Survivors Network, 'Drafting Working Group Daily Summaries 14–15 Jan 2004' (n 32).

65 Landmine Survivors Network, 'Drafting Working Group Daily Summaries 14–15 Jan 2004' (n 32).

monitored,[66] including through the collection of '[s]ystematic and reliable anonymised statistical information on the application of mental health law and on complaints'.[67] This guideline provides an example of *counting the practice* rather than the person. The aim is to keep health professionals and institutions accountable for using restrictive practices in order to, one hopes, eliminate these practices. Nonetheless, as integration is one of the core tenets of the *CRPD*, this approach to data production may work to monitor deinstitutionalisation but is unlikely to be useful in a more integrated society in the future.

Furthermore, while concerns were raised about people being required to identify their disability in an integrated environment, other delegations argued that it is important for people with disability to be more visible in datasets.[68] Visibility in datasets was viewed as important to understand how people with disability were faring compared to the broader population and to inform advocacy about resourcing and barriers to realising rights. Nonetheless, visibility may be harmful to some. For instance, the World Network of Users and Survivors of Psychiatry expressed concerns that collecting data that identifies people with disability may cause harm:

> In relation to the issue of statistics, that there was concern about issues of privacy when people could be deprived of life, liberty, autonomy, on the basis of disability. In this regard, states could use the data against PWD [people with disability]. The recognition of right to life or survival, in this context, could be implicated by a policy of keeping data.[69]

In 2017, a Human Rights Council Resolution about *Mental Health and Human Rights* recognised that people with psychosocial disability are subject to 'widespread discrimination, stigma, [and] prejudice'.[70] Within this context of 'widespread discrimination', identifying people with psychosocial disability in integrated settings is potentially harmful. Harm may occur directly to an individual who is sharing their disability information; the harm may be perpetrated by those who collect the information or by those who can access the information on government databases, for example, to discriminate against

66 Rehabilitation International, 'Daily Summary of Discussion at the Sixth Session 11 August 2005', *UN Convention on the Human Rights of People with Disabilities Ad Hoc Committee – Daily Summaries* (United Nations Enable, 11 August 2005) <https://www.un.org/esa/socdev/enable/rights/ahc6sum11aug.htm>.

67 Council of Europe Committee of Ministers, *Recommendation No REC(2004)10 of the Committee of Ministers to Member States Concerning the Protection of the Human Rights and Dignity of Persons with Mental Disorder and Its Explanatory Memorandum*, 896th mtg of Ministers' Deputies (adopted 22 September 2004) art 38.

68 See later Section 4.3.

69 Landmine Survivors Network, 'Drafting Working Group Daily Summary 7 Jan 2004' (n 32).

70 United Nations Human Rights Council, *Mental Health and Human Rights* (26 September 2017).

future work opportunities.[71] Harm may also occur at a group level against people with psychosocial disability; governments may use data and existing community prejudice to justify draconian policies, such as restrictive practices against people with psychosocial disability.

People with disability's experience of harm from data varies. The degree of harm may be influenced by type of disability. Likewise, as explored in Part III of this monograph, people with disability who experience multiple and aggravated discrimination, such as those with refugee or asylum seeker status, also experience different degrees of harm from data production and processing. Therefore, greater visibility in datasets is not universally welcomed by people with disability.

In conclusion, the difficulty in reaching a consensus about data's role in society and human rights law was evident during the *CRPD* article 31 negotiations. Due to the rapidly emerging possibilities that technology had presented, there were growing opportunities for data use. For this reason, the drafters of the *CRPD* did not make data production and processing obligations subordinate to monitoring; instead, they imagined further possibilities. Nonetheless, data production and processing's unresolved role in society and human rights law was also evident in the negotiations about the form and content of the data to be collected. This discussion is progressed further in the next section, which explores the beneficial and harmful effects of data production and processing by examining the negotiations about classification and disaggregation.

4.3 Data Are Useful and Harmful: Negotiations About Classification and Disaggregation

Disaggregation is the process of dividing data into categories enabling quick comparison. For example, if data were collected about gender and income, analysis of this data could determine the difference in income between men and women. Governments may use these comparisons to identify inequalities and rectify them with targeted policies.[72] Understandably, there was broad support for such a tool at the *CRPD* negotiations. Nonetheless, echoing the concerns raised in the previous section about counting people versus practice, dissenting voices highlighted that disaggregation is not without implications, as it requires the production and processing of detailed information about people and their lives. This section follows the negotiations about the obligation to disaggregate data in *CRPD* article 31(2) to illustrate that the drafters grappled with the tension that human classification may be harmful and useful. This

71 'As a manager, she witnessed HR [human resources] openly discuss which staff had accessed EAP [employee assistance program] through that process'. Sarah Alley and Sophie Kesteven, 'When Her Employers Were Cutting Staff, Laura Witnessed HR Discussing Who Had Accessed the EAP', *ABC News* (online, 9 November 2022) <https://www.abc.net.au/news/2022-11-10/employee-assistance-program-and-workers-privacy/101607634>.

72 See earlier Section 3.3 for a critique of indicators and data-driven policy.

section is divided into three themes: intersectionality and data disaggregation, defining and counting disability and formulating an obligation to disaggregate.

4.3.1 Intersectionality and Data Disaggregation

Intersectionality describes the multiple layers of human identity and how these interact to impact people's life chances.[73] Delegations to the *CRPD* drafting that raised the impact of intersectionality on unequal access to rights were also strong advocates for data production and processing obligations with prescriptive instructions about disaggregation. This advocacy was not surprising, as data are integral to 'intersectional methodologies' that measure disadvantages and identify strategies to reduce inequalities that result from intersectional discrimination.[74]

Aside from impairment and disability, age and gender were the most common data variables requested by delegations at the *CRPD* negotiations.[75] Delegations advocating for the rights of women and children had guidance about the utility of data production and processing from the Committee on the Elimination of Discrimination Against Women ('CDAW Committee') and the Committee on the Rights of the Child ('CRC Committee'). The CDAW Committee had previously advised 'that statistical information is necessary in order to understand the real situation of women'.[76] Similarly, the CRC Committee had highlighted 'the need for data collection to be disaggregated to enable discrimination or potential discrimination to be identified'.[77] These human rights committees had associated data production and processing about the bodies and lives of rights-holders with measuring progress towards substantive equality.

During the 7th session of the Ad Hoc Committee, five meetings were held under the auspices of the Facilitators of Women and Children.[78] Following these sessions, the Facilitator of Women, Theresia Degener, reported a strong consensus for separate provisions for women with disability and children

73 Committee on the Rights of Persons with Disabilities, *General Comment No 3 (2016) on Women and Girls with Disabilities*, UN Doc CRPD/C/GC/3 (25 November 2016) [11].

74 Pioneered in 2001 at the United Nations Commission on the Status of Women, the work on intersectional methodologies was undertaken in the Working Group on Women and Human Rights. See Center for Women's Global Leadership, *A Women's Human Rights Approach to the World Conference Against Racism* (2001).

75 Eg, in the third session of the Ad Hoc Committee, the Republic of Korea proposed text for an article about women with disabilities. One of the five steps the delegation included 'to ensure that women with disabilities are able to live with dignity in freedom, safety, and autonomy' was to incorporate 'women with disabilities in social surveys and statistics collection efforts and collect gender-disaggregated data on persons with disabilities'. Landmine Survivors Network, 'Daily Summary of Discussion at the Third Session 28 May 2004', *UN Convention on the Human Rights of People with Disabilities Ad Hoc Committee – Daily Summaries* (United Nations Enable, 28 May 2004) <https://www.un.org/esa/socdev/enable/rights/ahc3sum28may.htm>.

76 Committee on the Elimination of Discrimination Against Women (n 27).

77 Committee on the Rights of the Child (n 27) [12].

78 The first was a joint meeting, then there were two meetings on women and two on children.

with disability, either within the article on general obligations or placed close afterwards. These articles were to have a 'horizontal effect on all the rights enshrined in the convention'.[79] The Facilitator of Women reported: 'There was also strong agreement that women and children with disabilities should be explicitly mentioned in the provisions related to awareness raising, statistics, data collection and monitoring'.[80] Later in the feedback, it was specifically noted that a state obligation should be created in 'Article 31, on statistics and data collection, . . . to involve women and children with disabilities in data collection, and that the data must be disaggregated were recognized'.[81] Data production and processing was one of five actions identified as fundamental to progressing the rights of women and children with disability.

Gender and child rights advocates were some of the strongest supporters of data disaggregation. Delegations advocated for detailed data to build knowledge about overcoming the diverse barriers that people with disability experience in realising their rights. Within the negotiation's plenary, there was significant support for the utility of disaggregated data; nonetheless, there was division about whether the *CRPD* should prescribe the categories by which data should be disaggregated and if disability data was of the same nature as data about age and gender. The next subsection describes the negotiations about defining and counting disability.

4.3.2 Defining and Counting Disability

In the decades leading up to the *CRPD* negotiations, improving data production and processing about people with disability was identified as a critical area of action at numerous conferences and working groups.[82] Despite agreement during this time that data was an important tool to build understanding about the inequalities experienced by people with disability and

79 This feedback was provided by the Facilitator on Women with Disabilities, Theresia Degener. Rehabilitation International, 'Daily Summary of Discussion at the Seventh Session 31 January 2006', *UN Convention on the Human Rights of People with Disabilities Ad Hoc Committee – Daily Summaries* (United Nations Enable, 31 January 2006) <https://www.un.org/esa/socdev/enable/rights/ahc7sum31jan.htm> ('Ad Hoc Committee Daily Summary 31 January 2006').

80 Ibid., ('Ad Hoc Committee Daily Summary 31 January 2006').

81 Ibid., ('Ad Hoc Committee Daily Summary 31 January 2006').

82 Eg: 'An expert group meeting on the development of impairment, disability and handicap statistics will be organized by the Division from 7 to 11 November 1994 at Voorburg, the Netherlands, hosted by the Netherlands Central Bureau of Statistics. The meeting will review existing disability data collection methods and standards and prepare a guiding set of principles for use in census, surveys and registration systems . . . The Statistical Division and the North America Collaborating Centre (National Centre for Health Statistics) jointly organized an international meeting on the scientific review of applications of the International Classification (Harbour Town, Maryland, USA, 31 May–3 June 1994) . . . A consultant study was prepared during 1994, entitled "A Human Development Agenda for Disability: Statistical Considerations" '. Report of the Secretary-General, *Implementation of the World Programme of Action Concerning Disabled Persons*, UN Doc A/49/435 (27 September 1994).

to inform action, there was no agreement about the best approach to data production and processing to support the realisation of rights for people with disability.[83] These same tensions were present during the drafting of the *CRPD*.

Drafters' conceptualisations of disability informed their beliefs about the utility of disability data production and processing and, hence, their proposed approaches to data. Despite broad agreement that the *CRPD* should be based on the social model of disability, delegations had diverse understandings of this model. The lack of agreement about how to conceptualise and define disability had implications for drafting the entire treaty,[84] including article 31. This subsection considers the debates surrounding the inclusion of definitions of 'disability' and 'persons with disabilities' in the *CRPD*, the controversy about referencing the International Classification of Functioning, Disability and Health (ICF) and the various views about disaggregating data by disability. All sub-subsections illustrate the tensions of data production and processing's beneficial and harmful effects.

a) The CRPD *Negotiations About Defining Disability*

Integral to data disaggregation are data definitions describing and categorising the phenomena being counted, for example, race vs. ethnicity data definitions. Conceptual frameworks inform these data definitions. The conceptualisation of disability had evolved significantly over the decades preceding the drafting of the *CRPD*.[85] Despite the extensive work undertaken to reframe disability, or perhaps because of it, delegations at the negotiations had divergent concepts of disability. This divergence resulted in extensive negotiations regarding a definition of 'disability' and 'persons with disabilities', as described in this subsection.

Early in the negotiations, the Drafting Working Group's text had 'disability' and 'persons with disabilities' listed as terms to be defined under draft article 3, 'Definitions'.[86] A corresponding footnote stated: 'Some members were of the view that no definition of "disability" should be included in the Convention, given the complexity of disability and the risk of limiting the ambit of the Convention'.[87] Nonetheless, '[t]here was general agreement that

83 Report of the Secretary-General, *Overview of Issues and Trends Related to Advancement of Persons with Disabilities*, UN Doc A/AC.265/2003/2 (7 April 2003) 24.

84 See especially Kayess and French for a discussion of the implications of the lack of agreement on a definition of disability during the drafting of the *CRPD*. Rosemary Kayess and Phillip French, 'Out of Darkness into Light – Introducing the Convention on the Rights of Persons with Disabilities' (2008) 8 *Human Rights Law Review* 1, 21.

85 See earlier Section 1.1.1.

86 Working Group to the Ad Hoc Committee (n 14) annex 1 art 3.

87 Working Group to the Ad Hoc Committee (n 14) annex 1 art 3. Annex 1 n 12.

if a definition was included, it should be one that reflected the social model of disability, rather than the medical model'.[88]

Two years later, in the Ad Hoc Committee's 7th session's final report, the newly numbered draft article 2, 'Definitions', still contained the title 'Disability'/'Persons with disabilities' but no definition.[89] At this late stage, they were the only undefined terms. The delegations were divided. Those in favour of including a definition believed it was important to clarify to whom the convention applied.[90] Those against inclusion were concerned that a definition may become outdated and limit the application of the convention.[91] Kayess and French recalled that some states were also anxious that the definition might include groups not previously defined as 'persons with disabilities' in their jurisdictions and impact state resources.[92] These debates also included discussions about who has the power to define disability. The International Disability Caucus emphasised 'the notion of persons having the choice to self-identify as persons with disabilities but not being so identified . . . contrary to their choice'.[93]

No daily summaries exist for the 8th session. Nonetheless, the 8th session's interim report contains a description of 'persons with disabilities' inserted into article 1, 'Purpose', rather than article 2, 'Definitions'.[94] The final text reads:

> Persons with disabilities include those who have long-term physical, mental, intellectual or sensory impairments which in interaction with

88 Working Group to the Ad Hoc Committee (n 14) annex 1 art 3. Annex 1 n 12.

89 Ad Hoc Committee, *Report of the Ad Hoc Committee on a Comprehensive and Integral International Convention on the Protection and Promotion of the Rights and Dignity of Persons with Disabilities on Its Seventh Session* (n 7) annex II art 2.

90 Eg, the National Human Rights Institutions (represented by the South African Human Rights Institutions delegation) stated: 'There is a danger in not defining disability – States may refuse to ratify the convention if its meaning and obligations are uncertain, it would fail to provide a template for national law and policy and for guiding disability awareness, and states which lack legal or policy protections for some types of disability would not be stimulated to develop more inclusive policies'. Disabled Peoples' International, Handicap International and International Service for Human Rights, 'Ad Hoc Committee Daily Summary 23 August 2004' (n 43).

91 Eg, the Chairman stated in a letter before the 7th session: 'I tend to think that we don't [include a definition of "disability" or "persons with disabilities"], as this will be very difficult, and there is a risk that we will unintentionally exclude someone'. MacKay (n 17) [17]. The Austrian delegation on behalf of the EU stated: 'It agreed with the Chair that definitions for "disability" and "persons with disabilities" were not needed, noting that including these definitions would risk exclusion. The EU proposed an amendment to the Purpose of the Convention to include the word "all" so no disabled person would be excluded'. Rehabilitation International, 'Ad Hoc Committee Daily Summary 31 January 2006' (n 79).

92 Kayess and French (n 84) 23.

93 Rehabilitation International, 'Ad Hoc Committee Daily Summary 31 January 2006' (n 79).

94 Ad Hoc Committee, *Interim Report of the Ad Hoc Committee on a Comprehensive and Integral International Convention on the Protection and Promotion of the Rights and*

> various barriers may hinder their full and effective participation in society on an equal basis with others.[95]

Many scholars maintain that this text is not intended to be a definition;[96] however, some scholars use it as one,[97] suggesting some ambiguity.

Whether article 1 contains a definition or not, the paragraph describing 'persons with disabilities' was inserted too late to inform the article 31 negotiations. Given the broad formulation of article 31, the late insertion likely had a negligible impact.[98] Nonetheless, it is worth noting that some of the concerns raised in the negotiations about defining disability remain today, such as disability is an evolving concept,[99] defining disability 'would inevitably derive from the medical model, and would be externally imposed and disempowering'[100] and disability varies between societies.[101] The reticence about defining disability has implications for creating an operational definition to categorise and count disability. One conceptual framework that had grappled with these concerns, but perhaps not well enough, was the International Classification of Functioning, Disability and Health (ICF). Given the contemporary influence of this tool on the implementation of the *CRPD*, it is worth examining why the ICF was not referenced in the *CRPD*.

Dignity of Persons with Disabilities on Its Eighth Session, UN Doc A/AC.265/2006/4 (1 September 2006) annex II art 1.

95 *CRPD* (n 1) art 1.

96 Eg, Kayess and French distinctly differentiate a definition of disability from the description in *CRPD* art 1. Kayess and French (n 84) 23. Bickenbach similarly describes art 1 as a characterisation of disability rather than a definition. Jerome E Bickenbach, 'The ICF and Its Relationship to Disability Studies' in Nick Watson and Simo Vehmas (eds), *Routledge Handbook of Disability Studies* (Taylor & Francis Group, 2nd ed, 2019) 55, 65.

97 Eg, Crock and colleagues state: 'it was very difficult to find reliable statistics on the total number of persons who would meet the CRPD definition of disability'. Mary Crock et al, *The Legal Protection of Refugees with Disabilities: Forgotten and Invisible?* (Edward Elgar Publishing, 2017) 75. Interestingly Kazou points to the Preamble para e as containing the *CRPD* definition of disability. Katerina Kazou, 'Analysing the Definition of Disability in the UN Convention on the Rights of Persons with Disabilities: Is It Really Based on a "Social Model" Approach?' (2017) 23 *International Journal of Mental Health and Capacity Law* 25, 26.

98 See later Chapter 5 for an interpretation of the art 31 text.

99 'Recognizing that disability is an evolving concept and that disability results from the interaction between persons with impairments and attitudinal and environmental barriers that hinders their full and effective participation in society on an equal basis with others'. *CRPD* (n 1) Preamble para e.

100 Kayess and French (n 84) 23.

101 Kayess and French (n 84) 23.

b) The International Classification of Functioning, Disability and Health

Endorsed by 191 World Health Organization (WHO) member states in 2001,[102] the International Classification of Functioning, Disability and Health (ICF), among other purposes, was meant 'as an appropriate instrument for the implementation of . . . human rights mandates'.[103] Despite considerable support for the inclusion of the ICF in the *CRPD*,[104] it was ultimately viewed as controversial and not included in the treaty.[105] This absence is notable given the ICF's significant role in documenting the situation of people with disability worldwide. The ICF is the conceptual framework for the Washington Group questions that DPOs and the Committee on the Rights of Persons with Disabilities have endorsed as the best method for producing disability data.[106] Understanding the controversies around the ICF at the time of the *CRPD* drafting provides insights into some potential harms of data production that drafters identified.

102 World Health Assembly, *International Classification of Functioning, Disability and Health*, WHA Res 54.21, 54th sess, 9th plenary mtg, Agenda Item 13.9, UN Doc WHA54.21 (adopted 22 May 2001).

103 World Health Organization (WHO), *International Classification of Functioning, Disability and Health* (2001) 6.

104 The report of the Working Group noted that 'delegations pointed to existing definitions used in the international context, including the World Health Organization's International Classification of Functioning, Disability and Health (ICF)'. Working Group to the Ad Hoc Committee (n 14) 10 n 12. During the 4th session of the Ad Hoc Committee, the Korean delegation noted that 'The definition of disability has evolved and ICF now embraces a broad, social model definition'. Disabled Peoples' International, Handicap International and International Service for Human Rights, 'Daily Summary of Discussion at the Fourth Session 24 August 2004', *UN Convention on the Human Rights of People with Disabilities Ad Hoc Committee – Daily Summary* (United Nations Enable, 24 August 2004) <https://www.un.org/esa/socdev/enable/rights/ahc4sum24aug.htm>. 'Australia discussed the WHO's International Classification of Functioning, Disability and Health (ICF) as a possible source of a definition for disability and as a framework within which human functioning can be understood and applied in a policy concept'. This was supported by the Delegation from Serbia and Montenegro, Norway, Jamaica and China. Rehabilitation International, 'Ad Hoc Committee Daily Summary 31 January 2006' (n 79).

105 The International Disability Caucus 'noted that ICF is a very controversial definition of disability that many disability organizations do not accept'. Rehabilitation International, 'Ad Hoc Committee Daily Summary 31 January 2006' (n 79).

106 'Conceptual Framework', *Washington Group on Disability Statistics* (Web Page, 2023) <https://www.washingtongroup-disability.com/about/conceptual-framework/>. Notably, as discussed earlier in Section 1.3.1, since 2017, the *Washington Group Short Set of Questions on Disability* has featured in 65 of 82 Concluding Observations. This was the count at the time of writing August 2024. See the Committee on the Rights of Persons with Disabilities website for links to all of their concluding observations to states. 'Committee on the Rights of Persons with Disabilities', *Office of the High Commissioner for Human Rights* (Web Page) <https://www.ohchr.org/en/treaty-bodies/crpd>. See later Sections 7.2.2 and 7.3.1 for a critique of the human rights compliance of the *Washington Group Short Set of Questions on Disability*.

There appeared to be many reasons for the drafters to include a reference to the ICF in the *CRPD*. The ICF was widely endorsed and updated by the WHO regularly.[107] Moreover, the ICF acknowledged that disability resulted from the interaction between a 'health condition and contextual factors (i.e. environmental and personal factors)'.[108] The reason for the controversy about the inclusion of the ICF in the *CRPD* is difficult to discern from the daily summaries. Opposition to the inclusion of the ICF appears to have been led by the International Disability Caucus. Nonetheless, the daily summaries include no explanation about the caucus' concerns other than their statement that the 'ICF is a very controversial definition of disability that many disability organizations do not accept'.[109]

The nature of the ICF controversies may be gleaned from documents and literature published up to the *CRPD* negotiations. The predecessor to the ICF was the 1980 International Classification of Impairments, Disabilities and Handicaps (ICIDH), developed during the 1970s to accompany the World Health Organization's well-established classification system, the International Statistical Classification of Diseases, Injuries, and Causes of Death (ICD).[110] Reference to the ICIDH was included in the 1993 *Standard Rules on Equalization of Opportunities for Persons with Disabilities*, which recognised its broad use and the ICIDH's conceptual differentiation between 'impairment', 'disability' and 'handicap'.[111] However, following this reference was a significant disclaimer:

> Some users have expressed concern that the Classification, in its definition of the term 'handicap', may still be considered too medical and too centred on the individual, and may not adequately clarify the interaction between societal conditions or expectations and the abilities of the individual. Those concerns, and others expressed by users during the 12 years since its publication, will be addressed in forthcoming revisions of the Classification.[112]

107 The WHO advises on their website that 'Official updates to the ICF are available as annual lists of changes. These updates are approved annually at the October meeting of the WHO Family of International Classifications (WHO-FIC) Network'. WHO, 'International Classification of Functioning, Disability and Health (ICF)', *World Health Organization* (2023) <https://www.who.int/standards/classifications/international-classification-of-functioning-disability-and-health>.

108 WHO, *International Classification of Functioning, Disability and Health* (n 103) 19.

109 Rehabilitation International, 'Ad Hoc Committee Daily Summary 31 January 2006' (n 79).

110 The 11th iteration/update of the ICD came into effect on 1 January 2022. 'International Statistical Classification of Diseases and Related Health Problems (ICD)', *World Health Organization* (Web Page, 2023) <https://www.who.int/standards/classifications/classification-of-diseases>.

111 *Standard Rules on the Equalization of Opportunities for Persons with Disabilities*, GA Res 48/96, 48th sess, 85th plen mtg, Agenda Item 109, UN Doc A/RES/48/96 (adopted 20 December 1993) [20].

112 *Standard Rules on the Equalization of Opportunities for Persons with Disabilities*, GA Res 48/96, 48th sess, 85th plen mtg, Agenda Item 109, UN Doc A/RES/48/96 (adopted 20 December 1993) [20].

The foreword to the 1993 ICIDH reprint acknowledges some of these issues, noting that '[a]n important task in the revision of the ICIDH will be to clarify the role and interrelationships of environmental factors in the definition and development of different aspects addressed by the ICIDH, most notably – but not exclusively – handicap'.[113] The WHO acknowledged the shortcomings of the ICIDH and indicated that it intended to address them.

During the mid to late 1990s, the WHO made a concerted effort to work with DPOs to address concerns and remodel the ICIDH classification systems with a greater emphasis on the impact of the environment on disability. Rachel Hurst recounted their experience as the World Council of Disabled Peoples' International's representative and subsequent chair of the Environmental Task Force in the revision of the ICIDH.[114] Hurst acknowledged the negative effect that the ICIDH had on the lives of people with disability: 'It had a negative effect on assessments for services and benefits, assessing people in relation to their impairment rather than their living conditions'.[115] Hurst conceded that the 'resulting revision [of the ICF] is inevitably a compromise'.[116] Nonetheless, they explained optimistically that the ICF 'can now be used as an international example of how the environmental impacts are the key to understanding the nature of disability and how solutions must come through social change'.[117] Hurst considered that the ICF's 'interactive model of disability' was considerably different from its predecessor.[118]

Despite the WHO's efforts to work with people with disability to develop the ICF to be congruent with the contemporary understandings of disability, the ICF was still viewed as controversial by DPOs during the drafting of the *CRPD* (2002–2006). Hurst's account of their time with the WHO includes two clues to explain DPOs' distrust of the updated tool. Hurst explained that there was a broader mistrust of the WHO due to the different conceptual framework of disability that underpinned another WHO metric, the Disability Adjusted Life Years (DALY). Based on the medical model of disability, the DALY equates disability to impairment and the burden of disease.[119] Hurst

113 WHO, *International Classification of Impairments, Disabilities, and Handicaps: A Manual of Classification Relating to the Consequences of Disease* (1980) 4.

114 Rachel Hurst, 'The International Disability Rights Movement and the ICF' (2003) 25(11–12) *Disability and Rehabilitation* 572.

115 Ibid., 573.

116 Ibid., 575.

117 Ibid., 575.

118 Ibid., 574.

119 'The DALY is a summary measure which combines time lost through premature death and time lived in states of less than optimal health, loosely referred to as "disability". The DALY is a generalization of the well-known Potential Years of Life Lost measure (PYLLs) to include lost good health. One DALY can be thought of as one lost year of "healthy" life and the measured disease burden is the gap between a population's health status and that of a normative reference population'. World Health Organization, *WHO Methods and Data Sources for Global Burden of Disease Estimates 2000–2011* (Technical Paper, November 2013) 4.

stated: 'Most regrettably, the use of the DALY as a measurement provides the Disability Rights Movement with another bone of contention with WHO'.[120] Hurst also argued that the new conceptual framework behind the ICF might not have been well understood because of the tool's complexity and the lack of training about the new tool.[121]

Others who engaged in the WHO dialogues felt that the ICF contained the same fundamental issues as its predecessor. Throughout the mid-90s, disability scholar David Pfeiffer also consulted with the WHO about updating ICIDH. Despite the considerable revisions to the tool, Pfeiffer continued to see the new iteration of the ICIDH as championing the medical model and 'a declaration of the ideal of eugenics'.[122] Pfeiffer argued that the updated tool was improved without 'handicapist language'; however, this did not 'excuse the other problems with it'.[123] Pfeiffer assessed that the ICIDH2, later renamed the ICF, gave 'control of the lives of people with disabilities to medical professionals' who make judgments about people's quality of life and, therefore, who is 'deserving of society's resources' or 'candidates for euthanasia', or less provocatively, 'who shall or shall not receive treatment based on the present and/or future quality of life'.[124] This argument is echoed in that presented by the International Disability Caucus during the *CRPD* negotiations that 'the use of statistical indicators that presuppose a lesser value of the lives of PWD [people with disability] . . . can and have been used to discriminate against PWD [people with disability] in terms of accessing health services and other services'.[125]

The ICF developers mostly responded to Pfeiffer's assertions with offence and claims of absurdity.[126] Nonetheless, there was some attempt from ICF

120 Hurst (n 114) 575.

121 Hurst (n 114) 575.

122 Pfeiffer's assertion that the new iteration of ICIDH champions the medical model may be partly due to their conceptualisation of the social model of disability in which impairment has no role in disability. David Pfeiffer, 'The Devils Are in the Details: The ICIDH2 and the Disability Movement' (2000) 15(7) *Disability & Society* 1079, 1081.

123 Ibid., 1081.

124 Ibid., 1081.

125 Rehabilitation International, 'Daily Summary of Discussion at the Seventh Session 27 January 2006', *UN Convention on the Human Rights of People with Disabilities Ad Hoc Committee – Daily Summaries* (United Nations Enable, 27 January 2006) <https://www.un.org/esa/socdev/enable/rights/ahc7sum27jan.htm> ('Ad Hoc Committee Daily Summary 27 January 2006').

126 Eg, 'This has been especially distorting when spurious links are made between the ICIDH, medical care and eugenics, even to the point of invoking Nazism (Pfeiffer, 1998, p. 511). In such instances the scheme has, in effect, been used as an "aunt sally", in order to create what has frequently seemed to me to be a confusing and confused "radical" alternative to disablement: by turns Marxist, constructionist and deeply individualistic'. Mike Bury, 'A Comment on the ICIDH2' (2000) 15(7) *Disability & Society* 1073, 1075. 'In the early days the ICF attracted bizarre criticisms, for example that the ICF was a precursor to eugenics and the elimination of people with disabilities': Bickenbach (n 96) 67 (citations omitted).

supporters to engage on whether the ICF is based on the medical model of disability. Disability studies scholar and ICF developer Jerome Bickenbach explained that the ICF 'characterises a person with disabilities as someone with an impairment who *is* hindered by social barriers that limit full and effective participation'.[127] Bickenbach argued that the description of people with disability in the *CRPD* is more aligned with the medical model than the ICF characterisation, stating: 'the CRPD defines a "person with disabilities" as someone with long-term impairments which in interaction with barriers *may* hinder their full and effective participation'.[128] Bickenbach explained that the literal interpretation of the *CRPD* description of 'persons with disabilities' implies that people may experience disability without any environmental barriers, plainly put, that impairment is disability.

However, Bickenbach's response does not get to the heart of Pfeiffer's, and likely the International Disability Caucus', concerns, which were fundamentally about the classification system's power over people with disability to define them and their circumstances. Pfeiffer's unwillingness to recognise the change to the ICIDH after the significant work undertaken by the WHO to reform the tool demonstrates their concerns were not about what conceptual model informs that classification system but rather that the process of an expert classifying a person into a category is inextricably linked to the medical model. In Pfeiffer's eyes, classification was fundamentally harmful to people with disability and resulted in outcomes like that seen through eugenics.

Despite the International Disability Caucus' concerns about the classification of people with disability, during the *CRPD*'s drafting, the caucus, among other delegations, grappled with the unreconcilable truths about the usefulness and harmfulness of data production and processing. This tension is demonstrated in the seemingly contradictory stance taken by those wanting to exclude the ICF from the *CRPD* while advocating the inclusion of specific provisions about data production and processing about the bodies and lives of people with disability.[129] The following explores the diverse perspectives of delegations about disability data production.

127 Bickenbach (n 96) 66 (emphasis in original).

128 It is of note that Bickenbach characterises the description in *CRPD* art 1 as a definition, again demonstrating the confusion about whether this comprises a definition or not. Bickenbach (n 96) 66 (emphasis in original). See earlier nn 90–91 for more on the definition of disability.

129 'International Disability Caucus recommended moving Article 6 to Monitoring with amendments taking into account the importance of: safeguarding the rights of PWD [people with disability] in line with ethical standards on data collection; detailing information on access to public services and programs relevant for PWD as well as barriers faced by PWD in exercising their rights; gender, age, indigenous status and other factors. States Parties must promote international cooperation in collecting and gathering statistics'. Disabled Peoples'

c) Disability Data Production and Processing

The *CRPD* drafters' inability to develop an agreed definition of disability during the negotiations was somewhat consistent with the debates about formulating obligations regarding disability data production and processing. Perplexingly, even though the drafters could not define the phenomenon of disability, many state and non-state delegations advocated for disability to be counted. Nevertheless, there was also considerable dissent about producing disability data – with one delegation attempting to reconcile the tensions between data's useful and harmful qualities by proposing giving greater control to people with disability through self-identification. The following describes the debates about including an obligation to disaggregate by disability.

States that advocated for disability data asserted they are necessary for evidence-informed policy consistent with observations made in Chapter 3 of this book about the digital state.[130] Some delegations argued that the article's purpose could not be fulfilled without collecting information about disability.[131] For these delegations, disability data were viewed as a neutral, value-free instrument to inform decisions.[132] In contrast, other state delegations viewed disability data as sensitive,[133] with a couple highlighting that disability data collection may be illegal in some jurisdictions.[134]

International, Handicap International and International Service for Human Rights, 'Ad Hoc Committee Daily Summary 25 August 2004' (n 44).

130 See earlier Section 3.3 for a critique of evidence-based policy.

131 Save the Children Alliance stated that they 'supported defining disability in the convention which will be important for data collection and monitoring and implementation'. It is important to note that Save the Children is a service provider rather than a DPO like the World Network of Users and Survivors of Psychiatry. Disabled Peoples' International, Handicap International and International Service for Human Rights, 'Ad Hoc Committee Daily Summary 23 August 2004' (n 43). As late as the 7th session of the Ad Hoc Committee, the delegation from Mexico continued to argue for the need for data to be disaggregated by disability. Rehabilitation International, 'Ad Hoc Committee Daily Summary 27 January 2006' (n 125).

132 Eg, the delegation from Uganda were in favour of collecting data about the types of impairments people had, likening collecting data about disability to collecting data on age and sex. Disabled Peoples' International, Handicap International and International Service for Human Rights, 'Ad Hoc Committee Daily Summary 1 September 2004' (n 55).

133 Eg, the delegation from Yemen argued that 'privacy issues . . . may vary among communities' and 'that the details of disabilities should not be specified unless it is essential to have those details'. Landmine Survivors Network, 'Ad Hoc Committee Daily Summary 25 May 2004' (n 35).

134 Eg, the delegation from Korea stated: 'There have been constitutional challenges regarding collection of data (regarding privacy), which could create problems if the convention obliges States to undertake activities that have been found to be unconstitutional in their countries', and the delegation from the World Federation of the Deafblind 'noted that in Denmark, it is forbidden to collect data around disabilities, in terms of identifying who is deafblind'.

Nonetheless, even the most vocal opponent of disability data collection, the delegation from the World Network of Users and Survivors of Psychiatry, conceded that 'data collection, if done, should focus on the human rights and participation'.[135] This concession, though subtle, implicitly endorsed the need for people with disability to be identifiable within an integrated dataset so their participation rates may be counted. Echoing Pfeiffer's concern that disability data production and processing equated to medical model thinking, the World Network of Users and Survivors of Psychiatry stridently argued that the 'collection on the medical or impairment conditions of PWD [people with disability] should not be allowed'.[136]

Importantly, DPOs also made submissions about *who* should be undertaking the classification. The International Disability Caucus argued for self-identification by people with disability rather than classification by others.[137] Changing the classifying person alters the power dynamic and may address Pfeiffer's concern about experts imposing classifications. Disability data production and processing congruent with the human rights model of disability is not straightforward and requires more attention than developing a taxonomy that reflects the social model of disability: *who* is undertaking the categorisation and *who* is ultimately responsible for the data production and processing matter.

In conclusion, this subsection has explained that the drafters could not agree on a definition of disability and that the ICF was omitted from the *CRPD* despite the work to reform it. Disability data was viewed in a range of ways by delegations as essential, harmless, sensitive and illegal. Nonetheless, diverse delegations could see the benefit of disability data if it was produced under the right conditions. The text of *CRPD* article 31 does not prescribe the production and processing of data about disability. The following subsection describes the negotiations surrounding the text about the obligation to disaggregate.

4.3.3 Formulating an Obligation to Disaggregate

During the *CRPD* negotiations, there were extensive debates about including prescriptive data categories for disaggregation. A desire for 'data harmonisation' likely underpinned the advocacy for the enumeration of data categories in the treaty text. Data harmonisation means using the same data categories over multiple jurisdictions to enable comparisons. The delegations were divided between those advocating for data variables to be enumerated in the text and

---

Landmine Survivors Network, 'Drafting Working Group Daily Summaries 14–15 Jan 2004' (n 32).

135 Landmine Survivors Network, 'Drafting Working Group Daily Summary 7 Jan 2004' (n 32).

136 Landmine Survivors Network, 'Drafting Working Group Daily Summary 7 Jan 2004' (n 32).

137 Rehabilitation International, 'Ad Hoc Committee Daily Summary 31 January 2006' (n 79).

those arguing that categories were too prescriptive.[138] The following describes the debates about enumerating variables for disaggregation in the *CRPD* text.

The early drafts of the article on statistics and data collection listed variables by which the data should be disaggregated. In the Drafting Working Group's text, the paragraphs on disaggregation prescribed data should be 'disaggregated according to the purpose of the collection of information and should include age, sex and type of disability'[139] and 'include detailed information on their access to public services, rehabilitation programmes, education, housing and employment'.[140] During the 4th session of the Ad Hoc Committee, a growing number of data variables were listed in the draft text. The additional data that delegations wanted states to produce included, *inter alia*, the following: indigenous status,[141] geographical distinction,[142] access to communication (eg, sign language),[143] victims of crime,[144] development indicators,[145] living conditions,[146] public transport and subsidised medications.[147]

Delegations began to concede that agreeing on variables would be too difficult, and several states raised concerns about the article becoming 'too detailed and prescriptive'.[148] The delegation from South Africa noted that list-

138 Eg, in the third session of the Drafting Working Group, the delegation from Japan 'expressed concerns about dictating the statistical categories into much detail . . . because each government has different concerns about information. Decisions about data should be left to individual countries'. Landmine Survivors Network, 'Ad Hoc Committee Daily Summary 25 May 2004' (n 35).

139 Working Group to the Ad Hoc Committee (n 14) annex I art 6(d).

140 Working Group to the Ad Hoc Committee (n 14) annex I art 6(e).

141 Proposed by the delegation from the International Disability Caucus. Disabled Peoples' International, Handicap International and International Service for Human Rights, 'Ad Hoc Committee Daily Summary 25 August 2004' (n 44).

142 Proposed by the delegation from Mexico. Disabled Peoples' International, Handicap International and International Service for Human Rights, 'Ad Hoc Committee Daily Summary 1 September 2004' (n 55).

143 Proposed by the delegation from Venezuela. Disabled Peoples' International, Handicap International and International Service for Human Rights, 'Ad Hoc Committee Daily Summary 25 August 2004' (n 44).

144 Proposed by the delegation from the Save the Children Alliance. Disabled Peoples' International, Handicap International and International Service for Human Rights, 'Ad Hoc Committee Daily Summary 25 August 2004' (n 44).

145 Proposed by the delegation from Chile in support of the delegation from Lebanon. Disabled Peoples' International, Handicap International and International Service for Human Rights, 'Ad Hoc Committee Daily Summary 25 August 2004' (n 44).

146 Delegation from Cuba. Disabled Peoples' International, Handicap International and International Service for Human Rights, 'Ad Hoc Committee Daily Summary 1 September 2004' (n 55).

147 Proposed by the delegation from Chile. Disabled Peoples' International, Handicap International and International Service for Human Rights, 'Ad Hoc Committee Daily Summary 25 August 2004' (n 44).

148 The quotation is from the delegation from the EU represented by the Netherlands. The delegation from Japan also supported an article that was 'not overly prescriptive or too detailed'. Disabled Peoples' International, Handicap International and International Service for Human Rights, 'Ad Hoc Committee Daily Summary 31 August 2004' (n 49). The delegation from Australia also submitted that they do 'not favor the inclusion of prescriptive

ing all the variables would counterintuitively limit the provision, as it implied an exhaustive list of variables.[149] In place of this, broader categories were proposed by some delegations, including 'full inclusion indicators such as access to public policy',[150] or 'access to public services and facilities',[151] and 'detailing information on access to public services and programs relevant for PWD [people with disability] as well as barriers faced by PWD [people with disability] in exercising their rights'.[152] However, this approach was contested, with some delegations still feeling it was important to specify variables by which data should be disaggregated.[153]

Concerned about the time the negotiations were taking on this 'relatively simple' provision,[154] the Coordinator highlighted text from the CRC Committee: 'Collection of sufficient and reliable data on children, disaggregated to enable identification of discrimination and/or disparities in the realization of rights'.[155] This intervention was followed a year later with draft text (from the former Coordinator, now Chair) that was even less prescriptive and did not include reference to disaggregation in an attempt to address concerns about the text's bias towards quantitative data.[156] Despite these interventions, delegations again began to list data variables that they felt were important to enumerate in the text, such as gender,[157] age, ethnicity and economics.[158]

---

and operational measures within the body of a convention'. Disabled Peoples' International, Handicap International and International Service for Human Rights, 'Ad Hoc Committee Daily Summary 1 September 2004' (n 55).

149 Disabled Peoples' International, Handicap International and International Service for Human Rights, 'Ad Hoc Committee Daily Summary 1 September 2004' (n 55).

150 Proposed by the delegation from Canada. Disabled Peoples' International, Handicap International and International Service for Human Rights, 'Ad Hoc Committee Daily Summary 25 August 2004' (n 44).

151 Proposed by the delegation from Jamaica. Disabled Peoples' International, Handicap International and International Service for Human Rights, 'Ad Hoc Committee Daily Summary 25 August 2004' (n 44).

152 Proposed by the delegation from the International Disability Caucus. Disabled Peoples' International, Handicap International and International Service for Human Rights, 'Ad Hoc Committee Daily Summary 25 August 2004' (n 44).

153 The delegation from Lebanon suggested that enumerating demographic or intersectional categories in the article prevented 'stereotypical disease or medically driven categories by which data on PWD [people with disability] is often enumerated'. Disabled Peoples' International, Handicap International and International Service for Human Rights, 'Ad Hoc Committee Daily Summary 1 September 2004' (n 55).

154 Disabled Peoples' International, Handicap International and International Service for Human Rights, 'Ad Hoc Committee Daily Summary 1 September 2004' (n 55).

155 Committee on the Rights of the Child (n 27) [48].

156 See earlier Section 4.2.2.

157 Delegations from Chile and the International Disability Caucus. Rehabilitation International, 'Ad Hoc Committee Daily Summary 27 January 2006' (n 125).

158 Delegation from the International Disability Caucus. Rehabilitation International, 'Ad Hoc Committee Daily Summary 27 January 2006' (n 125).

Informed by advocacy from the 'disability community', the delegation from Canada proposed the text 'disaggregated where necessary'.[159] Advocates had reportedly informed the delegation that disaggregation of data is necessary 'to use information effectively'.[160] Other delegations supported this approach.[161] In the final text, the phrase 'disaggregated as appropriate' was viewed to 'cover the critical ideas without adding unnecessary detail'.[162]

In conclusion, as discussed in the previous section, during the *CRPD* drafting, data was taking a greater role in many realms of society; it was evolving at such a rate that delegations at the treaty drafting held hope for its potential and could not fully define its purpose and function. Despite the lack of clarity of data's role, this section demonstrated that many delegations advocated that the more data produced and processed through disaggregation, the more useful they can be at measuring inequalities and targeting special measures. However, collecting more data comes at a cost, including the harms associated with human classification. The potential benefits and harms caused by data are considerations that need to be held together and cannot be separated. The next section looks at measures discussed by *CRPD* drafters to mitigate the harms of data production and processing.

4.4 Measures to Moderate the Data Controllers' Power and Control

Data production and processing give the data controller power over data subjects.[163] Human rights law, conceived after the World War II atrocities, acts to moderate a state's power over people within its jurisdiction. The *CRPD* drafters appreciated that the data production and processing obligations could exacerbate the power asymmetry between the duty-bearer and the right-holder because it cast people with disability as data subjects and states as the data controller. Drafters were aware that an obligation that provides more power to states, in theory to support the realisation of human rights, may be misused.[164]

159 Rehabilitation International, 'Ad Hoc Committee Daily Summary 27 January 2006' (n 125).

160 Rehabilitation International, 'Ad Hoc Committee Daily Summary 27 January 2006' (n 125).

161 Eg, the delegation from Mexico. Rehabilitation International, 'Ad Hoc Committee Daily Summary 27 January 2006' (n 125).

162 Rehabilitation International, 'Ad Hoc Committee Daily Summary 27 January 2006' (n 125). For more on the phrase 'as appropriate', see later Sections 5.2.6 and 7.2.

163 See earlier Chapter 3 for a critique of data and power.

164 Eg, the Swedish delegation 'expressed hesitancy' about 'the inclusion of this [article] . . . in the Convention, as history has shown the danger of "registering" race . . . in central databases'. Landmine Survivors Network, 'Afternoon Session Daily Summary of the Working Group – 5 January 2004', *Disability Information Resources* (Web Page, 5 January 2004) <https://www.dinf.ne.jp/doc/english/rights/040105.html>. In the Drafting Working Group, 'Serbia and Montenegro supported Sweden that this [an article on statistics and data collection] is not relevant to a human rights convention and raises serious concerns about privacy issues'. The Sierra Leonne delegation stated that 'any data collected on PWD, in whatever form, must not infringe on the human rights of' people with disability. The World

The potential misuse of data and measures to moderate the data controller's (states') power were discussed extensively during the negotiations. This section explores three themes that emerged during the discussions related to moderating the data controller's power. The first subsection examines the negotiations about data production and processing regulation. The second explores the discussions around people with disability participating in data production and processing. The last subsection outlines the discussion about the dissemination of statistics.

4.4.1 Regulation of Data Production and Processing

Safeguards to avoid the potential misuse of data were a prominent theme during the negotiations.[165] Some delegations viewed this article as primarily about the protection and privacy of data.[166] As discussed in this subsection, several measures to restrict data collection and use were proposed, inserted into the text and deleted. Rather than being viewed as unimportant, it was often assessed that these provisions were implicit in the article or covered elsewhere in the convention or international law.

Network of Users and Survivors of Psychiatry delegation 'expressed concerns related to privacy and the possible use of such statistics'. Landmine Survivors Network, 'Drafting Working Group Daily Summaries 14–15 Jan 2004' (n 32). The South African delegation stated that data should only serve 'to enhance the quality of life' of people with disability. Disabled Peoples' International, Handicap International and International Service for Human Rights, 'Ad Hoc Committee Daily Summary 25 August 2004' (n 44).

165 During the 4th session of the Ad Hoc Committee, the Coordinator acknowledged that 'safeguards in the use and collection of data was a primary concern for many delegations'. Disabled Peoples' International, Handicap International and International Service for Human Rights, 'Ad Hoc Committee Daily Summary 31 August 2004' (n 49).

166 The footnote to the Drafting Working Group's article 6 stated: 'Other delegations suggested that the draft article should be re-titled. One suggestion was "Collection and protection of statistics and data". It was clearly considered that any data collected on disabilities must not infringe on the human rights of persons with disabilities'. Landmine Survivors Network, 'Drafting Working Group Daily Summaries 14–15 Jan 2004' (n 32). The alternative name was supported by the delegations from Uganda, Colombia and Sierra Leone in the 3rd session of the Ad Hoc Committee. During this session, the South African delegation 'supported this Article, especially the provision on respect for the right to privacy'. Landmine Survivors Network, 'Ad Hoc Committee Daily Summary 25 May 2004' (n 35). In the 4th session, the delegations from Chile and Kenya also expressed their support for the alternative name. Disabled Peoples' International, Handicap International and International Service for Human Rights, 'Ad Hoc Committee Daily Summary 25 August 2004' (n 44). The European Union delegation stated: 'It would be wiser for the Article to limit itself to establishing strict safeguards to ensure there will be no misuse of the information, and leave it up to States to decide the methods and types of information to be collected and what to do with it. This will increase the likelihood that policies will be aligned with the goals of the overall Convention'. The Lebanese delegation shared this view, stating the article served 'the purpose of limiting any possible damage that may occur from the misuse of data'. Disabled Peoples' International, Handicap International and International Service for Human Rights, 'Ad Hoc Committee Daily Summary 1 September 2004' (n 55).

Early drafts of the article contained specific and prescriptive provisions to protect the privacy of the data subjects, people with disability. The text from the Drafting Working Group specified 'information collected from persons with disabilities should be on a voluntary basis' and that production and processing should '[a]dhere to established ethics regarding respect for anonymity and confidentiality in the collection of statistics and data'.[167] This draft also provided instructions about data being 'kept only in a statistical format without identifying individuals and should be kept secure to prevent unauthorized access or misuse of information'.[168]

Over time, particularly after the presentation by the United Nations Statistical Commission and the circulation of the 1994 *Fundamental Principles of Official Statistics* ('*1994 Statistics Principles*'), states argued that the text should refer to international norms and principles.[169] Delegations debated whether specific instruments, such as the *1994 Statistics Principles*,[170] should be named in the text, whether specific provisions from these instruments should be duplicated in the article, that is, 'explicit reference to the specific ethical principles in the UN standards',[171] or whether a general reference should be

167 Working Group to the Ad Hoc Committee (n 14) annex I art 6(a), (f).

168 Working Group to the Ad Hoc Committee (n 14) annex I art 6(b).

169 During the 4th session of the Ad Hoc Committee, the Eritrean delegation sought to strengthen the protections in the article, proposing the addition of the text 'existing internationally accepted human rights norms and standards and ethical principles of statistics in order to maintain confidentiality of records and to avoid undue intrusion'. This was supported by the delegation from Canada, which argued: 'The need to protect privacy and confidentiality through legislative standards should be specified'. Likewise, the delegation from Kenya 'called for the inclusion of ethical standards to ensure anonymity, protection of privacy and confidentiality, and human rights standards'. Disabled Peoples' International, Handicap International and International Service for Human Rights, 'Ad Hoc Committee Daily Summary 25 August 2004' (n 44).

170 The Canadian delegation sought to strengthen the text on protections, submitting that the provision on privacy 'should recognize international norms and principles in addition to human rights to read "comply with internationally accepted norms and principles, including or in particular those relating to the protection of human rights and fundamental freedoms" but without specifically identifying any particular standard by name'. The delegation from South Africa proposed that the *1994 Statistics Principles* should be referenced in the Preamble of the convention and was supported by the delegation from Serbia-Montenegro. The Norwegian delegation proposed: 'The current language on confidentiality [in draft article 6 Data and Statistics] could be strengthened using language from the UN Fundamental Principles without referring to a specific instrument'. Disabled Peoples' International, Handicap International and International Service for Human Rights, 'Ad Hoc Committee Daily Summary 1 September 2004' (n 55).

171 Delegation from Kenya. Disabled Peoples' International, Handicap International and International Service for Human Rights, 'Ad Hoc Committee Daily Summary 1 September 2004' (n 55).

made to international norms and standards. The final text adopted the general reference approach:

> The process of collecting and maintaining this information shall:
>
> a) Comply with legally established safeguards, including legislation on data protection, to ensure confidentiality and respect for the privacy of people with disabilities;
> b) Comply with internationally accepted norms to protect human rights and fundamental freedoms and ethical principles in the collection and use of statistics.[172]

The strength of this approach is that it can continue to be relevant over time as contexts change (ie, technology) and as community expectations and laws evolve (eg, the introduction of the European Union's General Data Protection Regulation).[173] Conversely, this approach relies on significant knowledge and expertise about data protection laws and other regulatory instruments. It is reasonable to expect that not all states have equal capacity, knowledge and expertise of 'legislation on data protection' and 'ethical principles in the collection and use of statistics'.[174] Moreover, some states may choose to apply this selectively. Consequently, in these circumstances, data controllers will have increased power without regulation.

Furthermore, relying on other international law instruments is a missed opportunity to consider and ameliorate the specific harms that people with disability may experience from data production and processing. Article 31 is silent about the significant amount of data states produce and process about people with disability to assess eligibility for social security benefits and the impact that this has on the data subject. Perhaps the ensuing years since the drafting of the *CRPD* have sharpened our understanding of these harms.[175] Nonetheless, there has been little scholarship, jurisprudence and practice devoted to the protections in article 31 compared with the focus on the obligations to collect and disaggregate data.[176] This neglect over time may have harmful consequences for people with disability.

172 *CRPD* (n 1) art 31(1).

173 *Regulation (EU) 2016/679 of the European Parliament and of the Council of 27 April 2016 on the Protection of Natural Persons with Regard to the Processing of Personal Data and on the Free Movement of Such Data, and Repealing Directive 95/46/EC (General Data Protection Regulation)* [2016] OJ L 119/1.

174 *CRPD* (n 1) art 31(1).

175 See, eg, the Special Rapporteur on Extreme Poverty and Human Rights' work on the human rights implications of the digital welfare state. Philip Alston, *Report of the Special Rapporteur on Extreme Poverty and Human Rights*, UN Doc A/74/48037 (11 October 2019).

176 A recent exception is the Special Rapporteur on the Rights of Persons with Disabilities' report about the implications of artificial intelligence on disability rights. Quinn cites art 31 provisions as data protection obligations rather than data production and processing obligations. Gerard Quinn, *Report of the Special Rapporteur on the Rights of Persons with Disabilities*, UN Doc A/HRC/49/52 (28 December 2021) [45].

4.4.2 Participation of People With Disability

States, civil society organisations and other delegations argued that people with disability should be actively involved in implementing the data production and processing obligations and identified several reasons why their participation was important.[177] The arguments can broadly be categorised into two themes: participation of people with disability in the implementation of this article will (1) lead to better data[178] and (2) act as a safeguard against harmful practices.[179] The negotiations about the participation of people with disability in the data production and processing obligations focused on the placement of the provision in the treaty text[180] and *who* should participate in the implementation.[181]

The draft article on statistics and data collection produced by the Drafting Working Group included a provision to 'Ensure that the design and

177 During the 3rd session of the Ad Hoc Committee, the International Rehabilitation Centre argued that 'Disabled peoples' organizations should always be involved in the design, gathering and follow-up of statistical activities'. Disabled Peoples' International stated the article 'needs to stress working in partnership'. The National Human Rights Institutions proposed including the text 'to ensure that the collection of information is done in partnership with PWD, their respective organizations, and all other relevant stakeholders'. Landmine Survivors Network, 'Ad Hoc Committee Daily Summary 25 May 2004' (n 35). During the 4th session, the Chinese delegation provided support for keeping the obligation to consult with people with disabilities in the article: 'China agrees with the inclusion of (c), given the "teamwork" required between the Government and the people from whom information is collected'. Disabled Peoples' International, Handicap International and International Service for Human Rights, 'Ad Hoc Committee Daily Summary 1 September 2004' (n 55).

178 At the 3rd session of the Ad Hoc Committee, the World Network of Users and Survivors of Psychiatry stated that the article 'needs to say the preferred method of design and data collection is in partnership with PWD [people with disability] because this not only creates better data, but also this helps create disability movement'. Landmine Survivors Network, 'Ad Hoc Committee Daily Summary 25 May 2004' (n 35). During the 7th session, the Ugandan delegation stated 'that the article should reflect the need to consult PWD in data collection. It noted its experience in which PWD were not consulted and the resulting data did not reflect the reality of PWD'. Rehabilitation International, 'Ad Hoc Committee Daily Summary 27 January 2006' (n 125).

179 During the 3rd session of the Ad Hoc Committee, the delegation from the European Union (represented by Ireland) said that 'States should comply with international norms to protect human rights and fundamental freedoms and that such processes should be undertaken in collaboration with and following consultations with organizations of persons with disabilities'. Landmine Survivors Network, 'Ad Hoc Committee Daily Summary 25 May 2004' (n 35).

180 See later n 183.

181 The World Network of Users and Survivors of Psychiatry objected to text that said the data should 'be collected in close collaboration with all stakeholders in contact with PWD [people with disability]'. The network argued 'PWD are the primary stakeholders in all of the issues "affecting us". Problems may arise in collecting information through people who may have conflicting interests to the PWD themselves, such as members of the family or medical professionals'. Landmine Survivors Network, 'Drafting Working Group Daily Summaries 14–15 Jan 2004' (n 32).

implementation of data collection is done in partnerships with persons with disabilities, their representative organizations and all other relevant stakeholders'.[182] This text was later deleted, as it was argued that this provision was covered by the participation provisions in article 4, 'General obligations'.[183] The text produced by the Drafting Working Group had an early but very similar version of *CRPD* article 4(3) that obligates states to ensure the participation of people with disability in the implementation of the convention.[184] Later drafts expanded the 'General Obligations' provision to enumerate situations where people with disability and their representative organisations should be actively involved, including in the 'the design and implementation of data collection'.[185] When this was inserted, the corresponding provision about participation was deleted from the 'Statistics and data collection' draft article. The chair noted that this was a strategy to consolidate several provisions across articles into the general obligations that apply to all articles in the convention.[186] It is not clear from the drafting records why the sentence that enumerated the contexts for participation was subsequently deleted,[187] perhaps for brevity or because it was viewed as too prescriptive and limited the potential application of article 4(3).

The final article 31 text has no reference to participation. Nevertheless, states must ensure that people with disability 'are closely consulted and actively involve[d]' in implementing article 31.[188] It is clear from the negotiations that

182 Working Group to the Ad Hoc Committee (n 14) annex I art 6(c).

183 During the 4th session of the Ad Hoc Committee, the New Zealand delegation proposed deleting reference to consultation with people with disability in draft article 6, as it 'is better covered in Article 4'. Disabled Peoples' International, Handicap International and International Service for Human Rights, 'Ad Hoc Committee Daily Summary 25 August 2004' (n 44). The Ad Hoc Committee Coordinator summarised during the 4th session that the participation of people with disability and their representative organisations in statistics and data collection would be incorporated into article 4. The European Union delegation said later during an informal consultation about the statistics and data collection obligations: 'There was a strong expression of will in the Committee this morning that consultation with PWD [people with disability] and DPOs . . . is a cross cutting issue that is more appropriately dealt with elsewhere'. In the same consultation, the Mexican delegation, which was responsible for the drafting of the text, summarised that, '[a]s all delegations noted, consultations with PWD . . . are sufficiently covered elsewhere in the Convention especially Article 4'. Disabled Peoples' International, Handicap International and International Service for Human Rights, 'Ad Hoc Committee Daily Summary 1 September 2004' (n 55).

184 Working Group to the Ad Hoc Committee (n 14) annex I art 4(2).

185 MacKay (n 17) annex I art 4(3).

186 MacKay (n 17) annex I art 4(3) [26].

187 A written submission from the European Union proposed deleting the second sentence of art 4(3). European Union, *Initial EU Position Paper for 7th Ad Hoc Committee: EU Proposals Based on Chair's Text* (16 January 2006) 6 <https://www.un.org/esa/socdev/enable/rights/ahc7docs/ahc7eu1.doc>.

188 *CRPD* (n 1) art 4(3). See later Section 5.2.8.

the level of involvement intended was substantial: 'the design and implementation of data collection'.[189]

4.4.3 Transparency: Dissemination of Statistics

An advantage arises when one party holds information that the other party does not. The third paragraph of *CRPD* article 31, about the dissemination of statistics, required the briefest negotiations. During the 4th session of the Ad Hoc Committee, there was a growing endorsement for including an obligation for states to disseminate aggregated and de-identified information. During this discussion, the delegation from Israel argued that transparency was important in data production and processing and that the data should be made 'available to the public in general and to PWD [people with disability] . . . in particular'.[190] Likewise, the delegation from Thailand proposed that 'Data and statistics should be made accessible to PWD [people with disability], consistent with access to information in [draft] Article 13'.[191] Towards the end of the 4th session of the Ad Hoc Committee, the Coordinator summarised that there seemed to be support for the article:

> [to] expressly refer to the need of PWD [people with disability] to access this information: 'Subject to complying with safeguards to ensure confidentiality and respect for privacy as previously mentioned in this Article, States Parties shall make the information collected pursuant to this Article available to the public in general and PWD [people with disability] and their organizations in particular in accessible formats'.[192]

This clause was removed during the Chair's reformulation of the article (and the treaty) that focused on brevity.[193] There was no explanation provided for this deletion. As seen in other instances of deletion, perhaps it was viewed to be covered elsewhere in the convention, such as in article 21, 'Freedom of Expression and Opinion and Access to Information'.[194]

Nonetheless, during the 7th session of the Ad Hoc Committee, the delegation from the International Labour Organization submitted that article 31 should 'cover the dissemination of data, including publication and making

189 Working Group to the Ad Hoc Committee (n 14) annex I art 6(c); MacKay (n 17) annex I art 4(3).
190 Disabled Peoples' International, Handicap International and International Service for Human Rights, 'Ad Hoc Committee Daily Summary 1 September 2004' (n 55).
191 Disabled Peoples' International, Handicap International and International Service for Human Rights, 'Ad Hoc Committee Daily Summary 25 August 2004' (n 44).
192 Disabled Peoples' International, Handicap International and International Service for Human Rights, 'Ad Hoc Committee Daily Summary 1 September 2004' (n 55).
193 MacKay (n 17).
194 MacKay (n 17).

data and data sets available to users'.[195] The delegation from the International Disability Caucus added that '[d]issemination and access by PWD [people with disability] to data collected – including in accessible formats – should be stressed in this article'.[196] At the end of the session, the Chair's summary stated: 'There was a reasonable level of support for adding a new [paragraph] . . . about the dissemination of statistics as proposed by the IDC [International Disability Caucus]'.[197] The third paragraph of *CRPD* article 31 reads: 'States Parties shall assume responsibility for the dissemination of these statistics and ensure their accessibility to persons with disabilities and others'.[198]

In conclusion, the previous two sections examined themes that arose from the negotiations about the undetermined nature of data and its dichotomous harmful and helpful effects. This section explored the drafters' response to the increased power of states as data controllers. Article 31's codification of an asymmetrical power relationship was antithetical to the purpose of human rights law. This section described three methods drafters employed to moderate state power: regulation, participation and dissemination. Nonetheless, not all states have the same capacity for regulation; therefore, there is a need for care in prescribing data production and processing about the bodies and lives of people with disability.

Further, while the moderation of state power as data controllers was a significant part of the negotiations, there appears to have been little discussion on this topic in the subsequent years. More interpretive advice from human rights committees, scholarship and good practice examples are required about moderating the power amassed by states as data controllers and ameliorating the particular harms experienced by people with disability as data subjects. As argued throughout this monograph, people with disability experience specific harms associated with data production and processing; therefore, this should not be viewed as the domain of generic data regulation instruments.

4.5 Conclusion

The goodwill surrounding the *CRPD*'s drafting is often spoken about: civil society, states and other organisations came together to draft a treaty that ensured people with disability had access to their rights. Despite delegations' diverse motivations for an article on statistics and data collection, there were many areas of agreement. However, a close reading of the article 31 negotiations uncovers unresolved tensions that go to the heart of the incongruencies in the article's text. This chapter examined the impact of the unresolved role

195 European Union (n 187) 6.

196 Rehabilitation International, 'Ad Hoc Committee Daily Summary 27 January 2006' (n 125).

197 Rehabilitation International, 'Ad Hoc Committee Daily Summary 27 January 2006' (n 125).

198 *CRPD* (n 1) art 31(3).

of data in society and human rights law and the coexistence of beneficial and harmful effects of data on the drafting of the article. It also identified measures employed to moderate the power amassed by the data controller (states).

Data production and processing have the potential to hold states to account for their human rights records and identify disparities to help states to target positive measures. Nonetheless, people with disability experience particular and exacerbated harms associated with data production and processing. As this and previous chapters have demonstrated, human classification inevitably creates hierarchies, and people with disability have long experienced discrimination in those hierarchies that have caused significant and even fatal harm. Increased data production and processing also increases the power of the data controller over data subjects. Many states already collect large amounts of data about people with disability through their interactions with services such as health care and social security. More data collection about the bodies and lives of people with disability exacerbates the power asymmetry.

The article 31 text reflects the drafter's manoeuvring around the tensions inherent in obligations about data production and processing. It is perplexing, therefore, that there has been minimal debate, commentary and scholarship about article 31 in the ensuing years. The following chapter adds to scholarship on article 31 by proposing a *Vienna Convention on the Law of Treaties* – adherent alternative interpretation of the text.[199] This alternative interpretation may go some way in addressing some of the tensions raised in this chapter.

199 *Vienna Convention* (n 2).

5 Interpreting *CRPD* Article 31

The *Convention on the Rights of Persons with Disabilities* ('*CRPD*') article 31 is often used to authorise and demand large-scale data production and processing.[1] Despite this, there is little analysis of the doctrinal or normative nature of the state obligations in article 31. The two commentaries about article 31 by Pedersen, the second with a co-author Ferretti,[2] focus on how to produce and process disability data rather than examining states' legal obligations. This lack of analysis likely stems from Pedersen's view that 'the obligations specified in Article 31 . . . are somewhat unambiguous'.[3] These commentaries support the view that article 31 requires states to produce and process 'robust, consistent and comparable [quantitative] data on disability',[4] that 'encompasses all areas of society'[5] and that are 'systemize[d] and harmonize[d]' to enable national

1 *Convention on the Rights of Persons with Disabilities*, opened for signature 24 January 2007, 2515 UNTS 3 (entered into force 3 May 2008) ('*CRPD*') art 31. Consider the Committee on the Rights of Persons with Disabilities' Concluding Observations, which have called for the disaggregation of data about people with disability by numerous variables which requires states to undertake systemic data production and processing. See, eg, the Committee on the Rights of Persons with Disabilities' Concluding Observations to Korea: 'The Committee recalls the Washington Group short set of questions on disability . . . and recommends that the State party: Expeditiously develop a system and procedures for collecting data on persons with disabilities disaggregated by age, sex, sexual orientation, gender identity, race, ethnicity, income, migration status, level of education, employment situation and place of residence'. Committee on the Rights of Persons with Disabilities, *Concluding Observations on the Combined Second and Third Periodic Reports of the Republic of Korea*, UN Doc CRPD/C/KOR/CO/2-3 (6 October 2022) [64]. See also earlier Chapter 1 n 3, Section 1.2.2 at nn 70–80 and Section 1.3.1 at nn 87–88.

2 Mads Pedersen and Federico Ferretti, 'Article 31: Statistics and Data Collection' in Ilias Bantekas, Michael Ashley Stein and Dimitris Anastasiou (eds), *The UN Convention on the Rights of Persons with Disabilities: A Commentary* (Oxford University Press, 2018) 924; Mads Pedersen, 'Article 31: Statistics and Data Collection' in Valentina Della Fina, Rachele Cera and Giuseppe Palmisano (eds), *The United Nations Convention on the Rights of Persons with Disabilities: A Commentary* (Springer International Publishing, 2017) 557.

3 Pedersen (n 2) 559.

4 Pedersen (n 2) 564.

5 Pedersen (n 2) 561.

DOI: 10.4324/9781003506140-7

and international comparisons.[6] If we take Pedersen and, more recently, Ferretti's account of article 31, this article obligates states to surveil the bodies and lives of people with disability in great detail.

This chapter complicates Pedersen and Ferretti's interpretation of article 31 by proposing a novel argument. It asserts that the *CRPD* article 31, interpreted in context and congruent with the treaty's purpose, emphasises information production and processing ***about state actions and barriers to rights attainment***. It argues that article 31 is not concerned with information production and processing about the bodies and lives of people with disability. Article 31 should not lead to greater surveillance of people with disability where external experts quantify the bodies and lives of people with disability to measure progress in realising rights. This practice reflects the medical model and is incompatible with the purpose of the *CRPD*. Instead, the *CRPD* provides for the close consultation and active involvement of people with disability to identify barriers to rights attainment. Information, therefore, may be created and processed about identified barriers, state actions and resources invested in implementing the treaty.

Nonetheless, this monograph's interpretation of article 31 conflicts with the Committee on the Rights of Persons with Disabilities' ('CRPD Committee') recommendations which routinely cite the authority of article 31 to call on states to disaggregate data for more detailed information about people with disability and their lives.[7] This contradiction between the treaty provisions and the CRPD Committee's recommendations demonstrates that this is an unsettled area in disability human rights law to which this chapter contributes. Another area of scholarship to which this chapter contributes is the debate about group rights in human rights law. Data's power increases through aggregation. This monograph, therefore, argues that harm and protection may need to be conceptualised at a group rather than individual level. A group right to choose to be visible in data sets, to be counted, may be one such group protection.

These arguments will be progressed through the three substantive sections of this chapter. Section 5.1 fleshes out the context of *CRPD* article 31 and the treaty's purpose. Section 5.2 interprets the ordinary meaning of article 31 and enumerates its state obligations. Accepting that no individual rights exist within article 31, Section 5.3 explores the possibility of a group right in this article: the group right to be counted.

5.1 Article 31's Context and the *CRPD*'s Object and Purpose

The detailed framing around the rights and obligations in the *CRPD* underscores the extensive paradigm and practice shift required by states and society

6 Pedersen (n 2) 562.
7 See earlier n 1.

to enable people with disability to realise their rights. The paradigm shift is detailed in *CRPD* article 1, 'Purpose', article 2, 'Definitions', article 3, 'General principles', and article 4, 'General obligations', which are all preceded by a lengthy 25-paragraph Preamble.[8] This background is vital to understanding the convention and necessary for its interpretation. The *Vienna Convention on the Law of Treaties* ('*Vienna Convention*') states that '[a] treaty shall be interpreted . . . in their context and in the light of its object and purpose'.[9] Context may be derived from the treaty's text, including the preamble and annexes, as well as subsequent agreements and practices between the parties.[10]

Common themes are threaded through the Preamble and the early articles of the *CRPD*. This section explores some of these themes to establish article 31's context and the *CRPD*'s object and purpose to assist in interpreting the ordinary meaning of article 31's text in Section 5.2. The themes explored in this section include (1) the paradigm shift from the medical model of disability, (2) the *CRPD*'s model of disability, (3) respect for the inherent dignity, autonomy and independence of the person, (4) remediation of disparity and discrimination and (5) the diversity of people with disability.

5.1.1 Break From the Medical Model of Disability

The *CRPD*'s Preamble locates the convention in the human rights framework and highlights some of the previous instruments that have progressed the rights of people with disability.[11] Despite numerous global instruments and extensive campaigns to improve the conditions for people with disability,[12] only two international instruments that focus on the progression of disability rights are named in the *CRPD*'s Preamble: the *World Programme of Action concerning Disabled Persons* and the *Standard Rules on the Equalization of Opportunities for Persons with Disabilities*.[13] The omission of other instruments intentionally

8 At 25 paragraphs long, the *CRPD*'s Preamble is the longest of all international human rights treaties.

9 *Vienna Convention on the Law of Treaties*, opened for signature 23 May 1969, 1155 UNTS 331 (entered into force 27 January 1980) art 31(1).

10 Ibid., art 31(2)–(4).

11 *CRPD* (n 1) Preamble paras a–d, f.

12 See, eg, *Declaration on the Rights of Mentally Retarded Persons*, GA Res 2856(XXVI), 26th sess, Agenda Item 12, UN Doc A/RES/26/2856 (adopted 20 December 1971); *Declaration on the Rights of Disabled Persons*, GA Res 3447(XXX), UN GAOR Supp (No 34) at 88, 30th sess, 2433rd plen mtg, UN Doc A/RES/3447(XXX) (adopted 9 December 1975).

13 *World Programme of Action Concerning Disabled Persons*, GA Res 37/52, UN Doc A/RES/37/52 (adopted 3 December 1982); *Standard Rules on the Equalization of Opportunities for Persons with Disabilities*, GA Res 48/96, 48th sess, 85th plen mtg, Agenda Item 109, UN Doc A/RES/48/96 (adopted 20 December 1993).

signalled a break with the old approach to conceptualising disability,[14] a break from the medical model.[15]

The exclusion of the newly updated *International Classification of Functioning, Disability and Health* ('ICF') from the *CRPD*'s Preamble was a significant snub and requires consideration in the interpretation of article 31, 'Statistics and data collection'. As discussed in Chapter 4,[16] the ICF was meant 'as an appropriate instrument for the implementation of . . . human rights mandates'.[17] During the drafting of the *CRPD*, some stakeholders held strong views that the ICF represented the medical model. These views are still held, despite the significant work undertaken to consult people with disability and reform the tool.[18] For example, Kakoullis and Ikehara, in their 2018 *CRPD* article 1 commentary, stated that consideration of the ICF as the tool to monitor the *CRPD* needs 'to be treated with utmost caution', as it does not accord with article 1, 'Purpose', of the *CRPD* due to its 'medicalised understanding of disability'.[19] Kakoullis and Ikehara argued that the 'exclusion of the ICF from any reference in the CRPD suggests that it is not compatible with the CRPD'.[20] They substantiate their position by highlighting an example they claim demonstrates the CRPD Committee queries the ICF's compatibility with the *CRPD*.[21] Nonetheless, the CRPD Committee has never referred to the ICF directly in its Concluding Observations.[22]

14 'When the GA adopted the Declaration on the Rights of Mentally Retarded Persons 1971 (1971 Declaration) and the Declaration on the Rights of Disabled Persons 1975 (1975 Declaration), persons with disability may have become explicit subjects of international human rights law, but this status was heavily qualified by the individual model of disability within which they were couched. As a result, these instruments tend to be paternalistic, and legitimise segregation through specialised services and institutions'. Rosemary Kayess and Phillip French, 'Out of Darkness into Light – Introducing the Convention on the Rights of Persons with Disabilities' (2008) 8 *Human Rights Law Review* 1, 14–15.

15 See earlier Section 1.1.1 for an introduction to the models of disability.

16 See earlier Section 4.3.2(b).

17 World Health Organization (WHO), *International Classification of Functioning, Disability and Health* (2001) 6.

18 Ibid., 6.

19 Emily Kakoullis and Yoshikazu Ikehara, 'Article 1: Purpose' in Ilias Bantekas, Michael Ashley Stein and Dēmētrēs Anastasiou (eds), *The UN Convention on the Rights of Persons with Disabilities: A Commentary* (Oxford University Press, 2018) 35, 60–61. In the second quotation in this sentence Kakoullis and Ikehara are quoting Steven R Smith, 'Social Justice and Disability' in Kristjana Kristiansen, Simo Vehmas and Tom Shakespeare (eds), *Arguing About Disability* (Routledge, 2009) 17.

20 Kakoullis and Ikehara (n 19) 61.

21 'Furthermore, the Committee has expressed concern regarding how the ICF is implemented and its compatibility with the CRPD in its concluding observations on Mongolia'. Kakoullis and Ikehara (n 19) 61.

22 The CRPD Committee's Concluding Observation to Mongolia, which Kakoullis and Ikehara cite, states: 'The Committee is concerned that while the State party adheres to the concept of disability of the World Health Organization and focuses on conditions arising from inherent

Arguing that the ICF contravenes the *CRPD* is not as straightforward as some suggest. This line of argument ignores the fact that the ICF is embedded in an instrument cited in the *CRPD*'s Preamble, the ***Standard Rules of Equalization of Opportunities for Persons with Disabilities***. Furthermore, the ICF is the conceptual framework for the Washington Group questions that disabled persons organisations ('DPOs') have endorsed as the best disability data production method, and since 2017, the CRPD Committee have recommended its use to states in 65 of 82 Concluding Observations.[23] Kakoullis and Ikehara do not argue that data and statistics are inherently linked to the medical model.[24] Indeed, nothing in the treaty may contradict the purpose of the treaty.[25] Therefore, it can only be assumed that the obligations in article 31 may be implemented in a way that does not reflect or reinforce the medical model. Nonetheless, further work is required to understand people's concerns about the ICF and why they think it reflects the medical model.[26]

The medical model disempowers people with disability, takes away control over their lives and does not value their participation in life-altering decisions. Acknowledging that the medical model leads to the marginalisation of people with disability, the drafters of the *CRPD* codified a model of disability that was human rights promoting. The following subsection explores the conceptualisation of disability in the *CRPD*.

5.1.2 The CRPD*'s Conceptualisation of Disability*

The *CRPD*'s model of disability is vital context for interpreting article 31. The treaty's Preamble includes a description of disability stating that 'disability results from the interaction between persons with impairments and attitudinal and environmental barriers that hinder their full and effective participation in society'.[27] Lord stated that this paragraph is the most important statement in the Preamble, 'instantiating the decisive shift from a medical and/or

personal or medical impairment, it overlooks environmental factors'. Committee on the Rights of Persons with Disabilities, *Concluding Observations on the Initial Report of Mongolia*, UN Doc CRPD/C/MNG/CO/1 (13 May 2015) [5].

23 This was the count at the time of writing in August 2024. 'Conceptual Framework', *Washington Group on Disability Statistics* (Web Page, 2023) <https://www.washingtongroup-disability.com/about/conceptual-framework/>. See the Committee on the Rights of Persons with Disabilities website for links to all of their concluding observations to states. 'Committee on the Rights of Persons with Disabilities', *Office of the High Commissioner for Human Rights* (Web Page) <https://www.ohchr.org/en/treaty-bodies/crpd>. See later Section 7.2.2 and 7.3.1 for a critique of the Washington Group questions.

24 They recommend the tools developed by the Disability Rights Promotion International and Academic Network of European Disability Experts for data collection and monitoring. Kakoullis and Ikehara (n 19) 61.

25 *CRPD* (n 1) art 46.

26 See earlier Section 4.3.2(b).

27 *CRPD* (n 1) Preamble para e.

charity modelled approach to one that understands the disabling impact of socio-contextual factors exogenous to individuals with disability'.[28]

The *CRPD*'s conceptualisation of disability was heavily influenced by the social model of disability, which characterises disability as the result of the interaction between an individual and 'an environment that does not accommodate that individual's difference'.[29] Therefore, the marginalisation of people with disability results from society's inability to eliminate barriers.[30] While the social model of disability may have been important in shaping the conceptualisation of disability in the *CRPD*,[31] it is important to differentiate the model of disability in the *CRPD* from the social model as the latter has some limitations.[32] Former chair of the CRPD Committee Theresia Degener proposed that the *CRPD* has created the human rights model of disability.[33] The human rights model emphasises that people with disability are rights-holders, and states have obligations to fulfil these rights; 'it treats the barriers in society as discriminatory and provides avenues for persons with disabilities to complain when they are faced with such barriers'.[34]

The *CRPD* drafters left no ambiguity about the importance of this new paradigm by including a description of disability in article 1, 'Purpose', reflecting the new model: 'impairments which in interaction with various barriers may hinder . . . full and effective participation in society'.[35] The drafters' inclusion of the new paradigm in article 1 was strategically important as states are prohibited from making '[r]eservations incompatible with the [convention's] object and purpose'.[36] States parties are obligated to conceptualise disability as resulting from an unaccommodating social and physical environment, not as a problem inherent in a person.

The obligations in article 31 must be implemented in a way that is congruent with the *CRPD*'s conceptualisation of disability. Without delving into the specifics of what information states should produce and process, it seems likely that a greater focus should be on attitudinal and environmental change rather than on the characteristics of people with disability. Nonetheless, this model explains that disability occurs when there is a mismatch between the individual and the environment; therefore, some data about individuals may be

28 Janet E Lord, 'Preamble' in Ilias Bantekas et al (eds), *The UN Convention on the Rights of Persons with Disabilities: A Commentary* (Oxford University Press, 2018) 1, 12.

29 United Nations Office of the High Commissioner for Human Rights (OHCHR), *The Convention on the Rights of Persons with Disabilities: Training Guide* (2014) 9.

30 OHCHR (n 29) 9.

31 See earlier Section 1.1.1.

32 Theresia Degener, 'Disability in a Human Rights Context' (2016) 5(3) *Laws* 35.

33 Ibid., 35.

34 OHCHR (n 29) 10.

35 *CRPD* (n 1) art 1.

36 *CRPD* (n 1) art 46. This is in line with a well-established practice articulated in art 19(c) of the *Vienna Convention*. *Vienna Convention* (n 9).

necessary. Producing and processing information about individuals and their lives in a way that reflects the *CRPD* model of disability rather than the medical model of disability is the challenge. As discussed in the next subsection, this process requires respect for people with disability's inherent dignity, individual autonomy and freedom to make their own uncoerced choices.

5.1.3 Respect for the Inherent Dignity, Individual Autonomy and Independence of the Person

The inherent dignity, individual autonomy and independence of the person are different but interrelated concepts. These concepts are also closely linked to *CRPD* article 12, which recognises the legal personhood of people with disability.[37] This subsection will look at each concept separately, concluding with the implications for interpreting *CRPD* article 31.

a) Inherent Dignity

The United Nations General Assembly Resolution that established the *CRPD* drafting committee identified the rights and dignity of people with disability as the central concern of a new convention.[38] During the drafting processes, it was recognised that the nature of rights and dignity are slightly different, 'as States can confer rights but not dignity, which is inherent in everyone'.[39] Therefore, the drafters deliberately moved away from including dignity in conjunction with rights.[40] Instead, the innate qualities of dignity were reinforced through the phrase 'promote respect for their inherent dignity' in *CRPD* article 1, 'Purpose', and repeated in article 3, 'General principles'.[41] 'Respect' is used in human rights law to communicate non-interference by states, individuals and non-state entities.[42] States are, therefore, not to interfere with the dignity of people with disability.

37 See Eilionoir Flynn and Anna Arstein-Kerslake, 'Legislating Personhood: Realising the Right to Support in Exercising Legal Capacity' (2014) 10(1) *International Journal of Law in Context* 81.

38 *Comprehensive and Integral International Convention to Promote and Protect the Rights and Dignity of Persons with Disabilities*, GA Res 56/168, UN Doc A/RES/56/168 (26 February 2002, adopted 19 December 2001).

39 Valentina Della Fina, 'Article 1 [Purpose]' in Valentina Della Fina, Rachele Cera and Giuseppe Palmisano (eds), *The United Nations Convention on the Rights of Persons with Disabilities: A Commentary* (Springer, 2017) 89, 91.

40 Ibid., 89, 91.

41 *CRPD* (n 1) art 1.

42 See Philip Alston and Ryan Goodman, *International Human Rights* (Oxford University Press, 2013) 182–183; Committee on Economic, Social and Cultural Rights, *General Comment No 15: The Right to Water (Arts, 11 and 12 of the Covenant)*, UN Doc E/C.12/2002/11 (adopted 20 January 2003) [21].

There is no universally accepted concept of dignity. To 'treat someone with dignity' is culturally relative. Arduin summarised that 'a basic minimum understanding of human dignity suggests that each human being possesses an intrinsic worth . . . and that some behaviours are inconsistent with respect for this intrinsic worth'.[43] This definition appears to be consistent with how 'inherent dignity' is used in the *CRPD*. The *CRPD*'s Preamble opens by recalling the inherent dignity of 'all members of the human family as the foundation of freedom, justice and peace in the world'[44] and continues, stating that discrimination 'on the basis of disability is a violation of the inherent dignity'.[45] 'Inherent dignity' also features in the substantive provisions of the *CRPD*.[46]

One criticism of information production, which is mainly undertaken by experts who have power over others, is that it objectifies people. 'Expert' assessments reduce people's complex and rich lives to codes within categories. This objectification can be viewed as inconsistent with respect for intrinsic worth. Conversely, it may be argued that a person's inherent worth may be acknowledged by ensuring they and their life experiences are included in national censuses and the like, that they 'count' and should be counted. Inherent dignity as a concept does not provide much clarity about information production and processing practices. Nonetheless, the tensions raised here are elaborated further throughout this section.

b) Individual Autonomy

'Individual autonomy' features in the *CRPD*'s Preamble paragraph n and as a general principle in article 3. This phrase has not appeared in any other human rights instrument prior to the *CRPD*, but the concept is not new to the human rights framework. Jurisprudence and scholarship exist about individual autonomy's normative provisions. These provisions were acknowledged during the drafting of the *CRPD*, most notably by the Danish Human Rights Institute. The institute noted that individual or personal autonomy in human rights law is linked to five existing rights, namely, the 'right to personal development, to create goals for life', the 'right to privacy', the 'right to integrity, liberty and freedom from coercion', the 'right to inclusion in community life' and the 'right to participate actively in the political process'.[47] In their detailed

43 Sarah Arduin, 'Article 3: General Principles' in Ilias Bantekas, Michael Ashley Stein and Dēmētrēs Anastasiou (eds), *The UN Convention on the Rights of Persons with Disabilities: A Commentary* (Oxford University Press, 2018) 84, 92, citing Christopher McCrudden, 'Human Dignity and Judicial Interpretation of Human Rights' (2008) 19 *European Journal of International Law* 655, 723.

44 *CRPD* (n 1) Preamble para a.

45 *CRPD* (n 1) Preamble para h.

46 Including in articles on awareness raising, freedom from exploitation, violence and abuse, the right to education and the right to health. *CRPD* (n 1) arts 8, 16, 24, 25.

47 Morten Kjærum, *Letter Dated 26 May 2003 From the Executive Director of the Danish Institute for Human Rights Addressed to the Secretary of the Ad Hoc Committee on a Comprehensive and*

submission, the institute highlighted how individual autonomy integrates rights that are traditionally viewed as positive or negative rights, assessing that positive duties are often required for people to realise their freedoms (historically termed negative duties/rights).

The Danish Human Rights Institute highlighted a handful of cases from the European Court of Human Rights that have drawn on personal autonomy as an interpretive lens on human rights law. One judgment of interest when considering *CRPD* article 31, 'Statistics and data collection', is *I v United Kingdom*, where the following was found:

> Under Article 8 [respect for private life] of the Convention in particular, where the notion of *personal autonomy* is an important principle underlying the interpretation of its guarantees, protection is given to the personal sphere of each individual, including *the right to establish details of their identity as individual human beings.*[48]

The court determined that a transgender woman could have official government records changed to reflect her identity as a woman. *Who* has the 'right to establish details of . . . identity' significantly affects how information is produced and processed. The concept of personal or individual autonomy ensures that this right to determine how to identify is held by the individual whose identity is being recorded.

One aspect of individual autonomy that the *CRPD* highlights is the 'freedom to make one's own choices'.[49] The *CRPD*'s emphasis on the freedom to make one's own choices, read with the judgment cited earlier, reinforces the notion that people have a right to choose how and when to identify. The choice to identify is vital to people who experience marginalisation, as they may experience stigma or discrimination if they disclose aspects of their identity. An individual's choice to disclose their identity is an essential protective provision.[50]

Nonetheless, exercising the freedom to identify (or not) is challenged by the need to demonstrate eligibility to access programs, for example, having a disability to access reasonable accommodations. The privacy principle of producing and processing the minimum amount of information necessary to ensure a person meets the access criteria should apply in these situations, also known as data minimisation.[51] Information about people and their lives should not be produced and processed unless it is fundamental to service provision. If

---

Integral International Convention on the Protection and Promotion of the Rights and Dignity of Persons with Disabilities, UN Doc A/AC.265/2003/CRP/9 (26 May 2003).

48 *I v United Kingdom* [2002] Eur Court HR 25680/94, [70].

49 *CRPD* (n 1) Preamble para n, art 3(a).

50 See later Sections 6.4 and 7.3.1.

51 United Nations High Commissioner for Refugees (UNHCR), *Guidance on the Protection of Personal Data of Persons of Concern to UNHCR* (2018) 5. See later Section 7.3.3 for more on data minimisation.

additional data are to be produced and processed for monitoring or research purposes, service users should have a choice about whether to opt in or out of providing that information. Freedom from coercion, another element of individual autonomy, ensures that people with disability should not be coerced into sharing information about themselves that is unnecessary to receiving services. However, in practice, people with disability routinely need to provide extensive information to receive essential services.[52]

Further, central to people's ability to make their own decisions is accessible information.[53] In situations where people with disability may be asked to provide information about themselves or their experiences, accessible information should be provided detailing what information is being produced and how it will be processed and used. Accessible information includes translations into other languages, Braille, sign languages and Easy Read, as well as the use of augmentative and alternative communications.

c) Independence of Persons

The 'independence of persons' codified in the *CRPD*'s Preamble and article 3, 'General principles', underscores people with disability's rights to live independently and make their own life choices, as discussed in the previous subsection. Physical and social environments need to be made accessible to facilitate independence, and some people with disability may require individual accommodations.

It is a state obligation to facilitate the independence of persons. This state obligation has implications for *CRPD* article 31 and how information is produced. Information production should be accessible to enable people with disability to participate independently. In some cases, accommodations may need to be made. The Stakeholder Advisory Group discussed the Australian census, noting that the online form was not accessible to people who were blind.[54] That national census should be made accessible to people who are blind, and this could be done through technology that is already available. Independence is important, as it enables a person with disability to respond how they would like and prevents interference.

The *CRPD* makes it clear that people with disability have inherent worth, they can decide how they identify, and they have a right to live independently. This context informs how article 31 is interpreted. People must have a choice about whether they provide information about their bodies and lives. Information should not be produced and processed routinely and coercively. People must understand the purpose or use of the information. People with disability must have access to services without providing information unnecessary to the service delivery. Fulfilling these fundamental rights would seem

52 Stakeholder Advisory Group meeting minutes, 16 July 2021.
53 *CRPD* (n 1) art 21.
54 Stakeholder Advisory Group meeting minutes, 20 August 2021.

straightforward, yet, as explored in the following subsection, there is a significant and urgent gap in rights attainment for people with disability. Measuring all people with disability is tempting, as it promises to measure inequality and inform the development of targeted measures.

5.1.4 Remediation of Inequality and Discrimination

Addressing the shortfall in the realisation of human rights by people with disability is a core objective of the *CRPD*. Paragraph b of the Preamble states that people with disability are 'entitled to all the rights and freedoms . . . without distinction of any kind'.[55] Despite this entitlement, paragraph c highlights the disparity in rights realisation for people with disability, stating there is a 'need for persons with disabilities to be guaranteed their full enjoyment without discrimination'.[56] The universal experience of marginalisation by people with disability is described in paragraph k, which states that people with disability 'face barriers in their participation as equal members of society and violations of their human rights in all parts of the world'.[57] The Preamble concludes by highlighting the 'profound social disadvantage' experienced by people with disability and the intended significant role of the *CRPD* in redressing this and promoting the participation of people with disability 'in civil, political, economic, social and cultural spheres'.[58] *CRPD* article 1, 'Purpose', explains that human rights and fundamental freedoms are owed to people with disability and that this convention is to promote, protect and ensure the equal enjoyment of these rights.[59]

The terms *promote*, *protect* and *ensure* have specific and significant meanings in human rights law. Alston and Goodman state that the duty to *promote* 'refers to bringing about changes in public consciousness or perception or understanding about a given problem or issue, with the purpose of alleviating the problem'.[60] The Committee on Economic, Social and Cultural Rights stated that *protect* 'requires States parties to prevent third parties from interfering in any way with the enjoyment of the right',[61] placing a positive obligation on states to create the required institutional framework to protect given rights.[62] Schulze recalled from the *CRPD* drafting that *ensure* was included 'to make certain that *all possible State actions* would be covered and to make certain that the outcome aimed for would be achieved'.[63] The verb *ensure*

55 *CRPD* (n 1) Preamble para b.
56 *CRPD* (n 1) Preamble para c.
57 *CRPD* (n 1) Preamble para k.
58 *CRPD* (n 1) Preamble para y.
59 *CRPD* (n 1) art 1.
60 Alston and Goodman (n 42) 185.
61 Committee on Economic, Social and Cultural Rights (n 42) [23].
62 Alston and Goodman (n 42) 183.
63 Marianne Schulze, *Understanding the UN Convention on the Rights of Persons with Disabilities: A Handbook on the Human Rights of Persons with Disabilities* (Handicap International, 3rd ed, 2010) 33 (emphasis in original).

features 55 times in the *CRPD*, including in the chapeau of article 4, 'General obligations', in a similar formulation to that of article 1, 'Purpose'.[64] Nonetheless, article 4(2) concedes that some of the rights within the convention may only be implemented to 'the maximum' of a state's resources and will need to be achieved 'progressively'.[65]

Read with article 31, 'Statistics and data collection', these obligations to promote, protect and ensure require information about state actions to change the public consciousness, measures taken to establish institutional systems to protect rights and measures taken by states and the resources invested in ensuring the realisation of the rights within the *CRPD*. These rights must be obtained 'on an equal basis with others'.[66] *Equal* is a word used in measurement. It also forms part of the word equality. The *CRPD* creates obligations on states to take action to bring about equality for people with disability. Information may assist in understanding the size and nature of these disparities and discrimination. *CRPD* article 2 states that discrimination based on disability can occur in any realm of life and may require reasonable accommodations to be remediated. The treaty is concerned with substantive equality (that is, equality of outcomes) rather than formal equality (that is, equal opportunity).

Considering *CRPD* article 31 with the substantive equality obligations to ensure 'full and effective participation',[67] recommendations for wide-scale surveillance that identifies people with disability to understand the disparities in outcomes and develop targeted measures is understandable.[68] However, this form of surveillance greatly impacts the privacy of people with disability, requiring them to disclose personal information when others do not. Further, as discussed in the previous subsection, people may choose to provide

64 'States Parties undertake to ensure and promote the full realization of all human rights and fundamental freedoms for all persons with disabilities without discrimination of any kind on the basis of disability'. *CRPD* (n 1) art 4.

65 *CRPD* (n 1) art 4(2).

66 This phrase is not in any other United Nations human rights treaty. Kakoullis and Ikehara (n 19) 58. It works not only to ensure that people with disability have full enjoyment of their human rights 'on an equal basis with others' but also to ensure that people with disability are not 'given more protection than others in a Member State', eg, from the death penalty. Schulze (n 63) 78. This phrase features in the *CRPD* 35 times: *CRPD* (n 1) Preamble paras e, r, arts 1, 2 (twice), 7 (twice), 9, 10, 12, 13, 14 (twice), 15, 17, 18, 19 (twice), 21, 22, 23 (twice), 24 (twice), 27 (four times), 29 (three times), 30 (four times).

67 *CRPD* (n 1) arts 1, 3(c). See earlier Section 3.3.2(a) for a discussion about using data in surveillance of social issues to develop policy.

68 See earlier n 1. DPOs and NGOs also cite art 31 as an obligation to produce and process data about the bodies and lives of people with disability. See, eg, CBM and International Disability Alliance (IDA), *What's Happening with Disability Data? Together We Will Count and Be Counted! A Brief Study and Overview of DPO Experiences Regarding Disability Data* (Report, n.d.) 2–3. See also Leonard Cheshire and Humanity & Inclusion, *Disability Data Collection: A Summary Review of the Use of the Washington Group Questions by Development and Humanitarian Actors* (Report, 2018) 2 n 2.

or withhold their information. Therefore, it is unlikely that a dataset will be complete and show a true picture. It also typically requires people with disability to be measured by others (experts in outcome measures and indicators, statisticians), which is medical model practice.[69]

The *CRPD* offers another method of understanding the experiences of people with disability, providing them with a more active role as participants in treaty implementation.[70] Rather than objectifying and counting individuals, disparities may be identified in partnership with people with disability through participatory mechanisms.[71] Barriers that hinder 'full and effective participation' may be identified.[72] State actions to remove these barriers to promote, protect and ensure the rights of people with disability may be measured. Ensuring the participation of people with disability in matters affecting them is closely associated with individual autonomy, discussed earlier, and is important in interpreting article 31. In addition to the general obligation in article 4(3) for states to closely consult and actively involve people with disability,[73] the *CRPD* Preamble highlights the importance of people with disability participating 'in decision-making processes about policies and programmes'.[74] Nonetheless, to be effective, broad participation is required to ensure the range of barriers encountered by people with disability are documented and their remediation measured. The following subsection briefly revisits the *CRPD*'s recognition of the diversity of people with disability.

5.1.5 *Diversity of People With Disability*

The *CRPD* goes to great lengths to acknowledge the heterogeneity of people with disability and to identify all people with disability as rights-holders. Article 1 states that the *CRPD* is to 'promote, protect and ensure . . . enjoyment of all human rights . . . by *all* persons with disabilities'.[75] The Preamble acknowledges 'the diversity of persons with disabilities'[76] and describes:

> the difficult conditions faced by persons with disabilities who are subject to multiple or aggravated forms of discrimination on the basis of race,

69 See earlier Section 5.1.1.

70 *CRPD* (n 1) art 4(3). See earlier Sections 2.2.2(b) and 4.4.2 and later Section 7.4 for discussions about of the nature of the *CPRD*'s participation obligations.

71 See especially Committee on the Rights of Persons with Disabilities, *General Comment No 7 (2018) on the Participation of Persons with Disabilities, Including Children with Disabilities, Through Their Representative Organizations, in the Implementation and Monitoring of the Convention*, UN Doc CRPD/C/GC/7 (9 November 2018) ('*General Comment 7 Participation*').

72 *CRPD* (n 1) Preamble para e, art 1.

73 *CRPD* (n 1) Preamble para e, art 4(3).

74 *CRPD* (n 1) Preamble para o.

75 *CRPD* (n 1) Preamble para o, art 1 (emphasis added).

76 *CRPD* (n 1) Preamble para i.

> colour, sex, language, religion, political or other opinion, national, ethnic, indigenous or social origin, property, birth, age or other status.[77]

As discussed in Section 1.1.2, the *CRPD* is the first human rights treaty to acknowledge multiple discrimination.[78] Bids to acknowledge the plight of displaced people were not accepted during the drafting.[79] Nonetheless, article 5 obligates states to provide 'equal and effective legal protection against discrimination on *all* grounds'.[80] Article 5's text is intentionally broad and creates obligations for states to provide 'reasonable accommodation' and '[s]pecific measures' for people with disability to access 'equal and effective legal protection' against discrimination for any reason, disability-related or not.[81]

The *CRPD* also acknowledges people's diverse experiences of disability. Broad, distinct categories of impairments experienced by people with disability are named in article 1: 'physical, mental, intellectual or sensory impairments'. Further, article 1's description of disability describes impairments interacting 'with various barriers' hindering 'full and effective participation in society'.[82] This description of disability acknowledges the infinitely different experiences of people with disability; two people with the same impairment may experience disability differently depending on barriers in their environment. Further, the *CRPD* also refers to promoting and protecting the human rights of 'those who require more intensive support'.[83] This text reminds us that the severity of impairment does not limit a person's rights.

CRPD article 31 provides for the disaggregation of information, potentially enabling the experiences of different subgroups to be explored.[84] However, disaggregation by multiple indicators assumes wide-scale surveillance of people with disability and their lives, raising the concerns discussed earlier. Given the infinite range of elements that impact disability and rights realisation, detailed surveillance of people's lives would be required to gain a granular

77 *CRPD* (n 1) Preamble para p.

78 *CRPD* (n 1) Preamble, art 6.

79 See later Section 6.2.2.

80 *CRPD* (n 1) art 5(2) (emphasis added).

81 *CRPD* (n 1) art 5(3)–(4). This interpretation is consistent with the CRPD Committee's *General Comment 6*: 'Protection against "discrimination on all grounds" means that all possible grounds of discrimination and their intersections must be taken into account. Possible grounds include but are not limited to: disability; health status; genetic or other predisposition towards illness; race; colour; descent; sex; pregnancy and maternity/paternity; civil; family or career status; gender expression; sex; language; religion; political or other opinion; national, ethnic, indigenous or social origin; migrant, refugee or asylum status; belonging to a national minority; economic or property status; birth; and age, or a combination of any of those grounds or characteristics associated with any of those grounds'. Committee on the Rights of Persons with Disabilities, *General Comment No 6 (2018) on Equality and Non-Discrimination*, UN Doc CRPD/C/GC/6 (26 April 2018) [21].

82 *CRPD* (n 1) art 1.

83 *CRPD* (n 1) art 1 Preamble para j.

84 See earlier Section 4.3.

picture of these circumstances. Therefore, it seems more likely that these issues should be identified and explored with smaller groups of people through disability human rights–promoting research or consultation with diverse DPOs.[85]

The *CRPD* signals a break from the medical model and introduces a new model of disability.[86] The treaty conceptualises disability as a product of the interaction between an individual and their environment, placing obligations on states to remove environmental barriers to ensure that people with disability can realise their rights. States are obligated to respect the inherent dignity of people with disability, their autonomy and their right to make choices about their own lives. Significant rights disparities for people with disability creates an urgency to act. Nevertheless, the wide-scale production of information about people with disability and their lives is unnecessary. Surveillance should be about the attitudinal and physical environmental barriers to rights attainments and state actions to implement the treaty. Barriers and issues may be identified through the active involvement and close consultation of people with disability and disability human rights–promoting research.[87] The following section will enumerate the state obligations in article 31 by examining the text's ordinary meaning in light of the themes discussed in this section.

5.2 The Ordinary Meaning of Article 31

The *Vienna Convention* places primary importance on the 'ordinary meaning' of the treaty's text, which is to be interpreted 'in their context and in the light of its object and purpose'.[88] The previous section explored the context of article 31 and unpacked the object and purpose of the *CRPD*. Building on that discussion, this section considers the ordinary meaning of *CRPD* article 31 and its state obligations. During the *CRPD* drafting, the text about statistics and data collection was initially in the 'General obligations' article and then moved to draft article 6.[89] After some negotiation, it moved to article 31 to be closer but still distinct from the obligations about monitoring. It is conventionally accepted that article 31 does not contain individual rights or substantive provisions but is essential for implementing substantive rights in the treaty.[90] This section is structured according to the sequence of the text in article 31, and the last subsection summarises the state duties in article 31.

85 See especially Anna Arstein-Kerslake et al, 'Introducing a Human Rights-Based Disability Research Methodology' (2020) 20(3) *Human Rights Law Review* 412; CRPD Committee, *General Comment 7 Participation* (n 71).

86 See earlier Sections 1.1.1, 5.1.1 and 5.1.2.

87 *CRPD* (n 1) art 4(1)(f), (g), 4.3; Arstein-Kerslake et al (n 85).

88 *Vienna Convention* (n 9) art 31(1).

89 See earlier Section 4.2.1.

90 See earlier Chapter 4 n 35. See also Schulze (n 63) 165.

5.2.1 *'Statistics and Data Collection'*

The title of *CRPD* article 31 is 'Statistics and Data Collection'. Numerical data may be known as statistics, but statistics also refers to 'the science which deals with the collection, classification, and use of numerical facts or data'.[91] 'Statistics' in the article's title suggests a focus on quantitative data. Nonetheless, the drafters intended data to be conceptualised broadly, including qualitative information.[92] The definition of data in the *Macquarie Dictionary* that most aligns with the drafters' intent defines data as 'information collected for analysis or reference',[93] confirming that data may be quantitative or qualitative. 'Collection' may be defined as *a set*. However, in this context, it is more likely meant in terms of *the act of collecting*. Therefore, the title indicates that this article is about collecting information.

5.2.2 *'Undertake to Collect Appropriate Information . . . to Formulate and Implement Policies to Give Effect to the Present Convention'*

> 1. States Parties undertake to collect appropriate information, including statistical and research data, to enable them to formulate and implement policies to give effect to the present Convention.

The term 'undertake' denotes 'an obligation of conduct'.[94] Determining what constitutes 'appropriate information' requires a process of identification before the 'collection' can occur. According to article 31(1), states are required to 'collect' all forms of information that are 'appropriate' to give effect to the convention. While all forms of information may be produced and processed, this must include 'statistical and research data'. This provision supports the state obligations in article 4(1[f–g]) that focus on research. Nonetheless, the drafters' use of the verb 'collect' obfuscates the true nature of data and information.[95]

As established earlier, collect means to 'gather together',[96] which assumes the gathering of existing phenomena. Information and data do not exist without a creator. Those who create and process information have world views and

91 *Macquarie Dictionary: Australia's National Dictionary Online* (Electronic Resource, Macquarie Library, 2003) <www.macquariedictionary.com.au>.

92 See earlier Section 4.2.2.

93 *Macquarie Dictionary: Australia's National Dictionary Online* (n 91).

94 Alston and Quinn argue that 'undertake' is 'less demanding than guarantee' but 'represents a clear legal undertaking'. Philip Alston and Gerard Quinn, 'The Nature and Scope of States Parties' Obligations Under the International Covenant on Economic, Social and Cultural Rights Symposium: The Implementation of the International Covenant on Economic, Social and Cultural Rights' (1987) 9 *Human Rights Quarterly* 156, 165–166.

95 See earlier Section 3.3.1.

96 *Macquarie Dictionary: Australia's National Dictionary Online* (n 91).

use methods that shape the data and information.[97] Information and data are, therefore, not neutral, inert or impartial reflections of the world. Recognising *who* creates the information and *how* this is to be done is vital to interpreting this article.

As the *CRPD* is a human rights treaty, the treaty obligations are ultimately the responsibility of states parties; therefore, states must *create appropriate information* or oversee this process. The creation of the information should adhere to the object and purpose of the *CRPD*, the principles and general obligations. These obligations include the active involvement of people with disability through their representative organisations[98] and a break from the medical model where 'experts' label people with disability.[99]

The use of the qualifying word 'appropriate' in the article's opening sentence provides limits and flexibility on the information that may be created. Information is not to be created indiscriminately but for a specific purpose: 'to formulate and implement policies to give effect to the present Convention'.[100] Further, the information that is deemed appropriate may vary across time and place.[101]

The similarities between *CRPD* article 4(3) and article 31 reinforce the pivotal role that people with disability, including children, through their representative organisations, have in creating appropriate information 'to formulate and implement policies to give effect to the present Convention'.[102] Article 4(3) states that '[i]n the *development and implementation of* legislation and *policies to implement the present Convention* . . . States Parties shall closely consult and actively involve persons with disabilities'.[103] In determining what information is appropriate to enable the formulation and implementation of policies to give effect to the convention, states must closely consult and actively involve people with disability.

The first paragraph of article 31 codifies information as vital to states' capacity to fulfil their obligations under the convention. Information has an 'enabling' role for states. Information 'enables [states] . . . to formulate and implement policies to give effect' to the *CRPD*. A narrow interpretation of this opening sentence may suggest that 'policy' is the tool chosen to

97 See earlier Chapter 3. Also see especially, Sally Engle Merry, *The Seductions of Quantification: Measuring Human Rights, Gender Violence, and Sex Trafficking* (University of Chicago Press, 2016).

98 *CRPD* (n 1) art 4(3).

99 See earlier Section 5.1.1.

100 *CRPD* (n 1) art 31(1).

101 See earlier Section 1.2.2, which demonstrates that the CRPD Committee have recommended the production of refugee data in select contexts. By way of another example, in select contexts, the CRPD Committee recommends the collection of Indigenous data. See, eg, Committee on the Rights of Persons with Disabilities, *Concluding Observations on the Initial Report of Sweden*, UN Doc CRPD/C/SWE/CO/1 (12 May 2014) [57]–[58].

102 *CRPD* (n 1) art 31(1).

103 *CRPD* (n 1) art 4(3) (emphasis added).

give effect to the convention. Nonetheless, article 4, 'General obligations', lists several measures that states must take to give effect to the convention, namely, the adoption of legislation, policies and programs, abolishing existing laws and practices and undertaking research. Therefore, 'policies' in article 31 should be read broadly as 'a course or line of action adopted and pursued by a government',[104] rather than narrowly as a written policy document or a lesser form of law (soft law).

5.2.3 *'The Process of Collecting and Maintaining This Information Shall'*

The subparagraphs of article 31(1) must be fully implemented before information may be created under the authority of this article. The last sentence of the paragraph 1 chapeau and the introductory phrase of the subparagraphs read: 'Collecting and maintaining this information shall: (a) comply with'.[105] As discussed in the previous subsection, information is better characterised as produced than collected. 'Maintain' may be defined as ongoing retention, preserving, continuance, keeping in a due condition of operation and keeping or holding against attack.[106] Therefore, before states parties produce and retain information for this article, they must 'ensure confidentiality and respect of the privacy' of people with disability and follow 'ethical principles in the collection and use of statistics', as discussed next.[107]

5.2.4 *'Respect for the Privacy of Persons With Disabilities'*

> (a) Comply with legally established safeguards, including legislation on data protection, to ensure confidentiality and respect for the privacy of persons with disabilities;

Article 22 of the *CRPD* is about 'Respect for Privacy' and is modelled on article 17 of the *International Covenant on Civil and Political Rights.*[108] According to Land and colleagues, respect for privacy is a manifestation of respect for a person's inherent dignity.[109] In their commentary about *CRPD* article 22, Land and colleagues suggest that 'For persons with disabilities, limiting access

104 *Macquarie Dictionary: Australia's National Dictionary Online* (n 91).

105 *CRPD* (n 1) art 31(1).

106 *Macquarie Dictionary: Australia's National Dictionary Online* (n 91).

107 *CRPD* (n 1) art 31(1).

108 *International Covenant on Civil and Political Rights*, opened for signature 16 December 1966, 999 UNTS 171 (entered into force 23 March 1976) ('*ICCPR*').

109 Land and colleagues stated: 'As an intrinsic value, privacy is an acknowledgement of the dignity owed to every individual – the idea that limiting access to the body, to information about the individual, and to the individual's relationships is an essential aspect of respect for the person'. Molly Land et al, 'Article 22: Respect for Privacy' in Ilias Bantekas et al (eds), *The UN Convention on the Rights of Persons with Disabilities: A Commentary* (Oxford University Press, 2018) 604, 605 (citations omitted).

to disability status or other medical or health information is necessary to ensure respect for autonomy and individual dignity'.[110]

Several scholars have written on the importance of privacy for reaching and pushing the boundaries of human potential and protecting against government and commercial interference.[111] Land and colleagues highlight that respect for privacy is important to people with disability to protect them from discrimination and stigma.[112] The right to privacy provides people with disability the right to 'control information about themselves, including information related to their disability status'.[113] Land and colleagues also highlight that people with disability often have to disclose more personal information than their peers to achieve their human rights.[114] This information is often viewed as necessary to receive reasonable accommodations. Respect for privacy obligations ensures that this information 'is not shared further than necessary and is not used for purposes other than the claimed accommodation or benefit'.[115]

Interference with privacy is permitted in limited circumstances, not as a routine part of life as is experienced by many people with disability. Interference must be lawful.[116] Interference cannot be arbitrary.[117] Lawful interference must be 'proportional to the end to be achieved'.[118] The limited provisions for interference with privacy are of interest to this research, as people with disability who are refugees may find themselves in emergency situations where interference is permitted.[119] Land and colleagues stated that the law allowing

110 Land et al (n 109) 605. See later Section 7.2.3(a) for a discussion about the nature of disability data and whether it should be characterised as sensitive.

111 See, eg, Julie E Cohen, 'What Privacy Is For' (2013) 126 *Harvard Law Review* 1904, cited in Molly Land et al, 'Article 22: Respect for Privacy' in Ilias Bantekas et al (eds), *The UN Convention on the Rights of Persons with Disabilities: A Commentary* (Oxford University Press, 2018) 604, 605.

112 Land et al (n 109) 605.

113 Land et al (n 109) 605–606.

114 Land et al (n 109) 606.

115 Land et al (n 109) 606.

116 *CRPD* art 22(1) states: 'No person . . . shall be subjected to arbitrary or unlawful interference with his or her privacy', implying there is a form of lawful interference. Art 17 of the *International Covenant on Civil and Political Rights* has the same provision. *CRPD* (n 1) art 22(1); *ICCPR* (n 108) art 17. The Human Rights Committee have advised that these are situations that are 'envisaged by the law. Interference authorized by States can only take place on the basis of law, which itself must comply with the provisions, aims and objectives of the Covenant'. Human Rights Committee, *General Comment No 16: Article 17 (Right to Privacy) The Right to Respect of Privacy, Family, Home and Correspondence, and Protection of Honour and Reputation*, 32nd sess (adopted 8 April 1988) [3].

117 The Human Rights Committee have advised that 'even interference provided for by law should be in accordance with the provisions, aims and objectives of the Covenant and should be, in any event, reasonable in the particular circumstances'. Human Rights Committee (n 116) [4].

118 Land et al (n 109) 610.

119 See later Section 7.2.3.

interference must be accessible before the interference, including details of the specific circumstances in which interference is legitimate.[120] Effective means for 'legal redress against arbitrary or incongruous interference by public authorities' must be provided.[121] These provisions also require attention to ensure information about the law is accessible[122] and that people with disability have avenues to access justice if their privacy is unlawfully breached.[123]

Not all states have competent laws to respect privacy, including avenues for redress in the case of breaches. In the context of article 31, information production about people with disability and their lives is prohibited unless states 'comply' with 'respect for privacy' provisions. Information may be produced and processed about state actions to implement the treaty, remediate barriers and allocate resources if it does not interfere with the privacy of people with disability.

5.2.5 *'Ethical Principles in the Collection and Use of Statistics'*

> (b) Comply with internationally accepted norms to protect human rights and fundamental freedoms and ethical principles in the collection and use of statistics.

Subparagraph 1(b) must also be fully implemented before data production and processing is undertaken for the article. States 'shall comply' with the provisions in this subparagraph. These include adherence to norms and principles established by the international community. The *CRPD* drafters' general reference to these tools was deliberate, allowing for norms and principles to evolve and for article 31 to remain relevant. One such example is the *Fundamental Principles of Official Statistics.* The 1994 version of the principles was consulted during the *CRPD* drafting.[124] The subsequent 2013 update of the principles is seamlessly recognised by article 31.[125]

Subparagraph 1(b) also broadens the protections to consider the 'use' of statistics, not just 'collection'. 'Use' includes analysis and dissemination, broadening the scope beyond that of the chapeau. While these principles are included in article 31 as safeguards, they are not the only protections that data subjects have. Measures to implement the article 31 obligations cannot harm people with disability, as this would not adhere to the purpose of the *CRPD.*[126] Rather than a comprehensive description of protections, subparagraphs 1(a) and (b) act as a reminder that the production and processing of information for the *CRPD* may cause harm and that protections are necessary

120 Land et al (n 109) 610–611.
121 Land et al (n 109) 611.
122 *CRPD* (n 1) art 21.
123 *CRPD* (n 1) art 13.
124 See earlier Section 4.4.1.
125 *Fundamental Principles of Official Statistics*, GA Res 68/261, UN Doc A/RES/68/261 (3 March 2014, adopted 29 January 2014).
126 *CRPD* (n 1) art 1.

and must be immediately and fully implemented before the information is produced and processed.

5.2.6 *'Information . . . Shall Be Disaggregated'*

> 2. The information collected in accordance with this article shall be disaggregated, as appropriate, and used to help assess the implementation of States Parties' obligations under the present Convention and to identify and address the barriers faced by persons with disabilities in exercising their rights.

Article 31 paragraph 2 states that information produced and processed for this article 'shall be disaggregated' or divided into categories. 'Shall' is defined by *Black's Law Dictionary* as 'is required to'.[127] The *CRPD* drafters deliberately strengthened the language in this provision, changing 'should' to 'shall'.[128] Nonetheless, it does not mean that information must be disaggregated in all instances. The language 'disaggregated, as appropriate' requires closer scrutiny, as it suggests that there may be situations where some types of disaggregation are inappropriate and that, in some settings, certain variables of disaggregation may be more relevant or appropriate than others. This qualification is consistent with discussions during the *CRPD* drafting where states could not agree on variables to disaggregate data.[129] Further, some states argued that producing and processing some data variables was inappropriate and illegal in their jurisdiction.[130]

The first purpose of the disaggregation is to 'help assess the implementation of State Parties' obligations'. Fulfilling this obligation requires a detailed understanding of each obligation within the convention and detailed information about states' actions to meet these obligations. Note that disaggregation's purpose is to assess the actions or the process of meeting the obligations' 'implementation'. 'Assessing the implementation' requires scrutiny of more than whether the obligations are met or not. It requires assessing the measures taken to meet the obligation. Nonetheless, the effectiveness of the implementation is implicit in this requirement, that is, to what degree the obligations have been fulfilled. Examples of steps that states may take to meet their obligations that can be measured include, among other things, identifying money spent on disability inclusion in government budgets, accessible versus inaccessible

127 Bryan A Garner and Henry Campbell Black (eds), *Black's Law Dictionary* (Thomson Reuters, 10th ed, 2014) 1585.

128 The Chair summarised at the start of the afternoon session that there was 'unopposed support . . . for changing "should" to "shall"' in the second paragraph. Rehabilitation International, 'Daily Summary of Discussion at the Seventh Session 27 January 2006', *UN Convention on the Human Rights of People with Disabilities Ad Hoc Committee – Daily Summaries* (United Nations Enable, 27 January 2006) <https://www.un.org/esa/socdev/enable/rights/ahc7sum27jan.htm>.

129 See earlier Section 4.3.3.

130 See earlier Chapter 4 n 134.

buses, materials published in Easy Read compared to those that are not and events where sign language interpreting is provided compared to where they are not.

The disaggregated information is also used to 'identify and address the barriers faced by persons with disabilities in exercising their rights'.[131] Identifying and addressing barriers is central to how the *CRPD* conceptualises disability. '[A]ttitudinal and environmental barriers' interact with a person's impairments to cause disability,[132] prevent 'equal membership of society'[133] and hinder 'full and effective participation'.[134] Individuals with disability will experience a range of different barriers. As discussed previously, barriers may be identified through close consultation and active involvement of diverse people with disability through their representative organisations and disability human rights research. These mechanisms may identify barriers that may be converted into data variables for disaggregation.

The *CRPD* drafters decided not to include variables by which data should be disaggregated. Nonetheless, the Preamble includes a non-exhaustive list of grounds by which people with disability face more significant barriers to realising their rights and specific conditions are noted as exacerbating rights violation, such as poverty.[135] Including these grounds and conditions in the Preamble was perhaps a concession to the states that wanted data variables or indicators listed in article 31.[136] Whether producing and processing information about these groups is 'appropriate' must be determined in each setting in consultation with the populations impacted. However, also consider that these groups have traditionally experienced greater marginalisation and persecution from the state (even in liberal democracies where they are often scapegoated) and have greater barriers to participating in DPOs, for example, people with disability who are refugees.

It should be noted that the CRPD Committee has recommended hundreds of variables by which states should disaggregate information, including refugee and asylum seeker status.[137] The macro rationale for these recommendations is clear and aligns with the movement towards data-driven policy,[138] but the micro-interactions that require individuals to disclose personal information about their lives have not been fully considered. Suppose population data that include variables that require people with disability to disclose personal

131 *CRPD* (n 1) art 31(2).
132 *CRPD* (n 1) Preamble para e.
133 *CRPD* (n 1) Preamble para k.
134 *CRPD* (n 1) art 1.
135 Grounds by which people with disability experience greater barriers noted in the Preamble include: 'race, colour, sex, language, religion, political or other opinion, national, ethnic, indigenous or social origin, property, birth, age or other status', *CRPD* (n 1) Preamble para p.
136 See earlier Section 4.3.3 for a discussion about the drafting of art 31(2).
137 See earlier n 1, 101. For the CRPD Committees recommendations about disaggregation by refugee status, see 1.2.2 nn 70–80.
138 For more on data-driven policy, see Section 3.3.

information are necessary to implement the treaty. More research is required to understand the individual impact of data production and processing by states. If there are concerns about states undertaking this surveillance but still a legitimate need for data, alternative methods of data production could be considered. For example, a third party may be entrusted to fulfil this obligation.[139] DPOs or other trusted non-government organisations may produce and process the data.[140] Obligations are often fulfilled through third parties who are provided with the resources by the state, such as the right to health and education. Third parties may also produce and process the information necessary to implement the treaty.[141]

5.2.7 *'Dissemination of These Statistics'*

> 3. States Parties shall assume responsibility for the dissemination of these statistics and ensure their accessibility to persons with disabilities and others.

The third and final paragraph of *CRPD* article 31 refers to 'statistics' rather than information. The term 'statistics' suggests the information has been processed. States must release the aggregated and processed information and take measures to ensure it is accessible. While the *CRPD* describes the processed information as statistics, it can be reasonably assumed that this applies to all processed (non-identifiable) information, both quantitative and qualitative.

The article identifies 'persons with disabilities and others' as the recipients of the information produced and processed for article 31. The drafters deliberately positioned people with disability as the primary audience for this information. Dissemination of processed information supports the effective functioning of *CRPD* article 4(3), which requires that people with disability should be 'closely consult[ed] with and actively involve[d]' in implementing the convention. Article 31 clarifies that information is necessary for the implementation of the convention; therefore, people with disability need access to the information to be actively involved in the implementation of the convention. As discussed earlier, it is a state obligation to ensure that the information

139 See later Section 7.3.3.

140 Office of the High Commissioner for Human Rights (OHCHR), *Statistics and Data Collection Under Article 31 of the Convention on the Rights of Persons with Disabilities*, UN Doc A/HRC/49/60 (28 December 2021) [34]–[35].

141 For example, the World Federation of the Deafblind Global Survey. 'The purpose of this survey is to gather information for WFDB's 2nd Global Report, which will be published during the third quarter of 2022, on the situation of persons with deafblindness and assess the current status of their inclusion at country levels. This report will build on the findings and recommendations of the first WFDB Global Report published in 2018. The aim is to strengthen the data and evidence base, as well as identify and propose good practices to resolve the issues identified in the first report'. Email from Lucia D'Arino to crpd-forum (including Philippa Duell-Piening), 25 January 2022.

is accessible to people with disability, including making information available in a range of accessible formats.[142]

5.2.8 *Summary of Article 31 State Duties*

The *CRPD* drafters asserted that article 31 contained no individual rights.[143] Therefore, this subsection goes directly to the state obligations. The next section of this chapter will consider whether article 31 contains a group right to control visibility in datasets, a group right to be counted.

In summary, the analysis in this chapter demonstrates that, to fulfil their duties under *CRPD* article 31, states parties to the convention must do the following:

1. Produce appropriate information to formulate and implement initiatives to promote, protect and ensure the full and equal enjoyment of all human rights and fundamental freedoms by all persons with disability and to promote respect for their inherent dignity.
    a. People with disability, including children with disability, through their representative organisations, must be closely consulted and actively involved in determining what information is appropriate for this purpose.
    b. The information produced and processed should include, *inter alia*, statistical and research data.
2. The information production and information storage, preservation and security must:
    a. be governed by laws that ensure confidentiality and respect for the privacy of people with disability and provide legal redress for unlawful interference with privacy;
    b. adhere to norms that protect human rights and fundamental freedoms; and
    c. adhere to ethical principles in the production and use of statistics.
3. Information produced for this article must be disaggregated only as appropriate.[144] The disaggregation is limited to that required to assess measures taken to fulfil treaty obligations and discover and rectify barriers faced by people with disability in realising their rights.
    a. People with disability, including children with disability, through their representative organisations, must be actively involved and closely consulted in determining 'appropriate' disaggregation.

142 *CRPD* (n 1) art 21.

143 See earlier Chapter 4 n 35. See also Schulze (n 63) 165.

144 See later Section 7.2 for a discussion about a test for 'appropriate' data production and processing.

4. Information produced and processed for this article must be made public in a format that all people with disability can access.
   a. This information should be processed, and data subjects should not be identifiable.

These procedural obligations in article 31 correspond and are important to implementing substantive rights throughout the convention.[145] Article 31's information production obligations 'enable' the realisation of all substantive rights within the convention. Take, for example, the right to health. People with disability have a right to 'the same range, quality and standard of free or affordable health care and programmes as provided to other persons'.[146] Article 31 creates corresponding obligations for states to produce and process information to enable initiatives that protect, respect and ensure this right. Working with people with disability, states may assess the implementation of the measures to ensure the right and identify barriers to rights attainment. Metrics about state performance may then be designed to measure the effectiveness of implementation, such as the number of accessible clinics.

While article 31 was not intended to create rights, an important group right may be read into this article, the group right to control visibility in datasets or the right to be counted. As discussed in the next section, this right is necessary to respond to the potential harms of data to groups, allowing groups to have greater control over the production and processing of data about their bodies and lives.

5.3 A Group Right to Be Counted

Group rights, rights that individuals cannot realise apart from a group, are controversial and under-theorised in human rights law. Nevertheless, they may be essential for creating the conditions necessary for people to realise their human rights. This section will take a cursory look at whether it could be argued that article 31 contains group rights. Given that information production and processing is a novel content area in human rights law, it is fertile for this form of exploration. Information's power comes through aggregation, the grouping of data. It is, therefore, possible that rights, harms and protections need to be conceptualised at a group rather than individual level. When individuals cannot be identified, such as in de-identified data, a group right may be the only way to offer protection from harm resulting from that data.

This section begins by exploring the definition of group rights in human rights law, which will be referred to as 'group (human) rights' for brevity.[147] It

145 For a discussion about the relationship between rights and duties, see Alston and Goodman (n 42) 181.

146 *CRPD* (n 1) art 25(a).

147 The parentheses around 'human' indicate that the notion of 'group human rights' is controversial. Some scholars argue that group rights are antithetical to human rights. Eg, Jeremy Waldron argues: 'Rights express limits on what can be done to individuals for the sake of

then uses Alston's framework for 'formulating and implementing' new human rights[148] to explore the group (human) right (not) to be counted.

5.3.1 *What Are Group (Human) Rights?*

As discussed earlier, respect for individual autonomy is integral to the purpose of the *CRPD*. This principle of individual autonomy informed international human rights law's development following World War II. In this rights paradigm, individual human rights are fundamental and should be protected, respected and fulfilled by the state. As political philosopher Ronald Dworkin concluded, individual human rights are 'political trumps' on which the state may not impinge.[149] Nonetheless, groups have received some recognition as rights-holders under international human rights law. For example, the Human Rights Committee recognised the rights of associations under the *International Covenant on Civil and Political Rights* article 22.[150]

At the turn of the millennium, human rights scholar Peter Jones tried to clarify what a group (human) right meant. Jones explained that a group (human) right is identifiable by 'its subject rather than its object – who it is that holds the right rather than what the right is a right to do'.[151] According to Jones, an individual cannot hold a group (human) right apart from the group, as rights that individuals hold apart from the group are simply individual human rights. Elaborating his theory, Jones identified two types of group (human) rights: collective and corporate group rights.

Jones observed that in the collective conceptualisation of group (human) rights, 'moral standing' remains with the individuals within the group.[152] Nonetheless, for a right to be a group right instead of an individual right, an

---

the greater benefit of others; they impose limits on the sacrifices that can be demanded from them as a contribution to the general good. Though we may reasonably be required to accept some losses and frustrations in social life along the lines that the utilitarians suggest, rights are designed to pick out those interests of ours that are not to be traded off against the interests of others in this way'. Jeremy Waldron, 'Rights in Conflict' (1989) 99(3) *Ethics* 503, 508.

148 Philip Alston, 'A Third Generation of Solidarity Rights: Progressive Development or Obfuscation of International Human Rights Law?' (1982) 29(3) *Netherlands International Law Review* 307, 308.

149 Ronald Dworkin, *Taking Rights Seriously* (Bloomsbury Academics, 2013) 4.

150 *ICCPR* (n 108) art 22. The Human Rights Committee stated that 'the Committee observes that the right to freedom of association relates not only to the right to form an association, but also guarantees the right of such an association freely to carry out its statutory activities. The protection afforded by article 22 extends to all activities of an association', *Kungurov* v. *Uzbekistan*, CCPR/C/102/D/1478/2006, 20 July 2011 [8.2]. The Human Rights Committee also stated that article 22 'guarantees the right of such an association freely to carry out its statutory activities. The protection afforded by article 22 extends to all activities of an association', *Korneenko et al.* v. *Belarus*, CCPR/C/88/D/1274/2004 31 October 2006 [7.2].

151 Peter Jones, 'Human Rights, Group Rights, and Peoples' Rights' (1999) 21(1) *Human Rights Quarterly* 82–83.

152 Ibid., 85.

individual may not hold this right apart from the group.[153] Therefore, collective rights have a threshold requirement; no single rights-holder meets the threshold for a right to be created.[154] In describing the collective conceptualisation of group (human) rights, Jones draws heavily on Joseph Raz's interest theory of rights. According to Raz's conceptualisation of rights, an individual interest may not meet the threshold to create a duty.[155] Nonetheless, Jones explains that 'the joint interest of a number of individuals [may provide] . . . sufficient justification for imposing duties', creating a collective group (human) right.[156]

In contrast, Jones' corporate conceptualisation of group (human) rights requires a group to pre-exist the right in order to engage a right.[157] Jones explained that a corporate conceptualisation of group (human) rights 'ascribes moral standing to the group';[158] the right holder is the group. Jones argued that the label 'corporate' 'does not imply that only groups that possess all of the features that we normally associate with legal corporations can possess "corporate rights" '.[159] Instead, 'corporate rights, like the rights of a legal corporation, are held by a single corporate entity rather than, as in the case of collective rights, jointly by a set of separately identifiable individuals'.[160] The following explores *CRPD* article 31's contribution to group (human) rights doctrine.

5.3.2 A New Group (Human) Right?

Preventing and responding to harm caused or exacerbated by de-identified, aggregated data is an emerging issue.[161] Therefore, this section uses Alston's framework for 'formulating and implementing' new human rights or 'new formulations of existing rights'.[162] The first step in the framework carefully considers the problem and need that the new right addresses. The second step translates these to specific legal norms.[163] The last step in Alston's framework is elaborating on means to promote the realisation of these newly identified rights.

a) The Problem and the Need

CRPD article 31 identifies information as an enabler for implementing the treaty. This chapter has argued that data about the bodies and lives of people

153 Ibid., 85.
154 Ibid., 84.
155 Ibid., 83–84 citing Joseph Raz, *The Morality of Freedom* (1986).
156 Ibid., 83.
157 Ibid., 87–88.
158 Ibid., 86.
159 Ibid., 87.
160 Ibid., 87.
161 See, for example, Linnet Taylor, Luciano Floridi and Bart van der Sloot (eds), *Group Privacy: New Challenges of Data Technologies* (Springer International Publishing, 2017).
162 Alston (n 148) 308.
163 Alston (n 148) 315–316.

with disability should be minimised and produced with caution. Nonetheless, the CRPD Committee and other advocacy groups maintain that data on certain variables about people and their lives are necessary to measure disparity in access to resources and rights attainment.[164] Following this reasoning, relevant information is required to target effective measures for people who experience diverse barriers. Therefore, it may be argued that the lack of information about specific groups prevents the effective implementation of the treaty. According to the CRPD Committee and others, there is a need to produce more information about these groups.

Visibility in datasets can be a powerful political tool to highlight disparity and demand action,[165] but it can also be problematic for some groups.[166] While individual protections exist to ameliorate some of the harm that may be exacerbated by data production and processing, this may not be sufficient. During the *CRPD* drafting, there was significant advocacy for greater visibility of people with disability and the barriers they face through the production and processing of data.[167] This advocacy was not about individual but group visibility. This visibility was not simply about representing people with disability as a homogenous group but about better understanding the diverse lives of people with disability.[168] However, some groups do not want greater visibility due to the negative consequences they may face.[169]

Groups need to be able to control their visibility in datasets to manage risks associated with aggregated data. In this scenario, groups are those with a shared identity as described by the data category or indicator that would make them 'visible' in a dataset, such as a type of impairment or migration status. While individuals have the right not to identify,[170] currently, a group has no recognised right to control its visibility in datasets. Though responding to this need, there is some support in policy documents for groups to 'self-define', such as in *A Human Rights-Based Approach to Data: Leaving No One Behind in the 2030*

164 See earlier n 137.

165 See generally Caroline Criado Perez, *Invisible Women: Exposing Data Bias in a World Designed for Men* (Vintage Books, a Division of Penguin Random House, 2019).

166 See later Section 6.4.

167 See earlier Section 4.3.

168 See earlier Section 4.3.1.

169 Jeff Crisp observes that '[n]eedless to say, authoritarian states that have produced large refugee and displaced populations – Myanmar, Sudan and Syria, for example – could make use of such data to identify individuals and groups whose loyalty is considered suspect, targeting them for surveillance, discrimination or punitive action'. Jeff Crisp, 'Beware the Notion That Better Data Lead to Better Outcomes for Refugees and Migrants', *Chatham House* (Web Page, 9 March 2018) <https://www.chathamhouse.org/2018/03/beware-notion-better-data-lead-better-outcomes-refugees-and-migrants>. Christopher Kuner and Marelli Massimo similarly explain that 'in armed conflicts and other situations of violence, many threats are collective rather than individual'. Christopher Kuner and Massimo Marelli (eds), *Handbook on Data Protection in Humanitarian Action* (International Committee of the Red Cross, 2nd ed, 2020) 24. Identification of disability in data may exacerbate risk to some communities, as certain impairments may be characteristic of combat injuries or torture.

170 See earlier Section 5.1.3(b) and later Section 7.3.

Agenda for Sustainable Development, explored further in 7.4.2.[171] The following subsection describes the important doctrinal contribution made by *CRPD* article 31, which addresses the need for groups to control their visibility in datasets.

b) *The Legal Norm to Control Group Visibility in Datasets: A Group Right (Not) to Be Counted*

Alston's second step in elaborating new human rights is the 'translation of needs into specific legal norms through recognition by the relevant legal forum'.[172] The following demonstrates that the legal norms for a group (human) right (not) to be counted exist in the *CRPD* text. It is a subsidiary right of article 4(3), which requires 'State Parties . . . closely consult with . . . persons with disabilities . . . through their representative organizations'.[173]

Consultation, like information production, is a procedural obligation to assist in realising substantive rights in the convention. Importantly, the convention names 'representative organisations' as the vehicle for consultation, giving them special status. A status that was further recognised and elaborated in *General Comment No 7 (2018) on the Participation of Persons with Disabilities, Including Children with Disabilities, through their Representative Organizations, in the Implementation and Monitoring of the Convention* ('*General Comment No 7*').[174]

It may be argued that the 'representative organizations' identified by the *CRPD*, known as 'organizations of persons with disabilities'[175] or DPOs, have *a right to be consulted*. The text of article 4(3) stipulates that individuals with disability cannot realise this right apart from the group. The right is accessed 'through their representative organisation'.[176] DPOs as described in article 4(3) appear to satisfy the necessary criteria for a collective group (human) right, as a certain proportion of DPO members need to have disability in order to engage the state obligation.[177] The state obligation is engaged when a number of people with the same right claim it from the state, fulfilling the collective conceptualisation of a group (human) right.[178]

171 Office of the High Commissioner for Human Rights (OHCHR), *A Human Rights-Based Approach to Data: Leaving No One Behind in the 2030 Agenda for Sustainable Development* (2018) 11 <https://www.ohchr.org/Documents/Issues/HRIndicators/GuidanceNoteonApproachtoData.pdf>.

172 Alston (n 148) 316.

173 *CRPD* (n 1) art 4(3).

174 CRPD Committee, *General Comment 7 Participation* (n 71).

175 CRPD Committee, *General Comment 7 Participation* (n 71) [10].

176 *CRPD* (n 1) art 4(3).

177 'A clear majority of their membership should be recruited among persons with disabilities themselves'. CRPD Committee, *General Comment 7 Participation* (n 71) [11].

178 There may be certain conditions where a DPO meets the corporate conceptualisation of group (human) rights, ie, where the group term of reference contains the necessary requirements contained in the CRPD Committee's *General Comment 7*. See CRPD Committee, *General Comment 7 Participation* (n 71).

The provisions in article 4(3) provide an umbrella group (human) right. A subsidiary group (human) right may be read into the text of article 31(2) the state obligation to disaggregate information 'as appropriate'.[179] Determining appropriate disaggregation requires closely consulting with the rights holders, DPOs. It may be argued that DPOs have a right to be consulted on how data is disaggregated under article 31.

Article 4(3) only obligates states to 'closely consult with and actively involve' DPOs; it does not provide control. Nonetheless, states are obligated to accept the paradigm change from the medical model to the *CRPD* model of disability.[180] The *CRPD* requires states to rethink how information is produced and processed. The medical model was characterised by experts labelling people with disability. The *CRPD* gives people with disability to control over how they are labelled and, therefore, the data variables produced and processed about them.

The normative nature of the group (human) right (not) to be counted in *CRPD* article 31(2) includes the following:

- The DPO formation precedes the state obligation.[181]
- The right applies only to information produced and processed under the authority of article 31.
- When information is about people with disability and their lives, people with disability and other intersectional identities represented by a DPO decide whether the data variable that identifies their group should be produced and processed.
- Groups of people with disability cannot be disadvantaged if they choose not to be visible in datasets.[182]

c) *Promotion of the Realisation of the Legal Norm*

The final step in Alston's formulation and implementation of new human rights is promoting the realisation of the legal norm.[183] The CRPD Committee has provided significant guidance in its *General Comment No 7*.[184] Nonetheless, within the democratic mechanism of DPOs, greater clarity is needed about who may speak for the diverse groups represented within DPOs and how priorities are negotiated. Within groups, there are often politics and diversity of

179 *CRPD* (n 1) art 31(2).
180 See earlier Sections 5.1.1 and 5.1.2.
181 This is true for both the corporate and collective conceptualisation of group (human) rights.
182 As discussed throughout this chapter, there are other ways to identify barriers to realising human rights and to measure progress.
183 Alston (n 148) 316.
184 CRPD Committee, *General Comment 7 Participation* (n 71).

opinions. Working through these issues is not unique to this group (human) right and deserves further attention.

It is important to note that marginalised groups, who are often less active in DPOs, may be disadvantaged in accessing information production and processing discussions, including whether certain data variables are produced and processed that may impact their visibility. Therefore, these marginalised groups are forgotten, or data variables are included without their consent. The *CRPD*'s granting of rights to DPOs emphasises the state's vital role in building the capacity of diverse DPOs to be active partners in implementing the treaty.[185]

5.4 Conclusion

CRPD article 31 codifies information's enabling function for implementing the treaty. It does not require that information about the bodies or lives of people with disability be produced and processed. In the production and processing of information, dignity, autonomy and privacy must be ensured and protected. Information is to be used to assess the implementation of states' obligations and to identify and address barriers to people with disability realising rights. The information produced needs to be accessible to people with disability in an aggregated and de-identified form.

The need to remediate disparity experienced by people with disability provides the urgency to act. However, many of the issues preventing rights realisations are already known. States should be investing in facilitating the participation of people with disability from diverse DPOs in partnering in the implementation of the treaty, not in 'systematic' data surveillance that intrudes into the lives of people with disability.[186] It is perplexing that the CRPD Committee routinely recommends producing information about the bodies and lives of people with disability. Given the authority of the CRPD Committee's interpretive advice, urgent and ongoing attention is required to understand the impact of surveillance on people with disability.

Nonetheless, greater control may be restored to people with disability by recognising the group (human) right (not) to be counted. The *CRPD* has codified a group right for DPOs to be closely consulted and actively involved

185 CRPD Committee, *General Comment 7 Participation* (n 71) [60], [94(b)(j)].

186 The CRPD Committee commonly uses a derivative of the word 'systematic' in its advice about the implementation of the obligations in art 31. Eg, 'The Committee also recommends that the State party *systematically* collect, analyse and disseminate data on persons with disabilities, disaggregated by sex, age, ethnicity, type of impairment, socioeconomic status, employment and place of residence, as well as on the barriers that persons with disabilities face in society, relying on the methodology of the Washington Group Short Set of Questions on Disability'. Committee on the Rights of Persons with Disabilities, *Concluding Observations on the Initial Report of Greece*, UN Doc CRPD/C/GRC/CO/1 (29 October 2019) [47] (emphasis added).

in implementing the *CRPD.*[187] This chapter sought to contribute modestly to the debate about group rights in human rights law by proposing that a subsidiary group right exists in article 31. This group (human) right responds to the harm that may occur when data are de-identified and aggregated according to variables that reflect people's identities. Groups with a shared identity may protect themselves by ensuring invisibility in datasets.[188] Conversely, groups may be interested in having greater visibility in datasets to assist in advocacy for policy reform.

The article 31 text allows for variation in interpretation depending on the setting, including refugee contexts. The next part of the monograph explores how refugee contexts inform the interpretation of article 31 and the implications of the article for the realisation of rights for people with disability in these contexts.

187 *CRPD* (n 1) art 4(3).
188 See later Section 7.4.2.

Part III

CRPD Article 31 in Refugee Contexts

> Data protection works for some communities but does not work for others.
> Stakeholder Advisory Group meeting minutes, 18 June 2021

DOI: 10.4324/9781003506140-8

6 People With Disability in Refugee Contexts as Rights-Holders and Data Subjects

The focus on disability rights during the *Convention on the Rights of Persons with Disabilities*' ('*CRPD*') drafting created greater visibility of the gaps that needed addressing. This greater scrutiny of the situation of people with disability was also true in refugee contexts. In 2008, the United Nations High Commissioner for Refugees, António Guterres, observed, '[t]oo often invisible, too often forgotten and too often overlooked, refugees with disabilities are among the most isolated, socially excluded and marginalized of all displaced populations'.[1]

This part of the monograph, Part III, utilises the theory and methods introduced in Part I and builds on the doctrinal analysis introduced in Part II to consider the implications of article 31 of the *CRPD* in refugee contexts and explores methods to prevent and mitigate harm from data.[2] In doing so, it explores the second and third research questions: How do refugee contextual considerations inform the interpretation of the state obligations and (potential) group right in *CRPD* article 31? And does the international human rights framework adequately balance the potential benefits of information production and processing with the potential harms?[3]

This chapter, the first of two in this part, explains that people with disability in refugee contexts experience multiple and aggravated discrimination. Since the *CRPD* drafting, there has been greater acknowledgement and efforts to remedy their marginalisation. Statistics and data collection were included in the *CRPD* as tools to assist in remediating disparity and have been adopted in refugee contexts to try and develop a better understanding of the situation of people with disability in these contexts. However, this chapter argues that the greater visibility created by data production and processing may

1 Women's Refugee Commission, *Disabilities Among Refugees and Conflict-Affected Populations* (Report, June 2008) 1.

2 *Convention on the Rights of Persons with Disabilities*, opened for signature 24 January 2007, 2515 UNTS 3 (entered into force 3 May 2008) ('*CRPD*') art 31. See earlier Prologue for further background about the motivation for this research and selection of this population group. See also Section 1.2, which describes refugee contexts.

3 See earlier Section 1.3.2 for all the research questions.

DOI: 10.4324/9781003506140-9

counterintuitively create conditions that enable subjugation. Indeed, individuals may use anonymity strategically to ensure they realise their human rights.

These arguments are executed through this chapter's four substantive sections. Section 6.1 highlights the multiple and aggravated discrimination experienced by people who are refugees with disability. Section 6.2 explores the legal and institutional contexts regulating the lives of people who are refugees with disability, in which disability rights have become more prominent since the *CRPD*. Section 6.3 describes how the operationalisation of article 31 obligations has omitted an important safeguard that requires data only to be produced and processed if 'appropriate'. Section 6.4 introduces a conceptual framework that considers how the locus of power influences when visibility may be useful in human rights attainment.

6.1 Multiple and Aggravated Discrimination: The Situation of People Who Are Refugees With Disability

As described throughout this monograph, addressing multiple and aggravated discrimination was a key concern of the drafters of the *CRPD*.[4] This section examines the conditions faced by people who are refugees with disability that create significant barriers to human rights attainment. It demonstrates how disability and refugee experience can work together to cause multiple and aggravated forms of discrimination.

Refugee contexts are present in almost every jurisdiction in the world.[5] This monograph employs the term 'people who are refugees' broadly to cover a range of experiences and legal statuses, including the 1951 *Convention Relating to the Status of Refugees* and its associated 1967 protocol's ('*Refugee Convention*') definition of a refugee,[6] people seeking asylum who are waiting for their claims to be assessed and people in refugee-like situations.[7] Where there is a need to differentiate these statuses, this is explained.

Disability may pre-exist or may be caused by or be exacerbated by the circumstances that pre-empt the search for protection, the refugee flight or the asylum location. Disability may be caused by the persecution and violence

4 See earlier Sections 1.1.2, 4.3.1 and 5.1.5.

5 See earlier Section 1.2.

6 See earlier Chapter 1 n 50 for the definition and n 49 for an explanation of the relationship between the convention and the protocol. Convention Relating to the Status of Refugees, opened for signature 28 July 1951, 189 UNTS 150 (entered into force 22 April 1954) ('Refugee Convention') art 1(A)(2), as modified by the Protocol Relating to the Status of Refugees, opened for signature 31 January 1967, 606 UNTS 267 (entered into force 4 October 1967) art 1(2).

7 'People in refugee-like situation refers to a category which is descriptive in nature and includes groups of people who are outside their country or territory of origin and who face protection risks similar to those of refugees, but for whom refugee status has, for practical or other reasons, not been ascertained'. 'Who Is Included in UNHCR Statistics?', UNHCR Refugee Data Finder (Web Page, 2023) <https://www.unhcr.org/refugee-statistics/methodology/definition/>.

people are escaping, such as torture or war.[8] Disability may be exacerbated because support mechanisms that enable rights attainment are ruptured due to war, disappearances of family members or denial of access to services.[9] As explained elsewhere in this monograph, the *CRPD* model of disability, derived from the social model, recognises disability as an interaction between a person's impairment and the environment.[10] As part of the refugee experience, impairments may or may not change, but the environment will certainly change; therefore, the degree of disability that people experience will undoubtedly be impacted throughout the refugee experience.[11] Consequently, refugee contexts are important sites to consider the human rights attainment of people with disability.[12]

People who are refugees with disability may be part of a large exodus from a region due to systematic violence or be individuals fleeing due to targeted persecution.[13] They may travel across land, sea or sky by various modes of transport.[14] People often report having little time to plan their escape and leave with few belongings.[15] For people with disability, this may include leaving without aids and equipment necessary for facilitating independence.[16] On

8 'Among persons who reported illness/disease, injury and malnutrition as causes of their disabilities, 24.7% considered the causes were related to the Syrian conflict'. Humanity & Inclusion and iMMAP, *Removing Barriers: The Path towards Inclusive Access: Disability Assessment among Syrian Refugees in Jordan and Lebanon: Jordan Report* (Report, July 2018) 1. For a description of the prevalence, types and impact of torture on people who are refugees see Ida Kaplan, *Rebuilding Shattered Lives: Integrated Trauma Recovery for People of Refugee Background* (Victorian Foundation for Survivors of Torture, 2nd ed, 2020) 54–63.

9 'Moreover, traditional community coping mechanisms, including extended families, neighbors and other caregivers, often break down during displacement. The loss of caregivers can leave persons with disabilities extremely vulnerable and exposed to protection risks'. Women's Refugee Commission (n 1) 2.

10 See earlier Section 1.1.1.

11 According to the *CRPD*, disability is a product of the interaction between an impairment and the environment. See *CRPD* (n 2) Preamble para e, art 1.

12 See earlier Section 1.2.2 for more about refugee contexts as sites to consider disability rights.

13 In 2022, almost 200,000 people a day left the Ukraine in search of protection in the early days of the war. United Nations High Commissioner for Refugees (UNHCR), *Mid-Year Trends 2022* (Report, 2022) 6. Cf the approximately 80 women from Saudi Arabia who have sought asylum in Australia over a number of years who, according to this article, were fleeing 'Saudi Arabia's oppressive male guardianship laws'. 'Australian Border Force Accused of Targeting Women Suspected of Fleeing Saudi Arabia', *ABC News* (online, 3 February 2019) <https://www.abc.net.au/news/2019-02-04/border-force-accused-of-targeting-saudi-women-traveling-alone/10768036>.

14 The citations earlier, n 13, also demonstrate different modes of leaving the country and seeking asylum by land border or air travel. UNHCR, *Mid-Year Trends 2022* (n 13) 6; 'Australian Border Force Accused of Targeting Women Suspected of Fleeing Saudi Arabia' (n 13).

15 Kaplan (n 8) 29.

16 See generally Victorian Refugee Health Network, *Service Responses for People with Disabilities from Refugee Backgrounds in Northern Melbourne* (Victorian Foundation for Survivors of Torture, 2018).

arrival in a country of asylum, there is often a phase of acute need.[17] Host countries are often overwhelmed, and vital services may be interrupted, delayed or unavailable.[18] Nonetheless, most people who are refugees, including those with disability, live in protracted refugee contexts.[19] Over time, given periods of stability and safety, barriers to access and inclusion may be identified and remediated.

Providing accessible services in refugee contexts presents logistical challenges. These challenges differ depending on whether someone lives in an urban or refugee camp setting. Typically, in an urban context, people who are refugees are dispersed throughout cities and are challenging to identify. This invisibility may be compounded for people with disability who may be confined to their homes for various reasons, such as inaccessible environments or families who believe their relative should remain at home for their safety or because of concerns regarding stigma.[20] Undertaking population needs assessments through household censuses or surveys is often more straightforward in refugee camp contexts. Likewise, services may be more targeted and accessible because camps have a 'captive audience'. However, within these contexts, camp populations often must deal with all the challenges of rural, low-infrastructure environments, often characterised by rugged inaccessible pathways that people with disability need to navigate to secure life-sustaining resources such as food rations.

In addition to the multiple and aggravated discrimination caused by disability and refugee experiences, organisations working with people who are refugees with disability have noted that other intersectional identities, such as gender, age, sexuality and type of disability, impact people's ability to access their rights.[21] For example, the 2006 Executive Committee of the High Commissioner's Programme ('ExCom') *Conclusion on Women and Girls at Risk* identified that women and girls with disability who have been forcibly

17 See, eg, United Nations High Commissioner for Refugees (UNHCR) and European Disability Forum, *Ensuring the Protection of Persons with Disabilities Fleeing From Ukraine* (Report, 2022).

18 Ibid.

19 Protracted situations are defined by UNHCR as 'where more than 25,000 refugees from the same country of origin have been in exile in a given low- or middle-income host country for at least five consecutive years' UNHCR, *Global Trends: Forced Displacement in 2023* (Report, 2024) 21.

20 The Stakeholder Advisory Group spoke about the stigma associated with disability within their communities and how people with disability were hidden away in family homes and not taken into the community. Stakeholder Advisory Group meeting minutes, 20 August 2021. An ExCom report also noted that 'adults and children with disabilities often face ostracism or marginalization within their immediate families and communities, which exacerbate their protection problems . . . Some families and communities see "disability" as a punishment, and parents may hide children with disabilities at home, or even tie them up'. Executive Committee of the High Commissioner's Programme, *The Protection of Older Persons and Persons with Disabilities*, UN Doc EC/58/SC/CRP.14 (6 June 2007) [12].

21 See, eg, Women's Refugee Commission (n 1).

displaced might be at greater risk due to interruptions in their support services.[22] This growing awareness of the diversity and complexity of the needs of displaced populations has been used as a rationale to undertake more detailed needs assessments and produce more data about people who experience multiple and aggravated forms of discrimination.[23]

6.2 Refugee Protection and the Human Rights of People With Disability

People who are refugees with disability have been marginalised in many realms of life, including in international law. The *Refugee Convention* does not reference disability, including in its non-discrimination provisions in article 3.[24] Likewise, the 2006 *CRPD* did not mention refugee contexts in its Preamble provisions about multiple discrimination or in article 11 on 'Situations of Risk and Humanitarian Emergencies'.[25] Despite the silence of these treaties, recent jurisprudence, policy and practice guidelines provide greater clarity about the rights of people who are refugees with disability under international law.

This section demonstrates the increased visibility of the rights of people who are refugees with disability in international law. This explanation is progressed through four subsections. The first subsection explains the lack of explicit provisions for people with disability in the *Refugee Convention.* The second subsection describes the drafting of the *CRPD* and the missed opportunity to clarify the rights of people who are refugees with disability. The third subsection examines the mandate given to the Office of the United Nations High Commissioner for Refugees ('UNHCR') to reform practices to be more disability inclusive. The last subsections demonstrate the explicit recognition of disability rights in refugee protection through the *Global Compact on Refugees.*[26]

6.2.1 The Refugee Convention and Disability Human Rights

Contemporary refugee protection has its legal foundation in the septuagenarian *Refugee Convention.*[27] Fewer states are party to the *Refugee Convention* than the *CRPD*, with some criticising the treaty's Europe-centric drafting.[28] Despite this, all states are bound by customary law prohibiting the return of

22 Executive Committee of the High Commissioner's Programme, *Conclusion on Women and Girls at Risk*, UN Doc A/AC.96/1035 (10 October 2006) [17(f)].

23 See later Section 6.3.

24 *Refugee Convention* (n 6) art 3.

25 *CRPD* (n 2) Preamble para p, art 11.

26 *Report of the United Nations High Commissioner for Refugees: Part II Global Compact on Refugees*, UN Doc A/73/12 (Part II) (13 September 2018, adopted 2 August 2018).

27 *Refugee Convention* (n 6).

28 See generally Maja Janmyr, 'Non-Signatory States and the International Refugee Regime' (2021) 67 *Forced Migration Review* 39.

people to states where they may be harmed, known as *non-refoulement*.[29] Two other instruments discussed later in this chapter are important to operationalising the protection regime and have had some effect in progressing the rights of refugees more broadly: the *Statute of the Office of the United Nations High Commissioner for Refugees* ('*UNHCR Statute*')[30] and the *Global Compact on Refugees*.[31]

Drafted in the aftermath of World War II, a considerable amount of jurisprudence, case law and academic work focuses on the *Refugee Convention*'s article 1A(2), which establishes the definition of a refugee.[32] Unlike the *CRPD*, assessing whether a person meets the definition of refugee is vital in determining whether a state owes them rights within the convention.[33] Predating the *International Covenant on Civil and Political Rights* and the *International Covenant on Economic, Social and Cultural Rights*,[34] the *Refugee Convention* grants civil, political and socio-economic rights to people who meet the definition of a refugee. While all human rights law applies to people who are refugees, the *Refugee Convention* allows for some rights to 'accrue as a function of the nature and duration of the attachment to the asylum state'.[35] For example, the right to work is a cumulative right gained after 'three years' residence in that country'.[36] Nonetheless, refugee law scholar James Hathaway observed that 'all refugees benefit from a number of core rights',[37] some of which are specific to people who have been determined to be refugees, such as the right to travel documents.[38]

The Preamble of the *Refugee Convention* references the *Universal Declaration of Human Rights* and affirms that 'human beings shall enjoy fundamental

29 See earlier Chapter 1 n 51.

30 *Statute of the Office of the United Nations High Commissioner for Refugees*, UNGA Res 428(V), UN Doc A/RES/428(V) (adopted 14 December 1950). For further discussion about the work of the UNHCR, see Section 6.2.3.

31 *Report of the United Nations High Commissioner for Refugees: Part II Global Compact on Refugees* (n 26).

32 See earlier Chapter 1 n 50 for the definition. For a comprehensive overview of the jurisprudence in this area, see James C Hathaway and Michelle Foster, *The Law of Refugee Status* (Cambridge University Press, 2nd ed, 2014). See also Motz who has reviewed the definition of refugee with a disability lens. Stephanie Anna Motz, *The Refugee Status of Persons with Disabilities* (Brill|Nijhoff, 2020).

33 This is because all the rights in the *CRPD* are derived from the 'bill of rights' and are owed to all people. See earlier Section 1.1.

34 *International Covenant on Civil and Political Rights*, opened for signature 16 December 1966, 999 UNTS 171 (entered into force 23 March 1976); *International Covenant on Economic, Social and Cultural Rights*, opened for signature 16 December 1966, 993 UNTS 3 (entered into force 3 January 1976).

35 James C Hathaway, *The Rights of Refugees Under International Law* (Cambridge University Press, 2nd ed, 2021) 174.

36 *Refugee Convention* (n 6) art 17(2)(a).

37 Hathaway (n 35) 174.

38 *Refugee Convention* (n 6) art 28.

rights and freedoms without discrimination'.[39] This reference signalled the drafters' intention for the *Refugee Convention* to be interpreted in light of the evolving human rights framework,[40] which since 2008 has included the *CRPD*.[41] Further, like the *CRPD*, the *Refugee Convention* is underpinned by the principle of non-discrimination. Article 3 of the *Refugee Convention* requires states to apply the convention 'without discrimination as to race, religion or country of origin'.[42] The *CRPD* reinforces this notion and ensures that the *Refugee Convention* is applied without discrimination according to disability.[43] The *CRPD* has created opportunities for a 'disability-sensitive interpretation of the refugee definition' and a disability-sensitive interpretation of the rights within the *Refugee Convention*.[44]

Nonetheless, the *CRPD* was a missed opportunity to enumerate the specific human rights violations experienced by people who are refugees with disability and to clarify state obligations to this population. The following briefly revisits how the rights of refugees with disability were discussed while drafting the *CRPD*.

6.2.2 *The* CRPD*'s Elaboration of Rights for People Who Are Refugees With Disability*

During the drafting of the *CRPD*, the elaboration of rights for people who are refugees with disability was raised in multiple forums by various parties.[45] The following highlights two missed opportunities. The *CRPD* drafters missed an opportunity to include the situations of people who are refugees with disability in the Preamble text about multiple discrimination.[46] Further, the drafters missed an opportunity to enumerate specific ways people with disability experience rights violations in refugee contexts and to reiterate the applicability of the *Refugee Convention* in *CRPD* article 11, 'Situations of risk and humanitarian emergencies'.[47]

Despite vocal advocacy for the inclusion of refugee rights in the *CRPD*, records of the drafting negotiations suggest that this population group and their corresponding rights were seen as too controversial for inclusion in the

39 *Refugee Convention* (n 6) art 28 Preamble.

40 For a comprehensive discussion about refugee law's place in the human rights framework, see Hathaway (n 35); Michelle Foster, *International Refugee Law and Socio-Economic Rights: Refuge From Deprivation* (Cambridge University Press, 2007).

41 The *CRPD* entered into force in 2008.

42 *Refugee Convention* (n 6) art 3.

43 *CRPD* (n 2) art 5.

44 See especially Motz (n 32). Mary Crock and colleagues have undertaken extensive fieldwork examining how people who are refugees with disability are faring in accessing their CRPD rights. Mary Crock et al, *The Legal Protection of Refugees with Disabilities: Forgotten and Invisible?* (Edward Elgar Publishing, 2017).

45 See earlier Section 4.1 for a description of the structure of the CRPD drafting negotiations.

46 *CRPD* (n 2) Preamble para p.

47 *CRPD* (n 2) Preamble art 11.

draft treaty.[48] Delegations who sought to have the rights of people who are refugees explicitly enumerated in the convention may have been motivated by the provisions made in the *Convention on the Rights of the Child* article 22, which enumerates the specific rights of children who are refugees.[49] Nonetheless, the following summarises the failed attempt to explicitly affirm the human rights of people who are refugees with disability in the *CRPD*.

Early in the drafting, several civil society organisations raised the need to highlight the rights of people who are refugees with disability.[50] Later, following the drafting working group and presentation of the draft text that included no reference to refugee contexts, specific interventions were made calling for the inclusion of a reference to people who are refugees with disability in the Preamble text about multiple and aggravated discrimination.[51]

48 Rehabilitation International, 'Daily Summary of Discussion at the Seventh Session 17 January 2006', *UN Convention on the Human Rights of People with Disabilities Ad Hoc Committee – Daily Summaries* (United Nations Enable, 17 January 2006) <https://www.un.org/esa/socdev/enable/rights/ahc7sum17jan.htm> ('Ad Hoc Committee Daily Summary 17 January 2006').

49 *Convention on the Rights of the Child*, opened for Signature 20 November 1989, 1577 UNTS 3 (entered into force 2 September 1990) art 22.

50 Two DPOs' submissions sent prior to the Drafting Working Group called for the explicit acknowledgement of state obligations to people who are refugees. In its position paper, Disabled Peoples' International called for further elaboration of the rights of people with disability who are refugees or internally displaced. Disabled Peoples' International, *DPI Position Paper Regarding a New International Human Rights Convention for Disabled People* (25 February 2003) <https://www.un.org/esa/socdev/enable/rights/contrib-dpi.htm>. The World Blind Union in their Manifesto under '5.3 Right to Judicial Equality and Protection' called for: 'The right to the same legal protection for disabled children, old people, refugees, asylum seekers, and other displaced, nomadic, indigenous or transient people as that given to other citizens without disabilities'. World Blind Union, Manifesto for a United Nations Convention on the Rights of People with Disabilities: 'Equal Rights and Full Inclusion as World Citizens' (January 2004) <https://www.un.org/esa/socdev/enable/rights/wgcontrib-wbu.htm>. The draft text from the Drafting Working Group included a footnote that proposed that draft article 16, 'Children with Disabilities', should focus on the 'vulnerability' of certain children with disabilities, including 'refugee children with disabilities'. Working Group to the Ad Hoc Committee, *Report of the Working Group to the Ad Hoc Committee*, UN Doc A/AC.265/2004/WG.1 (27 January 2004). During the 3rd session of the Ad Hoc Committee, the delegation from Disabled Peoples' International said: 'Disabled Peoples' International expressed concern that the draft Convention does not deal with some essential issues for children with disabilities, such as abuse and exploitation, and suggested that the Committee consider groups at risk, including refugees and orphans with disabilities'. Landmine Survivors Network, 'Daily Summary of Discussion at the Third Session 28 May 2004', *UN Convention on the Human Rights of People with Disabilities Ad Hoc Committee – Daily Summaries* (United Nations Enable, 28 May 2004) <https://www.un.org/esa/socdev/enable/rights/ahc3sum28may.htm>.

51 During the 3rd session of the Ad Hoc Committee, in a discussion about the Preamble, 'Kenya proposed three new paragraphs. The first would read: "Recognizing that many persons with disabilities suffer double or multiple discrimination because of their status as children, women, refugees or internally displaced, older persons, people living in rural areas and people living in informal settlements"'. Landmine Survivors Network, 'Daily Summary of Discussion at the

However, inexplicably, the paragraph in the *CRPD*'s Preamble that enumerates situations that may cause multiple and aggravated discrimination does not include reference to people who are asylum seekers, refugees or internally displaced.[52] It is difficult to understand this omission, as the negotiation records do not include any open dissent about the possible inclusion of the situation of refugees or refugee law in the *CRPD*.

The innovative inclusion of article 11, 'Situations of risk and humanitarian emergencies', in the *CRPD* presented another opportunity to raise the profile of the rights of people with disability in refugee contexts.[53] Article 11 emerged from negotiations about the right to life and the right to freedom from violence and abuse. During these negotiations, the situations of people who are refugees with disability were raised by several state delegations,[54] culminating in a proposal about a separate article to 'deal with the human rights of [people with disability] . . . in emergency situations, such as *refugees*'.[55] This proposal for a separate article was accepted. Despite the situation

---

Third Session 4 June 2004', *UN Convention on the Human Rights of People with Disabilities Ad Hoc Committee – Daily Summaries* (United Nations Enable, 4 June 2004) <https://www.un.org/esa/socdev/enable/rights/ahc3sum4june.htm>. At the 6th session of the Ad Hoc Committee, the Landmine Survivor's Network on behalf of the International Disability Caucus ('IDC') made a statement that included the following: 'The IDC also supported the substance of Kenya's proposed Article 20 bis and suggests that its content also include a reference protecting PWD who are refugees and asylum seekers from discrimination, as stated in para 20(e)'. Rehabilitation International, 'Daily Summary of Discussion at the Sixth Session 08 August 2005', *UN Convention on the Human Rights of People with Disabilities Ad Hoc Committee – Daily Summaries* (United Nations Enable, 8 August 2005) <https://www.un.org/esa/socdev/enable/rights/ahc6sum8aug.htm>.

52 *CRPD* (n 2) Preamble para p.

53 *CRPD* (n 2) art 11.

54 During the 3rd session of the Ad Hoc Committee in a discussion on draft article 8 about the right to life, the delegation from Yemen recommended inserting into the text: 'States Parties shall, in accordance to their obligations in the context of international law and the Universal Declaration of human rights and international treaties and conventions for the protection of civilians from armed conflicts, take all necessary measures to guarantee the protection and care for persons with disabilities that are affected by armed conflicts or are refugees or are internally displaced persons'. In the same session, the delegation from Jordan proposed similar but slightly briefer text. This was the text from the delegation from Jordan: 'in particular in situations of armed conflicts and natural disasters, in accordance with international law, human rights, refugee, and international humanitarian law'. Landmine Survivors Network, 'Daily Summary of Discussion at the Third Session 25 May 2004', *UN Convention on the Human Rights of People with Disabilities Ad Hoc Committee – Daily Summaries* (United Nations Enable, 25 May 2004) <https://www.un.org/esa/socdev/enable/rights/ahc3sum25may.htm>.

55 This was a submission by the Australian delegation. Landmine Survivors Network, 'Daily Summary of Discussion at the Third Session 27 May 2004', *UN Convention on the Rights of People with Disabilities Ad Hoc Committee – Daily Summaries* (United Nations Enable, 27 May 2004) <https://www.un.org/esa/socdev/enable/rights/ahc3sum27may.htm>. These calls were repeated during the 4th session of the Ad Hoc Committee. The delegation from Chile supported the text proposed by the delegation from Jordan for draft article 8 on the

of people with disability in refugee contexts being present in many of the proposals that led to article 11, refugee contexts and law do not appear in the final text.

The nature of the controversy about referencing refugee status, contexts and law in the *CRPD* was not documented in the daily summaries of the negotiations.[56] Nonetheless, the chair summarised at the end of the 7th session discussion on the draft article about 'Situations of Risk':

> Some delegations expressed the need to include reference to civilian populations in armed conflict, which is also dealt with in the preamble, and to specify situations such as natural disasters and refugees. Other delegations voiced concern that listing specific situations of risk would be *a controversial process.*[57]

Another clue in the daily summaries that may explain the exclusion of refugee status, contexts and law in article 11 is the United States delegation's statement that 'these issues are already under consideration by other bodies including the Security Council . . . this convention is not the forum to discuss them'.[58] While the nature of the controversy and the reason for the exclusion of refugee status, contexts and law is unclear, the records demonstrate there was division about the level of detail that should be included in the new article.

---

right to life, and the delegation from Yemen also proposed that '[l]anguage relating to refugees, armed conflict and those under foreign occupation should be included in a separate article'. Disabled Peoples' International, Handicap International and International Service for Human Rights, 'Daily Summary of Discussion at the Fourth Session 25 August 2004', *UN Convention on the Human Rights of People with Disabilities Ad Hoc Committee – Daily Summary* (United Nations Enable, 25 August 2004) <https://www.un.org/esa/socdev/enable/rights/ahc4sum25aug.htm>. In a subsequent session about the draft article on the right to life, the Coordinator of the Ad Hoc Committee stated that a decision needed to be made about 'whether to include protections for [people with disability] . . . during times when populations are at high risk, including armed conflict, natural disaster, refugee situations or mass displacement'. Rehabilitation International, 'Daily Summary of Discussion at the Fifth Session 24 January 2005', *UN Convention on the Human Rights of People with Disabilities Ad Hoc Committee – Daily Summaries* (United Nations Enable, 24 January 2005) <https://www.un.org/esa/socdev/enable/rights/ahc5sum24jan.htm>. The next day, after hearing submissions from delegations, the Coordinator summarised that there was wide support 'to include special measures for [people with disabilities] . . . at particular risk such as those facing natural disasters, war, foreign occupation and other events'. Rehabilitation International, 'Daily Summary of Discussions – 25 January 2005', *UN Convention on the Human Rights of People with Disabilities Ad Hoc Committee – Daily Summaries* (United Nations Enable, 25 January 2005) <https://www.un.org/esa/socdev/enable/rights/ahc5sum25jan.htm>.

56 See earlier Section 4.1.2 for a description of the limitations of the daily summaries.

57 Rehabilitation International, 'Ad Hoc Committee Daily Summary 17 January 2006' (n 48).

58 Rehabilitation International, 'Ad Hoc Committee Daily Summary 17 January 2006' (n 48).

After the creation of the new brief draft article about situations of risk,[59] several delegations made proposals to include the situation of people who are refugees. For instance, during the 7th session, the delegation from Yemen referred to a proposal it had made in the 3rd session in discussions about the right to life, 'which provided language to protect PWD [people with disability] affected by armed conflict and who live under foreign occupation, as well as refugees and displaced persons'.[60] Some delegations supported the inclusion of this text, as they felt ' "situations of risk" was too generic'.[61] Others argued for brevity.[62]

The final text contains a compromise. Nonetheless, the bodies of law and situations of risk included are somewhat telling. *CRPD* article 11, 'Situations of Risk and Humanitarian Emergencies', states:

> States Parties shall take, in accordance with their obligations under international law, including ***international humanitarian law and international human rights law***, all necessary measures to ensure the protection and safety of persons with disabilities in situations of risk, including ***situations of armed conflict, humanitarian emergencies and the occurrence of natural disasters***.[63]

The *CRPD*'s Preamble covers situations of armed conflict and occupation. Also, it references the 'applicable human rights instruments [that] are indispensable for the full protection of persons with disabilities' in these situations.[64] Nonetheless, refugee law and refugee contexts are not referenced in the Preamble nor the substantive text of the *CRPD*.

The Committee on the Rights of Persons with Disabilities ('CRPD Committee'), legal scholars and practitioners now read the rights of people who are refugees with disability into the *CRPD*'s text. For instance, despite the omission of the *Refugee Convention* from article 11, legal scholar Stephanie Motz observed that, while 'Article 11 specifically lists two international law regimes . . . the list is only exemplary, not exhaustive . . . and other international

59 The Chairman's draft text read: 'Article 11: Situations of risk[.] States Parties recognize that in situations of risk to the general population persons with disabilities are especially vulnerable and shall take all feasible measures for their protection'. Don MacKay, *Letter Dated 7 October 2005 From the Chairman to All Members of the Committee*, UN Doc A/AC.265/2006/1 (14 October 2005).

60 Rehabilitation International, 'Ad Hoc Committee Daily Summary 17 January 2006' (n 48).

61 Submission from the Syrian Arab Republic. Other delegations that supported this submission included Qatar and the Libyan Arab Jamahiriya. Rehabilitation International, 'Ad Hoc Committee Daily Summary 17 January 2006' (n 48).

62 A number of delegations supported the Chairman's brevity, eg, Israel, New Zealand, Japan, Australia, the United States of America and Austria on behalf of the EU. Rehabilitation International, 'Ad Hoc Committee Daily Summary 17 January 2006' (n 48).

63 *CRPD* (n 2) art 11 (emphasis added).

64 *CRPD* (n 2) Preamble para u.

law rules may be drawn upon'.[65] Motz contends that article 11 raises awareness about disability rights among those working in 'risk and disaster situations',[66] and it recognises people with disability 'as holders of non-derogable human rights also in risk situations'.[67]

While the rights of people who are refugees with disability are not explicitly enumerated in the *CRPD*, the convention has had a significant impact on refugee protection, including on the policies and operations of the UNHCR. A discussion of the UNHCR's growing awareness of disability human rights and an examination of its development of disability-inclusive practice follows.

6.2.3 The UNHCR's Response to the CRPD

Following World War II, a global refugee agency was established as a subsidiary organ of the United Nations General Assembly,[68] the Office of the United Nations High Commissioner for Refugees ('UNHCR'). The *UNHCR Statute* establishes and outlines the multilateral, intergovernmental institution's roles and responsibilities.[69] While the *Refugee Convention* enumerates state obligations, the *UNHCR Statute* 'outlines . . . tasks that supplement those of states'.[70] The mandate described in the *UNHCR Statute* has a greater reach than the *Refugee Convention*.[71] This broader mandate enables the UNHCR to operate in states not party to the *Refugee Convention* and, before 1967, in jurisdictions where the convention did not apply.[72]

Further, the *UNHCR Statute* enables some flexibility as directed by the General Assembly within the limits of the office's resources.[73] The flexibility of the UNHCR's mandate has enabled it to grow to be more extensive than the *Refugee Convention*. International refugee law scholar Marjoleine Zieck observed that, while the two mandates were initially reasonably aligned, they

65 Stephanie Motz, 'Article 11: Situations of Risk and Humanitarian Emergencies' in Ilias Bantekas et al (eds), *The UN Convention on the Rights of Persons with Disabilities: A Commentary* (Oxford University Press, 2018) 314, 320.

66 Ibid., 314.

67 Ibid., 315.

68 *Charter of the United Nations Art 22*; *Refugees and Stateless Persons*, UNGA Res 319 (IV), UN Doc A/RES/319 (adopted 3 December 1949).

69 *Statute of the Office of the United Nations High Commissioner for Refugees* (n 30).

70 Marjoleine Zieck, *UNHCR's Parallel Universe: Marking the Contours of a Problem* (Amsterdam University Press, 2010) 7.

71 *Statute of the Office of the United Nations High Commissioner for Refugees* (n 30) paras 6–7; *Refugee Convention* (n 6) art 1.

72 The General Assembly requested in its 1962 resolution that 'the United Nations High Commissioner for Refugees to continue to use his good offices, in agreement with the Governments of the countries concerned, to provide assistance to the Chinese refugees in Hong Kong'. *The Problem of Chinese Refugees in Hong Kong*, UNGA Res 1784 (XVII), UN Doc A/RES1784 (adopted 7 December 1962) para 3.

73 *Statute of the Office of the United Nations High Commissioner for Refugees* (n 30) para 9.

are now 'worlds apart'.[74] The UNHCR *Global Trends: Forced Displacement in 2023* report identified 122.6 million people that the UNHCR 'protects and/or assists', including the following:

> those who have been forcibly displaced (refugees, asylum-seekers, internally displaced people and other people in need of international protection); those who have returned home within the previous year; those who are stateless (most of whom are not forcibly displaced); and other groups to whom UNHCR has extended its protection or provided assistance on a humanitarian basis.[75]

This quote illustrates Zieck's point that the UNHCR's work goes well beyond assisting those owed protection under the *Refugee Convention.*

The *UNHCR Statute* stipulates that the UNHCR provides international protection and seeks permanent solutions for people under its mandate.[76] The permanent solutions include 'voluntary repatriation', 'assimilation within new national communities' and resettlement.[77] The effective fulfilment of this mandate 'depend[s] upon the co-operation of States with the High Commissioner'.[78] The *UNHCR Statute* requires the High Commissioner to report annually to the United Nations General Assembly through the Economic and Social Council.[79] The annual reporting plays a vital role in raising funds, as the UNHCR relies on voluntary contributions from states and other donors to finance its activities.[80]

Entrusted with overseeing the UNHCR's activities and budgets, the ExCom is comprised of states which are party and not party to the *Refugee Convention.*[81]

74 Zieck (n 70) 9.
75 People who are refugees from Palestine are under the United Nations Relief and Works Agency for Palestine Refugees in the Near East's (UNRWA) mandate. Ibid., 4. See also UNHCR, *Note on the Mandate of the High Commissioner for Refugees and His Office* (2013).
76 *Statute of the Office of the United Nations High Commissioner for Refugees* (n 30) para 1.
77 Repatriation and local integration are described in para 1 of the *UNHCR Statute.* Resettlement is less explicit but mentioned in para 8(e) with regard to transferring of assets and in para 9 in reference to potential additional activities. *Statute of the Office of the United Nations High Commissioner for Refugees* (n 30).
78 *Refugee Convention* (n 6) Preamble.
79 *Statute of the Office of the United Nations High Commissioner for Refugees* (n 30) para 11.
80 *Statute of the Office of the United Nations High Commissioner for Refugees* (n 30) para 20.
81 The General Assembly stipulated the membership of ExCom should be as follows: 'States Members of the United Nations or members of any of the specialized agencies, to be elected by the Council on the widest possible geographical basis from those States with a demonstrated interest in, and devotion to, the solution of the refugee problem', United Nations General Assembly Resolution, *International Assistance to Refugees Within the Mandate of the United Nations High Commissioner for Refugees*, GA Res 1166 (XII), UN Doc A/RES/1166 (XII) (adopted 26 November 1957) para 5. See also *Establishment of the Executive Committee of the Programme of the United Nations High Commissioner for Refugees*, UN ESC Res 672 (XXV), E/RES/672 (XXV) (adopted 30 April 1958). *The UNHCR Statute* allows for

Following the drafting of the *CRPD*, the ExCom released a report in 2007 entitled *The Protection of Older Persons and Persons with Disabilities*.[82] The report noted the discriminatory treatment experienced by people who are refugees with disability,[83] highlighted access issues[84] and observed the inadequacy of service responses.[85] Most significantly, this report demonstrated a change in the model of disability adopted by the ExCom and the UNHCR.[86] The report stated:

> Rather than considering them as passive recipients of aid, UNHCR and partner staff need to interact with older persons and persons with disabilities as equal partners, building on their skills, resources and abilities. Not only is an understanding of their specific needs related to age, gender roles and mental and/or physical condition required, but recognition of their right to be actively involved in all action undertaken to protect them and determine their future is also necessary.[87]

The report highlighted the extensive rights violations that people with disability experience in forced migration contexts by framing them as rights-holders,[88] not vulnerable and in need of care. The report recognised the need for disability-sensitive approaches to refugee status determination,[89] it committed to disseminating a copy of the *CRPD* to all UNHCR staff and partners to

---

additional activities and policy directives. The United Nations General Assembly and Economic and Social Council resolutions or ExCom conclusions determine additional activities and policy directives of the UNHCR. *Statute of the Office of the United Nations High Commissioner for Refugees* (n 30) paras 3, 9.

82 Executive Committee of the High Commissioner's Programme, *The Protection of Older Persons and Persons with Disabilities* (n 20).

83 Executive Committee of the High Commissioner's Programme, *The Protection of Older Persons and Persons with Disabilities* (n 20) [10].

84 'Older persons or persons with disabilities, who face difficulties in communication, concentration, understanding or mobility, may encounter serious barriers in accessing essential protection services. For example, they may be unable to access transport, understand written and verbal information, register with institutions for documentation and support, or recall and recount with accuracy relevant details during refugee status interviews'. Executive Committee of the High Commissioner's Programme, *The Protection of Older Persons and Persons with Disabilities* (n 20) [11].

85 Executive Committee of the High Commissioner's Programme, *The Protection of Older Persons and Persons with Disabilities* (n 20) [13].

86 Cf earlier UNHCR documents, such as the 2003 *Agenda for Protection* that adopted a charity/medical model referring to the 'special needs' of 'the disabled' and identifying 'the handicapped' as a 'vulnerable' group. United Nations High Commissioner for Refugees (UNHCR), *Agenda for Protection* (Report, 3rd ed, October 2003) 37, 38, 38 n 10, 40.

87 Executive Committee of the High Commissioner's Programme, *The Protection of Older Persons and Persons with Disabilities* (n 20) [2].

88 Executive Committee of the High Commissioner's Programme, *The Protection of Older Persons and Persons with Disabilities* (n 20) [16]–[18].

89 Executive Committee of the High Commissioner's Programme, *The Protection of Older Persons and Persons with Disabilities* (n 20) [21].

increase awareness of disability rights,[90] and it also stated that the UNHCR's future annual protection reports would include a section on people with disability.[91] Significantly, the report recommended that ExCom issue a conclusion about people with disability.[92]

In 2010 the ExCom issued the *Conclusion on Refugees with Disabilities and Other Persons with Disabilities Protected and Assisted by UNHCR* ('*2010 ExCom Conclusion*'), recognising the significant extent to which people who are refugees with disability experience human rights abuses.[93] The *2010 ExCom Conclusion* adopted the *CRPD*'s model of disability and reaffirmed the 'inherent dignity and equality of persons with disabilities'.[94] It highlighted the more significant risks experienced by people with disability and acknowledged the barriers they face in accessing support and permanent solutions to their displacement.[95]

The *2010 ExCom Conclusion* reaffirmed that it is the 'primary responsibility of States to take all appropriate measures to protect and assist persons with disabilities';[96] nonetheless, the conclusion acknowledged that states hosting people who are refugees are often 'developing countries' with limited resources.[97] It then highlighted international cooperation as a mechanism for fulfilling these responsibilities.[98]

The ExCom, through the *2010 ExCom Conclusion*, called upon states, the UNHCR and partner organisations to protect people with disability against all forms of discrimination and to provide appropriate support to meet their needs.[99] It also made several policy and programmatic recommendations, including ensuring the participation of people with disability in consultation

90 Executive Committee of the High Commissioner's Programme, *The Protection of Older Persons and Persons with Disabilities* (n 20) [32].

91 Executive Committee of the High Commissioner's Programme, *The Protection of Older Persons and Persons with Disabilities* (n 20) [32].

92 Executive Committee of the High Commissioner's Programme, *The Protection of Older Persons and Persons with Disabilities* (n 20) [38].

93 Executive Committee of the High Commissioner's Programme, *Conclusion on Refugees with Disabilities and Other Persons with Disabilities Protected and Assisted by UNHCR*, UN Doc A/AC.96/1095 (adopted 12 October 2010) ('*Conclusion on Refugees with Disabilities*').

94 Ibid.

95 Ibid.

96 Ibid.

97 Executive Committee of the High Commissioner's Programme, *The Protection of Older Persons and Persons with Disabilities* (n 20). The disproportionate 'burden' on the Global South has been highlighted by other scholars. Disability is greatest in the Global South, and people who are displaced due to war are concentrated in the Global South. Maria Pisani and Shaun Grech, 'Disability and Forced Migration: Critical Intersectionalities' (2015) 2(1) *Disability and the Global South* 421.

98 Executive Committee of the High Commissioner's Programme, *Conclusion on Refugees with Disabilities* (n 93) para h. The *Refugee Convention* and the *CRPD* both have provisions on international cooperation. *Refugee Convention* (n 6) Preamble; *CRPD* (n 2) art 32.

99 Executive Committee of the High Commissioner's Programme, *Conclusion on Refugees with Disabilities* (n 93) para a.

processes,[100] accessibility of information and services[101] and 'equality of opportunity for durable solutions'.[102] The conclusion also recommended awareness raising through staff training[103] and the 'swift and systematic identification and registration of refugees and other persons with disabilities . . . in order to identify their protection and assistance needs'.[104]

In response to the *CRPD*, the ExCom's 2007 report and *2010 ExCom Conclusion* marked a significant change in the policy and operations of the UNHCR. Guidelines for program staff supported these changes.[105] A decade after the *CRPD* was ratified, the 2018 *Global Compact on Refugees*,[106] an important soft law tool that aims to extend the reach of refugee protection and rights realisation, gave extensive attention to the situation of people with disability who are refugees or living in countries that host refugees. The following describes the disability rights advocacy during the *Global Compact on Refugees* drafting and the mechanisms the compact employs to engage stakeholders in refugee protection and rights realisation.

6.2.4 *Greater Visibility of Disability Rights in Refugee Protection: The Global Compact on Refugees*

In 2016, the United Nations General Assembly hosted a summit of the Heads of State and Government to discuss the 'large movements of refugees and migrants'.[107] This one-day summit culminated in a unanimously endorsed *New York Declaration for Refugees and Migrants* ('*New York Declaration*').[108]

100 Executive Committee of the High Commissioner's Programme, *Conclusion on Refugees with Disabilities* (n 93) para e.
101 Executive Committee of the High Commissioner's Programme, *Conclusion on Refugees with Disabilities* (n 93) paras f, g, h, j.
102 Executive Committee of the High Commissioner's Programme, *Conclusion on Refugees with Disabilities* (n 93) para k.
103 Executive Committee of the High Commissioner's Programme, *Conclusion on Refugees with Disabilities* (n 93) para b.
104 Executive Committee of the High Commissioner's Programme, *Conclusion on Refugees with Disabilities* (n 93) para c.
105 See, eg, Office of the United Nations High Commissioner for Refugees (UNHCR), *Working with Persons with Disabilities in Forced Displacement: Need to Know Guidance* (2011) ('*2011 Guide*'); Office of the United Nations High Commissioner for Refugees (UNHCR), *Working with Persons with Disabilities in Forced Displacement: Need to Know Guidance* (2019) ('*2019 Guide*').
106 *Report of the United Nations High Commissioner for Refugees: Part II Global Compact on Refugees* (n 26).
107 'UN Summit for Refugees and Migrants 2016', *UN Refugees and Migrants* (Web Page, 12 December 2014) <https://refugeesmigrants.un.org/summit>.
108 193 member states endorsed the declaration. 'UN Summit for Refugees and Migrants 2016', *UN Refugees and Migrants* (Web Page, 12 December 2014) <https://refugeesmigrants.un.org/summit>; *New York Declaration for Refugees and Migrants*, UNGA Res 71/1, UN Doc A/RES/71/1 (3 October 2016, adopted 19 September 2016).

The *New York Declaration* reaffirmed United Nations member states' commitment to fulfilling the human rights of people who are refugees and migrants, committed to supporting states who host refugees, endorsed the 'core elements of a Comprehensive Refugee Response Framework' and laid the foundations for global compacts around refugees and migrants.[109]

Following the *New York Declaration*, the CRPD Committee and the Committee on the Protection of the Rights of All Migrant Workers and Members of their Families made a joint statement.[110] This statement highlighted the importance of identifying people with disability and state obligations to ensure services are accessible.[111] The statement also noted that there was 'little information available on [the] . . . situation' of people who are refugees with disability and that '[w]ithout data on their specific requirements, States cannot fulfil their legal duty to ensure effective protection and safety in situations of risk and to provide services that meet their specific requirements'.[112] The committees stated they were concerned about the lack of 'formal procedures in many States to identify migrants and refugees with disabilities';[113] nonetheless, they acknowledged that 'migrants with disabilities are often hesitant to disclose their disabilities to authorities for fear of affecting their asylum applications'.[114]

Given that the joint statement was intended to influence the forthcoming global compacts on refugees and migrants, the recommendation for formal procedures to identify migrants with disability seems somewhat clumsy. People with disability found to be refugees are protected from deportation by states' *non-refoulement* obligations;[115] however, people who are migrants with disability are routinely denied visas due to the perceived burden of the disability on the state.[116] Further, countries offering refugee resettlement places to

109 *New York Declaration for Refugees and Migrants* (n 108).

110 Committee on the Protection of the Rights of All Migrant Workers and Members of their Families and Committee on the Rights of Persons with Disabilities, *Addressing Disabilities in Large-Scale Movements of Refugees and Migrants* (Joint Statement, 2017). This along with the CRPD Committee's 2015 statement for the World Humanitarian Summit comprise some of the most significant jurisprudence about the situation of people who are refugees with disability. Committee on the Rights of Persons with Disabilities, *Statement of the Committee on the Rights of Persons with Disabilities on Disability Inclusion for the World Humanitarian Summit* (14 September 2015).

111 Committee on the Protection of the Rights of All Migrant Workers and Members of their Families and the Committee on the Rights of Persons with Disabilities (n 110).

112 Committee on the Protection of the Rights of All Migrant Workers and Members of their Families and the Committee on the Rights of Persons with Disabilities (n 110) 1–2.

113 Committee on the Protection of the Rights of All Migrant Workers and Members of their Families and the Committee on the Rights of Persons with Disabilities (n 110) 2.

114 Committee on the Protection of the Rights of All Migrant Workers and Members of their Families and the Committee on the Rights of Persons with Disabilities (n 110) 2.

115 See earlier Chapter 1 n 51.

116 The Australian *Disability Discrimination Act* exempts 'discriminatory provisions in the *Migration Act 1958*', enabling the denial of visas based on failure to pass the mandated migration health assessment. *Disability Discrimination Act 1992* (Cth) s 52 (emphasis in

people who are refugees may place requirements such as successful completion of a health assessment that discriminate against people with disability.[117]

In 2018, the UNHCR presented the *Global Compact on Refugees* to the United Nations General Assembly.[118] The UNHCR reported that it had consulted with states, civil society, international organisations, people with lived experience and the private sector to develop the compact.[119] The *Global Compact on Refugees* is a soft law tool that reiterates the rights of people who are refugees. The compact aspires to engage states parties to the *Refugee Convention*, as well as those that are not parties, including non-state actors, in making pledges towards the compact's implementation.[120] These pledges are the means 'to provide a basis for predictable and equitable burden- and responsibility-sharing among all United Nations Member States, together with other relevant stakeholders'.[121]

Undoubtedly, the advocacy from the CRPD Committee and others significantly impacted the enumeration of rights for people with disability in the *Global Compact on Refugees*. The compact includes 20 references to disability across a wide range of areas. It acknowledges that disability discrimination may be the root cause of displacement,[122] highlights that partnership and participatory approaches should include people with disability[123] and explains that evidence-based responses require disaggregated data to identify people who are refugees and returnees with disability.[124]

Many of the *Global Compact on Refugees*' recommendations that reiterate the rights of people with disability address the situations of people who are refugees as well as those experienced by the host communities. The compact draws attention to the situation of people with disability in the breadth

original). For more on the impact of this discriminatory law, see Disabled People's Organisations Australia, *Factsheet: Discrimination Against Migrants and Refugees with Disability* (Fact Sheet, 8 March 2018) <https://dpoa.org.au/factsheet-migration/>. See also Philippa Duell-Piening, 'Refugee Resettlement and the Convention on the Rights of Persons with Disabilities' (2018) 33(5) *Disability & Society* 661. This article describes policy reforms that provide a health waiver to humanitarian entrants with disability. Nonetheless, it argues that these changes should be made in legislation.

117 See generally my article that describes the historical disability discrimination in the Australian humanitarian program. Duell-Piening (n 116).

118 *Report of the United Nations High Commissioner for Refugees: Part II Global Compact on Refugees* (n 26).

119 'The Global Compact on Refugees', *United Nations High Commissioner for Refugees* (Web Page) <https://www.unhcr.org/the-global-compact-on-refugees.html>.

120 *Report of the United Nations High Commissioner for Refugees: Part II Global Compact on Refugees* (n 26) paras 17–19.

121 *Report of the United Nations High Commissioner for Refugees: Part II Global Compact on Refugees* (n 26) para 3.

122 *Report of the United Nations High Commissioner for Refugees: Part II Global Compact on Refugees* (n 26) para 9.

123 *Report of the United Nations High Commissioner for Refugees: Part II Global Compact on Refugees* (n 26) paras 13, 34, 40, 44, 51, 106.

124 *Report of the United Nations High Commissioner for Refugees: Part II Global Compact on Refugees* (n 26) paras 46, 58.

of activities that the UNHCR and states undertake, such as reception,[125] registration,[126] education,[127] promotion of economic opportunities and vocational training,[128] health services (including for women and girls),[129] strategies to address the specific vulnerabilities of children,[130] food security,[131] support for countries of origin to reintegrate people who are returnees[132] and the sharing of good practices.[133] With the enumeration of these rights comes a call to measure the progress of their implementation.

This section demonstrated that, even though the situation of people with disability in refugee contexts was not explicitly included in the *Refugee Convention* or the *CRPD*, the dual regimes of refugee protection and disability human rights have effectively raised awareness about the rights of people with disability in refugee contexts. While refugee protection was previously (as good as) silent on the rights of people with disability, there has been considerable clarification about the rights of this population, evident in more recent guidance such as the ExCom conclusions and the *Global Compact on Refugees.* There is now an urgency to respond to these newly visible rights. The following explores how data have been employed to monitor rights implementation.

6.3 Disability Data in Refugee Contexts

Laws, policies and practice guidelines facilitate and reflect the apparent link between data and protecting, respecting and fulfilling human rights. The following demonstrates that disability data production and processing in refugee contexts were initially treated with care. Nonetheless, as the provisions have been translated into operational guidelines, nuances have been removed, and the opportunities to make context-based assessments are limited. Where cautions are included in operational guidelines, they are often incomplete and confusing.

125 *Report of the United Nations High Commissioner for Refugees: Part II Global Compact on Refugees* (n 26) para 54.
126 *Report of the United Nations High Commissioner for Refugees: Part II Global Compact on Refugees* (n 26) para 58.
127 *Report of the United Nations High Commissioner for Refugees: Part II Global Compact on Refugees* (n 26) para 69.
128 *Report of the United Nations High Commissioner for Refugees: Part II Global Compact on Refugees* (n 26) paras 70–71.
129 *Report of the United Nations High Commissioner for Refugees: Part II Global Compact on Refugees* (n 26) paras 72, 75.
130 *Report of the United Nations High Commissioner for Refugees: Part II Global Compact on Refugees* (n 26) para 76.
131 *Report of the United Nations High Commissioner for Refugees: Part II Global Compact on Refugees* (n 26) para 80.
132 *Report of the United Nations High Commissioner for Refugees: Part II Global Compact on Refugees* (n 26) para 89.
133 *Report of the United Nations High Commissioner for Refugees: Part II Global Compact on Refugees* (n 26) para 106.

These observations are progressed in this section by first examining the authorities for data collection in refugee contexts, including *Refugee Convention* article 35 and *CRPD* article 31.[134] The second subsection explores the authoritative interpretations of these articles by bodies such as the CRPD Committee, the ExCom and the UNHCR. The last subsection evaluates the guides and standards supplied to practitioners stipulating how disability data production should be undertaken in 'the field'.

6.3.1 *The Authority: Treaty Provisions About Data Production and Processing*

One of the newest and oldest human rights conventions, the 2006 *CRPD* and the 1951 *Refugee Convention*,[135] are amongst the few international human rights treaties with state obligations regarding statistical data.[136] Article 31 of the *CRPD* has been comprehensively examined in Chapters 4 and 5 of this monograph. This subsection will briefly examine *Refugee Convention* article 35 and compare the two articles.

Article 35 of the *Refugee Convention*, entitled 'Co-operation of the National Authorities with the United Nations', has two distinct paragraphs with different purposes. Paragraph 1 focuses on states parties' obligations to cooperate with the UNHCR in its role of 'supervising the application of the provisions of the Convention'.[137] Paragraph 2's purpose is to ensure the UNHCR receives the necessary information and statistics from states 'to make reports to the competent organs of the United Nations'.[138] Article 35 facilitates relationships between states and the United Nations and defines the roles and responsibilities of each. It requires states parties to support the UNHCR in doing its work.

States are only obligated to provide data to the UNHCR on request.[139] Unlike the periodic review reports, states must submit to other treaty bodies, *Refugee Convention* article 35(2)'s information and statistics gathering obligations have never been 'regularized'.[140] Nonetheless, due to the UNHCR's

134 *Refugee Convention* (n 6) art 35; *CRPD* (n 2) art 31.

135 The *Refugee Convention* is not under the mandate of the Office of the High Commissioner for Human Rights; nonetheless, it bestows individual rights on humans. It was the first international convention to do so following the *Universal Declaration of Human Rights*. *Refugee Convention* (n 6); *Universal Declaration of Human Rights*, GA Res 217A (III), UN GAOR, UN Doc A/810 (10 December 1948).

136 *CRPD* (n 2) art 31; *Refugee Convention* (n 6) art 35; see also the International *Convention for Protection of All Persons from Enforced Disappearance*, opened for signature 6 February 2007, 2716 UNTS 3 (entered into force 23 December 2010) art 19.

137 *Refugee Convention* (n 6) art 35(1).

138 *Refugee Convention* (n 6) art 35(2).

139 '[P]rovide [UNHCR] . . . in the appropriate form with information and statistical data requested'. *Refugee Convention* (n 6) art 35(2).

140 Walter Kälin, *Supervising the 1951 Convention on the Status of Refugees: Article 35 and Beyond* (UNHCR, 2002) 8.

substantial operations in the 'field', there is often regular communication and requests for information between the field offices and the governments of host countries.[141] This information, obtained somewhat ad hoc, is used to inform the UNHCR's annual protection reports.[142]

The subject matter of the statistical data required by article 35(2)(a) is 'the condition of refugees'.[143] The *UNHCR Statute* has slightly more detail in requiring states to provide 'information concerning ***the number*** and conditions of refugees'.[144] Zieck argues that 'condition' refers 'to the status and entitlements of refugees'.[145] Further, Zieck explains that the data describe the condition of a group rather than individuals.[146] Nonetheless, the concept of *statistics about groups* or *categories of people* take an end-of-processing view of data production and processing. Data about the 'conditions of groups' require producing data about the individual, which is then aggregated with others categorised similarly. It is impossible to see the whole without the units (individual data) that comprise the population data.

Zieck distinguishes between the convention's use of 'application' in article 35(1) and 'implementation' in article 35(2). Zieck argues that 'implementation' is 'of a much more general order' and that article 35(2)'s state obligation concerns the convention's implementation 'in the domestic legal order'.[147] This focus on the domestic legal order is clear in subparagraph (c) about information and statistical data describing '[l]aws, regulations and decrees which are, or may hereafter be, in force relating to refugees'.[148] However, subparagraph (b) only stipulates the need for information and statistical data about '[t]he implementation of this Convention'.[149]

Zieck's narrow interpretation of the information and statistical data states are obligated to produce and process regarding '[t]he implementation of this Convention' contrasts with how *CRPD* article 31(2) has been interpreted. *CRPD* article 31(2) has been interpreted as requiring states to produce and process extensive data about the bodies and lives of people with disability.[150] It

141 Ibid., 8.
142 Ibid., paras 10–11.
143 *Refugee Convention* (n 6) art 35(2)(a).
144 *Statute of the Office of the United Nations High Commissioner for Refugees* (n 30) para 8(f) (emphasis added).
145 Marjoleine Zieck, 'Article 35 of the 1951 Convention/Article II of the 1967 Protocol: A Commentary' in Andreas Zimmermann, Jonas Dörschner and Felix Machts (eds), *The 1951 Convention Relating to the Status of Refugees and Its 1967 Protocol: A Commentary* (Oxford University Press, 2011) 1459, 1505 ('Article 35').
146 Ibid., 1505 (citation omitted).
147 Zieck, 'Article 35' (n 145) 1505.
148 *Refugee Convention* (n 6) art 35(2)(c).
149 *Refugee Convention* (n 6) art 35(2)(b).
150 See also earlier Chapter 1 n 3, Section 1.2.2 at nn 70–80, Section 1.3.1 at nn 87–88, and Chapter 5 n 1, 101, 137, 186 for examples of the data production and processing requested by the CPRD Committee under the authority of *CRPD* art 31(2).

is beyond the scope of this monograph to provide an interpretation of *Refugee Convention* article 35. Nonetheless, one would expect that data production and processing for reporting to the United Nations organs would differ from data produced and processed to develop policy to enable the 'full and effective participation' of rights-holders.[151] The different data practices that manifest from *CRPD* article 31 and *Refugee Convention* article 35 obligations make sense due to the different purposes of the data production and processing obligations.

6.3.2 *The Details: What Data Variables Should Be Produced and Processed About Disability Rights in Refugee Contexts?*

The *Refugee Convention* and the *CRPD* impose state obligations for data to be produced and processed to assist in reporting and implementing the conventions.[152] The CRPD Committee, the ExCom and the UNHCR have produced authoritative interpretations of these obligations. Materials from these bodies demonstrate how *Refugee Convention* article 35 and *CRPD* article 31 are interpreted to promote the production and processing of data about the bodies and lives of people with disability in refugee contexts.[153] The *Global Compact on Refugees* promotes similar data production and processing. While most of these interpretations of the treaties' obligations specify the production of data about the bodies and lives of people with disability, they acknowledge that data production and processing may not be 'appropriate' in some contexts.[154]

The CRPD Committee has recommended disaggregation of data by refugee status to 20 states in Concluding Observations.[155] The attention this population receives in Concluding Observations demonstrates the committee's concern that this population experience marginalisation and that more information in the form of data may lead to states parties developing policies that will enable rights attainment.[156] Nonetheless, the committee has not provided reasoning about the conditions that may determine whether these data variables are 'appropriate' to produce and process.

Of a slightly different order, the *2010 ExCom Conclusion* recommends that states, the UNHCR and other stakeholders undertake 'where appropriate a swift and systematic identification and registration of refugees and other

151 *CRPD* (n 2) art 1.

152 *Refugee Convention* (n 6) art 35; *CRPD* (n 2) art 31.

153 Cf earlier Section 5.2, a doctrinal interpretation that demonstrates that the obligations in *CRPD* art 31 may be read as requiring data production and processing about state actions, not individuals' bodies and lives.

154 *CRPD* art 31(2) states that data should be 'disaggregated, as appropriate', suggesting that there are situations where the production and processing of some types of data is inappropriate. *CRPD* (n 2) art 31(2).

155 See earlier Section 1.2.2.

156 *CRPD* (n 2) art 31.

persons with disabilities'.[157] Identification and registration of people with disability require the production of disability data and, less explicitly, data about refugee status. A definition of disability and assessment methods are required to 'identify' people with disability.

In addition to identifying people with disability under the UNHCR mandate, the *2010 ExCom Conclusion* recommends that the UNHCR and other stakeholders 'identify protection and assistance needs'.[158] This assessment of protection and assistance needs is presumably used to respond individually to 'provide sustainable and appropriate support in addressing all their needs'.[159] The *2010 ExCom Conclusion* notes that 'the specific needs of persons with disabilities are often overlooked, especially in the early phases of humanitarian emergencies'.[160] This neglect is intended to be remedied by the 'swift and systematic identification' of people with disability.[161]

The *2010 ExCom Conclusion* specifies that the individual data points should contribute to 'a global needs assessment'.[162] 'Global needs assessments' require aggregated individual data to provide an overview that is assumed to represent the population's needs. Otherwise, the only explicit mention of data in the conclusion concerns the UNHCR providing periodic updates to the member states about the 'follow-up to this Conclusion, including relevant financial data'.[163]

The 2018 *Global Compact on Refugees* elaborated on the rationale for producing and processing data in refugee contexts over four paragraphs and provided guidance on which variables states and relevant stakeholders should produce and process. It included a commitment:

> To support evidence-based responses, States and relevant stakeholders will, as appropriate, promote the development of harmonized or interoperable standards for the collection, analysis, and sharing of age, gender, *disability*, and diversity disaggregated data on refugees and returnees.[164]

157 Executive Committee of the High Commissioner's Programme, *Conclusion on Refugees with Disabilities* (n 93) para c.

158 Executive Committee of the High Commissioner's Programme, *Conclusion on Refugees with Disabilities* (n 93) para c.

159 Executive Committee of the High Commissioner's Programme, *Conclusion on Refugees with Disabilities* (n 93) para a.

160 Executive Committee of the High Commissioner's Programme, *Conclusion on Refugees with Disabilities* (n 93) para a.

161 Executive Committee of the High Commissioner's Programme, *Conclusion on Refugees with Disabilities* (n 93) para c.

162 Executive Committee of the High Commissioner's Programme, *Conclusion on Refugees with Disabilities* (n 93) para c.

163 Executive Committee of the High Commissioner's Programme, *Conclusion on Refugees with Disabilities* (n 93) para n.

164 *Report of the United Nations High Commissioner for Refugees: Part II Global Compact on Refugees* (n 26) para 46 (emphasis added) (citation omitted).

The *Global Compact on Refugees*' data provisions are not about meeting individual needs but a broader agenda of 'evidence-based' responses. The compact also calls for the 'sharing of quality registration data, disaggregated by age, gender, disability, and diversity'.[165]

Zieck explained that the drafters of the *Refugee Convention* were acutely aware of the need to avoid creating more work for states through administrative requests for data.[166] These earlier concerns about administrative burden are addressed by the compact, which offers support to states 'to strengthen national data collection systems on the situation of refugees and host communities'.[167] The request for more statistical data and the offer of support to assist with the administrative burden of producing and processing data about people who are refugees seems entirely consistent with the *Refugee Convention* article 35 obligations and the Preamble, which includes the principles of burden sharing and international cooperation.[168]

Unlike the CRPD Committee's Concluding Observations to states, the *2010 ExCom Conclusion* and the *Global Compact on Refugees* temper their data production and processing recommendations with the qualifier 'where appropriate' and 'as appropriate'.[169] 'Where/as appropriate' suggests that decision-making is necessary to assess whether it is ethical, useful and in the data subject's best interest to produce and process data at a given time in each context. The *2010 ExCom Conclusion* and the *Global Compact on Refugees* provide no specific advice about how to assess whether it is appropriate. The following delves into the practice of disability data production and processing in refugee contexts to understand how the interpretations of *CRPD* article 31 and *Refugee Convention* article 35 are operationalised and, in turn, directly impact the lives of people who are refugees with disability.

6.3.3 *Operationalisation: Duty-Bearers' Disability Data Production and Processing Practices*

States are the duty-bearers in human rights treaties. While the duty remains with the state, sometimes states delegate the delivery or operationalisation

165 *Report of the United Nations High Commissioner for Refugees: Part II Global Compact on Refugees* (n 26) para 58.

166 *Refugee Convention* art 35 states that information must be provided 'in the appropriate form'. *Refugee Convention* (n 6) art 35(2); Zieck, 'Article 35' (n 145) 1504.

167 *Report of the United Nations High Commissioner for Refugees: Part II Global Compact on Refugees* (n 26) para 47.

168 *Refugee Convention* (n 6) Preamble, art 35.

169 Executive Committee of the High Commissioner's Programme, *Conclusion on Refugees with Disabilities* (n 93) para c; *Report of the United Nations High Commissioner for Refugees: Part II Global Compact on Refugees* (n 26) para 46.

of duties to other stakeholders, for example, private health services. International cooperation principles in the *Refugee Convention* and obligations in the *CRPD* acknowledge that states cannot always fulfil their human rights obligations alone.[170] In these instances, the international community often funds agencies to fulfil state duties, for example, refugee status determination undertaken by the UNHCR.

While states are the primary duty-bearers and will fulfil the data production and processing role in some jurisdictions, individual states' data production and processing practices are beyond the scope of this monograph. The following examines the international guidance on operationalising *Refugee Convention* article 35 and *CRPD* article 31. This guidance is developed to be used across multiple jurisdictions that often host large numbers of people who are refugees.

This subsection demonstrates that the operational guidance does not engage with the issue of whether it is appropriate to collect data in a given refugee context. The guidance contains no advice on assessing whether producing data about a given population in a certain context is appropriate. Commonly, the message in these guides and standards, explicit or not, is that all services and projects in all refugee contexts should produce disability data. This drive for disability data is demonstrated through the following two subsections, which examine, firstly, the UNHCR operational guides and, secondly, the guidelines and standards developed by global networks of agencies working in refugee contexts. It is beyond the scope of this monograph to assess the level of adherence to these guides, guidelines and standards.

a) UNHCR Operational Guides

The *2010 ExCom Conclusion* was followed swiftly by the UNHCR's 2011 *Working with Persons with Disabilities in Forced Displacement: Need to Know Guidance*, which was disseminated widely through the UNHCR field offices.[171] The guide stated its objective was to provide staff with guidance 'to ensure that the rights of persons with disabilities who are of concern to the Office [UNHCR] are met without discrimination'.[172]

The 2011 UNHCR guide notably provided much discretion to the field offices, including how to identify people with disability in that context. It noted that people with disability were often overlooked at registration and that '[i]t is therefore vital to introduce explicit procedures for identifying persons with disabilities'.[173] As an action, among others, the guide recommended field offices should '[p]ut in place procedures for identifying refugees with

170 Note the provisions in the *Refugee Convention* feature in the Preamble are not state obligations. *Refugee Convention* (n 6) Preamble; *CRPD* (n 2) art 32.
171 UNHCR, *2011 Guide* (n 105).
172 UNHCR, *2011 Guide* (n 105) 2.
173 UNHCR, *2011 Guide* (n 105) 9.

disabilities' and 'screen areas where many displaced persons live for persons with disabilities'.[174]

The 2019 update of the UNHCR guide reflected the evolution of thinking in disability data production and processing in refugee contexts.[175] The 2011 guide only featured the word 'data' twice. In contrast, the 2019 guide included the word 'data' 16 times. The stark change is evident from the outset, as the section heading changed from the 2011 title 'Ensure identification and registration' to the 2019 title 'Improve identification and *data collection*'.[176] The new title demonstrates disability data production and processing's growing prominence in refugee contexts and the solidifying belief that data are necessary to fulfil the rights of people with disability. The 2019 version of the UNHCR guide also features data production and processing in sections outside identification and registration. In the section titled 'Non-discrimination', the manual provides the example action of 'Disaggregate all data by disability status in order to make it possible to monitor access and inclusion'.[177] As noted earlier, to disaggregate data by disability, a method of identifying people with disability is required.

The 2019 UNHCR guide includes a paragraph about how people should be asked if they have a disability and how the response should be recorded in the UNHCR systems. Importantly, it describes some approaches as inadequate, such as 'identifying persons with disabilities based on visual cues'.[178] Nonetheless, the guide states it is insufficient to ask 'whether someone has a disability, with a yes/no response option',[179] likely because research has shown that fewer people self-identify when asked if they have a disability.[180] This approach raises ethical issues about using proxy measures to determine whether someone has a disability.

The 2019 guide critiques the medical model approach to diagnosing impairments as 'not giving information on lived experience and support needs'[181] but misses the broader point about how disempowering and damaging it is for experts to label people with disability.[182] This under-examination of the impact of the medical model categorisation culminates in the guide recommending a tool that categorises people by their impairments, the *Washington Group Short Set of Questions on Disability*, to 'identify people with disability'.[183]

174 UNHCR, *2011 Guide* (n 105) 9.
175 UNHCR, *2019 Guide* (n 105).
176 UNHCR, *2011 Guide* (n 105) 9; UNHCR, *2019 Guide* (n 105) 14.
177 UNHCR, *2019 Guide* (n 105) 11.
178 UNHCR, *2019 Guide* (n 105) 14.
179 UNHCR, *2019 Guide* (n 105) 14.
180 See, eg, Marguerite Schneider, 'The Difference a Word Makes: Responding to Questions on "Disability" and "Difficulty" in South Africa' (2009) 31(1) *Disability and Rehabilitation* 42.
181 UNHCR, *2019 Guide* (n 105) 14.
182 See earlier Sections 1.1.1 and 4.3.2(b) for more on the medical model and disability classification.
183 UNHCR, *2019 Guide* (n 105) 15. See later Section 7.2.2 for a critique of the *Washington Group Short Set of Questions on Disability*.

The 2019 guide also suggests that understanding the 'lived experience and support needs' of people with disability in refugee contexts will be enhanced by strengthening data production and processing.[184] The guide asserts that data will enable 'planning, implementation and monitoring'.[185] None of the reasons for producing data about people with disability in refugee contexts outlined in the guide appear to be for meeting individual needs.

The 2019 guide instructs field offices to update the UNHCR database proGres regularly. Centralised databases make it likely that data reuse and sharing will occur. Sharing appears to be the intent of the UNHCR, as indicated by the 'example approach', which directs field offices to 'adapt informed consent procedures for sharing data'.[186] While the 2019 guide also includes a paragraph on confidentiality and consent, it is questionable whether informed consent is possible in refugee contexts.[187]

Data sharing may reduce the burden on the data subject when travelling between services and improve efficiency. Conversely, it may exacerbate the harm experienced by people with disability in refugee contexts. Databases can be helpful as they retain information, and people are not repeatedly asked the same questions, which may be triggering or distressing. Nonetheless, authorities may trust databases as a more reliable source of information about an individual than their personal account.[188] Unquestioning trust in computer databases is highly problematic when database errors or unexpected or unusual changes in a person's life occur. People with disability in refugee contexts face many barriers in advocating for changes to erroneous databases.[189] Furthermore, the ability for rapid and extensive data sharing and reuse through databases exacerbates the potential for serious harm.

The 2019 guide recommends disaggregating program data by disability to monitor access by people with disability,[190] drawing on the authority of the *UNHCR Policy on Age, Gender and Diversity*'s ('*UNHCR AGD Policy*') Core Action 1.[191] The *UNHCR AGD Policy* states that '[a]t a minimum, all data collected by UNHCR will be disaggregated by age, sex and other diversity considerations, *as contextually appropriate* and possible, for the purposes

184 UNHCR, *2019 Guide* (n 105) 14.
185 UNHCR, *2019 Guide* (n 105) 14.
186 UNHCR, *2019 Guide* (n 105) 15.
187 See later Section 7.2.3(b).
188 See, eg, Marion Fourcade and Jeffrey Gordon, 'Learning Like a State: Statecraft in the Digital Age' (2020) 1(1) *Journal of Law and Political Economy* 78, 82.
189 For a discussion on the barriers people with disability from refugee backgrounds face in engaging with bureaucracy, see generally Samantha Furneaux and Dina Korkees, *'We Need to Raise Our Voices': Advice From People of Refugee Backgrounds Living with Disabilities and Their Carers* (Report, Victorian Foundation for Survivors of Torture, 2019).
190 UNHCR, *2019 Guide* (n 105) 15.
191 Office of the United Nations High Commissioner for Refugees (UNHCR), *UNHCR Policy on Age, Gender and Diversity* (2018).

of analysis and programming'.[192] The 2019 guide omits any reference to 'as contextually appropriate'. This omission in the 2019 guide erroneously suggests that the *UNHCR AGD Policy* requires disaggregation by disability in all contexts.

b) Global Networks' Standards and Guidelines on Disability Data Production in Refugee Contexts

In addition to the UNHCR guides, several other recent instruments drive the demand for data about the bodies and lives of people with disability in refugee contexts. The following will critique the data production and processing provisions in three such instruments that set standards in humanitarian responses: the 2016 *Charter on Inclusion of Persons with Disabilities in Humanitarian Action*,[193] the 2018 *Humanitarian Inclusion Standards for Older People and People with Disabilities* ('*2018 Humanitarian Disability-Inclusion Standards*')[194] and the 2019 *Inclusion of Persons with Disabilities in Humanitarian Action*.[195]

The 2016 *Charter on Inclusion of Persons with Disabilities in Humanitarian Action*,[196] launched at the World Humanitarian Summit (May 2016, Istanbul), invites states, UN agencies, humanitarian organisations and other civil society organisations, including DPOs, to commit to inclusive humanitarian action.[197] The charter promotes the 'importance of collection and analysis of disability data disaggregated by age and sex, as an important element in the design and monitoring of States' obligations, humanitarian programming and policy as a whole'.[198] Signatories commit to:

> Adopt policies and processes to improve quantitative and qualitative data collection on persons with disabilities that delivers comparable and reliable evidence and is ethically collected, respectful of confidentiality and privacy. Ensure that data collected on persons with disabilities is disaggregated by age and sex, and analysed and used on an ongoing basis to assess and advance accessibility of humanitarian services and assistance,

192 Office of the United Nations High Commissioner for Refugees (UNHCR), *UNHCR Policy on Age, Gender and Diversity* (2018) 10 (citation omitted) (emphasis added).
193 *Charter on Inclusion of Persons with Disabilities in Humanitarian Action* (2016) <http://humanitariandisabilitycharter.org/>.
194 CBM International, HelpAge International and Handicap International, *Humanitarian Inclusion Standards for Older People and People with Disabilities* (Report, 2018).
195 Inter-Agency Standing Committee (IASC), *Guidelines on Inclusion of Persons with Disabilities in Humanitarian Action* (2019) ('*Guidelines on Inclusion*').
196 *Charter on Inclusion of Persons with Disabilities in Humanitarian Action* (n 193).
197 'About', *Charter on Inclusion of Persons with Disabilities in Humanitarian Action* (Web Page, 2022) <http://humanitariandisabilitycharter.org/>.
198 *Charter on Inclusion of Persons with Disabilities in Humanitarian Action* (n 193) art 1.9.

as well as participation in policy and program design, implementation and evaluation.[199]

The production and processing of disability data are not qualified by 'as appropriate'. Data production and processing are necessary according to this charter. The over 250 charter endorsees include states, civil society organisations and international organisations, such as the UNHCR.[200]

The *2018 Humanitarian Disability-Inclusion Standards* were developed to 'address the gap in understanding the needs, capacities and rights of older people and people with disabilities, and promote their inclusion in humanitarian action'.[201] Endorsed by Sphere, which developed the widely accepted standards for humanitarian responses,[202] the *2018 Humanitarian Disability-Inclusion Standards* recommend data disaggregation by sex, age and disability across multiple assessment tools. For the production of disability data, it recommends using the *Washington Group Short Set of Questions on Disability*.[203] The standards support these recommendations by including case studies where data disaggregation by disability was pivotal in designing responses.[204]

Importantly, the *2018 Humanitarian Disability-Inclusion Standards* highlight the central role of people with disability in data production and processing. They state that information about barriers and enablers should be collected directly from people with disability, that people with disability should be included in collecting data, that they should be involved in training and that they should be involved 'in developing data collection and monitoring systems that are relevant, accessible and culturally appropriate'.[205] The *2018 Humanitarian Disability-Inclusion Standards* also recommend ensuring data systems enable the recording of disability data variables,[206] that enumerators receive training[207] and that data are shared to support practice development.[208]

In 2019, the Inter-Agency Standing Committee (IASC), the 'longest-standing and highest-level humanitarian co-ordination forum', published *Inclusion of Persons with Disabilities in Humanitarian Action* ('*IASC*

199 *Charter on Inclusion of Persons with Disabilities in Humanitarian Action* (n 193) art 2.3(c).
200 'About' (n 197).
201 CBM International, HelpAge International and Handicap International (n 194) 9.
202 See especially Sphere Association, *The Sphere Handbook: Humanitarian Charter and Minimum Standards in Humanitarian Response* (2018).
203 CBM International, HelpAge International and Handicap International (n 194) 21. See later Section 7.2.2 for a discussion on the *Washington Short Set of Questions on Disability*.
204 CBM International, HelpAge International and Handicap International (n 194) 19–31, 34, 97, 124, 145, 168, 192, 212, 232.
205 CBM International, HelpAge International and Handicap International (n 194) 22–23, 25, 43.
206 CBM International, HelpAge International and Handicap International (n 194) 30–31.
207 CBM International, HelpAge International and Handicap International (n 194) 81–82.
208 CBM International, HelpAge International and Handicap International (n 194) 24–25, 76, 148, 171.

Guidelines').[209] The *IASC Guidelines* identify four 'must do actions', one of which is 'Disaggregate data for monitoring inclusion'.[210] The guideline explains that '"Must do" actions are required if persons with disabilities are to be included successfully in all phases of humanitarian action and need to be taken by every stakeholder in every section and all contexts'.[211] According to the guidelines, data should be collected using the *Washington Group Short Set of Questions on Disability* and the equivalent survey for children.[212]

The *IASC Guidelines* also include a chapter on 'Data and information management',[213] which, alongside the *2018 Humanitarian Disability-Inclusion Standards*,[214] is the most comprehensive guidance on producing and processing data about people with disability in humanitarian contexts. The chapter contains guidance, recommendations and nuances, including recognising the difficulty of collecting disability data. The guidelines also recommend that 'budgeting for accessibility should not rely on data collection'.[215] Instead, '[w]hen robust quantitative data do not exist . . . assume that 15 per cent of the affected population has a disability'.[216] *IASC Guidelines* also include a table to assist in assessing the quality of existing disability data.[217]

Notably, the *IASC Guidelines* differentiate questions that identify people with disability (eg, *Washington Group Short Set of Questions on Disability*) and questions that elicit information about the barriers people with disability experience.[218] This distinction is notable because it acknowledges that counting people is not enough; the barriers to inclusion must be identified. Disappointingly, the *IASC Guidelines* recommend seeking information from humanitarian actors rather than people with disability directly.[219] In contrast, the *2018 Humanitarian Disability-Inclusion Standards* state that information on barriers should be collected 'directly from . . . people with disabilities of all ages'.[220]

209 The guidelines were an outcome of the 2016 *Charter on Inclusion of Persons with Disabilities in Humanitarian Action* (n 193) art 2.3(b), launched at the 2016 World Humanitarian Summit. They also included stakeholders involved in the drafting of the *Humanitarian Disability-Inclusion Standards*, suggesting a lot of overlap in the documents and projects. IASC, *Guidelines on Inclusion* (n 195).
210 IASC, *Guidelines on Inclusion* (n 195) 19, 21.
211 IASC, *Guidelines on Inclusion* (n 195) 19.
212 IASC, *Guidelines on Inclusion* (n 195) 21. See later Section 7.2.2 for a discussion on the *Washington Short Set of Questions on Disability*.
213 Inter-Agency Standing Committee (IASC), *IASC Guidelines on Mental Health and Psychosocial Support in Emergency Settings* (2007) 23–31.
214 CBM International, HelpAge International and Handicap International (n 194).
215 IASC, *Guidelines on Inclusion* (n 195) 29.
216 IASC, *Guidelines on Inclusion* (n 195) 27.
217 IASC, *Guidelines on Inclusion* (n 195) annex 4.
218 IASC, *Guidelines on Inclusion* (n 195) 28.
219 IASC, *Guidelines on Inclusion* (n 195) 28.
220 CBM International, HelpAge International and Handicap International (n 194) 21.

Some other aspects of the *IASC Guidelines* are also potentially problematic, such as the inclusion of provisions about disability data in funding agreements.[221] Utilising the donor–service provider relationship to produce disability data may create perverse outcomes. For example, what are the consequences if people with disability do not want to disclose their disability status? Does this impact the service's funding? Services may also become more coercive about extracting data from people, for example, stating that they cannot provide services without a person providing the data. The report calls for the promotion of 'systematic monitoring of access to assistance' that is reported through 'situation reports, humanitarian dashboards and other reporting mechanisms'.[222] While these initiatives may be motivated by disability inclusion and wanting to ensure funded services are accountable, care must be taken not to put undue pressure on people with disability in refugee contexts to disclose information about their bodies and lives. Otherwise, the exchange may become coercive.

Furthermore, the gravity of producing and processing personal data is often not well communicated by the guides, guidelines and standards amidst the enthusiasm to increase data production and processing. This lack of consideration of the impact on the data subjects was noted in the Women's Refugee Commission's report documenting the piloting of the Sexual and Gender-Based Violence section within the *IASC Guidelines*.[223] The first recommendation from the pilot was to strengthen the 'language on safe and ethical collection of data related to sexual violence'.[224] It recognised that care must be taken with data produced and processed, as it may significantly deleteriously impact data subjects.

The sensitivity and power of information are not entirely lost in the *IASC Guidelines*, with a brief note that is incongruently in a box with the heading 'The importance of informed consent in data collection and use'. It says: 'Information and data should be protected. For example, avoid identifying individuals who might subsequently as a result be harassed, persecuted or killed'.[225] Humanitarian contexts are broader than refugee contexts, including responses to natural disasters. Nonetheless, this single sentence without any further guidance seems somewhat underexamined, given that refugee contexts, by nature of the definition of refugees, will contain large numbers of people with a 'well-founded fear of persecution'.[226]

People with disability in refugee contexts may be survivors of torture and ex-combatants with impairments who may be highly identifiable to persecuting regimes in disability data sets. If we take the earlier statement from the

221 IASC, *Guidelines on Inclusion* (n 195) 31.

222 IASC, *Guidelines on Inclusion* (n 195) 29.

223 Women's Refugee Commission, *Piloting the IASC Guidelines on Inclusion of Persons with Disabilities in Humanitarian Action: Disability Inclusion in Gender-Based Violence Programming in Jordan, Sri Lanka, and Uganda* (Report, 2019).

224 Ibid., 7.

225 IASC, *Guidelines on Inclusion* (n 195) 26.

226 *Refugee Convention* (n 6) art 1(A)(2).

IASC Guidelines literally, people who meet the definition of refugee should not be identified. Given the work that has been undertaken to demonstrate how de-identified aggregated data may be re-identified, this may also have ramifications for so-called de-identified data sets.[227] Furthermore, the Red Cross has noted that persecutory regimes may use aggregated data about groups that is 'community identifiable' to target and harm data subjects.[228]

An essential nuance and safeguard, the phrase 'as appropriate', has been lost in operationalising data production and processing obligations.[229] The authoritative *2010 ExCom Conclusion*, the *Global Compact on Refugees* and the *UNHCR AGD Policy* retain the safeguard 'where appropriate' and 'as contextually appropriate' before recommending (disability) data production.[230] Nonetheless, the manuals designed to operationalise the obligations and the authoritative interpretations, the UNHCR Guides, the *Charter on Inclusion of Persons with Disabilities in Humanitarian Action*, the *2018 Humanitarian Disability-Inclusion Standards* and the *IASC Guidelines*, have failed to acknowledge that disability data should only be produced and processed if it is 'appropriate'. Concerningly, the CRPD Committee also issues its authoritative advice on article 31 in its Concluding Observations to states without the qualifying statement 'as appropriate'.

Removing nuance is likely to reduce ambiguity and create clear actions for busy practitioners in the field. Before the operational guidelines were issued, a decision (consciously or not) was made that disability data production and processing would occur in all refugee contexts rather than providing a process to determine whether it is appropriate. However, it is not clear why and how this decision was made. Chapter 7 proposes a three-step test to determine whether it is appropriate to produce and process disability data in refugee contexts. The next section introduces a new framework that seeks to deepen our understanding of the importance of rights holders exercising their autonomy in data production and processing practices.

227 See, eg, Christine Ashby, Benjamin IP Rubinstein and Vanessa Teague, 'Stop the Open Data Bus, We Want to Get Off' (No arXiv:1908.05004, arXiv, 14 August 2019) <http://arxiv.org/abs/1908.05004>; Chris Culnane, Benjamin Rubinstein and Vanessa Teague, *Health Data in an Open World: A Report on Re-Identifying Patients in the MBS/PBS Dataset and the Implications for Future Releases of Australian Government Data* (University of Melbourne, 18 December 2017) <https://arxiv.org/abs/1712.05627>.

228 Christopher Kuner and Massimo Marelli (eds), *Handbook on Data Protection in Humanitarian Action* (International Committee of the Red Cross, 2nd ed, 2020) 24–25.

229 *CRPD* (n 2) art 31(2).

230 The parentheses indicate that some of these instruments are more broadly about data disaggregation or diversity variables, rather than disability data. *CRPD* (n 2) art 31(2); *Report of the United Nations High Commissioner for Refugees: Part II Global Compact on Refugees* (n 26) para 46; Executive Committee of the High Commissioner's Programme, *Conclusion on Refugees with Disabilities* (n 93) para c; UNHCR, *UNHCR Policy on Age, Gender and Diversity* (n 191) 10.

6.4 Visibility and Human Rights Attainment: Considering the Locus of Power

> The government says that you do the census to make sure that they can make a budget to fund the services required. But, as a person on a temporary visa, I don't feel the government wants to look after us.[231]

Before the *CRPD*, people who were refugees with disability were legally and programmatically invisible.[232] There was an assumption by some that people who are refugees with disability do not exist, as they are not able to make the arduous journeys often required in refugee flights. There is now a greater understanding of disability in refugee contexts. It is recognised that people with disability are displaced across borders seeking protection. It is well established that these journeys can produce disability and that the conditions that people who are refugees live within may lead to disability. People with disability in refugee contexts are now visible. Furthermore, the instruments described in this chapter affirm the rights of people who are refugees with disability.

Visibility is often seen as the antidote or at least a step along the path to remedy marginalisation.[233] In the margins, people are less seen. Nonetheless, visibility alone cannot achieve human rights, and in some instances, visibility may be counter-productive to human rights attainment. Not disclosing personal information about one's identity may be a form of *strategic anonymity* that can enable human rights attainment. One of the research Stakeholder Advisory Group members stated that they would not answer any questions that they thought may prejudice their chances of resettlement, for example, about their religion, when asked in the context of resettlement programs that prioritise Christians.[234]

The locus of power over an individual must be considered to understand whether visibility may benefit or harm the rights-holder. The locus of power is influenced by laws, citizenship and other mechanisms of control, such as data.[235] If invisibility-visibility is a spectrum or an axis, consideration must be given to an intersecting axis that denotes the spectrum of individual autonomy *vis-à-vis* state power over the individual. Visibility combined with state power over an individual may lead to subjugation, such as Kimlik (Temporary Protection Identification) being used by Turkish police to identify and detain people who are refugees from Syria.[236]

231 Stakeholder Advisory Group meeting minutes, 20 August 2021.

232 See the quotation from António Guterres at the beginning of this chapter.

233 See, eg, the title of this report: Clara Straimer, *Vulnerable or Invisible? Asylum Seekers with Disabilities in Europe* (Research Paper No 194, Office of the High Commissioner for Refugees, November 2010).

234 Stakeholder Advisory Group meeting minutes, 8 July 2022.

235 See earlier Chapter 3 and later Chapter 7 for more on how power operates to control data subjects.

236 Human Rights Watch, 'Syrian Refugees in Turkey Fear Turkish Police' (YouTube, 25 October 2022) <https://www.youtube.com/watch?v=4_HoMO0PMz4&t=16s>.

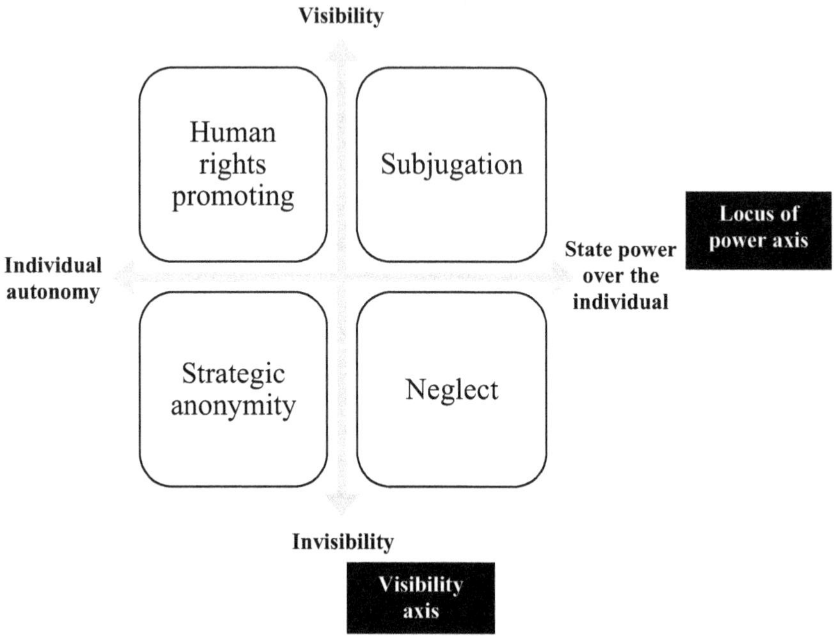

Figure 6.1 Conceptual framework depicting the intersecting axes of locus of power and visibility axes

Emergency responses, such as those experienced by people who are refugees, suspend some human rights provisions, giving responders and states more control over those affected by the emergency. When a person is being 'protected', others make decisions for them, enforcing their will over the rights-holder. Power dynamics in emergencies are very similar to the medical model of disability, which led to the subjugation of people with disability.[237] As discussed earlier, most people who are refugees are living in prolonged displacement contexts, in many cases without a pathway to citizenship rights. In non-emergency situations, state actions to fulfil human rights may sometimes counterintuitively lead to greater power over people's lives. One of these actions is the production and processing of data. In contrast, when people have greater autonomy, they can control their own lives and make decisions without external interference.[238]

I developed a conceptual framework, Figure 6.1, to critique the relationship between visibility and power. It depicts the intersecting axes of visibility and locus of power. The labels on the four quadrants describe the conditions that are created when these axes interact.

237 See earlier Section 1.1 for a description of the medical model of disability.
238 See earlier Section 5.1.3 for more on the *CRPD* and individual autonomy.

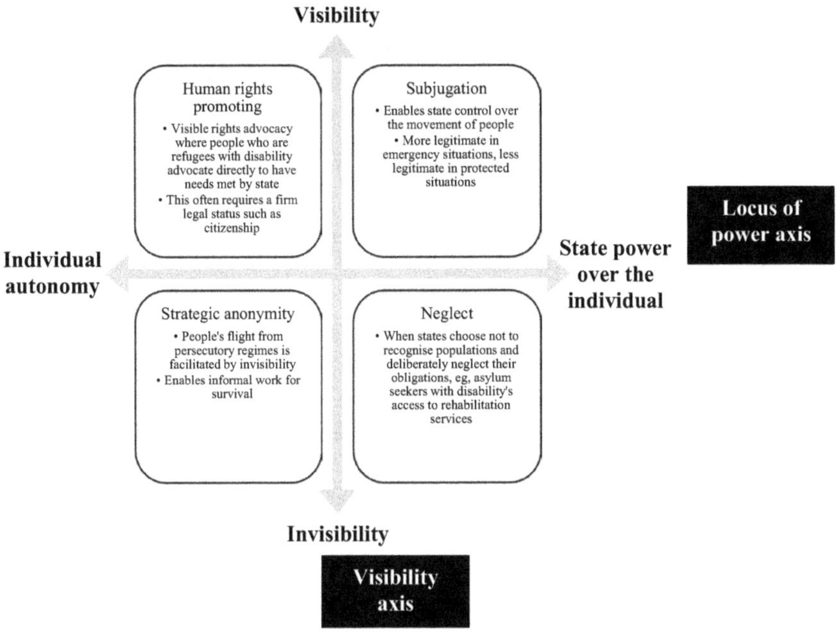

Figure 6.2 Conceptual framework depicting the intersecting axes of locus of power and visibility overlayed with considerations from refugee contexts

Individual autonomy is enhanced when people can self-identify and choose whether to make themselves visible. Figure 6.1 illustrates that when state power and invisibility are greater, there is a situation of neglect. In these circumstances, the state does not attempt to identify the population, their needs and their rights. From the state's perspective, if the individual and population do not exist, the state has no obligations towards them.

To illustrate the usefulness of this conceptualisation and the importance of considering the locus of power when discussing visibility, the following Figure 6.2 considers the refugee context. It demonstrates that visibility is only ideal when people have a firm legal status, such as citizenship. It illustrates how visibility with state control may limit a person's ability to move freely. At times, states neglect their obligations by maintaining a population as invisible, perhaps with the implicit threat of more significant restrictions should they speak up. Nonetheless, sometimes people who are refugees with disability exercise their agency and gain some control over their situation by managing their level of visibility to authorities through strategic anonymity. Examples of strategic anonymity include engaging in informal work for survival or fleeing persecutory regimes.

As discussed in Section 5.1.3(b), a general principle of the *CRPD* is individual autonomy, which is essential to curtail states' and others' control over the bodies and lives of people with disability. The *CRPD*'s explicit mechanisms to curtail state power are a response to people with disability's experiences of subjugation and neglect under state control legitimised through the medical model of disability. Now that greater visibility of disability rights has been achieved, including in refugee contexts, the urge to make individuals and groups with disability visible to measure rights attainment must be considered carefully. Strategic anonymity is essential to realising human rights. The framework introduced in this chapter is used in Chapter 7 to consider methods to curtail state power and restore autonomy to people with disability in refugee contexts.

6.5 Conclusion

The dual regimes of refugee protection and disability human rights have worked together to raise the profile of the rights of people with disability in refugee contexts. The greater prominence of rights was accompanied by a tool intended to support the realisation of those rights: data. Previous chapters have argued that the *CRPD* article 31 obligations require data production and processing about states' actions to implement the *CRPD*. Nonetheless, authoritative bodies have interpreted these obligations to focus on data production and processing about the bodies and lives of people with disability. Recent operational manuals reflect these interpretations, recommending systemic and comprehensive data production and processing about the bodies and lives of people with disability in refugee contexts. Further, an important nuance has been lost in the translation of obligations to operational guidance: the requirement to only produce and process data 'as appropriate'.

This chapter introduced a new framework to deepen the analysis of the implications of *CRPD* article 31 in refugee contexts. The framework considers the relationship between visibility and the locus of power over a person's life. It demonstrates that people may need to remain strategically anonymous to realise their human rights. Strategic anonymity requires a person to be able to exercise the human rights principle of individual autonomy.[239]

The enthusiasm for harnessing data to improve human rights attainment must be tempered by ensuring human rights principles are adhered to in the production and processing of data. The next chapter, Chapter 7, proposes a test for assessing whether producing and processing data are 'appropriate'. It uses the framework introduced in this chapter to explore two critical human rights principles often omitted in data production and processing: self-identification and self-defining.

239 *CRPD* (n 2) art 3(a).

7 A Balancing Act

Mitigating the Harms of Human Rights Data Production and Processing

Data as a source of knowledge to govern is not new,[1] but technology has made data prolific. States have transformed in recent decades to rely heavily on data and technology for policy development and bureaucratic administration.[2] Since states have an instrumental role in the international human rights framework and the international development agenda, it is unsurprising that international organisations have followed suit, investing in data to define and address problems. Despite data's shortcomings and potential for harm, their power may also benefit humanity.

This chapter, the monograph's penultimate and last substantive chapter, momentarily sets aside one of the core arguments, that article 31 of the *Convention on the Rights of Persons with Disabilities* ('*CRPD*') does not require data to be produced and processed about the bodies and lives of people with disability.[3] Doing so allows an exploration of harm minimisation measures that can be employed when producing and processing data about the bodies and lives of people with disability in refugee contexts. This exploration recognises that human rights protections are in tension with comprehensive, harmonious and interoperable data. These protections include obligations to only produce and process data 'as appropriate' and the human rights principles of self-defining and self-identifying. This chapter argues that the *CRPD* contributes to the doctrinal understanding of these protections by progressing the normative understanding of individual autonomy and group rights.[4] The chapter also explains that the *CRPD* has underutilised tools that work in tandem with data production and processing to facilitate the convention's implementation, such as awareness raising,[5] active involvement and close

1 See earlier Chapter 3 n 12.

2 See earlier Section 3.3.2.

3 *Convention on the Rights of Persons with Disabilities*, opened for signature 24 January 2007, 2515 UNTS 3 (entered into force 3 May 2008) ('*CRPD*'). See especially Section 5.2 for the reasoning behind this argument.

4 *CRPD*, arts 3(a), 4(3).

5 *CRPD*, art 8.

DOI: 10.4324/9781003506140-10

consultation with people with disability,[6] disability human rights research[7] and universal design.[8]

These arguments are progressed through four sections of this chapter. Section 7.1 explores the utility of producing and processing data about the bodies and lives of people with disability. Section 7.2 introduces a test for determining whether it is 'appropriate' to produce data about the bodies and lives of people with disability in a given context. Section 7.3 proposes that greater control may be given to people with disability in data production and processing by emphasising the right to self-identify. Finally, Section 7.4 discusses approaches to increasing the power of marginalised groups in data production and processing practices, including through the right to self-define and community-controlled data.

7.1 The Arguments for Disability Data Production

Assuming harm is not a consideration, this section explores the benefits of data about the bodies and lives of people with disability to realise their human rights. The following examines the evidence about the utility of data to protect, promote and ensure the human rights of people who are refugees with disability. It also explores the support provided for disability data production and processing by people with disability and their representative organisations.

7.1.1 Disability Data Are Useful

If we accept that data are powerful and can predict certain outcomes given specific inputs,[9] it is likely that data may also be useful in informing actions to

6 *CRPD*, art 4(3).

7 *CRPD*, arts 4(1)(f), (g), 31(1), 32(1)(c). See also Anna Arstein-Kerslake et al, 'Introducing a Human Rights-Based Disability Research Methodology' (2020) 20(3) *Human Rights Law Review* 412.

8 *CRPD* (n 3) art 4(1)(f).

9 'Predictive analytics' are statistical models that estimate the likelihood of a given outcome occurring. This process is happening at faster and greater rates with the assistance of machine learning. Commercial tools that offer predictive analytics include IBM's i2 Enterprise Insight Analysis, marketed as a tool that 'turn(s) disparate data into comprehensive and actionable intelligence to support timely decision making'. 'IBM I2 Enterprise Insight Analysis – Overview – Australia', *IMB* (Web Page, 27 November 2019) <https://www.ibm.com/au-en/marketplace/enterprise-insight-analysis>. See also Tucker who explains that 'But the more data i2 EIA gets, the more helpful it becomes. And that could put pressure on lawmakers and others to keep feeding new, and potentially sensitive, data streams to the beast'. Patrick Tucker, 'A New Tool to Turn Unstructured Data into Actionable Intelligence Could Change the Way Law Enforcement Fights Terrorism, and Challenge the Data-Collection Debate', *Nextgov.com* (online, 28 January 2016) <https://www.nextgov.com/cio-briefing/2016/01/refugee-or-terrorist-ibm-thinks-its-software-has-answer/125506/>.

create positive change. Even commentators who are aware of data's harmful effects concede that they have utility for good:

> While we do not wish to advance arguments that seek to further quantify disability within immigrant categories and feed into the 'cost burden' arguments that dominate the area, understanding the prevalence of disability within these communities is particularly important in mobilising local community groups to drive policy change towards inclusion.[10]

This quotation from Soldatic and colleagues demonstrates that quantification reduces the bodies and lives of people who are migrants with disability to a cost calculation by states; however, the same data may be used to advocate for policy changes that benefit people who are migrants with disability.[11]

The *Humanitarian Inclusion Standards for Older People and People with Disabilities* ('*2018 Humanitarian Disability-Inclusion Standards*') provides some details about how data may be useful for people who are refugees with disability.[12] The standards provide case studies illustrating disability data production and processing's role in disability-inclusive humanitarian planning and programming. It is important to note that these examples assume high levels of participation and disclosure by data subjects. Further, there is not enough information at times to determine whether the data production and processing benefits flow to the data subject, people in similar situations or the broader community. Examples covered in the standards about the power of data to promote, protect and ensure human rights for people with disability may be categorised as follows: (1) identifying who may be missing, (2) verifying programs are engaging with people with disability, (3) identifying when people are disproportionately impacted and (4) understanding the changing needs of a population.

In one such example, the *2018 Humanitarian Disability-Inclusion Standards* assessed that low response rates from a population group in datasets might indicate access issues. The standards point to the low numbers of people with disability identified in the Office of the United Nations High Commissioner for Refugees ('UNHCR') registration data as evidence that people with disability may not be accessing a camp.[13] Therefore, data were used to prompt further investigations of possible access issues.

10 Karen Soldatic et al, '"Nowhere to Be Found": Disabled Refugees and Asylum Seekers Within the Australian Resettlement Landscape' (2015) 2(1) *Disability and the Global South* 501, 507.

11 Note that these data are not collected under the authority of *CRPD* art 31, rather, the administrative process states undertake to assess visa applications. Therefore, while it may be illustrative of how data may be used to be harmful and helpful, it was collected for a different purpose.

12 See earlier Section 6.3.3(b) for a critique of CBM International, HelpAge International and Handicap International, *Humanitarian Inclusion Standards for Older People and People with Disabilities* (Report, 2018).

13 Ibid., 31.

Data may also be used as a method of accountability for delivering inclusive services. In the example shared in the *2018 Humanitarian Disability-Inclusion Standards*, a funding body required the disaggregation of beneficiaries' data by sex, age and disability.[14] The example concluded: 'what started with the collection of disaggregated data led to a comprehensive delivery of a response designed with the whole community in mind'.[15] The funding body used the data to verify that people with disability were receiving benefits from the funds.

Funds may be directed towards disability-inclusive programming because it has been identified that a particular event or context may disproportionately impact people with disability. The *2018 Humanitarian Disability-Inclusion Standards* described a scenario where data were used to determine that people with disability disproportionately lacked access to potable water and hygienic sanitation facilities.[16] Data may highlight disparity, communicate needs and determine target populations for positive measures, including foreign aid.[17]

Lastly, the *2018 Humanitarian Disability-Inclusion Standards* propose that disability data are necessary to understand a population's changing needs.[18] Populations on the move likely have changing demographics from their community of origin. People experience different levels of persecution and adversity and have access to varying resources. Therefore, individuals and families decide whether it is in their interest to stay or go. Furthermore, conditions faced during the flight to safety may impact the degree of disability a person experiences.[19] Disability data about populations on the move, including displaced populations in prolonged contexts, allow states, international organisations and civil society to understand the changing needs of a population and plan accordingly.[20]

Accepting that disability data in refugee contexts and beyond may be useful provides a rationale for exploring some strategies to minimise the harm caused by data production and processing.[21] The human rights promoting uses of data illustrated in this subsection provide the impetus to explore human rights–based data production and processing about the bodies and lives of people with disability in the following sections. The next subsection about support for disability data production and processing by people with disability and their representative organisations provides another important

14 Ibid., 78.

15 Ibid., 79.

16 Ibid., 138–139.

17 See generally Marcia H Rioux, Paula Campos Pinto and Gillian Parekh (eds), *Disability, Rights Monitoring, and Social Change: Building Power Out of Evidence* (Canadian Scholars' Press, 2015).

18 CBM International, HelpAge International and Handicap International (n 12) 207.

19 See Section 6.1 for a description of factors that will alter disability.

20 See, eg, United Nations Children's Fund (UNICEF), *Included, Every Step of the Way: Upholding the Rights of Migrant and Displaced Children with Disabilities* (Report, 2023).

21 See earlier Chapter 3.

source of analysis to inform how data may be produced and processed about people with disability while minimising harm.

7.1.2 *Support for Disability Data Production and Processing from People With Disability and Their Representative Organisations*

Another essential reason to consider the benefits of disability data production and processing is the support it receives from people with disability and their representative organisations.[22] Given the diversity of people with disability and their varied experiences of data production and processing, it is striking that public dissent about disability data production and processing today is rare, even nonexistent. Despite the concerns this monograph has raised about the production and processing of data about the bodies and lives of people with disability, I do not want this monograph, informed by the Disability Human Rights Research Protocol,[23] to be paternalistic. I want it to support the wishes of people with disability and their representative organisations.

People with disability must be closely consulted and actively involved in 'the development and implementation of legislation and policies to implement' the *CRPD*.[24] The humanitarian sector, adhering to this obligation, included people with disability and their representative organisations in developing the tools, manuals and standards described in Section 6.3.3(b) that operationalise disability data production and processing. The considerable support that disability data production and processing now receives from prominent disability rights advocates,[25] disabled persons organisations ('DPOs')[26] and the Committee on the Rights of Persons with Disabilities ('CRPD Committee')[27]

22 *CRPD* (n 3) art 4(3).

23 See earlier Section 2.2.2(b); Arstein-Kerslake et al (n 7).

24 *CRPD* (n 3) art 4(3).

25 Disability activists are asking for disability data and methods by which to collect it: 'There is finally a realization that if action is not disability inclusive, it will not deliver change or progress for everyone . . . organisations [delivering programs] need data collection tools and methodologies to be able to plan effectively, they need evidence and insights to know which tools to use and when to use them'. Judith E Heumann, 'Foreword' in Leonard Cheshire and Humanity & Inclusion (ed), *Disability Data Collection: A Summary Review of the Use of the Washington Group Questions by Development and Humanitarian Actors* (Report, 2018) 1.

26 The International Disability Alliance, which represents over 1,100 DPOs worldwide, has a Disability Data Advocacy Working Group. The group's website asserts that 'if persons with disabilities are not counted, then they don't count'. 'Disability Data Advocacy Working Group', *International Disability Alliance* (Web Page) <https://www.internationaldisabilityalliance.org/content/disability-data-advocacy-working-group>. See later Section 7.4.1 for a discussion about the complexity of representation through DPOs.

27 The Committee on the Rights of Persons with Disabilities comprises a majority of people with disability. 'Membership: Committee on the Rights of Persons with Disabilities', *Office of the High Commissioner for Human Rights* (Web Page) <https://www.ohchr.org/en/treaty-bodies/crpd/membership>. See also earlier Chapter 1 n 3, Section 1.2.2 at nn 70–80,

signifies a substantial change in position from the drafting negotiations in the early 2000s.[28]

In the public sphere, finding a voice of dissent or caution among people with disability and their representative organisations about the production and processing of disability data is difficult. The lack of dissent is unusual, given the diversity of jurisdictions, people and experiences in the disability rights movement. Data to identify those not accessing services, verify disability-inclusive programs, measure disparity and target needs are valuable for advocates engaging with governments worldwide. Understandably, DPOs champion the collection of data to fulfil these needs.

In conclusion, data is powerful and may be used to promote human rights. Production and processing of data about the bodies and lives of people with disability appears to receive almost universal support from DPOs and those charged with monitoring the implementation of the treaty, the CRPD Committee. Nonetheless, advocates who seek to harness the useful qualities of data to promote, protect and ensure human rights have not paid enough attention to the potential harms. The remainder of the chapter looks at measures to ensure human rights protections are in place when producing and processing data about the bodies and lives of people with disability. The following section examines how to test whether it is 'appropriate' to produce disability data.

7.2 When Is It Appropriate to Count People With Disability in Refugee Contexts?

This project's Stakeholder Advisory Group members noted in their fourth meeting, which was the first to concentrate on the *CRPD* article 31 text, that the term 'appropriate' left considerable scope for discretion.[29] Chapter 6 argued that this discretion has not been exercised transparently or systematically by the UNHCR, the CRPD Committee and other networks that operationalise disability data production and processing in refugee contexts. The operationalisation in all instances removed the directions to only produce data 'as appropriate', without explanation or assessment of how it was determined that disability data production and processing in these instances would be appropriate.

Responding to the lack of a test to assess whether data production and processing is appropriate, the following explores whether disability data can and should be produced and processed in refugee contexts, that is, whether it is

---

Section 1.3.1 at nn 87–88, and Chapter 5 n 1, 101, 137, 186 for examples of the committee's recommendations regarding data production and processing.

28 See earlier Section 4.3.2.

29 [While reviewing the CRPD article 31 text], [t]he group highlighted the word 'appropriate' in the text of paragraph 1 and wrote the note: 'appropriate'. This is vague. Defined by who? What is the standard of 'appropriate'? Define the standard 'appropriate'. Stakeholder Advisory Group meeting minutes, 18 June 2021.

appropriate. This chapter proposes that a test of appropriateness requires that data production and processing must be as follows:

(a) Necessary. Can the information be obtained through other, less invasive means?
(b) Achievable. Is it likely to achieve the specified purpose?
(c) Legal. Does it comply with human rights law? If not, is there a legal basis for derogation or limitation?

This three-part test for 'appropriateness' will be explored by examining approaches to population needs assessment to consider 'necessity' in 7.2.1. Next, to consider 'achievability', Section 7.2.2 critiques the disability data survey of choice in refugee contexts, the *Washington Group Short Set of Questions on Disability.*[30] Section 7.2.3 explores 'legality' by reviewing the nature of disability data and the complexity of consent in humanitarian contexts.

7.2.1 Necessary: Measuring Disability Prevalence

Disability data in refugee contexts appear to be produced for two primary reasons: (1) to identify and meet individual needs and (2) to identify and respond to population needs. The population needs category can be divided further, as was differentiated by the *Guidelines on Inclusion of Persons with Disabilities in Humanitarian Action* ('*IASC Guidelines*'),[31] into (a) prevalence/participation data (identifying people with disability, what they do and where they are) and (b) barrier information. The following analysis will examine the necessity of producing and processing disability prevalence and participation data (2a). As the *2018 Humanitarian Disability-Inclusion Standards* recommended, information about barriers (2b) should be sourced directly from people with disability in smaller self-selecting groups.[32]

In considering the necessity of data production and processing, it is relevant to consider whether population and participation data are available elsewhere that enables planning to meet the needs of people with disability in a given refugee context. The *IASC Guidelines* suggest that a proxy of 15% may be used when population data are unavailable.[33] Compared with most population surveys undertaken by specialist agencies,[34] this proportion underestimates the

30 See earlier Sections 6.3.2 and 6.3.3.

31 Inter-Agency Standing Committee (IASC), *Guidelines on Inclusion of Persons with Disabilities in Humanitarian Action* (2019) 28.

32 CBM International, HelpAge International and Handicap International (n 12) 22.

33 IASC (n 31) 27.

34 Handicap International and Help Age International interviewed a random sample of 3,202 people who had fled to Jordan and Lebanon from Syria and found that 22% of those surveyed reported having impairments, and 6% reported that their impairments were severe. HelpAge International and Handicap International, *Hidden Victims of the Syrian Crisis: Disabled, Injured and Older Refugees* (Report, 2014) 6. Consistent with the earlier study, Humanity

total number of people with disability and is silent on the intensity of support required. Nonetheless, it is significantly higher than the number of people registered as having disability with the UNHCR.[35]

An assessment of necessity should be informed by the benefit and cost to the data subject. The omission of mental health questions in the UNHCR screening is somewhat illustrative of this point.[36] Mental health impairments are generally the most prevalent impairment reported in population needs assessments in refugee contexts.[37] Nevertheless, there are often not enough services to meet the need.[38] Considering if it is necessary to ask people about their mental health raises an important question: Is it ethical to request information from people who will receive little or no benefit from disclosing their information?

Humanity & Inclusion and Leonard Cheshire, in their review of the Washington Group questions on disability in humanitarian settings, found 'that organisations felt asking the WGQ [Washington Group Questions] raised expectations of beneficiaries for support; often without there being programme capacity to meet these expectations'.[39] How remote can the benefit be to the

---

and Inclusion (formerly Handicap International) and iMMAP reported in 2018 that 22.9% of a sample of over 6,000 Syrian refugees in Jordan experienced disability. Humanity & Inclusion and iMMAP, *Removing Barriers: The Path Towards Inclusive Access: Disability Assessment Among Syrian Refugees in Jordan and Lebanon: Jordan Report* (Report, July 2018). Interestingly, the VASyR 2020 survey reported disability prevalence within the Syrian refugee population in Lebanon at 9%, which is dramatically different to the earlier surveys. United Nations Children's Fund (UNICEF), United Nations High Commissioner for Refugees (UNHCR) and United Nations World Food Program (WFP), *VASyR2020: Vulnerability Assessment of Syrian Refugees in Lebanon* (Report, February 2021).

35 'Just 1.4 per cent of UNHCR-registered refugees in Lebanon are recorded as having a disability' HelpAge International and Handicap International (n 34) 6.

36 The UNHCR has not adopted the *Washington Group Extended Set on Functioning* questions about depression and anxiety. Washington Group on Disability Statistics, *The Washington Group Extended Set on Functioning (WG-ES)* (11 October 2022) 12.

37 'For adults, the prevalence estimates for anxiety (10.6%) and depression (6.3%) were similar to those from Jordon and Lebanon (11.4% and 5.9% respectively). Anxiety and depression were among the most commonly reported of the WG functional domains in both studies, highlighting the need for quality Mental Health and Psychosocial Support (MHPSS) for displaced Syrians. However, our estimates are considerably lower than those of a 2018 survey conducted among adult Syrians in Sultanbeyli, which used specific mental health screening tools (Hopkins Symptoms Checklist) for anxiety (36.1%) and depression (34.7%) [23]. This suggests that the WG questions, using the recommended cut-off, may under-estimate prevalence of symptomatic anxiety and depression'. Sarah Polack et al, 'Disability among Syrian Refugees Living in Sultanbeyli, Istanbul: Results From a Population-Based Survey' (2021) 16(11) *PLoS One* e0259249, 10.

38 See generally Charles W Cange et al, 'Considering Chronic Uncertainty Among Syrian Refugees Resettling in Europe' (2019) 4(1) *The Lancet Public Health* e14; Breanne L Grace, Rajeev Bais and Benjamin J Roth, 'The Violence of Uncertainty – Undermining Immigrant and Refugee Health' (2018) 379(10) *New England Journal of Medicine* 904.

39 Leonard Cheshire and Humanity & Inclusion, *Disability Data Collection: A Summary Review of the Use of the Washington Group Questions by Development and Humanitarian Actors* (Report, 2018) 22.

person to demonstrate that it is necessary to request their information? Toleration of burden or cost to the data subject should reduce as the direct benefits become more remote. Further, the threshold for the cost to data subjects in refugee contexts should be very low, even negligible, for reasons explored earlier in this monograph about multiple and aggravated discrimination.[40]

The *Guidance on the Protection of Personal Data of Persons of Concern to UNHCR* includes the data protection principles of necessity and proportionality.[41] The guidance highlights that data minimisation is central to these principles.[42] Data minimisation is widely recognised as a fundamental principle of personal data protection. It ensures that 'data collected, shared or otherwise processed is necessary and relevant to achieve a specified purpose'.[43]

Ensuring the inclusion of people with disability is an important purpose that may be used to justify disability data production and processing, but there are other methods to ensure that programs are inclusive. Data may be unnecessary because other disability-inclusion strategies in the *CRPD* may fulfil the purpose. These strategies include awareness raising,[44] active involvement and close consultation with people with disability,[45] disability human rights research[46] and universal design.[47] In situations where the purpose of data production may be met otherwise, it is an unnecessary risk to produce and process information about the bodies and lives of people with disability in refugee contexts.[48]

7.2.2 *Achievable: A Critique of the Washington Group Questions in Refugee Contexts*

If data production is deemed necessary,[49] consideration must be given to whether data can be produced to meet the specified purpose. The following critiques a tool widely endorsed for use in refugee contexts,[50] the *Washington Group Short Set of Questions on Disability*. This critique contributes to a broader question about whether disability can be measured in refugee contexts: Is it achievable?

40 See earlier Section 6.1.

41 United Nations High Commissioner for Refugees (UNHCR), *Guidance on the Protection of Personal Data of Persons of Concern to UNHCR* (2018).

42 Ibid., 19.

43 Ibid., 5.

44 *CRPD* (n 3) art 8.

45 *CRPD* (n 3) art 4(3).

46 *CRPD* (n 3) arts 4(1)(f), (g), 31(1), 32(1)(c). See also, Arstein-Kerslake et al (n 7).

47 *CRPD* (n 3) art 4(1)(f).

48 See later Section 7.2.3(b) for an exploration of the considerations around 'necessity' when consent cannot be gained.

49 See earlier Section 7.2.1.

50 See earlier Sections 6.3.2 and 6.3.3.

Data variables are constructs to which definitions have been attributed. To understand what is being counted when measuring disability prevalence, it is useful to return to the *CRPD*'s description of disability. Disability, according to the *CRPD*, results from the interaction between impairments and barriers external to the person (ie, in the social and physical environment), the impact of which reduces 'full and effective participation in society'.[51] Disability prevalence statistics, such as those generated by the *Washington Group Short Set of Questions on Disability*, may be evaluated against this description. Adhering to the *CRPD*'s description of disability is essential if the data production is for *CRPD* article 31.

The *Washington Group Short Set of Questions on Disability* was developed 'to generate usable data for government' in population surveys such as censuses.[52] Since then, it has gained endorsement for use within humanitarian contexts.[53] The survey includes six questions intended to identify people with disability.[54] Respondents select from a scale: 'No – no difficulty', 'Yes – some difficulty', 'Yes – a lot of difficulty', 'Cannot do at all'. The *2018 Humanitarian Disability-Inclusion Standards* recommended that responses 'Yes – a lot of difficulty' and 'Cannot do at all' to any question should be the 'cut-off point for classification of a person with a disability for data disaggregation purposes'.[55]

The *Washington Group Short Set of Questions on Disability* begins with '[b]ecause of a health problem'. This phrase is likely intended to cover the 'impairment' aspect of the *CRPD* definition of disability.[56] Beyond the chapeau, the first four questions of the survey are as follows: (1) 'Do you have difficulty seeing, even if wearing glasses?' (2) 'Do you have difficulty hearing, even if using a hearing aid?' (3) 'Do you have difficulty walking or climbing steps?' and (4) 'Do you have difficulty remembering or concentrating?'[57] While the survey developers describe all the questions as 'functional', these first four questions do not account for the environment in which these activities occur. Instead, they focus on the body's ability to undertake the activity and are, therefore, impairment focused. Furthermore, the third and fourth questions do not consider the aids and equipment that people may use to enable them to do these activities.

51 *CRPD* (n 3) Preamble para e, art 1.
52 Leonard Cheshire and Humanity & Inclusion (n 39) 3.
53 Office of the United Nations High Commissioner for Refugees (UNHCR), *Working with Persons with Disabilities in Forced Displacement: Need to Know Guidance* (2019) ('*2019 Guide*') 15–16.
54 Earlier conceptual notes caution that 'it is imperative to recognize that the general disability measure developed to suit our proposed purpose may not suit other purposes. Nor will it provide a comprehensive assessment of disability or identify the "true" disabled population . . . Users must be aware of the limitations that accompany the proposed purpose and its operationalization in order for outcomes to be meaningful and comparable'. Barbara M Altman and Elizabeth K Rasch, 'Purpose of an International Comparable Census Disability Measure' in Barbara M Altman (ed), *International Measurement of Disability: Purpose, Method and Application* (Springer International Publishing, 2016) 55, 65.
55 CBM International, HelpAge International and Handicap International (n 12) 21.
56 UNHCR, *2019 Guide* (n 53) 16.
57 UNHCR, *2019 Guide* (n 53) 16.

Question 5 does reflect concepts that consider the impairment-environment interaction: (5) 'Do you have difficulty (with self-care) such as washing all over or dressing?' To illustrate how the environment is accounted for in this question, consider a person who had an accessible bathroom at their home from which they fled. If the survey had been undertaken before their flight, they might have responded that they experienced 'no difficulty' in undertaking their self-care. Within their new context, they may have shared facilities away from their home, which may be inaccessible, and now they may find they have 'a lot of difficulty' or 'cannot do at all' due to the change in environment. This scenario exemplifies how refugee flight has increased disability without changing the level of impairment a person experiences.

The sixth question again does not account adequately for the environment: (6) 'Using your usual (customary) language, do you have difficulty communicating, for example understanding or being understood?'[58] Consider a Deaf person who uses Iraqi Sign Language to communicate. Following displacement and resettlement to Australia, they may feel isolated and unable to participate in society, as they cannot use Auslan (Australian sign language). However, it would be reasonable for this person to respond that they have 'no difficulty' communicating in their 'usual language'. This example demonstrates that this question has an impairment focus, does not account for the environment and, therefore, is not a measure of disability.

This critique of the *Washington Group Short Set of Questions on Disability* brings into focus the second element of the 'appropriateness' test, achievability. Is the recommended survey to identify disability in refugee contexts achieving its purpose? This critique demonstrated that the *Washington Group Short Set of Questions on Disability* is not measuring disability as described in the *CRPD*.

Even if one accepts that the *Washington Group Short Set of Questions on Disability* may be a 'good-enough' proxy tool to measure disability, achieving representative disability data is heavily contingent on the enumerating organisation's capacity and data subjects' views on whether it is in their best interest to disclose their information. There is a vast variation in disability prevalence measured by specialist organisations compared to generalist humanitarian organisations when using the *Washington Group Short Set of Questions on Disability*.[59] Further, even though the survey does not have explicit provisions for people to choose not to identify, that is, the response 'I prefer not to say' or similar,[60] some people will choose not to disclose their information and remain strategically anonymous.[61]

This subsection raises important questions about whether it is achievable to measure disability prevalence in refugee contexts using the *Washington Group*

58 UNHCR, *2019 Guide* (n 53) 16.

59 See earlier n 34.

60 See later Section 7.3.1 for an exploration of the *Washington Group Short Set of Questions on Disability*'s compliance with the human rights principle of self-identification.

61 See earlier Section 6.4.

Short Set of Questions on Disability. The following explains the final part of the 'appropriateness' assessment: legal basis, including a discussion about the ethics of using a proxy to collect data on disability status.

7.2.3 Legal Basis: The Nature of Disability Data and the Impact of Context

> We come from countries where we keep our mouths shut about personal data. Whole tribes have been wiped out because of data.[62]

This quotation from the Stakeholder Advisory Group reflects how context may change the nature of data. Variables that seem innocuous in one context, such as ethnicity, may be extremely harmful in other contexts. One of the advisory group members said they had a good friend whose surname they did not know because this information would communicate the friend's ethnicity.[63] The friend's life experience of ethnic genocide had taught them to be cautious with this information.

The *IASC Guidelines* include a chapter on 'Data and Information Management'.[64] As stated in Section 6.3.3(b), the guidelines require 'every stakeholder in every sector and all contexts' to disaggregate data by disability for monitoring and inclusion.[65] They equate the production and processing of disability data to the production and processing of sex and age data.[66] The guidelines also emphasise '[t]he importance of informed consent in data collection and use' with a dedicated box with the same title.[67]

The earlier reflections from the advisory group and the excerpts from the *IASC Guidelines* raise two critical questions: (1) *What is the nature of disability data?* Are disability data the same as data on age and sex? Or are they more sensitive, of a similar nature to health and biometric data? Does refugee context alter the nature of disability data? (2) *When consent is impossible, should disability data be collected?* The following explores these questions in two sub-subsections. The first sub-subsection is a discussion about the nature of disability data. The nature of data is significant in that different legal protections exist for more sensitive data. The second sub-subsection explores the legal basis for data collection.

a) Is Disability Data Sensitive Data?

The International Committee of the Red Cross' *Handbook on Data Protection in Humanitarian Action* ('*ICRC Handbook on Data Protection*') defines

62 Stakeholder Advisory Group meeting minutes, 16 July 2021.
63 Stakeholder Advisory Group meeting minutes, 8 July 2022.
64 IASC (n 31) 23–31.
65 IASC (n 31) 19.
66 IASC (n 31) 25.
67 IASC (n 31) 26.

sensitive data as 'personal data which, if disclosed, may result in discrimination against or the repression of the individual concerned'.[68] Disability data may be sensitive given their potential to be used for discrimination. The *ICRC Handbook on Data Protection* explains that data's sensitivity may be altered by the 'specific situations in which Humanitarian Organizations work'.[69] This context-dependent view of data sensitivity requires organisations to make assessments of a data variable's sensitivity based on their operational context.[70]

Despite this context-dependent view of data sensitivity, the *ICRC Handbook on Data Protection* identifies health data as 'particularly sensitive'.[71] Due to the sensitive nature of this data, they require 'specific guarantees'.[72] Health data have corresponding procedures, including that they 'should be kept separate from other Personal Data' and only made accessible to health providers and those that manage health data.[73] Similarly, biometric data were identified as sensitive, requiring 'special protection'.[74]

Disability data often overlaps with health data, where a health condition may contribute to an impairment. Likewise, biometric data, 'measurable, unique human signatures that may include fingerprints, iris scans or behavioural characteristics such as the way a person walks',[75] also overlap with data that quantifies the bodies and lives of people with disability. Nonetheless, disability data are not categorised as sensitive data in any operational guides, guidelines or standards that promote disability data collection in refugee contexts.

Interestingly, the Stakeholder Advisory Group for this research project felt that disability data differ from age and gender; they are more sensitive.[76] This view is also reflected in the *Washington Group Short Set of Questions on Disability*'s instructions, which state that enumerators should avoid asking people if they or their family have a disability.[77] Enumerators are meant to ask questions about 'difficulty'.[78] This avoidance of asking about disability appears related to concerns about low response rates due to data subjects who may assess a high risk of deleterious effects of disclosing disability. However, to some extent, using a proxy to elicit information dismisses or circumvents people's genuine

68 Personal data is 'information relating to an identified or identifiable natural person'. Christopher Kuner and Massimo Marelli (eds), *Handbook on Data Protection in Humanitarian Action* (International Committee of the Red Cross, 2nd ed, 2020) 14.
69 Ibid., 14.
70 Ibid., 15.
71 Ibid., 39.
72 Ibid., 39.
73 Ibid., 40.
74 Ibid., 131.
75 Ibid., 128.
76 Stakeholder Advisory Group meeting minutes, 16 July 2021.
77 See, eg, Leonard Cheshire and Humanity & Inclusion (n 39) 25.
78 Marguerite Schneider, 'The Difference a Word Makes: Responding to Questions on "Disability" and "Difficulty" in South Africa' (2009) 31(1) *Disability and Rehabilitation* 42.

concerns about protecting themselves from being labelled as having a disability. Labelling people with disability without their participation in the process diminishes their autonomy to determine whether they want their disability to be visible.[79]

Likewise, some people are careful about disclosing age and gender in refugee contexts due to discrimination they may face or to access certain entitlements. For instance, some people may want to gain entitlements only available to younger people – such as family reunification entitlements for minors. Some people conceal their gender to enable freedom of movement. For example, female children in female-headed households may leave their gender ambiguous to allow freedom of movement to enable survival. Refugee contexts are characterised by limited access to legal recourse and struggles for survival. Therefore, people take measures to protect themselves in these situations, including censoring the information they disclose.

Identifying openly and being proud of one's identity is a feature of the minority rights movement.[80] Identity pride has been an essential element of the LGBTIQ+ and Indigenous rights movements, among others. Similarly, some people with disability have advocated for disability identity to be celebrated and for disabled people to be visible and proud.[81] Nonetheless, openly identifying comes at a calculated risk for all people who face discrimination. People who are refugees with disability make the calculated decision whether to identify or not. They decide whether their information is too sensitive to share or not. Of course, with trusted conduits, people will disclose the difficulties that they are facing.[82] However, this reluctance and the need to build trust reflects that the data should be kept in trust – away from others that a person may not trust with their data, such as state entities. Furthermore, collecting information under one banner (difficulty) and then deciding whether it indicates another form of information (disability) calls into question whether the nature of the information changes, that is, it becomes sensitive data.

It is unclear whether the lack of discussions about the nature of disability data is an oversight or if these discussions are being actively avoided. Potentially,

79 See earlier Section 6.4.

80 A minority rights approach 'characterizes disabled people as a social minority group who must seek out their basic civic rights and fight against discrimination'. Jerome E Bickenbach et al, 'Models of Disablement, Universalism and the International Classification of Impairments, Disabilities and Handicaps' (1999) 48 *Social Science & Medicine* 1173, 1179. The minority disability rights approach views 'disability as a group-defining characteristic'. Sandra Fredman, 'Disability Equality: A Challenge to the Existing Anti-Discrimination Paradigm?' in Anna Lawson and Caroline Gooding (eds), *Disability Rights in Europe: From Theory to Practice. Essays in European Law* (Hart Publishing, 2005) 199, 206.

81 See, eg, Zach Christensen, *Generating Disability Statistics: Models of Disability Measurement, History of Disability Statistics and the Washington Group Questions: Background Paper* (Development Initiatives, September 2020) 4; Jenny Morris, *Pride Against Prejudice: Transforming Attitudes to Disability* (New Society, 1991).

82 Stakeholder Advisory Group meeting minutes, 18 June 2021, 20 August 2021.

these debates are being avoided due to the difficult discussions about disability identity and the potential for some to view labelling disability data as 'sensitive' as akin to feeling shame about disability. A way forward would be to recast these discussions and direct the focus to people with disability having more control over their data. Moving data production and processing towards the individual autonomy end of the spectrum (depicted in Figure 6.1) enables conditions that allow for strategic anonymity or human rights advocacy.[83] Giving people greater control over their data aligns with the human rights–based approach to data that allows people to self-define and choose to identify.[84]

b) Consent and Other Legal Bases for Personal Data Production and Processing

There is no comprehensive international legal regime that governs data protection. Data privacy legal scholar Lee Bygrave explains that data sharing between jurisdictions often requires the receiving countries to have similar data protection laws to that of the country of origin.[85] Over time, this has resulted in 'international codes . . . embody[ing] the bulk of the central rules in national and sub-national codes'.[86] This regulatory reality is reflected in the 307-page *ICRC Handbook on Data Protection* that 'seeks to raise awareness and assist Humanitarian Organizations in ensuring that they comply with Personal data protection standards in carrying out humanitarian activities'.[87]

The *ICRC Handbook on Data Protection* is written for operations and does not include citations to the authorities from which it makes legal claims; instead, it provides a list of the legal sources on which it relies.[88] The nature of legal advice about data protection in refugee contexts and broader humanitarian responses is further complicated by the range of actors: 'Humanitarian Organizations, local authorities and private entities'.[89] Some of these actors are 'subject to the jurisdiction of the country in which they operate, while

83 See earlier Section 6.4.

84 See later Sections 7.3 and 7.4.

85 Lee A Bygrave, *Data Privacy Law in Context* (Oxford University Press, 2014) xxv.

86 Lee A Bygrave, *Data Privacy Law in Context* (Oxford University Press, 2014) xxv.

87 Kuner and Marelli (n 68) 23–24.

88 Kuner and Marelli (n 68) 22. These sources include United National General Assembly Resolution, *Guidelines for the Regulation of Computerized Personal Data Files*, GA Res 45/95 (14 December 1990); UN High-Level Committee on Management, *Personal Data Protection and Privacy Principles* (11 October 2018); International Conference of Data Protection and Privacy Commissioners, *International Standards on the Protection of Personal Data and Privacy* (5 November 2009); Organisation for Economic Co-Operation and Development, *The OECD Privacy Framework* (2013) 154; Council of Europe, *Convention for the Protection of Individuals with Regard to Automatic Processing of Personal Data*, opened for signature 28 January 1981, ETS No 108 (entered into force 1 October 1985).

89 Kuner and Marelli (n 68) 34.

others . . . [have] privileges and immunities'.[90] The *ICRC Handbook on Data Protection* acknowledges the jurisdictional variation and provides general guidance on the interpretation of 'data protection principles in the context of Humanitarian Action'.[91]

The *ICRC Handbook on Data Protection* suggests six legal bases on which personal data may be produced and processed in humanitarian contexts.[92] These include the following: 'vital interest of the Data Subject or of another person',[93] 'public interest',[94] 'consent', 'performance of contract',[95] 'legal obligation'[96] and 'legitimate interest'.[97] The *ICRC Handbook on Data Protection* suggests that in most humanitarian emergencies, including refugee contexts, it will not be possible to 'rely on Consent for most . . . Personal Data Processing'.[98]

The *ICRC Handbook on Data Protection* highlights various operational imperatives that interfere with consent: time, location and available personnel, among others.[99] Nonetheless, even when these logistical challenges may be overcome, gaining consent within refugee contexts will often be impossible because a person has 'no real choice to refuse Consent due to a situation of need and vulnerability, including a lack of alternative to the specific assistance being offered and the data Processing involved'.[100] Further, consent is hampered by the complex nature of data transactions across multiple jurisdictions typical of humanitarian responses, which makes it 'difficult for an individual to fully appreciate the risks and benefits of a Processing operation and, therefore, take the responsibility for it as entailed by giving Consent'.[101]

As refugee contexts often do not afford the opportunity for consent, humanitarian agencies must draw on other legal bases to legitimise the production and processing of personal data. According to the *ICRC Handbook on Data Protection*, the alternative legal bases only allow for the production and processing of 'necessary' information that must be 'truly necessary, rather than just convenient, to fulfil the relevant purpose'.[102] Data production must be truly necessary to meet the immediate humanitarian need. As demonstrated earlier in Section 7.2.1, there are limited circumstances where disability data production and processing are 'truly necessary'.

90 Kuner and Marelli (n 68) 34.
91 Kuner and Marelli (n 68) 21.
92 'Personal data' is defined earlier at n 68.
93 Kuner and Marelli (n 68) 66.
94 Kuner and Marelli (n 68) 67.
95 Kuner and Marelli (n 68) 70.
96 Kuner and Marelli (n 68) 70–71.
97 Kuner and Marelli (n 68) 68–69.
98 Kuner and Marelli (n 68) 61.
99 Kuner and Marelli (n 68) 61.
100 Kuner and Marelli (n 68) 61.
101 Kuner and Marelli (n 68) 62.
102 Kuner and Marelli (n 68) 67.

Further, there is an argument that the production of sensitive data should not occur without the data subject's consent.[103] Nonetheless, the *ICRC Handbook on Data Protection* concedes that there may be limited circumstances where sensitive data collection is necessary and consent cannot be gained.[104] Where consent cannot be gained, data should be held for a limited time.[105] Suppose disability data are sensitive,[106] in refugee contexts where consent is unlikely, data must be produced and processed for a clear and limited purpose to meet a vital interest, and its use and storage must be finite.

Given the concerns raised in this section about the difficulty in counting 'disability', the ambiguous nature of disability data and the barriers to informed consent, questions should be asked about whether data production and processing about the bodies and lives of people with disability in refugee contexts is 'appropriate'. Services may plan for at least 15% of people with disability accessing programs, and they may undertake consultation with their target group to understand barriers to rights attainment. Labelling people as having a disability and counting them is unnecessary for developing accessible services. Alternative methods for developing disability-inclusive humanitarian responses include closely consulting and actively involving people with disability and awareness raising,[107] which are explored in the following section about self-identification.

7.3 Giving Individuals With Disability More Control Over Data Production: Self-Identification

In philosophy, individual autonomy refers to living 'one's life according to reasons and motives that are taken as one's own and not the product of manipulative or distorting external forces'.[108] Individual autonomy is foundational to human rights law, and the *CRPD*'s Preamble and article 3, 'General principles', establish that article 31 must be interpreted according to this principle.[109] Nonetheless, individual autonomy is inconsistent with comprehensive and systematic data production practices, which require high levels of participation and compliance. This tension has been somewhat ignored and under-explored in human rights data and 'data for good' movements, which advocate for more comprehensive data production to ensure the needs of marginalised groups are reflected in representative datasets.[110]

103 Kuner and Marelli (n 68) 132.
104 Kuner and Marelli (n 68) 132–135.
105 Kuner and Marelli (n 68) 134.
106 See previous subsection for a discussion on this, 7.2.3(a).
107 *CRPD* (n 3) arts 4(3), 8.
108 John Christman, 'Autonomy in Moral and Political Philosophy' in Edward N Zalta (ed), *The Stanford Encyclopedia of Philosophy* (Metaphysics Research Lab, Stanford University, Fall 2020) <https://plato.stanford.edu/archives/fall2020/entries/autonomy-moral/>.
109 *CRPD* (n 3) Preamble para n, art 3(a). For the general rules of treaty interpretation, see *Vienna Convention on the Law of Treaties*, opened for signature 23 May 1969, 1155 UNTS 331 (entered into force 27 January 1980) art 31.
110 See earlier Section 6.3.3.

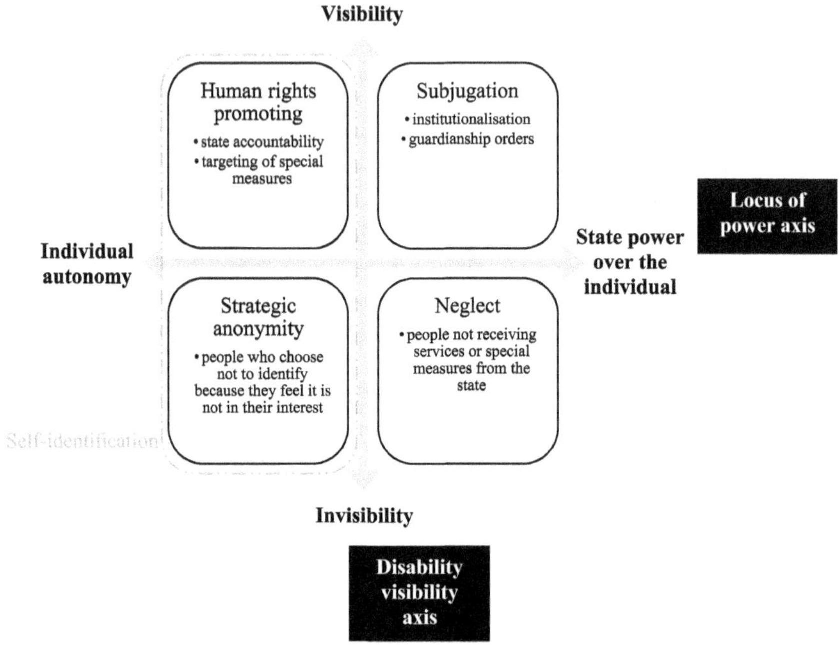

Figure 7.1 Framework with the intersecting axes of locus of power and disability visibility indicating the role of self-identification within this dynamic

In Section 6.4, this monograph introduced a new framework that illustrated the relationship between the locus of power and visibility on intersecting axes. This framework enabled consideration of the conditions that people with disability experience when states hold significant power over their lives compared to when people have greater individual autonomy. The framework enabled reflection on how experiences of visibility differ according to a person's legal status and context.

According to the framework, visibility combined with state control creates conditions that enable subjugation through practices such as institutionalisation and guardianship orders. Invisibility combined with state control enables conditions that allow neglect, which takes the form of inaccessible or absent government services and a lack of special measures to address disadvantages. This monograph is not arguing that these are causal relationships but that power combined with different levels of visibility creates enabling conditions for various actions and outcomes. Figure 7.1 is an updated framework reflecting these examples.

This framework is also helpful in determining the rationale and method of intervening to restore power to people with disability. Self-identification, the central topic of this section, enables people with disability to control their visibility. Self-identification suggests that the locus of power is with the individual rather than the state, as denoted in Figure 7.1.

This section argues that self-identification is an essential but forgotten principle in the human rights–based approach to data. Self-identification is often viewed as impractical due to concerns associated with under-identification and fraud. These concerns are not insurmountable and do not justify violating the principle of self-identification. These arguments will be progressed by first investigating why self-identification has become forgotten in data production and processing, followed by two subsections that respond to anxiety about under-identification and concerns about fraud.

7.3.1 Self-Identification: The Forgotten Principle of the Human Rights–Based Approach to Data

> Any information that an individual is not comfortable disclosing – this should be respected, and they should not be pushed for that data.[111]

'[I]ndividual autonomy including freedom to make one's own choices' includes the right to decide whether to disclose information about one's body and life.[112] Individual autonomy's importance in disability data production and processing was raised during the *CRPD* drafting in the International Disability Caucus' submission, which advocated for 'persons having the choice to self-identify as persons with disabilities but not being so identified . . . contrary to their choice'.[113] Externally imposing a categorisation was viewed as disempowering and ultimately linked to the medical model.[114]

Self-identification emerged from the understanding that categorising personal identity characteristics is not norm or value free.[115] To ensure people have the option to self-identify, the United Nations Office of the High Commissioner for Human Rights' ('OHCHR') guide, *A Human Rights-Based Approach to Data: Leaving No One Behind in the 2030 Agenda for Sustainable Development* ('*2018 Human Rights-Based Approach to Data Guide*'), stipulates that '[q]uestions about personal identity characteristics should be voluntary

111 Stakeholder Advisory Group meeting minutes, 16 July 2021.

112 *CRPD* (n 3) art 3(a).

113 Rehabilitation International, 'Daily Summary of Discussion at the Seventh Session 31 January 2006', *UN Convention on the Human Rights of People with Disabilities Ad Hoc Committee – Daily Summaries* (United Nations Enable, 31 January 2006) <https://www.un.org/esa/socdev/enable/rights/ahc7sum31jan.htm>.

114 'The IDC also objected on the basis that any definition would inevitably derive from the medical model, and would be externally imposed and disempowering (at various points in the debate, IDC spokespersons sought to assert a right to "self determine" identity as a "disabled person")'. Rosemary Kayess and Phillip French, 'Out of Darkness into Light – Introducing the Convention on the Rights of Persons with Disabilities' (2008) 8 *Human Rights Law Review* 1, 23.

115 Office of the High Commissioner for Human Rights (OHCHR), *A Human Rights-Based Approach to Data: Leaving No One Behind in the 2030 Agenda for Sustainable Development* (2018) 11 <https://www.ohchr.org/Documents/Issues/HRIndicators/GuidanceNoteonApproachtoData.pdf>.

and a non-response option should be provided; this is especially important where personal characteristics may be sensitive'.[116]

Self-identification is not a novel proposition. As noted in Section 5.1.3, in *I v United Kingdom*, a case brought by a transgender woman seeking to have her government documents reflect her gender, the European Court of Human Rights found she had a 'right to establish details of [her] . . . identity'.[117] Another area of international law that has grappled with identification is Indigenous rights. A fundamental element of Indigenous identity is a person self-identifying as Indigenous. To be accepted as so, they must also be identified as Indigenous by an Indigenous community.[118] Indigenous identification is a two-part process. Nonetheless, a person cannot be identified as Indigenous without self-identification.

Alongside self-identification, the *2018 Human Rights-Based Approach to Data Guide* outlines other essential principles of a human rights–based approach to producing and processing data. These principles include participation, data disaggregation, transparency, privacy and accountability.[119] The principles are interconnected and rely on each other to ensure that data production and processing are congruent with human rights. If a human rights–based approach to data is to be taken, all principles must be employed. However, projects often cite these principles individually to bolster claims that data production and processing are human rights compliant.

This tendency to prefer some *2018 Human Rights-Based Approach to Data Guide* principles over others is even seen in the OHCHR's work, such as in its recent report *Statistics and Data Collection under Article 31 of the Convention on the Rights of Persons with Disabilities*.[120] The report aimed to provide 'guidance on a human rights-based approach to data, specifically for persons with disabilities'.[121] The report includes legal and policy advice and case studies referencing participation,[122] transparency and accountability.[123] It also includes

116 Ibid., 12. See earlier Section 7.2.3(a) for a discussion on what constitutes sensitive data.

117 *I v United Kingdom* [2002] Eur Court HR 25680/94, [70].

118 See, eg, United Nations Permanent Forum on Indigenous Issues, *Fact Sheet: Who Are Indigenous Peoples?* (Fact Sheet, n.d.).

119 OHCHR, *A Human Rights-Based Approach to Data* (n 115).

120 Office of the High Commissioner for Human Rights (OHCHR), *Statistics and Data Collection Under Article 31 of the Convention on the Rights of Persons with Disabilities*, UN Doc A/HRC/49/60 (28 December 2021) ('*Article 31*').

121 Ibid., 1.

122 'Participation is a principle of the human rights-based approach to data and an obligation under article 4 (3) of the Convention'. Ibid., ('*Article 31*') [34]. 'A human rights-based approach to data calls for a redoubling of efforts to ensure that data are processed and provided to persons with disabilities in a way that they can immediately use to conduct independent analyses': at [52] (citations omitted).

123 'States should require greater transparency and accountability in respect of algorithms used in disability-related services, and adopt a human rights-based approach to big data, including on persons with disabilities and their human rights'. Ibid., [42]. 'States should, as part

entire sections on disaggregation[124] and privacy.[125] However, notably missing is self-identification.

Another example where little or no attention has been paid to self-identification is the *Washington Group Short Set of Questions on Disability*.[126] This chapter earlier challenged the claim that the tool is a measure of disability and problematised the tool's practice of categorising a person as disabled while avoiding the word disability.[127] It will now consider whether the *Washington Group Short Set of Questions on Disability* affords self-identification.

The *2018 Human Rights-Based Approach to Data Guide* states that self-identification requires that (a) questions about personal identity characteristics are voluntary and (b) a non-response option is provided.[128] The first part of this test is difficult to ascertain in an abstract exercise because context is critical to understanding whether the question is voluntary. The second part of the test is more straightforward to assess. Does the *Washington Group Short Set of Questions on Disability* allow for a non-response? It does not. As described in Section 7.2.2, respondents must select from the following: 'No, no difficulty; Yes, some difficulty; Yes, a lot of difficulty; Cannot do it at all'.[129] A fifth response option is required to meet the *2018 Human Rights-Based Approach to Data Guide* recommendations for self-identification, such as 'I prefer not to say' or similar.[130] According to this assessment, the *Washington Group Short Set of Questions on Disability* is incompatible with the *CRPD*'s obligations. It, therefore, should not be used to collect 'disability' data under the authority of article 31.[131]

Self-identification is challenging for data advocates, as datasets are more predictive and powerful if they are complete.[132] Self-identification threatens this predictive power because it inevitably accepts that datasets will be incomplete. Furthermore, concerns exist that self-identification may lead to people fraudulently identifying to receive material support intended for marginalised groups. Despite these concerns, human rights–adherent data production and

---

of the human rights-based approach, uphold the principle of transparency in respect of data to ensure accountability in policy implementation and to enhance the capacity of persons with disabilities to engage in policy design and implementation': at [46] (citations omitted).

124 Ibid., ('*Article 31*') 5–8.

125 Ibid., ('*Article 31*') 10–13.

126 Washington Group on Disability Statistics, *The Washington Group Short Set on Functioning (WG-SS)* (2018) 2.

127 See earlier Section 7.2.2.

128 OHCHR, *A Human Rights-Based Approach to Data* (n 115) 12.

129 Ibid.

130 The exact words should be tested to ensure they do not have any unintended consequences and that no value judgments are placed on the 'non-response' option other than indicating that a person would like to skip this question.

131 The quotation marks denote that questions have been raised earlier in this monograph about what is being measured. See earlier Section 7.2.2.

132 See earlier n 9.

processing require provision for self-identification. It is, therefore, vital that the root causes of these concerns that impede self-identification are examined and addressed.

7.3.2 Responding to Anxiety About Under-Identification

A human rights–based approach to data trusts that people with accessible information can make choices about self-identifying according to their beliefs and values, including their perception of personal safety. People who experience multiple and aggravated discrimination have reasons to remain anonymous. The following argues that strategies can be employed to increase the number of people willing to identify. Nonetheless, it also concedes that a human rights–based approach to data will mean that representative data are never achieved. Therefore, we need to look to other methods of achieving our aims that do not require coercing people to share information about their bodies and lives.

a) Trust Building

The principle of self-identification does not absolve states of their obligations to promote, protect and ensure human rights for people with disability.[133] Instead, it requires states, and those fulfilling obligations on their behalf, to create conditions where people with disability feel safe enough to identify and believe they will receive some benefit in doing so. Trust building with people who experience multiple and aggravated discrimination may take concerted and targeted efforts.

Open identification increases as marginalised communities feel safer and see the benefit of disclosing their status. The increased number of people identifying as Aboriginal in the recent Australian census was credited to a perceived reduction in 'some of the dangers of identifying as Aboriginal'.[134] This sense of safety and belief that there may be a benefit in openly identifying may be enhanced by duty-bearers' engagement with DPOs and awareness raising activities, discussed later.

b) Awareness Raising

Some academics, policy-makers and practitioners argue that, because of the stigma associated with disability, some survey respondents choose not to

133 *CRPD* (n 3) art 1.

134 Jackie Dent and Anna Kelsey-Sugg, 'Indigenous Australian Population Figures Jumped in Latest Census as Pride Increases and Fears Abate', *ABC News* (online, 6 July 2022) <https://www.abc.net.au/news/2022-07-07/indigenous-population-census-aboriginal-torres-strait-islander/101212240>.

identify or do not identify with this term.[135] The *CRPD* recognises that stigma creates barriers to people with disability realising their human rights. An entire article of the *CRPD* is dedicated to awareness raising, with states parties obligated to adopt the following:

> immediate, effective and appropriate measures . . . to raise awareness throughout society . . . to foster respect for the rights and dignity of persons with disabilities . . . [t]o combat stereotypes, prejudice and harmful practices . . . [t]o promote awareness of the capabilities and contributions of persons with disabilities.[136]

Awareness raising creates a mandate to engage with one of the root causes of disability – stigma. If tools that purport to identify disability avoid using the word disability because it is stigmatising, this creates no motivation to raise awareness and modify the social environment.

The *2018 Humanitarian Disability-Inclusion Standards* included a case study about funders responding to the needs of displaced people in Pakistan. The case study noted that 'villagers voiced concerns about sharing information on disabilities, due to taboos and a sense of shame around the subject'.[137] The funders discussed the data production process with the community and described how the data would be used. These steps reassured the community that the funders 'were genuinely interested in identifying barriers to accessing services'.[138] The *2018 Humanitarian Disability-Inclusion Standards* also highlight that disability data production activities may be practical methods of awareness raising, as they offer a systemic way of talking about the rights of people with disability to various actors and communities.[139]

c) Closely Consulting and Actively Involving People With Disability

Despite efforts to communicate and build trust with the community, some people may still decide not to provide their personal information because they do not view it as in their best interest. Others may not view their experience as disability despite their body and life reflecting a data definition formulated by experts. These complexities do not bolster claims for practices that avoid the term disability by using proxies such as difficulties.[140] Rather, they require us to focus on the actual obligation, which is not counting people and their

135 See, eg, Schneider (n 79).

136 *CRPD* (n 3) art 8(1).

137 CBM International, HelpAge International and Handicap International (n 12) 78.

138 CBM International, HelpAge International and Handicap International (n 12) 78.

139 See, eg, disability inclusion training for data enumerators. CBM International, HelpAge International and Handicap International (n 12) 31.

140 Schneider (n 78).

identity characteristics but identifying barriers to people with disability 'in exercising their rights'.[141] Barriers may be identified in close consultation and with the active involvement of people with disability. States may then be held accountable by producing and processing data on their actions to alleviate these barriers.[142]

States and those who fulfil obligations on their behalf should be held accountable for disability inclusion by being required to provide a narrative description of how people with disability, through their representative organisations, have been closely consulted and actively involved.[143] Obligation holders and fulfillers could be routinely asked: How do you closely consult and actively involve people with disability in fulfilling these obligations? How do you ensure diverse and marginalised voices are included? What changes were made as a result of this consultation and active involvement? What impact have these changes had on the realisation of rights for people with disability?

Datasets will be less comprehensive when people have a choice to self-identify. Nonetheless, trust building and awareness raising will improve response rates. However, counting people is not the ultimate purpose of article 31 data production and processing obligations. Effective implementation of the *CRPD* is possible with the other measures provided by the *CRPD*, including the close consultation and active involvement of DPOs.

7.3.3 Responding to Concerns About Fraud While Minimising Impost on Data Subjects: Data Minimisation and Neutral Third-Party Verification

States, international organisations and civil society use data to differentiate people and distribute resources to those deemed eligible. Resources are often finite, particularly in refugee contexts. Therefore, states, international organisations and civil society justify assessments (with externally imposed categorisation) to validate a person's material situation. External verification, including the biometric system introduced by the UNHCR, is often justified on the grounds of reducing fraud.[144] Self-identification can be exploited by people who may fraudulently claim an identity characteristic to gain resources allocated for marginalised groups. How should fraud be minimised without states, international organisations and civil society overreaching into the private lives of people with disability? In what instances is external verification of identity and need necessary?

141 *CRPD* (n 3) art 31(2).

142 See earlier Section 5.2 for an alternative doctrinal interpretation of *CRPD* art 31 that emphasises data production and processing about state actions to implement the treaty.

143 *CRPD* (n 3) arts 4(3), 33(3).

144 *Report of the United Nations High Commissioner for Refugees: Part II Global Compact on Refugees*, UN Doc A/73/12 (Part II) (13 September 2018, adopted 2 August 2018) para 58.

While states must fulfil obligations, such as providing social security benefits 'to the maximum of [their] . . . available resources',[145] human rights committees have acknowledged that states may face 'constraints owing to the limits of available resources'.[146] Further, even when the fiscal restraints are not significant, 'public authorities must take responsibility for the effective administration or supervision of the system' and 'ensure their sustainability'.[147] To ensure that a system is fiscally sustainable, eligibility criteria to determine those viewed as needing social security are necessary (eg, a criterion may be that a benefit is for people older than 70 years old).[148] Some people would likely exploit self-identification processes to access payments or benefits. Therefore, verifying that people meet the eligibility criteria is necessary.

Likewise, the UNHCR is entrusted with responsibly managing funds donated by states to fulfil its mandate. Therefore, like states, it must employ transparent methods of determining how to allocate funds, including eligibility criteria for special and targeted measures directed to people who experience marginalisation. Determining who fulfils these criteria requires some form of independent verification. Nonetheless, consideration should be given to avoid overreaching into the private lives of people who are refugees with disability. External verification must be balanced against the impost on people's lives. This balance may be achieved through data minimisation, which requires that 'data collected, shared or otherwise processed is necessary and relevant to achieve a specified purpose'.[149]

Lastly, the need for verification raises the question of who should undertake these assessments. Could a trusted, neutral third party undertake verification? This role may be similar to that the International Committee of the Red Cross plays in 'collect[ing] and centraliz[ing] information on the fate and whereabouts of POWs, dead or alive, for onward transmission to the parties and to the families'.[150] A trusted, neutral third party may act as an intermediary to verify that individuals meet eligibility criteria for state or UNHCR-targeted measures and hold the information in trust for the necessary period of time.

145 *International Covenant on Economic, Social and Cultural Rights*, opened for signature 16 December 1966, 993 UNTS 3 (entered into force 3 January 1976) art 2(1).

146 Committee on Economic, Social and Cultural Rights, *General Comment 19: The Right to Social Security (Art 9)* (2007) [40].

147 Ibid., [67].

148 Eligibility may be established, so long as 'Qualifying conditions for benefits must be reasonable, proportionate and transparent. The withdrawal, reduction or suspension of benefits should be circumscribed, based on grounds that are reasonable, subject to due process, and provided for in national law'. Ibid., [24] (citations omitted).

149 UNHCR, *Guidance on the Protection of Personal Data of Persons of Concern to UNHCR* (n 41) 5.

150 'Prisoners of War: What You Need to Know', *International Committee of the Red Cross* (Web Page, 19 May 2022) <https://www.icrc.org/en/document/prisoners-war-what-you-need-know>. See especially *Geneva Convention (III) Relative to the Treatment of Prisoners of War*, opened for signature 12 August 1949, 75 UNTS 135 (entered into force 21 October 1950) art 123.

In conclusion, self-identification is essential to the human rights approach to data. Self-identification requires responses to be voluntary and a non-response option to be provided for each question. There appears to be a low uptake by data controllers, policy officers and program managers of this fundamental aspect of a human rights approach to data due to concerns about under-identifying and fraud.

Under-identifying may be addressed by creating an environment where people view self-identifying as safe and congruent with their values and beliefs. Awareness raising about the rights of people with disability may also promote self-identification and is critical in modifying the environment to be less disabling. People may choose not to identify if they feel unsafe or view it as not in their interest; nonetheless, they are owed human rights.

Employing trusted third-party conduits may address concerns about people who will not self-identify to the state and anxieties about fraud. Those who do not wish to be visible, even to third-party conduits, benefit from state actions to improve accessibility and alleviate barriers identified through close consultation and active involvement of people with disability. The following explores how marginalised groups may gain more control over data production and processing.

7.4 Marginalised Groups Gaining and Maintaining Control Over Their Data

The *CRPD* contributes doctrine to the human rights–based approach to data. This section demonstrates further the *CRPD*'s contributions by exploring marginalised groups' autonomy in data production and processing practices. The *Macquarie Dictionary* definition of autonomy will be adopted for brevity, 'a self-governing community'.[151] The following is concerned with group self-governance or control over their data.

This section, building on Section 5.3, will continue to argue that the *CRPD* contributes doctrine to a legal basis for marginalised groups to have greater power to control their community data. This group (human) right protects against group harm from data production and processing. Community-generated and controlled data may also be a means to safeguard individuals from data harm. Nonetheless, community-generated and controlled data is currently undervalued.

These arguments will be progressed by examining the functioning of DPOs as democratic organisations that act as the vehicle for close consultation and

151 Exploring group autonomy could lead to a significant theoretical, philosophical and doctrinal enquiry beyond the scope of this monograph. For brevity, the *Macquarie Dictionary* definition of autonomy will be adopted, with a focus on self-governance of group data. *Macquarie Dictionary: Australia's National Dictionary Online* (Electronic Resource, Macquarie Library, 2003) <www.macquariedictionary.com.au>.

active involvement in matters affecting people with disability, as well as the holders of group (human) rights in the *CRPD*. This section will then revisit the group (human) right (not) to be counted, introduced in Chapter 5, to consider how it relates to the human rights principle of self-defining. It will conclude by exploring possible solutions that promote group autonomy, such as community-controlled data.

7.4.1 DPOs as Representative Organisations

People have multilayered identities. Data can provide some insight into the complexity of identity. As depicted in Figure 7.2, a person's identity may be defined by any combination of gender, sexuality, migration status, disability status, age and language spoken, among other characteristics and statuses.

When it comes to representation on issues related to a person's identity, they may not necessarily associate with organisations representing one, two or three aspects of their identity because intersectionality creates marginalisation unique to their experience.[152]

Groups cannot represent all individual interests. They often represent some form of consensus, compromise, majority opinion or the will of those who wield power within the group. Groups may be an effective method of collective bargaining and advocacy. Nonetheless, within groups, individual interests may not resonate with others and may be overlooked, or a group interest may even actively work to harm an individual group member's interest. Groups with significant heterogeneity may contain diverse and unaligned interests. Individual interests need to be carefully balanced with the interest of the collective.

DPOs must contain a majority of people with disability.[153] Aside from that, they may have other criteria to make them inclusive or representative of a particular identity, for example, women with disability, migrants with disability, Indigenous people with disability, autistic people, people who are blind and Deaf people, among others. The value of groups representing narrower interests is that they can more easily determine common needs and formulate a plan of action. However, groups representing the interests of a larger number of people can often speak with greater authority. Advocating with one voice for change can be powerful. Nonetheless, the drive for cohesion can be at the cost of creating spaces for dissenting views.

152 See earlier Sections 1.1.2 and 6.1.

153 Committee on the Rights of Persons with Disabilities, *General Comment No 7 (2018) on the Participation of Persons with Disabilities, Including Children with Disabilities, Through Their Representative Organizations, in the Implementation and Monitoring of the Convention*, UN Doc CRPD/C/GC/7 (9 November 2018) ('*General Comment 7 Participation*') [11].

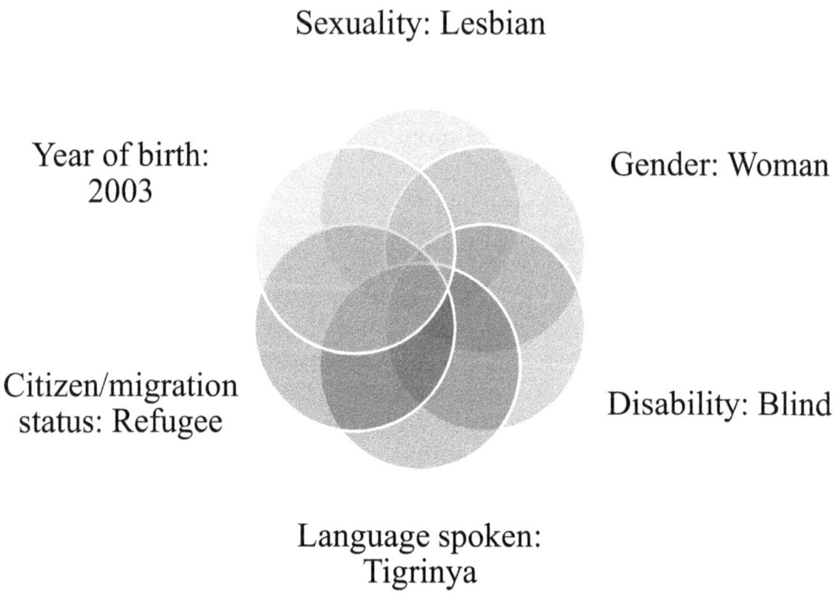

Figure 7.2 An image depicting a fictitious person's identity that has been captured through data categories

a) Lack of Dissent in DPOs About Disability Data Production and Processing

As raised throughout this monograph, it is surprising that diverse views about the production and processing of disability data are not represented amongst contemporary disability studies scholars, DPOs and other advocates. During the drafting of the *CRPD*, considerable dissent existed amongst DPOs about quantifying the bodies and lives of people with disability. Dissenters were acutely aware that the state gained more power over people with disability through data production and processing.[154]

One possibility for the current lack of dissent is the considerable funding allocated to operationalising disability data production and processing. State practice places considerable value on data for decision-making.[155] Funding initiatives to increase disability data production are, therefore, congruent with state priorities. Funding to operationalise disability data production, in turn, provides time and resources for scholars, policy advisors and program officers to write and speak about the import, benefits and methods of collecting data about the bodies and lives of people with disability.

154 See earlier Section 4.4.
155 See earlier Section 3.3.2.

Furthermore, critical examination of data practices is likely not an area that DPOs prioritise, given that *CRPD* article 31 contains procedural rather than substantive obligations. Article 31 may be viewed as a vehicle or authority to gather evidence to build arguments for delivering substantive obligations within the *CRPD*. This focus on the procedural may have allowed the possible harms of data production and processing to avoid scrutiny.

b) Representation of People Who are Refugees Within DPOs

Assuming greater power to control data production and processing is given to DPOs, the next issue that emerges is ensuring representation for marginalised groups. The CRPD Committee has issued comprehensive guidance in *General Comment 7* about the structure, functioning and resource needs of DPOs.[156] In *General Comment 7*, the committee proclaimed: 'The effective and meaningful participation of persons with disabilities, through their representative organizations, is . . . at the heart of the Convention'.[157] Nonetheless, they observed 'an important gap between the goals and the spirit of articles 4(3) and 33(3) and the degree to which they have been implemented'.[158] The General Comment endorses democratic methods. It also promotes diversity and advises carefully observing who is missing from forums and considering measures to improve accessibility to those groups.[159]

People who are refugees with disability are often a group not (well) represented in DPOs. In Australia, people who are refugees are largely absent from DPOs, facing numerous barriers to their participation, including language, culture, systems knowledge, unmet material need and discriminatory policies.[160] Furthermore, in Australia, people who are refugees with disability continue to face attitudinal barriers due to years of discriminatory migration policies;[161] for example, there is a belief that there are no people who are refugees with disability in Australia, so they are not missed from DPOs. Crock and

156 CRPD Committee, *General Comment 7 Participation* (n 153).

157 CRPD Committee, *General Comment 7 Participation* (n 153) [1].

158 CRPD Committee, *General Comment 7 Participation* (n 153) [8].

159 'To ensure that no one is left behind in relation to consultation processes, States parties should appoint persons with the role of following up on attendance, noticing underrepresented groups, and ensuring that accessibility and reasonable accommodation requirements are met'. CRPD Committee, *General Comment 7 Participation* (n 153) [54].

160 See Samantha Furneaux and Dina Korkees, *'We Need to Raise Our Voices': Advice From People of Refugee Backgrounds Living with Disabilities and Their Carers* (Report, Victorian Foundation for Survivors of Torture, 2019).

161 See Philippa Duell-Piening, 'Refugee Resettlement and the Convention on the Rights of Persons with Disabilities' (2018) 33(5) *Disability & Society* 661.

colleagues' book documenting extensive fieldwork exploring the rights of people who are refugees with disability described a similar encounter in Malaysia:

> In a memorable meeting that brought together representatives from Malaysian DPOs and leaders from organizations representing refugees from Myanmar, we listened with curiosity to a Malaysian man who asserted that in his region there were no wars and therefore no refugees.[162]

People who are refugees with disability are often not included in DPOs and face more significant barriers to developing their own advocacy organisations.[163] Therefore, their unique interests are not represented.

The lack of DPOs representing people who are refugees or asylum seekers is a crucial issue, as DPOs have significant power granted to them under *CRPD* article 4(3). As raised throughout this monograph, most people who are refugees live in prolonged displacement contexts where there is greater stability and potential to establish DPOs. Establishing DPOs in these contexts requires leadership, technical support and resourcing.[164] This prospect does not seem insurmountable with the current movement towards valuing the knowledge of people with lived experience in forced displacement contexts.[165]

Work is being undertaken to create mechanisms for people who are refugees to participate in decision-making processes affecting them.[166] However, it is rare in these forums to have a broad representation of people who are refugees with disability. Why does this matter? As discussed earlier, people who are refugees and asylum seekers with disability experience multiple and aggravated discrimination.[167] The detail of how this discrimination intersects to create further oppression is best understood from first-hand experience.

162 Mary Crock et al, *The Legal Protection of Refugees with Disabilities: Forgotten and Invisible?* (Edward Elgar Publishing, 2017) 274.

163 I met with Handicap International in Germany in 2019. They were working towards resourcing self-advocacy groups for people who were Syrian refugees. They noted that the demands of early settlement left little time for people to attend to systemic advocacy. Author's meeting notes, meeting with Dr Susanne Schwalgin and Wolfram Buttschardt, *Humanity and Inclusion Germany* (Formerly Handicap International Germany, Berlin, 3 September 2019). Similar observations have been made in Australia: see, eg, Furneaux and Korkees (n 160); Victorian Refugee Health Network, *Service Responses for People with Disabilities From Refugee Backgrounds in Northern Melbourne* (Victorian Foundation for Survivors of Torture, 2018).

164 This may include paying people for their time if they are giving up work or livelihood activities to attend.

165 See, eg, the recent issue of the *Forced Migration Review* about initiatives to increase the visibility of the lived experience knowledge of people in forced displacement in forums of power. 'Knowledge, Voice and Power' (2022) 70 *Forced Migration Review*.

166 Tristan Harley and Harry Hobbs, 'The Meaningful Participation of Refugees in Decision-Making Processes: Questions of Law and Policy' (2020) 32(2) *International Journal of Refugee Law* 200.

167 See earlier Section 6.1.

The interests of people who are refugees and asylum seekers with disability are not adequately represented. The consequence of neglecting to rectify the lack of participation of people who are refugees in DPOs is that group (human) rights enjoyed by DPOs may not be realised by people who are refugees with disability.[168] The lack of access to the group (human) right to be counted (discussed later) is significant because, as suggested throughout this monograph, people with disability have diverse experiences of data production and processing.

7.4.2 Revisiting the Group (Human) Right (Not) to Be Counted

This monograph proposes that the *CRPD* gives greater control to marginalised groups through a group (human) right to be counted or not.[169] The group (human) right to be counted enables a self-advocacy organisation to decide whether data may be collected about a characteristic shared by group members to enable their human rights. Before this group (human) right can be realised, the self-advocacy group must exist.[170] If the group choose not to have data collected about their common characteristic, the state still owes them human rights. Data are not a condition of human rights.

The following will first explore the human rights principle of self-defining. It will then discuss the group (human) right not to be counted. Both sub-subsections argue that human rights–based approaches to data allow marginalised groups to take greater control over data production and processing about their common trait.

a) The Human Rights Principle of Self-Defining

Data definitions are required for data production and processing.[171] During the drafting of the *CRPD*, concerns were raised that a definition of disability 'would inevitably derive from the medical model, and would be externally imposed and disempowering'.[172] The *2018 Human Rights-Based Approach to Data Guide* acknowledges the historical misuse of data and asserts that human rights–based data production must be 'used only for the benefit of the groups it describes'.[173] The guide also stipulates that 'populations of interest should be self-defining'.[174] The principle states that the 'parameters of the population

168 See earlier Section 5.3.

169 See earlier Section 5.3.

170 The importance of marginalised groups' interests being represented through DPOs, discussed earlier, is underscored by the normative provisions of this group (human) right. Nonetheless, to continue the exploration of the group (human) right, this issue will be set aside here.

171 See earlier Section 4.3.2.

172 Kayess and French (n 114) 23.

173 OHCHR, *A Human Rights-Based Approach to Data* (n 115) 11.

174 OHCHR, *A Human Rights-Based Approach to Data* (n 115) 12.

cannot be imposed by an external party'.[175] Self-defining does not simply mean that a group must choose from definitions developed by external experts. Instead, it means a group may develop a description of their common trait.

Unfortunately, as discussed earlier, in the years since the adoption of the *CRPD*, the principle of self-identification has been scarcely acknowledged in disability data production and processing practice. Similarly, there has been no concerted effort to develop data practices that enable groups to self-define. The principle of self-identification is linked to individual autonomy and enables people to choose to identify or not with a given data definition.[176] In comparison, self-defining is a principle that applies to groups, enabling them to develop a data definition that reflects their group trait. Decisions about the parameters of the group, the common trait(s), the words used to describe the commonality and determining which data will be useful should be controlled by the group from whom the data are being extracted.

There is resistance to groups self-defining, as it produces data that are not comparable across settings and jurisdictions. Interoperable data is a significant agenda for some of those in the disability human rights movement to compare and rank how states are progressing with meeting their obligations.[177] Nevertheless, the questions need to be asked: What is the aim of data harmonisation? Moreover, ultimately, what value does it add? And at what cost? Imposing a data definition on a community is not human rights promoting. Nonetheless, indicators about government outputs have a much lower impost on the lives of people with disability. Comparable indicators about state performance in fulfilling obligations, such as government spending on inclusion programs, may enable comparison between jurisdictions.

b) The Group (Human) Right Not to Be Counted: Strategic Anonymity

Groups with disability and other intersectional identities need to control the visibility of their status in datasets. Giving control of visibility in datasets to a marginalised group allows it to assess the risk to foresee and mitigate harm that may come from that data. The *ICRC Handbook on Data Protection* identified the possibility of group harm through aggregated data:

> in armed conflicts and other situations of violence, many threats are collective rather than individual . . . just focusing on the proper management of Personal Data may not be sufficient. In some cases, Processing of non-Personal Data may raise specific threats at the collective level.[178]

175 OHCHR, *A Human Rights-Based Approach to Data* (n 115) 12.
176 See earlier Section 7.3.1.
177 This is referred to as 'data harmonization' in the report OHCHR, *Article 31* (n 120) [30]–[31].
178 Kuner and Marelli (n 68) 24.

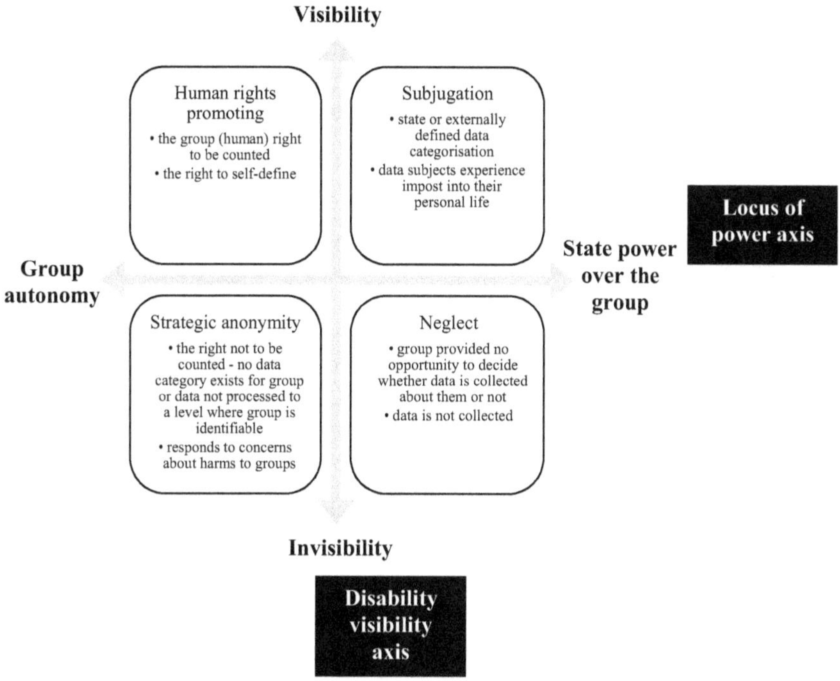

Figure 7.3 Framework with the intersecting axes of locus of power and disability visibility overlayed with considerations of group rights for people who are refugees with disability

Groups may also enact strategic anonymity.[179] While an individual may exercise their strategic anonymity by choosing not to identify, a group may exercise its strategic anonymity by enacting the group (human) right not to be counted. The group (human) right not to be counted means that no data category exists to record the common trait of the group, for example, blindness. The group (human) right not to be counted may allow for data production but prohibit processing to a level that enables the identification of a group. For example, at one time, most blind adult men in the Mae La refugee camp in Thailand were ex-soldiers injured by landmines; therefore, the data categories sex, age and blindness may be prohibited if this group decides it makes them vulnerable.[180] Figure 7.3 is an updated framework depicting the locus of power and visibility with consideration of group autonomy and disability visibility.

The *CRPD* has added doctrine that empowers marginalised groups to take more control over data production and processing about their members. It has elevated the role of rights-holders in producing knowledge to inform the treaty's implementation. Community control over their data is important because

179 See earlier Section 6.4.

180 Personal observations during my time working in the Mae La refugee camp in 2012.

knowledge is constructed, and depending on who is doing the constructing, there will be different outcomes.[181] The substantive part of this monograph will conclude with a brief discussion of community control over the production and use of data: community-controlled data.

7.4.3 Community-Controlled Data

Advocates who promote data production and processing about the bodies and lives of people with disability do so hoping to address neglected obligations and monitor policies that subjugate people. In this narrative, data are used to keep state power accountable. However, states producing data to keep themselves accountable assumes cooperation and transparency. In reality, states often use data to support their political agenda,[182] and civil society or others must deconstruct what that data measures to challenge or verify states' claims. Are states best placed to produce and process data to enable the implementation of human rights?

Control over the production and processing of data has been a significant area of concern for marginalised communities in responding to HIV, where community-led data collection emerged.[183] Similarly, Indigenous data sovereignty has been a significant movement to retain control of Indigenous data,[184] and there are emerging examples of community-controlled data in refugee contexts, such as R-ID.[185] During the *CRPD*'s drafting, delegations emphasised the importance of DPOs being involved in 'the design and implementation of data collection'.[186] Specific provisions relating to participation in data production and processing were deleted from the draft treaty, as it was seen to be covered in article 4(3).[187] Concerningly, community control of data about the bodies and lives of people with disability is not valued in the current climate.

Community-controlled data are often written about as temporary or a concession when the preferred comprehensive state data system is unavailable. The OHCHR report *Statistics and Data Collection under Article 31 of the Convention on the Rights of Persons with Disabilities* stated: 'While data systems continue to be strengthened, citizen-driven and community-based data-collection

181 See especially earlier Chapters 2, 3.

182 Vittert explained that 'I've heard many politicians, commentators, consultants say: "Give me the statistics that prove my argument"'. Liberty Vittert, 'The Problem with Official Statistics – And Three Ways to Make Them Better', *The Conversation* (online, 18 September 2018) <http://theconversation.com/the-problem-with-official-statistics-and-three-ways-to-make-them-better-103448>.

183 See generally Sara LM Davis, *The Uncounted: Politics of Data in Global Health* (Cambridge University Press, 2020).

184 See Tahu Kukutai and John Taylor, *Indigenous Data Sovereignty: Toward an Agenda* (ANU Press, 2016).

185 'What is R-ID?' (Web Page, 2022) <https://rohingyaproject.com/r-id/>.

186 Don MacKay, *Letter Dated 7 October 2005 From the Chairman to All Members of the Committee*, UN Doc A/AC.265/2006/1 (14 October 2005) annex I, art 4(3). See earlier Section 4.4.2 for a description of these debates.

187 *CRPD* (n 3) art 4(3).

processes and analyses led by or involving persons with disabilities are valuable sources of data'.[188] This quotation suggests that community-led/controlled data is a temporary measure rather than part of a robust framework for data collection. Imagine if state systems were viewed as temporary until DPOs can manage necessary data production, processing and storage. This change in emphasis would redirect resources and capacity building from state bureaucracies to DPOs.

As discussed throughout this monograph, disability data production and processing congruent with the human rights model of disability requires more attention than developing a taxonomy that reflects the social model of disability. *Who* is categorising and *who* is ultimately responsible for the data production and processing matters. Furthermore, personal data produced and processed by trusted conduits should be held in trust. Trustworthiness is important to people disclosing parts of their identity that may make them vulnerable to discrimination. Those who are stewards of the data must also be trustworthy.[189] Community-controlled data may be perceived as trustworthy when state bureaucracies are not.

Further, as has become increasingly clear, comprehensive data is a utopian or dystopian vision, depending on one's leaning, that will never entirely be realised in human rights–compliant data production and processing. Therefore, the only way to identify the barriers that people face is through partnerships with communities as trusted conduits of information:

> Governments increasingly recognise that official data sources alone are not enough. And that if they are to gather more robust disaggregated data that accurately reflects the needs of different population groups, then partnerships and collaborations with civil society organisations, marginalised groups and others are important to enable knowledge exchange, learning and spark innovative approaches.[190]

In a human rights–abiding system, comprehensive representative data are impossible. Acknowledging this limitation enables explorations of other information- and knowledge-generation approaches to implement the *CRPD*, such as

188 OHCHR, *Article 31* (n 120) [59].

189 Trustworthiness includes close attention to ensuring limited use of data and restricting data sharing. For an example of a harmful practice, see 'UN Shared Rohingya Data Without Informed Consent', *Human Rights Watch* (Web Page, 15 June 2021) <https://www.hrw.org/news/2021/06/15/un-shared-rohingya-data-without-informed-consent>. The UNHCR responded to Human Rights Watch's claims here: United Nations High Commissioner for Refugees, 'News Comment: Statement on Refugee Registration and Data Collection in Bangladesh' (Press Release, 15 June 2021) <https://www.unhcr.org/news/press/2021/6/60c85a7b4/news-comment-statement-refugee-registration-data-collection-bangladesh.html>.

190 Aissata Ndiaye and Tichafara Chisaka, 'How Can Inclusive Data Advocacy Help Us to Achieve the SDGs?', *Sightsavers* (Blog Post, July 2022) <https://www.sightsavers.org/blogs/2022/07/how-can-inclusive-data-advocacy-help-us-achieve-the-sdgs/>.

close consultation and active involvement of DPOs and disability human rights research.[191]

In conclusion, greater focus is required on creating pathways for people who are refugees with disability to have their interests represented through DPOs. Groups may be complicated, as the common interest may sometimes be in tension with an individual interest. Nonetheless, human rights law provides both group and individual data production and processing safeguards. A group of people with a common trait may choose to include (or not) a data category in a dataset that describes how they identify. If an individual is uncomfortable disclosing this information, they may choose not to self-identify. Inevitably, by adhering to these two human rights principles, states will have less comprehensive datasets that cannot be compared universally, but this should have no bearing on people with disability's human rights attainment.

7.5 Conclusion

It is a core contention of this monograph that *CRPD* article 31 does not require the production of data about the bodies and lives of people with disability but rather the quantification of state actions. Nonetheless, support for data production and processing about the bodies and lives of people with disability from the CRPD Committee, DPOs and evidence that data may be a powerful tool for human rights realisation suggested an enquiry into individual and group protections was necessary.

In accepting that the production and processing of data about the bodies and lives of people with disability in refugee contexts may be human rights promoting, a test was proposed to assess when it is 'appropriate' to produce and process this data. This test included an assessment of necessity, achievability and legality. Assuming there will be some circumstances where it is 'appropriate' to produce data, the human rights principles that act as safeguards against individual and group harm were explored: self-identification and self-defining. Self-identification requires surveys to have a non-response option, such as 'I prefer not to say' or similar. Further, the right to self-define requires that a group exists that represents the interests of people that share the trait being describe by the data variable. These measures that act as safeguards make comprehensive representative data unlikely.

Abandoning the vision of comprehensive and interoperable data brings into focus the other important strategies that enable the implementation of the *CRPD*, including the participation of people with disability through their representative organisations, awareness raising and disability human rights research.[192] The powerful group (human) rights provisions within the *CRPD* make it necessary to exert greater effort to ensure that people who are refugees with disability have avenues to participate in DPOs.

191 *CRPD* (n 3) arts 4(1)(f), (g), 4(3), 31(1), 32(1)(c). See also Arstein-Kerslake et al (n 7).
192 *CRPD* (n 3) art 4(1)(f).

8 Conclusion

Indiscriminate, large-scale data production and processing about the bodies and lives of people with disability in the name of human rights attainment is problematic. Systematic surveillance of diseases and impairments reflects public health practice and is a remnant of the medical model of disability.[1] This drive for data is also bolstered by the digital state, which looks to data to define problems and inform solutions.[2] Within this context, the imperative for disability human rights advocates is to demonstrate that other forms of knowledge and methods for implementing the *Convention on the Rights of Persons with Disabilities* ('*CRPD*') are of equal and even greater value, such as lived-experience knowledge through active participation of rights-holders, awareness raising, universal design and disability human rights research.[3]

8.1 Monograph Summary

The analysis presented in this monograph has challenged the dominant interpretation of *CRPD* article 31,[4] which many believe creates state obligations to produce and process extensive data about the bodies and lives of people with disability. It has done so by exploring the dual hypotheses that (a) *CRPD* article 31 may benefit people who are refugees with disability by rendering individuals and their rights more visible through information production and processing and (b) that information production and processing may be harmful to people who are refugees with disability. To explore these seemingly contradictory positions, this monograph asked: How should *CRPD* article 31 be interpreted? How do refugee contextual considerations inform the interpretation of the state obligations and (potential) group rights in *CRPD* article 31? And lastly,

1 See earlier Section 1.1.1.

2 See earlier Section 3.3.2.

3 *Convention on the Rights of Persons with Disabilities*, opened for signature 24 January 2007, 2515 UNTS 3 (entered into force 3 May 2008) ('*CRPD*') arts 2, 4(1)(f), (g), 4(3), 8; Anna Arstein-Kerslake et al, 'Introducing a Human Rights-Based Disability Research Methodology' (2020) 20(3) *Human Rights Law Review* 412.

4 *CRPD* (n 3) art 31.

DOI: 10.4324/9781003506140-11

does the international human rights framework adequately balance the potential benefits of information production and processing with the potential harms?

These questions were addressed through six substantive chapters. Chapter 2 deconstructed knowledge production and demonstrated the critical role of rights-holders in implementing the *CRPD*. Chapter 3 argued that data are not neutral and inert but powerful and potentially dangerous. Chapter 4 uncovered tensions that emerged while drafting *CRPD* article 31, including data's concurrently harmful and useful effects and the need to moderate the power amassed by states, the data controller. Chapter 5 assessed that the legal interpretation of article 31 emphasises information production and processing about state actions and barriers to rights attainment, not about the bodies and lives of people with disability.

Chapter 6 explored disability data production and processing obligations in refugee contexts. It demonstrated that the operationalisation of disability data production and processing in refugee contexts omits the article 31 safeguard that data are only produced and processed 'as appropriate'. It also proposed a framework that considers the locus of power when critiquing laws, policies and practices that enhance the visibility of rights-holders. This framework highlighted that strategic anonymity is vital for human rights realisation for people with disability in refugee contexts. Chapter 7 concluded the substantive part of the monograph. It argued that data production and processing often violate critical human rights protections because they are incompatible with comprehensive, harmonious and interoperable data. A test was proposed to determine whether a data variable is 'appropriate' to produce and process in a given context. The chapter also explored methods to remedy the underutilisation of the human rights protections that enable data subjects to self-identify and self-define.

Rather than repeating the comprehensive summaries of the chapters and key interventions found in the introduction,[5] this brief conclusion will explore the implications of this research and consider the next steps.

8.2 Implications of This Research and Next Steps

Data are dangerous, but not necessarily harmful, and must be treated cautiously. Data's dual potential for harm and benefit is the most important message of this research and informs all of the following recommendations. The recommendations have implications for a wide range of actors, including, first and foremost, people with disability in refugee contexts. They also have implications for people with disability more broadly, disabled persons organisations ('DPOs'), non-disabled allies, advocates, civil society, the Committee on the Rights of Persons with Disabilities ('CRPD Committee'), states, international organisations, other actors working in the broader human rights framework and legal scholars. These actors have various power and levers to change

5 See earlier Sections 1.3.3 and 1.4.

current policy and practice regarding data production and processing about the bodies and lives of people with disability.

Recommendation 1: States, International Organisations and Civil Society Need to Modify Their Data Practices to Immediately Adhere to Human Rights Law

This monograph demonstrated the poor adherence to the human rights principles of self-identification and self-defining.[6] All surveys conducted under the authority of article 31 should immediately allow people to self-identify by including a non-response option, such as 'I prefer not to say' or similar.[7] Both principles promote increased autonomy and allow for strategic anonymity.[8] Further work is required to understand how self-defining may be achieved, for example, ways to determine which groups represent certain interests. Further, amongst the enthusiasm to harness data for good, a core principle of personal data protection appears to have been neglected: data minimisation.[9] Data minimisation relates to whether it is necessary to collect data, and the lack of attention to this is likely related to the content of the next recommendation.

Recommendation 2: The CRPD Committee, States, DPOs, International Organisations and Scholars Should Work Together to Clarify How to Determine When It Is 'Appropriate' to Produce and Process Various Data Variables

This monograph demonstrated that the safeguard 'as/where (contextually) appropriate' in *CRPD* article 31, the Executive Committee of the High Commissioner's Programme's 2010 *Conclusion on Refugees with Disabilities and Other Persons with Disabilities Protected and Assisted by UNHCR*, the *Global Compact on Refugees* and the Office of the High Commissioner for Refugees' *Policy on Age, Gender and Diversity* was omitted from operational guidance.[10] Either an opaque decision has been made that it is appropriate to produce and process all data in all given contexts, or this provision has been neglected. Guidance is urgently required to determine when it is 'appropriate' to produce

6 See earlier Sections 7.3.1 and 7.4.2.

7 The exact language should be tested to avoid unintended consequences.

8 See earlier Section 6.4.

9 United Nations High Commissioner for Refugees (UNHCR), *Guidance on the Protection of Personal Data of Persons of Concern to UNHCR* (2018) 19.

10 See earlier Section 6.3.; *CRPD* (n 3) art 31(2); *Report of the United Nations High Commissioner for Refugees: Part II Global Compact on Refugees*, UN Doc A/73/12 (Part II) (13 September 2018, adopted 2 August 2018) para 46; Executive Committee of the High Commissioner's Programme, *Conclusion on Refugees with Disabilities and Other Persons with Disabilities Protected and Assisted by UNHCR*, UN Doc A/AC.96/1095 (adopted 12 October 2010) para c; Office of the United Nations High Commissioner for Refugees (UNHCR), *UNHCR Policy on Age, Gender and Diversity* (2018) 10.

data about the bodies and lives of people with disability. Consideration is also needed for contexts where people cannot consent.[11]

Recommendation 3: The CRPD Committee, DPOs, States and Scholars Should Recognise and Work to Promote the Realisation of the Group (Human) Right to Be Counted[12]

This research argued that people with disability and their representative organisations must have greater control over data production and processing about their bodies and lives. The group (human) right to be counted is a way to encapsulate the human rights principle of self-defining and to enable groups to be strategically anonymous.[13] As discussed later, further consideration is required to facilitate the inclusion of people with disability in refugee contexts in representative organisations due to these organisations having a pivotal role in the group (human) right to be counted, the human rights principle of self-defining and, more broadly, in the implementation of the *CRPD*.

Recommendation 4: States Should Resource and Adopt Creative Approaches to Enable the Development of Self-Advocacy Organisations for People With Disability in Refugee Contexts[14]

Representation for people with disability in refugee contexts may involve refugee self-led agencies who have developed methods of engaging with people in refugee contexts.[15] Working with refugee-led agencies will likely require awareness raising of disability human rights and disability inclusion.[16] Alternatively, national DPOs may require capacity building in cross-cultural and trauma-informed approaches to welcome people who are refugees with disability into their organisations.

Recommendation 5: DPOs, the CRPD Committee and States Should Develop Metrics About State Actions to Implement the CRPD *and Ameliorate Barriers to Rights Attainment*

This monograph provided an alternative interpretation of article 31, emphasising data production about state actions to implement the *CRPD* and remove barriers to rights attainment.[17] Identifying barriers to rights attainment for people with disability in refugee contexts must be based on close consultation and active involvement with people with disability in refugee contexts through

11 See earlier Section 7.2.3.
12 See earlier Section 5.3.
13 See earlier Section 7.4.2.
14 See earlier Section 7.4.
15 See, eg, Mustafa Alio et al, 'By Refugees, for Refugees: Refugee Leadership During COVID-19, and Beyond' (2020) 32(2) *International Journal of Refugee Law* 370.
16 *CRPD* (n 3) art 8.
17 See earlier Section 5.2.

their representative organisations,[18] reinforcing the importance of the previous recommendation. Statistics about state actions to implement the *CRPD* and address barriers to rights attainment must be disseminated in accessible formats to people with disability.[19]

Recommendation 6: The CRPD Committee Should Exercise Caution in Its Concluding Observations to States and Avoid Prescribing the Production of Data About the Bodies and Lives of People With Disability

It may be prudent not to recommend the production of any data variables about the bodies and lives of people with disability unless this is done to support a representative organisation to gain leverage with a state. Moreover, no data variables about the bodies and lives of people with disability should be prescribed until advice has been provided by the committee on how to determine 'appropriate' data production and processing (see recommendation earlier). Furthermore, given the authority of the CRPD Committee's interpretive advice, urgent and ongoing attention is required to understand the impact of data production and processing on individuals with disability.

Recommendation 7: An Urgent Dialogue Is Needed on Data Production and Processing About the Bodies and Lives of People With Disability That Includes a Range of Views

Critique is necessary to hold power to account. Concerningly, dissent has disappeared from discussions about disability data production and processing.[20] The lack of dissent seems unusual, given the considerable concern about disability data production and processing during the drafting of the *CRPD*.[21] It is promising to see two recent Special Rapporteurs' reports about data and technology's impact on human rights and digital rights labs established in major human rights non-government organisations.[22] Discussions regarding data production and processing about the bodies and lives of people with disability need to engage with the tension of data's potential for harm and benefit. Hopefully, this monograph may provoke discussion about the interpretation and practices stemming from article 31.

18 *CRPD* (n 3) art 4(3).

19 *CRPD* (n 3) art 31(3).

20 See, eg, Office of the High Commissioner for Human Rights (OHCHR), *Statistics and Data Collection under Article 31 of the Convention on the Rights of Persons with Disabilities*, UN Doc A/HRC/49/60 (28 December 2021).

21 See earlier Section 4.3.

22 On the digital welfare state, see Philip Alston, *Report of the Special Rapporteur on Extreme Poverty and Human Rights*, UN Doc A/74/48037 (11 October 2019). On artificial intelligence and disability rights, see Gerard Quinn, *Report of the Special Rapporteur on the Rights of Persons with Disabilities*, UN Doc A/HRC/49/52 (28 December 2021). For a human right lab in a major NGO, see 'Technology and Rights', *Human Rights Watch* (Web Page, 2023) <https://www.hrw.org/topic/technology-and-rights>.

Recommendation 8: The CRPD Committee, DPOs and States Should Explore How CRPD *Article 31 Protections Could Prevent People With Disability From Experiencing Harm From Existing Data Production and Processing Practices*

States already produce and process large amounts of data about people with disability to assess eligibility for social security benefits. Social security is a right;[23] therefore, article 31 may be used to ensure data minimisation, amongst other protections. More interpretive advice from human rights committees, scholarship and good practice examples is required about moderating the power amassed by states as data controllers and ameliorating the particular harms experienced by people with disability as data subjects.[24]

Recommendation 9: States Should Support the Development of Alternative Methods of Implementing the CRPD

Abandoning the vision of comprehensive and interoperable data brings into focus the other important strategies that enable the implementation of the *CRPD*, including the participation of people with disability through their representative organisations, awareness raising, universal design and disability human rights research.[25] Energy and resources assigned to developing comprehensive data systems to produce and process data about the bodies and lives of people with disability may be redirected to these strategies. The benefit of these approaches is that they centre individuals and groups with disability as experts on barriers to inclusion rather than objects to be counted.

8.3 Final Remarks

The *CRPD* is an important treaty that recognises the specific ways people with disability experience human rights violations.[26] It restores people with disability's control over their bodies and lives. People with disability in refugee contexts face significant barriers to realising their rights due to the multiple and aggravated discrimination they experience. Duty-bearers may only understand and address these barriers with close consultation and active involvement of rights-holders. As described by a Stakeholder Advisory Group member: 'Meeting with people who have a disability is important to give us knowledge about what can be done'.[27]

23 *International Covenant on Economic, Social and Cultural Rights*, opened for signature 16 December 1966, 993 UNTS 3 (entered into force 3 January 1976) art 9.

24 See earlier Sections 3.3.2 and 4.4.

25 *CRPD* (n 3) art 4(1)(f).

26 Rosemary Kayess and Phillip French, 'Out of Darkness into Light – Introducing the Convention on the Rights of Persons with Disabilities' (2008) 8 *Human Rights Law Review* 1, 14.

27 Stakeholder Advisory Group meeting minutes, 20 August 2021.

Bibliography

A) Article/Books/Reports

Adams, David, 'Usable Knowledge in Public Policy' (2004) 63(1) *Australian Journal of Public Administration* 29

AI Now, *Algorithmic Accountability Policy Tool Kit* (Report, October 2018)

Alio, Mustafa et al, 'By Refugees, for Refugees: Refugee Leadership During COVID-19, and Beyond' (2020) 32(2) *International Journal of Refugee Law* 370

Alston, Philip, 'A Third Generation of Solidarity Rights: Progressive Development or Obfuscation of International Human Rights Law?' (1982) 29(3) *Netherlands International Law Review* 307

Alston, Philip and Ryan Goodman, *International Human Rights* (Oxford University Press, 2013)

Alston, Philip and Gerard Quinn, 'The Nature and Scope of States Parties' Obligations Under the International Covenant on Economic, Social and Cultural Rights Symposium: The Implementation of the International Covenant on Economic, Social and Cultural Rights' (1987) 9 *Human Rights Quarterly* 156

Altman, Barbara M and Elizabeth K Rasch, 'Purpose of an International Comparable Census Disability Measure' in Barbara M Altman (ed), *International Measurement of Disability: Purpose, Method and Application* (Springer International Publishing, 2016) 55

Arduin, Sarah, 'Article 3: General Principles' in Ilias Bantekas, Michael Ashley Stein and Dēmētrēs Anastasiou (eds), *The UN Convention on the Rights of Persons with Disabilities: A Commentary* (Oxford University Press, 2018) 84

Arstein-Kerslake, Anna et al, 'Introducing a Human Rights-Based Disability Research Methodology' (2020) 20(3) *Human Rights Law Review* 412

Arthurs, HW, *Law and Learning: Report to the Social Sciences and Humanities Research Council of Canada by the Consultative Group on Research and Education in Law* (Social Sciences and Humanities Research Council of Canada, 1983)

Başak, Çalı, 'Specialized Rules of Treaty Interpretation: Human Rights' in Duncan B Hollis (ed), *The Oxford Guide to Treaties* (Oxford University Press, 2nd ed, 2020) 504

Beduschi, AC, 'The Big Data of International Migration: Opportunities and Challenges for States Under International Human Rights Law' (2018) 49 *Georgetown International Law Journal* 981

Bell, Chris, 'Is Disability Studies Actually White Disability Studies?' in Lennard J Davis (ed), *The Disability Studies Reader* (Routledge, 5th ed, 2017) 406

Ben-Moshe, Liat and Sandy Magaña, 'An Introduction to Race, Gender, and Disability: Intersectionality, Disability Studies, and Families of Color' (2014) 2(2) *Women, Gender, and Families of Color* 105

Bickenbach, Jerome E, 'The ICF and Its Relationship to Disability Studies' in Nick Watson and Simo Vehmas (eds), *Routledge Handbook of Disability Studies* (Taylor & Francis Group, 2nd ed, 2019) 55

Bickenbach, Jerome E et al, 'Models of Disablement, Universalism and the International Classification of Impairments, Disabilities and Handicaps' (1999) 48 *Social Science & Medicine* 1173

Broderick, Andrea, 'Of Rights and Obligations: The Birth of Accessibility' (2020) 24(4) *The International Journal of Human Rights* 393

Bury, Mike, 'A Comment on the ICIDH2' (2000) 15(7) *Disability & Society* 1073

Bygrave, Lee A, *Data Privacy Law in Context* (Oxford University Press, 2014)

Campbell, Jane and Michael Oliver, *Disability Politics: Understanding Our Past, Changing Our Future* (Routledge, 1996)

Campbell, Timothy and Adam Sitze, 'Introduction: Biopolitics an Encounter' in Timothy Campbell and Adam Sitze (eds), *Biopolitics: A Reader* (Duke University Press, 2013) 1

Cange, Charles W et al, 'Considering Chronic Uncertainty Among Syrian Refugees Resettling in Europe' (2019) 4(1) *The Lancet Public Health* e14

CBM and International Disability Alliance, *What's Happening with Disability Data? Together We Will Count and Be Counted! A Brief Study and Overview of DPO Experiences Regarding Disability Data* (Report, n.d.)

CBM International, HelpAge International and Handicap International, *Humanitarian Inclusion Standards for Older People and People with Disabilities* (Report, 2018)

Center for Women's Global Leadership, *A Women's Human Rights Approach to the World Conference Against Racism* (2001)

Charlesworth, Hilary, 'Feminist Methods in International Law' (1999) 93(2) *American Journal of International Law* 379

Charlesworth, Hilary, 'Human Rights as Men's Rights' in Julie Peters and Andrea Wolper (eds), *Women's Rights, Human Rights* (Routledge, 2018) 103

Charlton, James I, *Nothing About Us Without Us: Disability Oppression and Empowerment* (University of California Press, 1998)

Christensen, Zach, *Generating Disability Statistics: Models of Disability Measurement, History of Disability Statistics and the Washington Group Questions: Background Paper* (Development Initiatives, September 2020)

Christman, John, 'Autonomy in Moral and Political Philosophy' in Edward N Zalta (ed), *The Stanford Encyclopedia of Philosophy* (Metaphysics Research Lab, Stanford University, Fall 2020) <https://plato.stanford.edu/archives/fall2020/entries/autonomy-moral/>

Chynoweth, Paul, 'Legal Research' in Andrew Knight and Leslie Ruddock (eds), *Advanced Research Methods in the Built Environment* (Wiley-Blackwell, 2008) 28

Coomans, Fons, Fred Grünfeld and Menno T Kamminga, 'Methods of Human Rights Research: A Primer' (2010) 32(1) *Human Rights Quarterly* 179

Costello, Cathryn and Michelle Foster, 'Non-Refoulement as Custom and Jus Cogens? Putting the Prohibition to the Test' in Maarten den Heijer and Harmen van der Wilt (eds), *Netherlands Yearbook of International Law 2015: Jus Cogens: Quo Vadis?* (TMC Asser Press, 2016) 273

Crawford, James and Amelia Keene, 'Interpretation of the Human Rights Treaties by the International Court of Justice' (2020) 24(7) *International Journal of Human Rights* 935

Crock, Mary and Laura Smith-Khan, 'Swift and Systematic? Identifying and Recording Disability in Forced Migration' in Barbara M Altman (ed), *International Measurement of Disability: Purpose, Method and Application* (Springer, 2016) 305

Crock, Mary et al, *Syrian Refugees with Disabilities in Jordan and Turkey* (University of Sydney, 2015)

Crock, Mary et al, *The Legal Protection of Refugees with Disabilities: Forgotten and Invisible?* (Edward Elgar Publishing, 2017)

Crock, Mary, Christine Ernst and Ron McCallum, 'Where Disability and Displacement Intersect: Asylum Seekers and Refugees with Disabilities' (2012) 24(4) *International Journal of Refugee Law* 735

Culnane, Chris, Benjamin Rubinstein and Vanessa Teague, *Health Data in an Open World: A Report on Re-Identifying Patients in the MBS/PBS Dataset and the Implications for Future Releases of Australian Government Data* (University of Melbourne, 18 December 2017) <https://arxiv.org/abs/1712.05627>

Davis, Lennard J, *Enforcing Normalcy: Disability, Deafness, and the Body* (Verso, 1995)

Davis, Sara LM, *The Uncounted: Politics of Data in Global Health* (Cambridge University Press, 2020)

de Búrca, Gráinne, 'The EU in the Negotiation of the UN Disability Convention' (2010) 35(2) *European Law Review* 2010

Dean, Mitchell, *Governmentality: Power and Rule in Modern Society* (Sage, 2nd ed, 2010)

Deane, Phyllis, 'Political Arithmetic' in Matias Vernengo, Esteban Perez Caldentey and Barkley J Rosser Jr (eds), *The New Palgrave Dictionary of Economics* (Palgrave Macmillan UK, 2017) 1 <https://doi.org/10.1057/978-1-349-95121-5_1313-2>

Degener, Theresia, 'Disability in a Human Rights Context' (2016) 5(3) *Laws* 35

Della Fina, Valentina, 'Article 1 [Purpose]' in Valentina Della Fina, Rachele Cera and Giuseppe Palmisano (eds), *The United Nations Convention on the Rights of Persons with Disabilities: A Commentary* (Springer, 2017) 89

Department of Health, *The Victorian Refugee and Asylum Seeker Health Action Plan 2014–2018* (Action Plan, 2014)

Disability Human Rights Research Network, *Protocol for Rights-Based Disability Research in All Fields* (February 2018)

Duell-Piening, Philippa, 'Refugee Resettlement and the Convention on the Rights of Persons with Disabilities' (2018) 33(5) *Disability & Society* 661

Duell-Piening, Philippa, *Response to a Discussion Paper of the Victorian State Disability Plan 2017–2020* (Victorian Refugee Health Network, July 2016)

Dworkin, Ronald, *Taking Rights Seriously* (Bloomsbury Academics, 2013)

Erevelles, Nirmala and Andrea Minear, 'Unspeakable Offenses: Untangling Race and Disability in Discourses of Intersectionality' in Lennard J Davis (ed), *The Disability Studies Reader* (Routledge, 5th ed, 2017) 381

Eubanks, Virginia, *Automating Inequality: How High-Tech Tools Profile, Police, and Punish the Poor* (St Martin's Press, 2018)

Finlay, Steven, *Predictive Analytics, Data Mining and Big Data: Myths, Misconceptions and Methods* (Palgrave Macmillan, 2014)

Flegar, Veronika, 'UNHCR's Shifting Frames in the Social Construction of Disabled Refugees: Two Case Studies on the Organization's Work During the World Refugee Year (1959–1960) and the International Year of Disabled Persons (1981)' (2019) 1(2) *Diplomatica* 157

Flynn, Eilionoir and Anna Arstein-Kerslake, 'Legislating Personhood: Realising the Right to Support in Exercising Legal Capacity' (2014) 10(1) *International Journal of Law in Context* 81

Foster, Michelle, *International Refugee Law and Socio-Economic Rights: Refuge From Deprivation* (Cambridge University Press, 2007)

Foucault, Michel, 'Chapter 1 (Reproduction) Right of Death and Power Over Life' in Timothy Campbell and Adam Sitze (eds), *Biopolitics: A Reader* (Duke University Press, 2013) 41

Foucault, Michel, *Discipline and Punish: The Birth of the Prison*, tr Alan Sheridan (Vintage Books, a Division of Penguin Random House, 2nd ed, 1995)

Foucault, Michel, 'The Subject and Power' (1982) 8(4) *Critical Inquiry* 777

Fourcade, Marion and Jeffrey Gordon, 'Learning Like a State: Statecraft in the Digital Age' (2020) 1(1) *Journal of Law and Political Economy* 78

Fredman, Sandra, 'Disability Equality: A Challenge to the Existing Anti-Discrimination Paradigm?' in Anna Lawson and Caroline Gooding (eds), *Disability Rights in Europe: From Theory to Practice. Essays in European Law* (Hart Publishing, 2005) 199

Freire, Paulo, *Pedagogy of the Oppressed*, tr Myra Bergman Ramos (Penguin Classics, 1970)

Furneaux, Samantha and Dina Korkees, *'We Need to Raise Our Voices': Advice From People of Refugee Backgrounds Living with Disabilities and Their Carers* (Report, Victorian Foundation for Survivors of Torture, 2019)

Galton, Francis, *Essays in Eugenics* (Eugenics Education Society, 1909)

Galton, Francis, *Inquiries into Human Faculty and Its Development* (Macmillan, 1883)

Gardiner, Richard, 'The Vienna Convention Rules on Treaty Interpretation' in Duncan B Hollis (ed), *The Oxford Guide to Treaties* (Oxford University Press, 2nd ed, 2020) 459

Garner, Bryan A and Henry Campbell Black (eds), *Black's Law Dictionary* (Thomson Reuters, 10th ed, 2014)

Gian Maria Greco, 'On Accessibility as a Human Right, with an Application to Media Accessibility' in Anna Matamala and Pilar Orero (eds), *Researching Audio Description: New Approaches* (Palgrave Macmillan UK, 2016)

Gibbs, Graham, *Learning by Doing: A Guide to Teaching and Learning Methods* (Oxford Centre for Staff and Learning Development, Oxford Brookes University, 1988)

Grace, Breanne L, Rajeev Bais and Benjamin J Roth, 'The Violence of Uncertainty – Undermining Immigrant and Refugee Health' (2018) 379(10) *New England Journal of Medicine* 904

Gutting, Gary and Johanna Oksala, 'Michel Foucault' in Edward N Zalta (ed), *The Stanford Encyclopedia of Philosophy* (Metaphysics Research Lab, Stanford University, Spring 2019) <https://plato.stanford.edu/archives/spr2019/entries/foucault/>

Handicap International, *Data on Persons with Disabilities in Humanitarian Action: Collecting Quantitative Data with the Washington Group Questions* (May 2019)

Haraway, Donna Jeanne, *Primate Visions: Gender, Race, and Nature in the World of Modern Science* (Routledge, 1989)

Harley, Tristan and Harry Hobbs, 'The Meaningful Participation of Refugees in Decision-Making Processes: Questions of Law and Policy' (2020) 32(2) *International Journal of Refugee Law* 200

Harris, Jennifer and Keri Roberts, 'Not Our Problem: The Provision of Services to Disabled Refugees and Asylum-Seekers' in Debra Hayes and Beth Humphries (eds), *Social Work, Immigration and Asylum: Debates, Dilemmas and Ethical Issues for Social Work and Social Care Practice* (Jessica Kingsley, 2004) 151

Hathaway, James C, *The Rights of Refugees Under International Law* (Cambridge University Press, 2nd ed, 2021) <https://www.cambridge.org/core/books/rights-of-refugees-under-international-law/A7533B16F033C9FA03612B4F829B74E2>

Hathaway, James C and Michelle Foster, *The Law of Refugee Status* (Cambridge University Press, 2nd ed, 2014)

HelpAge International and Handicap International, *Hidden Victims of the Syrian Crisis: Disabled, Injured and Older Refugees* (Report, 2014)

Humanity & Inclusion and iMMAP, *Removing Barriers: The Path Towards Inclusive Access: Disability Assessment Among Syrian Refugees in Jordan and Lebanon: Jordan Report* (Report, July 2018)

Hurst, Rachel, 'The International Disability Rights Movement and the ICF' (2003) 25(11–12) *Disability and Rehabilitation* 572

Jacobsen, Katja Lindskov, *The Politics of Humanitarian Technology: Good Intentions, Unintended Consequences and Insecurity* (Routledge, 2015)

Janmyr, Maja, 'Non-Signatory States and the International Refugee Regime' (2021) 67 *Forced Migration Review* 39

Jasanoff, Sheila, *States of Knowledge: The Co-Production of Science and the Social Order* (Taylor & Francis Group, 2004)

Jasanoff, Sheila S, 'Contested Boundaries in Policy-Relevant Science' (1987) 17(2) *Social Studies of Science* 195

Jones, Peter, 'Human Rights, Group Rights, and Peoples' Rights' (1999) 21(1) *Human Rights Quarterly* 80

Kakoullis, Emily and Yoshikazu Ikehara, 'Article 1: Purpose' in Ilias Bantekas, Michael Ashley Stein and Dēmētrēs Anastasiou (eds), *The UN Convention on the Rights of Persons with Disabilities: A Commentary* (Oxford University Press, 2018) 35

Kälin, Walter, *Supervising the 1951 Convention on the Status of Refugees: Article 35 and Beyond* (UNHCR, 2002)

Kaplan, Ida, *Rebuilding Shattered Lives: Integrated Trauma Recovery for People of Refugee Background* (Victorian Foundation for Survivors of Torture, 2nd ed, 2020)

Kayess, Rosemary and Phillip French, 'Out of Darkness into Light – Introducing the Convention on the Rights of Persons with Disabilities' (2008) 8 *Human Rights Law Review* 1

Kazou, Katerina, 'Analysing the Definition of Disability in the UN Convention on the Rights of Persons with Disabilities: Is It Really Based on a "Social Model" Approach?' (2017) 23 *International Journal of Mental Health and Capacity Law* 25

Kevles, Daniel J, *In the Name of Eugenics: Genetics and the Uses of Human Heredity* (Harvard University Press, 1995)

'Knowledge, Voice and Power' (2022) 70 *Forced Migration Review* https://www.fmreview.org/issue70/

Kukutai, Tahu and John Taylor, *Indigenous Data Sovereignty: Toward an Agenda* (ANU Press, 2016)

Kuner, Christopher and Massimo Marelli (eds), *Handbook on Data Protection in Humanitarian Action* (International Committee of the Red Cross, 2nd ed, 2020)

Kymlicka, Will, *Contemporary Political Philosophy: An Introduction* (Oxford University Press, 2nd ed, 2002)

Land, Molly et al, 'Article 22: Respect for Privacy' in Ilias Bantekas et al (eds), *The UN Convention on the Rights of Persons with Disabilities: A Commentary* (Oxford University Press, 2018) 604

Ledwith, Margaret, 'Emancipatory Action Research as a Critical Living Praxis: From Dominant Narratives to Counternarratives' in Lonnie L Rowell et al (eds), *The Palgrave International Handbook of Action Research* (Palgrave Macmillan, 2017) 56

Leonard Cheshire and Humanity & Inclusion, *Disability Data Collection: A Summary Review of the Use of the Washington Group Questions by Development and Humanitarian Actors* (Report, 2018)

Lord, Janet E, 'Preamble' in Ilias Bantekas et al (eds), *The UN Convention on the Rights of Persons with Disabilities: A Commentary* (Oxford University Press, 2018) 1

Lövbrand, Eva, Roger Pielke and Silke Beck, 'A Democracy Paradox in Studies of Science and Technology' (2011) 36(4) *Science, Technology, & Human Values* 474

Macbride, EW, 'Sterilisation for Human Betterment: A Summary of Results of 6000 Operations in California, 1909–1929' (1930) 125(3141) *Nature* 40

Macquarie Dictionary: Australia's National Dictionary Online (Electronic Resource, Macquarie Library, 2003) <www.macquariedictionary.com.au>

Marks, Mason, *Algorithmic Disability Discrimination* (SSRN Scholarly Paper No ID 3338209, Social Science Research Network, 19 February 2019)

McKinnon, Catriona, *Toleration: A Critical Introduction* (Routledge, 2006)

McRae, John, *Becoming a Person: The Biography of Robert Martin* (Craig Potton Publishing, 2014)

Melbourne Social Equity Institute, *Guidelines for Equitable and Fair Remuneration for Community Research Participants* (Guidelines, 2019)

Merry, Sally Engle, *The Seductions of Quantification: Measuring Human Rights, Gender Violence, and Sex Trafficking* (University of Chicago Press, 2016)

Morris, Jenny, *Pride Against Prejudice: Transforming Attitudes to Disability* (New Society, 1991)

Morton, Rick, 'The Transmission of Shame: What the Robodebt Royal Commission Tells Us About Who Knew What and Why It Matters' *The Monthly* (December 2022–January 2023)

Motz, Stephanie, 'Article 11: Situations of Risk and Humanitarian Emergencies' in Ilias Bantekas et al (eds), *The UN Convention on the Rights of Persons with Disabilities: A Commentary* (Oxford University Press, 2018) 314

Motz, Stephanie Anna, *The Refugee Status of Persons with Disabilities* (Brill|Nijhoff, 2020)

Nowell, Lorelli S et al, 'Thematic Analysis: Striving to Meet the Trustworthiness Criteria' (2017) 16(1) *International Journal of Qualitative Methods* 1

Oliver, Michael, *Understanding Disability: From Theory to Practice* (Macmillan, 1996)

Oliver, Mike, 'Changing the Social Relations of Research Production?' (1992) 7(2) *Disability, Handicap & Society* 101

Otto, Dianne, 'Women's Rights' in Daniel Moeckli, Sangeeta Shah and Sandesh Sivakumaran (eds), *International Human Rights Law* (Oxford University Press, 2nd ed, 2014) 345

Pahuja, Sundhya, 'Methodology: Writing About How We Do Research' in Rossana Deplano and Nicholas Tsagourias (eds), *Research Methods in International Law: A Handbook* (Elgar, 2021) 60

Pedersen, Mads, 'Article 31: Statistics and Data Collection' in Valentina Della Fina, Rachele Cera and Giuseppe Palmisano (eds), *The United Nations Convention on the Rights of Persons with Disabilities: A Commentary* (Springer International Publishing, 2017) 557

Pedersen, Mads and Federico Ferretti, 'Article 31: Statistics and Data Collection' in Ilias Bantekas, Michael Ashley Stein and Dimitris Anastasiou (eds), *The UN Convention on the Rights of Persons with Disabilities: A Commentary* (Oxford University Press, 2018) 924

People with Disability Australia, *What Do I Say? A Guide to Language About Disability* (Guidelines, 2019) <https://pwd.org.au/resources/disability-info/language-guide/>

Perez, Caroline Criado, *Invisible Women: Exposing Data Bias in a World Designed for Men* (Vintage Books, a Division of Penguin Random House, 2019)

Pfeiffer, David, 'The Devils Are in the Details: The ICIDH2 and the Disability Movement' (2000) 15(7) *Disability & Society* 1079

Pisani, Maria and Shaun Grech, 'Disability and Forced Migration: Critical Intersectionalities' (2015) 2(1) *Disability and the Global South* 421

Polack, Sarah et al, 'Disability Among Syrian Refugees Living in Sultanbeyli, Istanbul: Results From a Population-Based Survey' (2021) 16(11) *PLoS One* e0259249

Porter, Theodore M, *The Rise of Statistical Thinking, 1820–1900* (Princeton University Press, 1986)

Quinn, Gerard and Theresia Degener (eds), *Human Rights and Disability: The Current Use and Future Potential of United Nations Human Rights Instruments in the Context of Disability* (Report, United Nations, 2002)

Rioux, Marcia H, Paula Campos Pinto and Gillian Parekh (eds), *Disability, Rights Monitoring, and Social Change: Building Power Out of Evidence* (Canadian Scholars' Press, 2015)

Robertson, Michael, Astrid Ley and Edwina Light, *The First into the Dark* (University of Technology Sydney ePress, 2019)

Schneider, Marguerite, 'The Difference a Word Makes: Responding to Questions on "Disability" and "Difficulty" in South Africa' (2009) 31(1) *Disability and Rehabilitation* 42

Schulze, Marianne, *Understanding the UN Convention on the Rights of Persons with Disabilities: A Handbook on the Human Rights of Persons with Disabilities* (Handicap International, 3rd ed, 2010)

Schwab, Klaus, *The Fourth Industrial Revolution* (World Economic Forum, 2016)

Shakespeare, Tom, 'The Social Model of Disability' in Lennard J Davis (ed), *The Disability Studies Reader* (Routledge, 5th ed, 2017) 195

Smits, Jan M, 'Redefining Normative Legal Science: Towards an Argumentative Discipline' in Fons Coomans, Fred Grünfeld and Menno T Kamminga (eds), *Methods of Human Rights Research* (Intersentia, 2009) 45

Soldatic, Karen, 'The Transnational Sphere of Justice: Disability Praxis and the Politics of Impairment' (2013) 28(6) *Disability & Society* 744

Soldatic, Karen et al, 'Disability and Migration in Urban Australia: The Case of Liverpool' (2020) 55(4) *Australian Journal of Social Issues* 456

Soldatic, Karen et al, '"Nowhere to Be Found": Disabled Refugees and Asylum Seekers Within the Australian Resettlement Landscape' (2015) 2(1) *Disability and the Global South* 501

Stone, Emma and Mark Priestley, 'Parasites, Pawns and Partners: Disability Research and the Role of Non-Disabled Researchers' (1996) 47(4) *British Journal of Sociology* 699

Straimer, Clara, *Vulnerable or Invisible? Asylum Seekers with Disabilities in Europe* (Research Paper No. 194, Office of the High Commissioner for Refugees, November 2010)

Taylor, Linnet, Luciano Floridi and Bart van der Sloot (eds), *Group Privacy: New Challenges of Data Technologies* (Springer International Publishing, 2017)

Tobin, John, 'Seeking to Persuade: A Constructive Approach to Human Rights Treaty Interpretation' (2010) 23(1) *Harvard Human Rights Journal* 1

Tremain, Shelley, 'Foucault, Governmentality, and Critical Disability Theory: An Introduction' in Shelley Tremain (ed), *Foucault and the Government of Disability* (University of Michigan Press, 2005) 1

United Nations High Commissioner for Refugees, *Note on the Mandate of the High Commissioner for Refugees and His Office* (2013)

Vasak, Karel, 'A 30-Year Struggle; the Sustained Efforts to Give Force of Law to the Universal Declaration of Human Rights – UNESCO Digital Library' (1977) 30(11) *UNESCO Courier* 29

Victorian Refugee Health Network, *Service Responses for People with Disabilities From Refugee Backgrounds in Northern Melbourne* (Victorian Foundation for Survivors of Torture, 2018)

Waldron, Jeremy, 'Rights in Conflict' (1989) 99(3) *Ethics* 503

Washington Group on Disability Statistics, *The Washington Group Extended Set on Functioning (WG-ES)* (11 October 2022)

Washington Group on Disability Statistics, *The Washington Group Short Set on Functioning (WG-SS)* (2018) 2

Women's Refugee Commission, *Disabilities Among Refugees and Conflict-Affected Populations* (Report, June 2008)

Women's Refugee Commission, *Piloting the IASC Guidelines on Inclusion of Persons with Disabilities in Humanitarian Action: Disability Inclusion in Gender-Based Violence Programming in Jordan, Sri Lanka, and Uganda* (Report, 2019)

World Health Organization, *WHO Methods and Data Sources for Global Burden of Disease Estimates 2000–2011* (Technical Paper, November 2013)

Yuval-Davis, Nira, 'Intersectionality and Feminist Politics' (2006) 13(3) *European Journal of Women's Studies* 193

Zieck, Marjoleine, 'Article 35 of the 1951 Convention/Article II of the 1967 Protocol: A Commentary' in Andreas Zimmermann, Jonas Dörschner and Felix Machts (eds), *The 1951 Convention Relating to the Status of Refugees Andits 1967 Protocol: A Commentary* (Oxford University Press, 2011) 1495

Zieck, Marjoleine, *UNHCR's Parallel Universe: Marking the Contours of a Problem* (Amsterdam University Press, 2010)

Zuboff, Shoshana, *The Age of Surveillance Capitalism: The Fight for a Human Future at the New Frontier of Power* (Profile Books, 2019)

B) Cases

I v United Kingdom [2002] Eur Court HR 25680/94

C) Legislation

Disability Discrimination Act 1992 (Cth)

D) Treaties

Charter of the United Nations

Convention on the Rights of Persons with Disabilities, opened for signature 24 January 2007, 2515 UNTS 3 (entered into force 3 May 2008)

Convention on the Rights of the Child, opened for signature 20 November 1989, 1577 UNTS 3 (entered into force 2 September 1990)

Convention Relating to the Status of Refugees, opened for signature 28 July 1951, 189 UNTS 150 (entered into force 22 April 1954)

Council of Europe, *Convention for the Protection of Individuals with Regard to Automatic Processing of Personal Data*, opened for signature 28 January 1981, ETS No 108 (entered into force 1 October 1985)

Geneva Convention (III) Relative to the Treatment of Prisoners of War, opened for signature 12 August 1949, 75 UNTS 135 (entered into force 21 October 1950)

International Covenant on Civil and Political Rights, opened for signature 16 December 1966, 999 UNTS 171 (entered into force 23 March 1976)

International Covenant on Economic, Social and Cultural Rights, opened for signature 16 December 1966, 993 UNTS 3 (entered into force 3 January 1976)

Protocol Relating to the Status of Refugees, opened for signature 31 January 1967, 606 UNTS 267 (entered into force 4 October 1967)

Regulation (EU) 2016/679 of the European Parliament and of the Council of 27 April 2016 on the Protection of Natural Persons with Regard to the Processing of Personal Data and on the Free Movement of Such Data, and Repealing Directive 95/46/EC (General Data Protection Regulation) [2016] OJ L 119/1

Statute of the International Court of Justice

Universal Declaration of Human Rights, GA Res 217A (III), UN GAOR, UN Doc A/810 (10 December 1948)

Vienna Convention on the Law of Treaties, opened for signature 23 May 1969, 1155 UNTS 331 (entered into force 27 January 1980)

E) United Nations General Assembly

Resolutions

Accreditation and Participation of Non-Governmental Organizations in the Ad Hoc Committee on a Comprehensive and Integral International Convention on Protection and Promotion of the Rights and Dignity of Persons with Disabilities, UNGA Res 56/510, UN Doc A/RES/56/510 (26 July 2002, adopted 23 July 2002)

Comprehensive and Integral International Convention to Promote and Protect the Rights and Dignity of Persons with Disabilities, GA Res 56/168, UN Doc A/RES/56/168 (26 February 2002, adopted 19 December 2001)

Convention on the Rights of Persons with Disabilities, GA Res 61/106, UN Doc A/RES/61/106 (24 January 2007, adopted 13 December 2006)

Declaration on the Rights of Disabled Persons, GA Res 3447(XXX), UN GAOR Supp (No 34) at 88, 30th sess, 2433rd plen mtg, UN Doc A/RES/3447(XXX) (adopted 9 December 1975)

Declaration on the Rights of Mentally Retarded Persons, GA Res 2856(XXVI), 26th sess, Agenda Item 12, UN Doc A/RES/26/2856 (adopted 20 December 1971)

Fundamental Principles of Official Statistics, GA Res 68/261, UN Doc A/RES/68/261 (3 March 2014, adopted 29 January 2014)

Guidelines for the Regulation of Computerized Personal Data Files, GA Res 45/95 (14 December 1990)

International Assistance to Refugees Within the Mandate of the United Nations High Commissioner for Refugees, GA Res 1166 (XII), UN Doc A/RES/1166 (XII) (adopted 26 November 1957)

New York Declaration for Refugees and Migrants, UNGA Res 71/1, UN Doc A/RES/71/1 (3 October 2016, adopted 19 September 2016)

The Problem of Chinese Refugees in Hong Kong, UNGA Res 1784 (XVII), UN Doc A/RES1784 (adopted 7 December 1962)

Refugees and Stateless Persons, UNGA Res 319 (IV), UN Doc A/RES/319 (adopted 3 December 1949)

Standard Rules on the Equalization of Opportunities for Persons with Disabilities, GA Res 48/96, 48th sess, 85th plen mtg, Agenda Item 109, UN Doc A/RES/48/96 (adopted 20 December 1993)

Statute of the Office of the United Nations High Commissioner for Refugees, UNGA Res 428(V), UN Doc A/RES/428(V) (adopted 14 December 1950)

World Programme of Action Concerning Disabled Persons, GA Res 37/52, UN Doc A/RES/37/52 (adopted 3 December 1982)

Other Official Documents

Report of the Secretary-General, *Implementation of the World Programme of Action Concerning Disabled Persons*, UN Doc A/49/435 (27 September 1994)

Report of the Secretary-General, *Overview of Issues and Trends Related to Advancement of Persons with Disabilities*, UN Doc A/AC.265/2003/2 (7 April 2003)

Report of the United Nations High Commissioner for Refugees: Part II Global Compact on Refugees, UN Doc A/73/12 (Part II) (13 September 2018, adopted 2 August 2018)

F) Human Rights Treaty Body and Related Materials

Committee on the Rights of Persons With Disabilities

Committee on the Protection of the Rights of All Migrant Workers and Members of Their Families and Committee on the Rights of Persons with Disabilities, *Addressing Disabilities in Large-Scale Movements of Refugees and Migrants* (Joint Statement, 2017)

Committee on the Rights of Persons with Disabilities, 'Annex II: Guidelines on the Participation of Disabled Persons' Organizations and Civil Society Organizations in the Work of the Committee' in *Report of the Committee on the Rights of Persons with Disabilities on Its Eleventh Session* (31 March–11 April 2014)

Committee on the Rights of Persons with Disabilities, *Communication No 1/2010*, UN Doc CRPD/C/9/D/1/2010 (21 June 2013, adopted 15–19 April 2013)

Committee on the Rights of Persons with Disabilities, *Concluding Observations on the Combined Second and Third Periodic Reports of Austria*, UN Doc CRPD/C/AUT/CO/2-3 (8 September 2023)

Committee on the Rights of Persons with Disabilities, *Concluding Observations on the Combined Second and Third Periodic Reports of Azerbaijan*, UN Doc CRPD/C/AZE/CO/2-3 (22 March 2024)

Committee on the Rights of Persons with Disabilities, *Concluding Observations on the Combined Second and Third Periodic Reports of China*, UN Doc CRPD/C/CHN/CO/2-3 (10 October 2022)

Committee on the Rights of Persons with Disabilities, *Concluding Observations on the Combined Second and Third Periodic Reports of Germany*, UN Doc CRPD/C/DEU/CO/2-3 (8 September 2023)

Committee on the Rights of Persons with Disabilities, *Concluding Observations on the Combined Second and Third Periodic Reports of Hungary*, UN Doc CRPD/C/HUN/CO/2-3 (20 May 2022)

Committee on the Rights of Persons with Disabilities, *Concluding Observations on the Combined Second and Third Periodic Reports of the Republic of Korea*, UN Doc CRPD/C/KOR/CO/2-3 (6 October 2022)

Committee on the Rights of Persons with Disabilities, *Concluding Observations on the Combined Second and Third Periodic Reports of Mexico*, UN Doc CRPD/C/MEX/CO/2-3 (20 April 2022)

Committee on the Rights of Persons with Disabilities, *Concluding Observations on the Combined Second and Third Periodic Reports of Sweden*, UN Doc CRPD/C/SWE/CO/2-3 (22 March 2024)

Committee on the Rights of Persons with Disabilities, *Concluding Observations on the Initial Report of Bangladesh*, UN Doc CRPD/C/BGD/CO/1 (9 September 2022)

Committee on the Rights of Persons with Disabilities, *Concluding Observations on the Initial Report of Canada*, UN Doc CRPD/C/CAN/CO/1 (8 May 2017)

Committee on the Rights of Persons with Disabilities, *Concluding Observations on the Initial Report of Chile*, UN Doc CRPD/C/CHL/CO/1 (13 April 2016)

Committee on the Rights of Persons with Disabilities, *Concluding Observations on the Initial Report of Czech Republic*, UN Doc CRPD/C/CZE/CO/1 (15 May 2015)

Committee on the Rights of Persons with Disabilities, *Concluding Observations on the Initial Report of France*, UN Doc CRPD/C/FRA/CO/1 (4 October 2021)

Committee on the Rights of Persons with Disabilities, *Concluding Observations on the Initial Report of Germany*, UN Doc CRPD/C/DEU/CO/1 (13 May 2015)

Committee on the Rights of Persons with Disabilities, *Concluding Observations on the Initial Report of Greece*, UN Doc CRPD/C/GRC/CO/1 (29 October 2019)

Committee on the Rights of Persons with Disabilities, *Concluding Observations on the Initial Report of Iraq*, UN Doc CRPD/C/IRQ/CO/1 (19 September 2019)

Committee on the Rights of Persons with Disabilities, *Concluding Observations on the Initial Report of Israel*, UN Doc CRPD/C/ISR/CO/1 (8 September 2023)

Committee on the Rights of Persons with Disabilities, *Concluding Observations on the Initial Report of Japan*, UN Doc CRPD/C/JPN/CO/1 (7 October 2022)

Committee on the Rights of Persons with Disabilities, *Concluding Observations on the Initial Report of Kazakhstan*, UN Doc CRPD/C/KAZ/CO/1 (22 March 2024)

Committee on the Rights of Persons with Disabilities, *Concluding Observations on the Initial Report of Kenya*, UN Doc CRPD/C/KEN/CO/1 (30 September 2015)

Committee on the Rights of Persons with Disabilities, *Concluding Observations on the Initial Report of Mongolia*, UN Doc CRPD/C/MNG/CO/1 (13 May 2015)

Committee on the Rights of Persons with Disabilities, *Concluding Observations on the Initial Report of Morocco*, UN Doc CRPD/C/MAR/CO/1 (25 September 2017)
Committee on the Rights of Persons with Disabilities, *Concluding Observations on the Initial Report of Sweden*, UN Doc CRPD/C/SWE/CO/1 (12 May 2014)
Committee on the Rights of Persons with Disabilities, *Concluding Observations on the Initial Report of Switzerland*, UN Doc CRPD/C/CHE/CO/1 (13 April 2022)
Committee on the Rights of Persons with Disabilities, *Concluding Observations on the Initial Report of the Former Yugoslav Republic of Macedonia*, UN Doc CRPD/C/MKD/CO/1 (29 October 2018)
Committee on the Rights of Persons with Disabilities, *Concluding Observations on the Initial Report of the Islamic Republic of Iran*, UN Doc CRPD/C/IRN/CO/1 (10 May 2017)
Committee on the Rights of Persons with Disabilities, *Concluding Observations on the Initial Report of the United Kingdom of Great Britain and Northern Ireland*, UN Doc CRPD/C/GBR/CO/1 (3 October 2017)
Committee on the Rights of Persons with Disabilities, *Concluding Observations on the Initial Report of Turkey*, UN Doc CRPD/C/TUR/CO/1 (9 April 2019)
Committee on the Rights of Persons with Disabilities, *Concluding Observations on the Initial Report of Uganda*, UN Doc CRPD/C/UGA/CO/1 (12 May 2016)
Committee on the Rights of Persons with Disabilities, *General Comment No 3 (2016) on Women and Girls with Disabilities*, UN Doc CRPD/C/GC/3 (25 November 2016)
Committee on the Rights of Persons with Disabilities, *General Comment No 6 (2018) on Equality and Non-Discrimination*, UN Doc CRPD/C/GC/6 (26 April 2018)
Committee on the Rights of Persons with Disabilities, *General Comment No 7 (2018) on the Participation of Persons with Disabilities, Including Children with Disabilities, Through Their Representative Organizations, in the Implementation and Monitoring of the Convention*, UN Doc CRPD/C/GC/7 (9 November 2018)
Committee on the Rights of Persons with Disabilities, *Statement of the Committee on the Rights of Persons with Disabilities on Disability Inclusion for the World Humanitarian Summit* (14 September 2015)

Other Human Rights Treaty Bodies

Committee on Economic, Social and Cultural Rights, *General Comment No 19: The Right to Social Security (Art 9)* (2007)
Committee on Economic, Social and Cultural Rights, *General Comment No 15: The Right to Water (Arts 11 and 12 of the Covenant)*, UN Doc E/C.12/2002/11 (adopted 20 January 2003)
Committee on the Elimination of Discrimination Against Women, *General Recommendation No 9: Statistical Data Concerning the Situation of Women*, 148th, 149th and 150th Comm, 8th sess, UN Doc A/44/38 V (13 February 1990, adopted 1989)
Committee on the Elimination of Discrimination Against Women, *General Recommendation No 25 (2004) on Temporary Special Measures*, UN Doc HRI/GEN/1/Rev.7 at 282 (2004)
Committee on the Elimination of Discrimination Against Women, *General Recommendation No 28 (2010) on the Core Obligations of States Parties Under Article 2 of the Convention on the Elimination of All Forms of Discrimination Against Women*, UN Doc CEDAW/C/GC/28 (16 December 2010)
Committee on the Elimination of Racial Discrimination, *General Recommendation XXIV Concerning Article 1 of the Convention*, 55th sess, 1371st mtg, UN A/54/18 annex V (adopted 27 August 1999)
Committee on the Rights of the Child, *General Comment No 5: General Measures of Implementation of the Convention on the Rights of the Child*, UN Doc CRC/GC/2003/5 (27 November 2003)

Human Rights Commission, *Human Rights of Persons with Disabilities*, CHR Res 2002/61, UN Doc E/CN.4/2002/61 (adopted 25 April 2002)
Human Rights Committee, *General Comment No 16: Article 17 (Right to Privacy) The Right to Respect of Privacy, Family, Home and Correspondence, and Protection of Honour and Reputation*, 32nd sess (adopted 8 April 1988)
Korneenko et al. v. *Belarus*, CCPR/C/88/D/1274/2004 (31 October 2006)
Kungurov v. *Uzbekistan*, CCPR/C/102/D/1478/2006 (20 July 2011)
Office of the High Commissioner for Human Rights (OHCHR), *Statistics and Data Collection Under Article 31 of the Convention on the Rights of Persons with Disabilities*, UN Doc A/HRC/49/60 (28 December 2021)

Special Rapporteur Reports

Alston, Philip, *Report of the Special Rapporteur on Extreme Poverty and Human Rights*, UN Doc A/74/48037 (11 October 2019)
Quinn, Gerard, *Report of the Special Rapporteur on the Rights of Persons with Disabilities*, UN Doc A/HRC/49/52 (28 December 2021)

Other OHCHR Materials

Office of the High Commissioner for Human Rights (OHCHR), *A Human Rights-Based Approach to Data: Leaving No One Behind in the 2030 Agenda for Sustainable Development* (2018) <https://www.ohchr.org/Documents/Issues/HRIndicators/GuidanceNoteonApproachtoData.pdf>
Office of the High Commissioner for Human Rights (OHCHR), *The Convention on the Rights of Persons with Disabilities: Training Guide* (2014)

G) Ad Hoc Committee on a Comprehensive and Integral International Convention on Protection and Promotion of the Rights and Dignity of Persons With Disabilities Materials

Official Documents

Ad Hoc Committee, *Ad Hoc Committee on a Comprehensive and Integral International Convention on Protection and Promotion of the Rights and Dignity of Persons with Disabilities*, UN Doc A/58/118 & Corr.1 (3 July 2003)
Ad Hoc Committee, *Final Report of the Ad Hoc Committee on a Comprehensive and Integral International Convention on the Protection and Promotion of the Rights and Dignity of Persons with Disabilities*, UN Doc A/61/611 (6 December 2006)
Ad Hoc Committee, *Interim Report of the Ad Hoc Committee on a Comprehensive and Integral International Convention on the Protection and Promotion of the Rights and Dignity of Persons with Disabilities on Its Eighth Session*, UN Doc A/AC.265/2006/4 (1 September 2006)
Ad Hoc Committee, *Report of the Ad Hoc Committee on a Comprehensive and Integral International Convention on Protection and Promotion of the Rights and Dignity of Persons with Disabilities*, UN Doc A/57/357 (27 August 2002)
Comprehensive and Integral International Convention to Promote and Protect the Rights and Dignity of Persons with Disabilities: Working Paper by Mexico, UN Doc A/AC.265/WP.1 (2002)
Kjærum, Morten, *Letter Dated 26 May 2003 From the Executive Director of the Danish Institute for Human Rights Addressed to the Secretary of the Ad Hoc Committee on a Comprehensive and Integral International Convention on the Protection*

and Promotion of the Rights and Dignity of Persons with Disabilities, UN Doc A/AC.265/2003/CRP/9 (26 May 2003)

MacKay, Don, *Letter Dated 7 October 2005 From the Chairman to All Members of the Committee*, UN Doc A/AC.265/2006/1 (14 October 2005)

Report of the Ad Hoc Committee on a Comprehensive and Integral International Convention on the Protection and Promotion of the Rights and Dignity of Persons with Disabilities on Its Seventh Session, UN Doc A/AC.265/2006/2 (13 February 2006)

Working Group to the Ad Hoc Committee, *Report of the Working Group to the Ad Hoc Committee*, UN Doc A/AC.265/2004/WG.1 (27 January 2004)

Daily Summaries (Unofficial)

Disabled Peoples' International, Handicap International and International Service for Human Rights, 'Daily Summary of Discussion at the Fourth Session 01 September 2004', *UN Convention on the Human Rights of People with Disabilities Ad Hoc Committee – Daily Summary* (United Nations Enable, 1 September 2004) <https://www.un.org/esa/socdev/enable/rights/ahc4sum01sep.htm>

Disabled Peoples' International, Handicap International and International Service for Human Rights, 'Daily Summary of Discussion at the Fourth Session 02 September 2004', *UN Convention on the Human Rights of People with Disabilities Ad Hoc Committee – Daily Summary* (United Nations Enable, 2 September 2004) <https://www.un.org/esa/socdev/enable/rights/ahc4sum02sep.htm>

Disabled Peoples' International, Handicap International and International Service for Human Rights, 'Daily Summary of Discussion at the Fourth Session 23 August 2004', *UN Convention on the Human Rights of People with Disabilities Ad Hoc Committee – Daily Summary* (United Nations Enable, 23 August 2004) <https://www.un.org/esa/socdev/enable/rights/ahc4sum23aug.htm>

Disabled Peoples' International, Handicap International and International Service for Human Rights, 'Daily Summary of Discussion at the Fourth Session 24 August 2004', *UN Convention on the Human Rights of People with Disabilities Ad Hoc Committee – Daily Summary* (United Nations Enable, 24 August 2004) <https://www.un.org/esa/socdev/enable/rights/ahc4sum24aug.htm>

Disabled Peoples' International, Handicap International and International Service for Human Rights, 'Daily Summary of Discussion at the Fourth Session 25 August 2004', *UN Convention on the Human Rights of People with Disabilities Ad Hoc Committee – Daily Summary* (United Nations Enable, 25 August 2004) <https://www.un.org/esa/socdev/enable/rights/ahc4sum25aug.htm>

Disabled Peoples' International, Handicap International and International Service for Human Rights, 'Daily Summary of Discussion at the Fourth Session 31 August 2004', *UN Convention on the Human Rights of People with Disabilities Ad Hoc Committee – Daily Summary* (United Nations Enable, 31 August 2004) <https://www.un.org/esa/socdev/enable/rights/ahc4sum31aug.htm>

Landmine Survivors Network, 'Afternoon Session Daily Summary of the Working Group – 5 January 2004', *Disability Information Resources* (Web Page, 5 January 2004) <https://www.dinf.ne.jp/doc/english/rights/040105.html>

Landmine Survivors Network, 'Daily Summary of Discussion at the Third Session 4 June 2004', *UN Convention on the Human Rights of People with Disabilities Ad Hoc Committee – Daily Summaries* (United Nations Enable, 4 June 2004) <https://www.un.org/esa/socdev/enable/rights/ahc3sum4june.htm>

Landmine Survivors Network, 'Daily Summary of Discussion at the Third Session 25 May 2004', *UN Convention on the Human Rights of People with Disabilities Ad Hoc Committee – Daily Summaries* (United Nations Enable, 25 May 2004) <https://www.un.org/esa/socdev/enable/rights/ahc3sum25may.htm>

Landmine Survivors Network, 'Daily Summary of Discussion at the Third Session 27 May 2004', *UN Convention on the Rights of People with Disabilities Ad Hoc Committee – Daily Summaries* (United Nations Enable, 27 May 2004) <https://www.un.org/esa/socdev/enable/rights/ahc3sum27may.htm>

Landmine Survivors Network, 'Daily Summary of Discussion at the Third Session 28 May 2004', *UN Convention on the Human Rights of People with Disabilities Ad Hoc Committee – Daily Summaries* (United Nations Enable, 28 May 2004) <https://www.un.org/esa/socdev/enable/rights/ahc3sum28may.htm>

Landmine Survivors Network, 'Daily Summary Related to Draft Article 6 Statistics and Data Collection (14–15 January 2004)', *UN Convention on the Human Rights of People with Disabilities Ad Hoc Committee – Daily Summaries* (United Nations Enable, 15 January 2004) <https://www.un.org/esa/socdev/enable/rights/wgsuma6.htm>

Landmine Survivors Network, 'UN Convention on the Rights of People with Disabilities: Working Group Daily Summary', *Disability Information Resources* (Web Page, 7 January 2004) <https://www.dinf.ne.jp/doc/english/rights/040107.html>

Rehabilitation International, 'Daily Summary of Discussion at the Fifth Session 24 January 2005', *UN Convention on the Human Rights of People with Disabilities Ad Hoc Committee – Daily Summaries* (United Nations Enable, 24 January 2005) <https://www.un.org/esa/socdev/enable/rights/ahc5sum24jan.htm>

Rehabilitation International, 'Daily Summary of Discussion at the Seventh Session 17 January 2006', *UN Convention on the Human Rights of People with Disabilities Ad Hoc Committee – Daily Summaries* (United Nations Enable, 17 January 2006) <https://www.un.org/esa/socdev/enable/rights/ahc7sum17jan.htm>

Rehabilitation International, 'Daily Summary of Discussion at the Seventh Session 27 January 2006', *UN Convention on the Human Rights of People with Disabilities Ad Hoc Committee – Daily Summaries* (United Nations Enable, 27 January 2006) <https://www.un.org/esa/socdev/enable/rights/ahc7sum27jan.htm>

Rehabilitation International, 'Daily Summary of Discussion at the Seventh Session 31 January 2006', *UN Convention on the Human Rights of People with Disabilities Ad Hoc Committee – Daily Summaries* (United Nations Enable, 31 January 2006) <https://www.un.org/esa/socdev/enable/rights/ahc7sum31jan.htm>

Rehabilitation International, 'Daily Summary of Discussion at the Sixth Session 1 August 2005', *UN Convention on the Human Rights of People with Disabilities Ad Hoc Committee – Daily Summaries* (United Nations Enable, 1 August 2005) <https://www.un.org/esa/socdev/enable/rights/ahc6sum1Aug.htm>

Rehabilitation International, 'Daily Summary of Discussion at the Sixth Session 08 August 2005', *UN Convention on the Human Rights of People with Disabilities Ad Hoc Committee – Daily Summaries* (United Nations Enable, 8 August 2005) <https://www.un.org/esa/socdev/enable/rights/ahc6sum8aug.htm>

Rehabilitation International, 'Daily Summary of Discussion at the Sixth Session 11 August 2005', *UN Convention on the Human Rights of People with Disabilities Ad Hoc Committee – Daily Summaries* (United Nations Enable, 11 August 2005) <https://www.un.org/esa/socdev/enable/rights/ahc6sum11aug.htm>

Rehabilitation International, 'Daily Summary of Discussions – 25 January 2005', *UN Convention on the Human Rights of People with Disabilities Ad Hoc Committee – Daily Summaries* (United Nations Enable, 25 January 2005) <https://www.un.org/esa/socdev/enable/rights/ahc5sum25jan.htm>

Other

Convention on the Rights of Persons with Disabilities: A Proposed Draft Text by China: For the Working Group of the Ad Hoc Committee on a Comprehensive and Integral International Convention on Protection and Promotion of the Rights and Dignity of

Persons with Disabilities (January 2004) <https://www.un.org/esa/socdev/enable/rights/wgcontrib-china.htm>
Disabled Peoples' International, *DPI Position Paper Regarding a New International Human Rights Convention for Disabled People* (25 February 2003) <https://www.un.org/esa/socdev/enable/rights/contrib-dpi.htm>
European Union, *Initial EU Position Paper for 7th Ad Hoc Committee: EU Proposals Based on Chair's Text* (16 January 2006) <https://www.un.org/esa/socdev/enable/rights/ahc7docs/ahc7eu1.doc>
International Labour Organization, *ILO Submission to Working Group Set Up by the United Nations Ad Hoc Committee to Consider Proposals for a Comprehensive and Integral International Convention on Protection and Promotion of the Rights and Dignity of Persons with Disabilities* (January 2004) <https://www.un.org/esa/socdev/enable/rights/wgcontrib-ilo.htm>
Regional Workshop Towards a Comprehensive and Integral International Convention on Protection and Promotion of the Rights and Dignity of Persons with Disabilities, 14–17 October 2003, Bangkok, Thailand, *Bangkok Draft: Proposed Elements of a Comprehensive and Integral International Convention to Promote and Protect the Rights of Persons with Disabilities* (2003) <https://www.un.org/esa/socdev/enable/rights/bangkokdraft.htm>
United Nations, *Press Conference by High Commissioner for Human Rights on Signing of Convention* (Media Release, 30 March 2007) <https://www.un.org/press/en/2007/070330_Disabilities.doc.htm>
World Blind Union, *Manifesto for a United Nations Convention on the Rights of People with Disabilities: 'Equal Rights and Full Inclusion as World Citizens'* (January 2004) <https://www.un.org/esa/socdev/enable/rights/wgcontrib-wbu.htm>

H) Office of the United Nations High Commissioner for Human Rights Materials

Executive Committee of the High Commissioners Program Materials

Establishment of the Executive Committee of the Programme of the United Nations High Commissioner for Refugees, UN ESC Res 672 (XXV), E/RES/672 (XXV) (adopted 30 April 1958)
Executive Committee of the High Commissioner's Programme, *Conclusion on Refugees with Disabilities and Other Persons with Disabilities Protected and Assisted by UNHCR*, UN Doc A/AC.96/1095 (adopted 12 October 2010)
Executive Committee of the High Commissioner's Programme, *Conclusion on Women and Girls at Risk*, UN Doc A/AC.96/1035 (10 October 2006)
Executive Committee of the High Commissioner's Programme, *The Protection of Older Persons and Persons with Disabilities*, UN Doc EC/58/SC/CRP.14 (6 June 2007)

Report/Guides/Press Releases/Webpages

'The Global Compact on Refugees', *United Nations High Commissioner for Refugees* (Web Page) <https://www.unhcr.org/the-global-compact-on-refugees.html>
Ministerial Meeting of States Parties, *Declaration of States Parties to the 1951 Convention and/or Its 1967 Protocol Relating to the Status of Refugees* (12 December 2001)
Office of the United Nations High Commissioner for Refugees (UNHCR), *UNHCR Policy on Age, Gender and Diversity* (2018)
Office of the United Nations High Commissioner for Refugees (UNHCR), *Working with Persons with Disabilities in Forced Displacement: Need to Know Guidance* (2011)

Office of the United Nations High Commissioner for Refugees (UNHCR), *Working with Persons with Disabilities in Forced Displacement: Need to Know Guidance* (2019)

'Refugee Camps Explained', *USA for UNHCR* (Web Page, 6 April 2021) <https://www.unrefugees.org/news/refugee-camps-explained/>

United Nations High Commissioner for Refugees (UNHCR), *Agenda for Protection* (Report, 3rd ed, October 2003)

United Nations High Commissioner for Refugees (UNHCR), *Global Trends: Forced Displacement in 2023* (Report, 2024)

United Nations High Commissioner for Refugees (UNHCR), *Guidance on the Protection of Personal Data of Persons of Concern to UNHCR* (2018)

United Nations High Commissioner for Refugees (UNHCR), *Mid-Year Trends 2022* (Report, 2022)

United Nations High Commissioner for Refugees (UNHCR), *News Comment: Statement on Refugee Registration and Data Collection in Bangladesh* (Press Release, 15 June 2021) <https://www.unhcr.org/news/press/2021/6/60c85a7b4/news-comment-statement-refugee-registration-data-collection-bangladesh.html>

United Nations High Commissioner for Refugees (UNHCR), *The Principle of Non-Refoulement as a Norm of Customary International Law. Response to the Questions Posed to UNHCR by the Federal Constitutional Court of the Federal Republic of Germany in Cases 2 BvR 1938/93, 2 BvR 1953/93, 2 BvR 1954/93* (31 January 1994) <https://www.refworld.org/docid/437b6db64.html>

United Nations High Commissioner for Refugees (UNHCR) and European Disability Forum, *Ensuring the Protection of Persons with Disabilities Fleeing From Ukraine* (Report, 2022)

'Who Is Included in UNHCR Statistics?', *UNHCR Refugee Data Finder* (Web Page, 2023) <https://www.unhcr.org/refugee-statistics/methodology/definition/>

I) Other United Nations Materials

Official Documents

World Health Assembly, *International Classification of Functioning, Disability and Health*, WHA Res 54.21, 54th sess, 9th plenary mtg, Agenda Item 13.9, UN Doc WHA54.21 (adopted 22 May 2001)

Other

UN High-Level Committee on Management, *Personal Data Protection and Privacy Principles* (11 October 2018)

United Nations Children's Fund (UNICEF), *Included, Every Step of the Way: Upholding the Rights of Migrant and Displaced Children with Disabilities* (Report, 2023)

United Nations Children's Fund (UNICEF), United Nations High Commissioner for Refugees (UNHCR) and United Nations World Food Program (WFP), *VASyR2020: Vulnerability Assessment of Syrian Refugees in Lebanon* (Report, February 2021)

United Nations Economic Commission for Europe, *UNECE Launches Knowledge Hub on Statistics for SDGs to Support Evidence-Driven Policies* (Press Release, 2 December 2019) <https://www.unece.org/info/media/presscurrent-press-h/statistics/2019/unece-launches-knowledge-hub-on-statistics-for-sdgs-to-support-evidence-driven-policies/doc.html>

United Nations Human Rights Council, *Mental Health and Human Rights* (26 September 2017)

United Nations Permanent Forum on Indigenous Issues, *Fact Sheet: Who Are Indigenous Peoples?* (Fact Sheet, n.d.)

World Health Organization (WHO), *International Classification of Functioning, Disability and Health* (2001)

World Health Organization (WHO), *International Classification of Impairments, Disabilities, and Handicaps: A Manual of Classification Relating to the Consequences of Disease* (1980)

J) Webpages/Blogs/Online News

'About', *Charter on Inclusion of Persons with Disabilities in Humanitarian Action* (Web Page, 2022) <http://humanitariandisabilitycharter.org/>

'Ad Hoc Committee on a Comprehensive and Integral International Convention on the Protection and Promotion of the Rights and Dignity of Persons with Disabilities', *United Nations Department of Economic and Social Affairs* (Web Page) <https://www.un.org/development/desa/disabilities/resources/ad-hoc-committee-on-a-comprehensive-and-integral-international-convention-on-the-protection-and-promotion-of-the-rights-and-dignity-of-persons-with-disabilities.html>

Adams, Rachel, 'Michel Foucault: Biopolitics and Biopower', *Critical Legal Thinking* (online, 10 May 2017) <http://criticallegalthinking.com/2017/05/10/michel-foucault-biopolitics-biopower/>

Alley, Sarah and Sophie Kesteven, 'When Her Employers Were Cutting Staff, Laura Witnessed HR Discussing Who Had Accessed the EAP', *ABC News* (online, 9 November 2022) <https://www.abc.net.au/news/2022-11-10/employee-assistance-program-and-workers-privacy/101607634>

Aratani, Lori, 'Secret Use of Census Info Helped Send Japanese Americans to Internment Camps in WWII', *Washington Post* (online, 7 April 2018) <https://www.washingtonpost.com/news/retropolis/wp/2018/04/03/secret-use-of-census-info-helped-send-japanese-americans-to-internment-camps-in-wwii/>

Ashby, Christine, Benjamin IP Rubinstein and Vanessa Teague, 'Stop the Open Data Bus, We Want to Get Off' (No arXiv:1908.05004, arXiv, 14 August 2019) <http://arxiv.org/abs/1908.05004>

'Australian Border Force Accused of Targeting Women Suspected of Fleeing Saudi Arabia', *ABC News* (online, 3 February 2019) <https://www.abc.net.au/news/2019-02-04/border-force-accused-of-targeting-saudi-women-traveling-alone/10768036>

Barroso, Carmen and Katell Le Goulven, 'A Rights-Based Data Revolution?', *UN Data Revolution* (online, 14 October 2014) <https://www.undatarevolution.org/2014/10/14/rights-based-revolution/>

Barry, Hannah, Isabel Moussalli and Evelyn Leckie, 'A Trial of the Controversial Cashless Welfare Card Will Run for Two More Years. Here's What People Think', *ABC News* (online, 10 December 2020) <https://www.abc.net.au/news/2020-12-10/mixed-response-to-cashless-debit-card-extension/12971626>

Booth, Robert, 'Benefits System Automation Could Plunge Claimants Deeper into Poverty', *The Guardian* (online, 14 October 2019) <https://www.theguardian.com/technology/2019/oct/14/fears-rise-in-benefits-system-automation-could-plunge-claimants-deeper-into-poverty>

Campanella, Nas, 'Disability Royal Commission Data Shows Indigenous and Culturally Diverse Groups Under-Represented in Submissions', *ABC News* (online, 23 July 2020) <https://www.abc.net.au/news/2020-07-23/disability-royal-commission-indigenous-cald-submissions-lacking/12476358>

'Committee on the Rights of Persons with Disabilities', *Office of the High Commissioner for Human Rights* (Web Page) <https://www.ohchr.org/en/treaty-bodies/crpd>

'Conceptual Framework', *Washington Group on Disability Statistics* (Web Page, 2023) <https://www.washingtongroup-disability.com/about/conceptual-framework/>

Consideration of Australia – 499th Meeting 22nd Session Committee on Rights of Persons with Disabilities (Video, Directed by UN Web TV, 12 September 2019) <https://media.un.org/en/asset/k1i/k1i5jtj8yk>

'Contributions Submitted by Governments in Electronic Format at the Fourth Session: Proposed Modifications to Draft Article 6', *United Nations Enable* (Web Page, 2004) <https://www.un.org/esa/socdev/enable/rights/ahc4da6.htm>

Crisp, Jeff, 'Beware the Notion That Better Data Lead to Better Outcomes for Refugees and Migrants', *Chatham House* (Web Page, 9 March 2018) <https://www.chathamhouse.org/2018/03/beware-notion-better-data-lead-better-outcomes-refugees-and-migrants>

'Data2X: Partnering for Better Gender Data', *Data2X* (Web Page) <https://data2x.org/>

Dent, Jackie and Anna Kelsey-Sugg, 'Indigenous Australian Population Figures Jumped in Latest Census as Pride Increases and Fears Abate', *ABC News* (online, 6 July 2022) <https://www.abc.net.au/news/2022-07-07/indigenous-population-census-aboriginal-torres-strait-islander/101212240>

'Disability Data', *CBM* (Web Page) <https://www.cbm.org.au/stories/disability-data>

'Disability Data Advocacy Working Group', *International Disability Alliance* (Web Page) <https://www.internationaldisabilityalliance.org/content/disability-data-advocacy-working-group>

Disabled People's Organisations Australia, *Factsheet: Discrimination Against Migrants and Refugees with Disability* (Fact Sheet, 8 March 2018) <https://dpoa.org.au/factsheet-migration/>

Dudovskiy, John, 'Purposive Sampling', *Business Research Methodology* (Web Page) <https://research-methodology.net/sampling-in-primary-data-collection/purposive-sampling/>

'Entry into Force', *United Nations Department of Economic and Social Affairs* (Web Page) <https://www.un.org/development/desa/disabilities/convention-on-the-rights-of-persons-with-disabilities/entry-into-force.html>

Harari, Yuval Noah, 'Why Technology Favors Tyranny', *The Atlantic* (online, October 2018) <https://www.theatlantic.com/magazine/archive/2018/10/yuval-noah-harari-technology-tyranny/568330/>

Henderson, Anna and Chris Uhlmann, 'Syrian Migrant Crisis: Christians to Get Priority as Abbott Faces Pressure to Take in More Refugees', *ABC News* (online, 8 September 2015) <https://www.abc.net.au/news/2015-09-08/christians-to-get-priority-in-syrian-refugee-intake/6757110>

Human Rights Watch, 'Syrian Refugees in Turkey Fear Turkish Police' (YouTube, 25 October 2022) <https://www.youtube.com/watch?v=4_HoMO0PMz4&t=16s>

'IBM I2 Enterprise Insight Analysis – Overview – Australia', *IMB* (Web Page, 27November2019) <https://www.ibm.com/au-en/marketplace/enterprise-insight-analysis>

'IDA's Compilations of CRPD Committee's Concluding Observations', *International Disability Alliance* (Web Page) <https://www.internationaldisabilityalliance.org/content/ida%E2%80%99s-compilations-crpd-committee%E2%80%99s-concluding-observations>

'International Classification of Functioning, Disability and Health (ICF)', *World Health Organization* (Web Page, 2023) <https://www.who.int/standards/classifications/international-classification-of-functioning-disability-and-health>

'International Statistical Classification of Diseases and Related Health Problems (ICD)', *World Health Organization* (Web Page, 2023) <https://www.who.int/standards/classifications/classification-of-diseases>

Marr, Bernard, 'How Much Data Do We Create Every Day? The Mind-Blowing Stats Everyone Should Read', *Forbes* (online, 21 May 2018) <https://www.forbes.com/sites/bernardmarr/2018/05/21/how-much-data-do-we-create-every-day-the-mind-blowing-stats-everyone-should-read/>

'Membership: Committee on the Rights of Persons with Disabilities', *Office of the High Commissioner for Human Rights* (Web Page) <https://www.ohchr.org/en/treaty-bodies/crpd/membership>

'National Health Survey', *Australian Bureau of Statistics* (Online Survey) <https://www.abs.gov.au/participate-survey/household-survey/national-health-survey>

Ndiaye, Aissata and Tichafara Chisaka, 'How Can Inclusive Data Advocacy Help Us to Achieve the SDGs?', *Sightsavers* (Blog Post, July 2022) <https://www.sightsavers.org/blogs/2022/07/how-can-inclusive-data-advocacy-help-us-achieve-the-sdgs/>

'Oxford Advanced Learner's Dictionary', *Oxford University Press* (online, 2023) <https://www.oxfordlearnersdictionaries.com/>

'Power/Knowledge: Michel Foucault', *Social Theory Re-Wired* (Web Page, 2016) <http://routledgesoc.com/category/profile-tags/powerknowledge>

'Prisoners of War: What You Need to Know', *International Committee of the Red Cross* (Web Page, 19 May 2022) <https://www.icrc.org/en/document/prisoners-war-what-you-need-know>

Reina, Maria Veronica, 'How the International Disability Caucus Worked During Negotiations for a UN Human Rights Convention on Disability', *Global Action on Aging* (Web Page, 6 February 2008) <http://globalag.igc.org/agingwatch/events/CSD/2008/maria.htm>

Royal Commission into Violence, Abuse, Neglect and Exploitation of People with Disabilities, *Connect* (Newsletter, 14 July 2020) <https://comms.external.royalcommission.gov.au/em/message/email/view.php?id=1559316&a=89073&k=gVRNtlWjstBVnI2h_teU0on0vniz1dMUvjjyNBNjaEk>

Rumi, 'The Elephant in a Dark Room', *Myth-Folklore* (Web Page, 9 October 2004) <http://www.mythfolklore.net/3043mythfolklore/reading/rumi/pages/01.htm>

'Technology and Rights', *Human Rights Watch* (Web Page, 2023) <https://www.hrw.org/topic/technology-and-rights>

'Thirteenth Conference of States Parties and 2020 Elections', *Office of the High Commissioner for Human Rights* (Web Page) <https://www.ohchr.org/en/events/events/2020/thirteenth-conference-states-parties-and-2020-elections>

Tucker, Patrick, 'A New Tool to Turn Unstructured Data into Actionable Intelligence Could Change the Way Law Enforcement Fights Terrorism, and Challenge the Data-Collection Debate', *Nextgov.com* (online, 28 January 2016) <https://www.nextgov.com/cio-briefing/2016/01/refugee-or-terrorist-ibm-thinks-its-software-has-answer/125506/>

'UN Shared Rohingya Data Without Informed Consent', *Human Rights Watch* (Web Page, 15 June 2021) <https://www.hrw.org/news/2021/06/15/un-shared-rohingya-data-without-informed-consent>

'UN Summit for Refugees and Migrants 2016', *UN Refugees and Migrants* (Web Page, 12 December 2014) <https://refugeesmigrants.un.org/summit>

Vittert, Liberty, 'The Problem with Official Statistics – And Three Ways to Make Them Better', *The Conversation* (online, 18 September 2018) <http://theconversation.com/the-problem-with-official-statistics-and-three-ways-to-make-them-better-103448>

'What is R-ID?', *Rohingya Project* (Web Page, 2022) <https://rohingyaproject.com/r-id/>

Williams, Oscar, 'How Palantir Is Quietly Extending Its Reach Through the British State', *New Statesman* (online, 5 January 2021) <https://www.newstatesman.com/science-tech/2021/01/how-palantir-quietly-extending-its-reach-through-british-state>

K) Other

Charter on Inclusion of Persons with Disabilities in Humanitarian Action (2016) <http://humanitariandisabilitycharter.org/>

Council of Europe Committee of Ministers, *Recommendation No REC(2004)10 of the Committee of Ministers to Member States Concerning the Protection of the Human Rights and Dignity of Persons with Mental Disorder and Its Explanatory Memorandum*, 896th mtg of Ministers' Deputies (adopted 22 September 2004)

Email from Lucia D'Arino to crpd-forum (Including Philippa Duell-Piening) (25 January 2022)

Inter-Agency Standing Committee (IASC), *Guidelines on Inclusion of Persons with Disabilities in Humanitarian Action* (2019)

Inter-Agency Standing Committee (IASC), *IASC Guidelines on Mental Health and Psychosocial Support in Emergency Settings* (2007)

International Conference of Data Protection and Privacy Commissioners, *International Standards on the Protection of Personal Data and Privacy* (5 November 2009)

Organisation for Economic Co-operation and Development (OECD), *OECD Information Technology Outlook* (2002)

Organisation for Economic Co-Operation and Development, *The OECD Privacy Framework* (2013)

Sphere Association, *The Sphere Handbook: Humanitarian Charter and Minimum Standards in Humanitarian Response* (2018)

Index

Page numbers in *italics* indicate figures and in **bold** indicate tables on the corresponding pages.

For Product Safety Concerns and Information please contact our EU representative GPSR@taylorandfrancis.com
Taylor & Francis Verlag GmbH, Kaufingerstraße 24, 80331 München, Germany

www.ingramcontent.com/pod-product-compliance
Lightning Source LLC
LaVergne TN
LVHW021121300926
849160LV00010B/811
9781032827735